Penguin Education

Attitudes
edited by Marie Jahoda and Neil Warren

Penguin Modern Psychology Reading

General Editor
B. M. Foss

Attitudes

Selected Readings

Edited by Marie Jahoda and Neil Warren

Penguin Books

Penguin Books Ltd, Harmondsworth,
Middlesex, England
Penguin Books Inc., 7110 Ambassador Road,
Baltimore, Maryland 21207, U.S.A.
Penguin Books Australia Ltd, Ringwood,
Victoria, Australia

First published 1966
Reprinted 1966, 1970
This selection copyright © Marie Jahoda
and Neil Warren, 1966
Introduction and notes copyright © Marie Jahoda
and Neil Warren, 1966

Made and printed in Great Britain by
Cox & Wyman Ltd, London, Reading
and Fakenham
Set in Monotype Times

Contents

Introduction

Not much more than a hundred years ago the term 'attitude' was used exclusively with reference to a person's posture. To describe someone as adopting 'a threatening attitude' or 'defiant attitude' was to refer to his physical mien. True, the word can still be used in this manner; but nowadays 'attitude' increasingly connotes the psychological rather than the immediately physical orientation of a person, his mental state rather than his bodily stance. In current usage the term is, of course, not a technicality of social science, but is readily understood by all English-speaking people. There is no great communication difficulty involved in speaking to anyone of attitudes towards China or towards democracy, to one's work or to one's boss. Much of the terminology employed by social scientists has been taken over directly from the everyday language of common sense. 'Attitude' is one such term: 'intelligence', 'personality' and 'role' are further examples of concepts which were linguistically available long before they were given operational definitions for research purposes.

Correspondence between scientific and everyday language is a mixed blessing. The scientific use of a term may not be intended to carry the identical connotations of the common sense word. The alternative course – the profligate invention of brand new technical terms of impeccable Greek or Latin etymology – may be equally deplorable, however; especially in the social sciences with their variety of approaches to the data and the consequent potential multiplicity of data-languages. There is one particular advantage in employing terms available to all in some sense, and we intend to make use of it here. This is that we can plunge into a discussion of attitudes without necessarily backing off at the outset to go through the difficult procedure of defining the term.

This is not to say, of course, that there are no problems in defining the concept of attitude. Indeed, there are. For several decades now there has been in the literature on attitudes a continuous undercurrent of controversy over both the theoretical and the operational definition of the term. Definitions are ultimately nothing but matters of convenience. But this makes it all the more important to examine precisely what one implies by a concept. If attitude is defined as a response to a specific stimulus or as the internal organization of past experiences with a class of objects in the external world, for whom or for what is either one of these definitions convenient? for a theory? a method? the solution of a problem? The answers to such questions lead straight into the as yet unresolved conflict between various assumptions about the nature of man on which different approaches to the social sciences rest.

The first part of this book includes readings which examine and highlight some of the conceptual issues of attitude research and theory; and in the suggestions for further reading on pp. 353–7 more detailed and more sophisticated treatment of the concept of attitude can be found. In view of these far-reaching problems, it is actually with certain reservations that we have devoted Part I to an examination of the conceptual aspects of 'attitude'. Such an arrangement appeared to be dictated by logical priorities. At the same time, however, attempts to come to terms with conceptual issues are best carried out as a continual procedure in conjunction with the usage of the concepts concerned; it is preferable to turn back on the concept, for a closer look with the benefit of hindsight, than to endeavour a precise specification in advance. The student is in a better position to enquire into and explicate the detailed meaning of the concept when he is already acquainted with some of the research which makes use of it, some of the theory which specifies its workings and relationships, and some of the methods involved in its measurement. This procedure can be readily followed if the term has some implicit meaning to begin with. When we speak of someone's attitude towards something we are actually forming a quite complex abstraction based on a number of observations or on a good deal of information. Rather different kinds of abstraction can be made from similar observational data, and this is what gives rise to problems of conceptualizing attitudes. But concepts are sometimes used concretely rather than abstractly, and then 'attitudes' are spoken of naïvely as if they were more like things or objects of which relatively direct knowledge is possible. Ultimately, science must use its concepts more and more abstractly. If at times one chooses to speak of attitudes as if they were things, that is, to 'reify' the notion, then it is necessary to remember that this can at best be no more than a temporary measure, and that reification is but a step on the way towards sophisticated abstraction. Nobody, after all, has seen an attitude with his eyes; and nobody ever will.

We would therefore encourage the reader of this book to look at the part dealing with conceptual aspects both before, during and after reading the later sections on research, theory and measurement. The suggested further readings on the concept of attitude should be taken up only after a perusal of Parts II and III. One example of an apparently empirical issue which in fact reflects back in a highly significant way on the problems of conceptualizing 'attitude' is the relationship between the attitudes and the behaviour of a person, of which three research investigations are presented in Part II.

The research reports in Part II illustrate a point of some importance for the development of the social sciences. It is occasionally difficult to say whether a particular article belongs to the literature of psychology or of sociology. Research on attitudes defies the meticulous division of the social sciences into separate disciplines with closed boundaries. In the history of thought concern with attitudes was once within the global field of philosophy. As the various social sciences acquired separate identities they staked – understandably and perhaps inevitably – property rights on certain themes and concepts. Sociologists, for example, 'own' what is known as 'social class', psychologists the concept of intelligence or the Rorschach test. But as knowledge proceeds these apparently distinct concepts yield a fuller meaning for either discipline by being used jointly. What is the relation of intelligence to social class? Only a combination of the approaches in both disciplines can fully answer this question. 'Attitude', however, is a concept of a somewhat different kind, one for which the property rights are not clear-cut in favour of one or other discipline. Here it is not a special research question which leads to a combination of separate branches of the social sciences. 'Attitude' is in itself an interdisciplinary term, bridging psychology and sociology; for attitudes have social reference in their origins, development and in their objects, while at the same time they have psychological reference in that they inhere in the individual and are a function of his psychological make-up. As such they are part of a relatively young field of study, social psychology, which sets out to interrelate psychological and social processes, thus straddling the distinction between psychology and sociology. At the current stage of development of the social sciences the rightful place of 'attitude' is, if anywhere, in social psychology.

Attitudes are related to, but to be distinguished from, 'personality'; and related to, but to be distinguished from, 'culture'. 'Personality' refers to the total organization of internal psychological functioning. 'Aggressiveness', for instance, might be said to be a general trait of personality – denoting a tendency to be hostile towards all and sundry. However, 'a hostile attitude towards coloured people' is much less global and has reference outside the person to the social object of the attitude. The man in the *New Yorker* cartoon who declared that he hated everybody regardless of race, creed or colour was referring to his personality, not to his attitude. To have an attitude you have to be more discriminating than that; nevertheless many investigators have examined the idea that the nature and content of a specific attitude is related to an individual's personality, and have found much confirmatory evidence. The studies of the authoritarian personality with its inclination to prejudicial attitudes is a case in point. This area of work has become known as the functional approach to the study of attitudes because the basic question it asks is: what is the function of a given attitude for maintaining the personality characteristics of an individual?

On the sociological side, 'culture' is a very general notion referring to the system of values and orientations common to a social or national group. Thus 'culture' refers to attitudes and beliefs which exist irrespective of individual differences; whereas for the social psychologist attitudes are located in the individual, and people may differ in their attitudes towards a whole range of social objects and practices. However, just as in the case of personality, the joint study of cultural factors and attitudes enlarges our knowledge of the determinants of human behaviour. The task of the social psychologist is ultimately that of setting personality, attitudes, and culture in a system of interdependent relationships.

Social psychology, as a distinct category of systematic research and theorizing, is younger than the twentieth century itself. And in the earlier decades of the century, as Gordon W. Allport points out, research into attitudes was the mainstay of empirical social psychology, enabling it to establish itself with some respectability as an independent discipline. In this period – let us say roughly the period between the two world wars – interest in attitudes manifested itself in two forms: first, in what we call research into content, in relatively unsophisticated and largely a-theoretical investigations of the attitudes of particular social groups towards issues or objects of current interest and social importance; and secondly, in the construction of scaling techniques for the quantification of attitude assessment. In later years, after 1940, as social psychology itself mellowed and established itself in many other areas, the study of attitudes became more ambitious and more systematic. Further developments have of course taken place in conceptualization, in measurement, and in the investigation of the content of attitudes. The study of prejudice, so much a part of the problem-centred approach of many American social psychologists, has been in post-war years enriched by the study of the more systematically elaborated syndrome of authoritarianism. But the most striking element of post-war work on attitudes has been a vast expansion in the study of attitude change. This has encompassed both experimental and field studies (see IIC), and has moreover given rise in recent years to various theoretical models of increasing elegance and usefulness, some of which are described in these readings.

A feature of the systematic theory of attitude structure and change now being developed is that it relates the structure of attitudes to general psychological theory. For some time, as stated before, attitude research was *the* mainstream of empirical social psychology. However, it was at the same time distant from the mainstream of general and experimental psychology. The dichotomy between social and experimental psychology, or between social and general psychology, is commonly made, but must be regarded as a historical survival of limited value. It ignores the fact, for instance, that much of the research reported or described in these readings is experimental in nature. In the earlier years of the century there was considerably more justification for making such a distinction than there is today. In the inter-war years experimental psychology was engaged upon its great age of rat research and theory-building, giving rise to the well-known systems of Hull, Tolman and others. From this arena the study of attitudes was far removed. The theoretical models of attitudes which are available today range from the neo-behaviouristic to the cognitive and psychoanalytic: each definitely attempts to set attitudes well within the sphere of general psychological functioning. This is particularly true of the various 'cognitive consistency' models reviewed in this book by Zajonc and elsewhere by Brown (see suggestions for further reading); and of the authoritarian personality studies, described here by Sanford and referred to by several other authors. No longer can the study of attitudes be said to be an encapsulated sub-area of psychology.

A similar point, moreover, can be made from the sociological point of view. Attitudes are today more firmly integrated, theoretically and empirically, with the concepts of social roles and norms, reference groups, and socialization processes than ever before. This is an implementation in terms of modern sociology of what Karl Marx, albeit in a different terminology, realized even in the nineteenth century: that a person's social conditions determine his attitudes.

11

An additional comment concerning the organization of this book is required. The sections on attitude theory and on methods of attitude measurement are at the very end, in Part III, even though theory and method are logically prior to substantive research. The major justification for this arrangement is the fact that the development of theory and of refined techniques of measurement in this area has been largely divorced from the main body of substantive attitude research. This is peculiar and unfortunate. Take, for instance, the enterprising cognitive consistency theories (see Zajonc) which are attracting so much interest today. The major theorists concerned (Heider, Osgood, Festinger, etc.) are not greatly identified with attitude research. And, in any case, these are theories whose main focus of convenience in the area of attitudes is on attitude *change*: equally necessary, perhaps more necessary are theories relating attitudes to behaviour, but this relationship has received very much less attention. If we turn to the area of measurement techniques, we find that quantitative methods of attitude scaling have become increasingly ambitious and sophisticated, but nonetheless seem to have been very little utilized in any of the substantively important research into attitudes. It would appear, in fact, that those scientists who develop measuring devices and those who carry out basic research on attitude processes are not at all the same kind of people, and have little influence on one another.

Thus we have felt it permissible to employ a slightly unorthodox order of presentation. The student particularly interested in attitude change may prefer to read that section in conjunction with the theoretical contributions which appear later. But in any case the division of the material into sections and the particular order of presentation are inevitably arbitrary, and largely dependent on the state of attitude research at the time of writing. We look forward to the day when the conceptual theoretical, methodological and substantive aspects of attitude research will be fully integrated and interdependent. The contemporary energetic developments may well produce in the future an integration of attitudes (perhaps using different terminology) with general theory in social science. We have attempted in these readings to highlight some of the problems involved in achieving this end, and at the same time to provide examples of the major advances and achievements in attitude research.

Part One THE CONCEPT OF ATTITUDE

The selections in this part constitute an introduction to the problems inherent in arriving at an adequate conceptualization of 'attitude'. Many of the issues raised are still open to dispute, and the student is encouraged to view their significance from a vantage-point of acquaintance with attitude research and theory. The first excerpt is from Gordon W. Allport, who has himself been a leading figure in the study of attitudes for three decades. Allport outlines the early history of the concept in psychology and sociology, and makes it clear that attitude research was 'the primary building stone in the edifice of social psychology'. Among the conceptions of 'attitude' cited by Allport is the very influential definition that he himself proposed in 1935. Theodore M. Newcomb, in providing a concise authoritative statement on the usage of the concept, finds it necessary, thirty years later, to quote this same definition of Allport's. Newcomb points out some contextual differences between psychologists and sociologists, and emphasizes that attitudes must of necessity be inferred from observed behaviour. The short extract from Donald T. Campbell and the longer discussion by Cooper and McGaugh deal with the conceptual overlap of many technical terms which are related to the notion of attitude. Campbell provocatively plunges us into the terminological jungle in order to indicate the similarity or mutual relevance of terms from disparate theoretical frameworks throughout the behavioural sciences. Cooper and McGaugh cite and define terms which are frequently used by social psychologists as specific variations of the attitude construct. Finally there is a careful expository discussion of the cognitive nature of attitudes by Solomon Asch. This is especially interesting in view of the more recent theories of attitude organization framed within the general cognitive orientation taken up here by Asch.

1 G. W. Allport

Attitudes in the History of Social Psychology

Excerpt from: G. W. Allport, *Handbook of Social Psychology*, G. Lindzey (ed.), Addison-Wesley, U.S.A., 1954, Vol. 1, pp. 43–5.

This concept is probably the most distinctive and indispensable concept in contemporary American social psychology. No term appears more frequently in experimental and theoretical literature. Its popularity is not difficult to explain. It has come into favor, first of all, because it is not the property of any one psychological school of thought, and therefore serves admirably the purposes of eclectic writers. Furthermore, it is a concept which escapes the controversy concerning the relative influence of heredity and environment. Since an attitude may combine both instinct and habit in any proportion, it avoids the extreme commitments of both the instinct theory and environmentalism. The term likewise is elastic enough to apply either to the dispositions of single, isolated individuals or to broad patterns of culture (common attitudes). Psychologists and sociologists therefore find in it a meeting point for discussion and research. This useful, one might almost say peaceful, concept has been so widely adopted that it has virtually established itself as the keystone in the edifice of American social psychology. In fact, several writers, starting with Thomas and Znaniecki (1918), have *defined* social psychology as 'the scientific study of attitudes'.

Like most abstract terms in the English language, *attitude* has more than one meaning. Derived from the Latin *aptus*, it has on the one hand the significance of 'fitness' or 'adaptedness', connoting, as does its by-form *aptitude*, a subjective or mental state of preparation for action. Through its use in the field of art, however, the term came to have a quite independent meaning; it referred to the outward or visible posture (the bodily position) of a figure in statuary or painting. The first meaning is clearly preserved in the phrase 'mental attitudes', and the second meaning in 'motor attitudes'. Since mentalistic psychology historically precedes response psychology, it is only natural to find that mental attitudes are given recognition earlier than motor attitudes. One of the earliest psychologists to employ the term was Herbert Spencer. In his *First Principles* (1862), he wrote:

Arriving at correct judgements on disputed questions, much depends on the attitude of mind we preserve while listening to, or taking part in, the controversy; and for the preservation of a right attitude it is needful that we should learn how true, and yet how untrue, are average human beliefs. (Vol. I, 1, i.)

Somewhat later, when psychologists were forsaking their exclusively mentalistic point of view, the concept of *motor attitudes* became popular. In 1888, for example, N. Lange developed a motor theory wherein the process of a perception was considered to be in large part a consequence of muscular preparation or 'set'. At about the same time Münsterberg (1889) developed his action theory of attention, and Féré (1890) maintained that a balanced condition of tension in the muscles was a determining condition of selective consciousness.

In recent years it is uncommon to find explicit labeling of an attitude as either 'mental' or 'motor'. Such a practice smacks of body-mind dualism, and is therefore distasteful to contemporary psychologists. In nearly all cases today the term appears without a qualifying adjective, and implicitly retains both its original meanings: a mental aptness and a motor set. Attitude connotes *a neuropsychic state of readiness for mental and physical activity*.

Perhaps the first explicit recognition of attitudes within the domain of laboratory psychology was in connection with a study of reaction time. In 1888 L. Lange discovered that a subject who was consciously prepared to press a telegraph key immediately upon receiving a signal reacted more quickly than did one whose attention was directed mainly to the incoming stimulus, and whose consciousness was not therefore directed primarily upon the expected reaction. After Lange's work, the task attitude, or *Aufgabe*, as it came to be called, was discovered to play a decisive part in nearly all psychological experiments. Not only in the reaction experiment, but in investigations of perception, recall, judgment, thought, and volition, the central importance of the subjects' *preparedness* became universally recognized. In Germany, where most of the early experimental work was done, there arose a swarm of technical expressions to designate the varieties of mental and motor 'sets' that influence the subjects' trains of thought or behavior during the experiment. In addition to the *Aufgabe*, there was the *Absicht* (conscious purpose), the *Zielvorstellung* (or idea of the goal), the *Bezugsvorstellung* (idea of the relation between the self and the object to which the self is responding), the *Richtungsvorstellung* (or idea of direction), the *determinierende Tendenz* (any disposition that brings in its train the spontaneous appearance of a determined idea), the *Einstellung*, a more general term (roughly equivalent to 'set'), the *Haltung* (with a more behavioral connotation), and the *Bewusstseinslage* (the 'posture or lay of consciousness'). It was perhaps the lack of a general term equivalent to 'attitude' that led the German experimentalists to discover so many types and forms. The lack may also explain why no systematic social psychology was written in Germany based upon a unified concept of 'attitude'.

Then came the lively controversy over the place of attitudes in consciousness. The *Würzburg* school was agreed that attitudes were neither sensation, nor imagery, nor affection, nor any combination of these states. Time and again attitudes were studied by the method of introspection, always with meager results. Often an attitude seemed to have no representation in consciousness other than a vague sense of need, or some indefinite and unanalyzable feeling of doubt, assent, conviction, effort, or familiarity (Titchener, 1909).

As a result of the *Würzburg* work all psychologists came to accept attitudes, but not all believed them to be impalpable and irreducible mental elements. In general, the followers of Wundt believed that attitudes could be accounted for adequately as *feelings*, particularly as some blend of striving and excitement. Clarke (1911), a pupil of Titchener, found that attitudes in large part *are* represented in consciousness through imagery, sensation, and affection, and that where no such states are reported there is presumably merely a decay or abbreviation of these same constituents.

However they might disagree upon the nature of attitudes as they appear in consciousness, all investigators, even the most orthodox, came to admit attitudes as an indispensable part of their psychological armamentarium. Titchener is a case in point. His *Outline of Psychology* in 1899 contained no reference to attitude; ten years later, in his *Textbook of Psychology*, several pages are given to the subject, and its systematic importance is fully recognized.

Many authors have reduced the phenomena of perception, judgment, memory, learning, and thought largely to the operation of attitudes (*cf.*, e.g. Ach, 1905; Bartlett, 1932). Without guiding attitudes the individual is confused and baffled. Some kind of preparation is essential before he can make a satisfactory observation, pass suitable judgment, or make any but the most primitive reflex type of response. Attitudes determine for each individual what he will see and hear, what he will think and what he will do.

17

To borrow a phrase from William James, they 'engender meaning upon the world'; they draw lines about, and segregate, an otherwise chaotic environment; they are our methods for finding our way about in an ambiguous universe. It is especially when the stimulus is not of great intensity nor closely bound with some reflex or automatic response that attitudes play a decisive role in the determination of meaning and of behavior.

The meagerness with which attitudes are represented in consciousness resulted in a tendency to regard them as manifestations of brain activity or of the unconscious mind. The persistence of attitudes that are totally unconscious was demonstrated by Müller and Pilzecker (1900), who called the phenomenon 'perseveration'. The tendency of the subject to slip into some frame of mind peculiar to himself led Koffka (1912) to postulate 'latent attitudes'. Washburn (1916) characterized attitudes as 'static movement systems' within the organs of the body and the brain. Other writers, still more physiologically inclined, subsumed attitudes under neurological rubrics: traces, neurograms, incitograms, brain patterns, and the like. The contribution of the Würzburger and of all other experimental psychologists was in effect the demonstration that the concept of attitude is indispensable.

But it was the influence of Freud that endowed attitudes with vitality, equating them with longing, hatred and love, with passion and prejudice, in short, with the onrushing stream of unconscious life. Without the painstaking labors of the experimentalists, attitudes would not today be an established concept in the field of psychology; but also without the influence of psychoanalytic theory they would certainly have remained relatively lifeless, and would not have been of much assistance to social psychology. For the explanation of prejudice, loyalty, patriotism, crowd behavior, control by propaganda, no anemic conception of attitudes will suffice.

As we have said, the instinct hypothesis did not satisfy social scientists for long, for the very nature of their work forced them to recognize the importance of custom and environment in shaping social behavior. The instinct hypothesis has precisely the contrary emphasis. What social scientists required was a new psychological concept that would escape on the one hand from the hollow impersonality of 'custom' and 'social force', and on the other from nativism. They gradually adopted the concept of *attitude*.

The credit for instituting the concept as a permanent and central feature in sociological writing must be assigned to Thomas and Znaniecki (1918), who gave it systematic priority in their monumental study of Polish peasants. Before this time the term had made only sporadic appearances in sociological literature, but immediately afterward it was adopted with enthusiasm by scores of writers.

According to Thomas and Znaniecki, the study of attitudes is *par excellence* the field of social psychology. Attitudes are individual mental processes which determine both the actual and potential responses of each person in the social world. Since an attitude is always directed toward some object, it may be defined as a 'state of mind of the individual toward a value'. Values are usually social in nature, that is to say, they are objects of common regard on the part of socialized men. Love of money, desire for fame, hatred of foreigners, respect for a scientific doctrine are typical attitudes. It follows that money, fame, foreigners, and a scientific theory are all values. A social value is defined as 'any datum having an empirical content accessible to the members of some social group and a meaning with regard to which it is or may be an object of activity'. There are, to be sure, numerous attitudes corresponding to every social value; there are, for example, many attitudes regarding the church or the state. There are also numerous possible values for any single attitude. The iconoclast may direct his attacks quite at random upon all established social values, or the Philistine may accept them all uncritically. Hence in the social world, as studied by the sociologist, both values and attitudes must have a place.

Following closely in the same vein of thought, Faris (1925) proposed additional refinements. He would distinguish between conscious and unconscious attitudes, between mental and motor attitudes, between individual and group attitudes, and between latent and kinetic attitudes. Park (see Young, 1931), who is likewise in essential agreement with this school of thought, suggests four criteria for an attitude: (1) it must have definite orientation in the world of objects (or values), and in this respect differ from simple and conditioned reflexes; (2) it must not be an altogether automatic and routine type of conduct, but must display some tension even when latent; (3) it varies in intensity, sometimes being regnant, sometimes relatively ineffective; (4) it is rooted in experience, and therefore is not simply a social instinct.

The following are typical definitions of attitude that emerged:

Attitude = the specific mental disposition toward an incoming (or arising) experience, whereby that experience is modified; or, a condition of readiness for a certain type of activity. (Warren, *Dictionary of Psychology*, 1934.)

19

An attitude is a mental disposition of the human individual to act for or against a definite object. (Droba, 1933.)

An attitude is a mental and neural state of readiness, organized through experience, exerting a directive or dynamic influence upon the individual's response to all objects and situations with which it is related. (G. W. Allport, 1935.)

As we have said, the attitude unit has been the primary building stone in the edifice of social psychology. It has, of course, had many critics. Especially in recent years, learning theorists, field theorists, phenomenologists have attempted to dislodge it. But it is questionable whether their combined efforts can do more than refine the concept for future use. After all, social behavior reflects so much organization, recurrent and habitual expectancy, that the doctrine of attitude (or some close equivalent) is necessary. Without some such concept, social psychologists could not work in the fields of public opinion, national character, or institutional behavior – to mention only a few areas; nor could they characterize the mental organization of social man. The term itself may not be indispensable, but what it stands for is.

References

Ach, N., *Ueber die Willenstätigkeit und das Denken*, Göttingen: Vanderhoeck and Ruprecht, 1905.

Allport, G. W., Attitudes. In C. M. Murchison (ed.), *Handbook of Social Psychology*. Worcester, Mass.: Clark Univ. Press, 1935.

Bartlett, F. C., *Remembering*. Cambridge: Cambridge Univ. Press, 1932.

Clarke, H. M., Conscious attitudes. *Amer. J. Psychol.*, 32, 214–49, 1911.

Droba, D. D., The nature of attitude. *J. Soc. Psych.*, 4, 444–63, 1933.

Faris, E., The concept of social attitudes. *J. applied Sociol.*, 9, 404–9, 1925.

Féré, C., Note sur la physiologie de l'attention. *Rev. Phil.*, 30, 393–405, 1890.

Koffka, K., Zur Analyse der Vorstellungen und ihren Gesetzen. Leipzig: Quelle and Meyer, 1912.

Lange, L., Neue Experimente über den Vorgang der einfachen Reaktion auf Sinneseindrücke. *Phil. Stud.*, 4, 472–510, 1888.

Lange, N., Beiträge zur Theorie der sinnlichen Aufmerksamkeit und der activen Apperception. *Phil. Stud.*, 4, 390–422, 1888.

Müller, G. E., and Pilzecker, A., Experimentelle Beiträge zur Lehre vom Gedächtnis. *Z. Psychol.*, Ergbd. 1, 1900.

Münsterberg, H., Beiträge zur Experimentellen Psychologie. Vol. 1. Freiburg: Morh., 1889.

Spencer, H., *First principles*. Preface dated 1862. New York: Appleton, 1895.

Thomas, W. I., and Znaniecki, F., *The Polish peasant in Europe and America*. Boston: Badger, 1918–20.

Titchener, E. B., *Experimental psychology of the thought processes*. New York: Macmillan. 1909.

Titchener, E. B., *A textbook of psychology*. New York: Macmillan, 1910.

Warren, H. C. (ed.), *Dictionary of psychology.* Boston: Houghton
Mifflin, 1934.
Washburn, M. F., *Movement and mental imagery.* Boston: Houghton
Mifflin, 1916.
Young, K. (ed.), *Social attitudes.* New York: Holt, 1931.

2   T. M. Newcomb

On the Definition of Attitude

Excerpt from: T. M. Newcomb, *A Dictionary of the Social Sciences*, J. Gould and W. L. Kolb (eds.), Tavistock, London, 1964.

The essential components of the concept of *attitude* are two:

(*a*) The notion of attitude has been found useful, if not indispensable, because it provides a conceptual bridge between persisting psychological states of the individual and persisting objects of orientation (including whole classes of objects) in that individual's world. To understand the conditions under which attitudes are formed, endure, and change is thus equivalent to understanding the conditions of a very great deal of behaviour.

(*b*) This important conceptual tool must be so defined as to come to grips with the facts of intra-individual psychological organization (including the individual's taxonomy of objects, whether concrete or abstract), and also with the facts of persistence and change. Since we understand things best when we understand the conditions under which they do and do not change, an adequate definition must face the Heraclitean problems of persistence in spite of change. It must, moreover, remain accessible to the empirical facts of observed behaviour, from which alone attitudes can be inferred.

Some such definition as the following therefore seems required: An *attitude* is the individual's organization of psychological processes, as inferred from his behaviour, with respect to some aspect of the world which he distinguishes from other aspects. It represents the residue of his previous experience with which he approaches any subsequent situation including that aspect and, together with the contemporary influences in such a situation, determines his behaviour in it. Attitudes are enduring in the sense that such residues are carried over to new situations, but they change in so far as new residues are acquired through experience in new situations.

Psychologists and sociologists, to whom the notion has more conceptual significance than to other social scientists, differ contextually rather than conceptually in their usage of the term. Historically, both disciplines have, in one way or another, regarded attitudes as tendencies to act with regard to some specifiable entity.

Many sociologists, following W. I. Thomas and F. Znaniecki, have viewed attitudes primarily in the context of social value which they define as 'any datum having an empirical content accessible to the members of some social group and a meaning with regard to which it is or may be an object of activity' (*The Polish Peasant in Europe and America*, New York: Knopf, 1927, Vol. I, p. 21). Attitudes and values are, in fact, defined interdependently: 'A value is the objective counterpart of the attitude' (ibid., p. 22); and 'The attitude is thus the individual counterpart of the social value' (ibid., p. 22). 'It is the individual tendency to react, either positively or negatively, to a given social value' (ibid., p. 24).

Psychologists have characteristically been concerned with relationships between attitudes and other psychological characteristics of individuals, and their social-psychological treatises, at least since the beginning of the 1930s (cf. G. and L. B. Murphy, *Experimental Social Psychology*, New York: Harper & Brothers, 1931), have devoted much space to such topics. Among their many definitions, two have probably been most influential: 'An attitude is a mental and neural state of readiness, organized through experience, exerting a directive or dynamic influence upon the individual's response to all objects and situations with which it is related' (G. W. Allport, 'Attitudes', in C. Murchison (ed.), *Handbook of Social Psychology*, Worcester, Mass.: Clark University Press, 1935, p. 810); and 'An attitude can be defined as an enduring organization of motivational, emotional, perceptual, and cognitive processes with respect to some aspect of the individual's world' (D. Krech and R. S. Crutchfield, *Theory and Problems of Social Psychology*, New York: McGraw-Hill, 1948, p. 152).

Attitudes have occasionally been defined, both by sociologists (cf. W. M. Fuson, 'Attitudes: A Note on the Concept and Its Research Context', *American Sociological Review*, vol. 7, 1942, pp. 856–7) and by psychologists (cf. D. T. Campbell, 'The Indirect Assessment of Social Attitudes', *Psychological Bulletin*, vol. 47, 1950, pp. 15–38) simply in terms of the probability of the occurrence of a specified behaviour in a specified situation. Such definitions, while relatively devoid of conceptual content, serve to remind us that the ultimate referent of attitudes is behaviour.

Often, though not invariably, motives, like attitudes, are distinguished from one another by labels which refer to objects of orientation. Perhaps the principal distinctions between motives and attitudes are the following: (*a*) motives are conceptualized as existing only during those periods in which organisms are actually being activated in some manner, while attitudes are thought of as persisting, even during periods of behavioural quiescence; and (*b*) a wide range of specific and transitory motives may be aroused in the same individual who may be said to have a single, general attitude toward a whole class of specific objects – e.g. an entomologist with a favourable attitude toward lepidoptera is, at a given moment, motivated to catch a particular butterfly. Thus attitudes are generally both more persistent and more inclusive than motives, and a 'motive' which is described as both persistent and general is indistinguishable from an attitude.

3 D. T. Campbell

Acquired Behavioral Dispositions

Excerpt from: D. T. Campbell, *Psychology: A Study of A Science*,
S. Koch (ed.) McGraw-Hill, U.S.A., 1963, Vol. 6, pp. 100–1.

[. . . .]

Here is a list of terms, all of which – in part, at least – call attention
to the fact that experience has modified the behavioral tendencies
of the organism:

acquired drive
adaptation
adjustment
Anschauung
anticipation
apperceptive mass
association
attitude
behavioral
    environment
belief
bent
canalization
cathectic orientation
cathexis
cell assembly
cognitive map
cognitive structure
concept
conditioned reflex
conviction
definition of the
    situation
determining tendency
disposition
engram
evaluation
expectancy

expectation
experience
fixation
frame of reference
goal
hab
habit
hypothesis
idea
imprinting
integrative field
intention
interest
judgment
knowledge
learning
life space
meaning
memory
mental image
motive
need disposition
neurobiotaxis
notion
object
opinion
orientation

past history of
    reinforcement
perceptual
    sensitization
percept
perseveration
personality trait
predisposition
    (acquired)
prejudgement
representation
response disposition
response latency
response probability
response threshold
role perception
schema
sentiment
set
stereotype
synaptic threshold
    change
tendency
tinsit
trace
valence
value

4 J. B. Cooper and J. L. McGaugh

Attitude and Related Concepts

Excerpt from: J. B. Cooper and J. L. McGaugh, *Integrating Principles of Social Psychology*, Schenkman, U.S.A., pp. 240–4.

While the term *attitude* is used most generally in contemporary psychology to designate psychological set, and we find it used psychologically in a generic sense, there are other terms that are often used with the intention of conveying more specific psychological meaning. Certain of these correlative terms seem to introduce more confusion than clarification of the basic concept of psychological set. On the other hand, though certain of these terms are often used in literary ways to convey quite variable meanings they are worth citing since we may safely assume that their long history in the language insures that they have some utility. The terms which are used most frequently as specific variations of the attitude construct are described in the next paragraphs.

Belief
A belief is an attitude which incorporates a large amount of cognitive structuring. Operationally, one has an attitude *toward* and a belief *in* or *about* a stimulus object (Krech and Crutchfield, 1948). One believes in another person, a political concept, or a theory. The stimulus object of a belief is relatively complex even though this may mean that the subject has differentiated the object into smaller and smaller sub-regions. Belief connotes an attitude which involves or identifies the subject deeply with the object. The individual uses his belief as a basis for predicting what will happen in the future.

Bias
Bias literally refers to that which is bent or oblique. A father may be correctly thought of as biased in favor of his own child when he overvalues the child's competitive behavior. In such an instance the outside observer more or less expects this. His evaluation of the father's attitude is that it is based upon incomplete, inaccurate, preconceived or deductive premises. Biases may also be described as weak prejudices, prejudices that do not carry conviction or great potency. Biases are often admitted by the subject; he is willing to admit that his attitude is not based on as firm ground as

it perhaps should be. This he has great difficulty doing with a prejudice. Thus, a biased attitude is a perception of a stimulus object from a slightly warped, inaccurate position.

Doctrine

Doctrine literally means that which is taught. Coutu (1949) puts the concept nicely when he says that it refers to that which we are taught and expected to believe; how things should be done and what should be believed. The 'doctrine of the Church', 'doctrine of the Republican Party', 'doctrine of Communism' are teachings, elaborate stimulus objects, toward which individuals have attitudes. A doctrine is a highly involved logical system concerning some complex phenomenon to which an individual subscribes or objects. A doctrine must be accepted or rejected – there are no shades of gray, since it is a way of interpreting an important phenomenon. A doctrine explicitly describes (by codification) the reasons for adherence and the ways in which those who subscribe to it should behave as a function of its validity.

Faith

Faith is a complex form of attitude involving deep affective meaning. It refers to a system of attitudes that describes a specific and fundamental belief in a person or principle or conception which may or may not be shared by others. 'Faith' stands between 'belief' and 'ideology'. It is belief in that it is a prediction, it tells what will happen in the future. It is ideology in that it may be an elaborate cognitive system which purports to explain some phenomenon. On the other hand, one may be said to have faith in a doctrine. Thus, the term is closely associated with other 'attitude species' terms. All theologies incorporate faith; in fact, religions are frequently referred to as faiths. Also, faith incorporates personal identification; the individual surrenders self to a predetermined future. While the term is infrequently used in current psychological parlance, it is quite possible that as psychology moves into a more intensive and systematic study of religious experience, the concept of faith will undergo rigorous scrutiny (Dunlap, 1946). If we can agree upon an operational definition there is no reason why faith cannot be measured and dealt with quantitatively.

Ideology

According to Gordon Allport (1954), the ideology construct can be traced back to Francis Bacon's 'idols'. In this sense an ideology is an elaborate cognitive system which may be used to justify certain forms of behavior – or, is a means of rationalization. Historically, ideology connotes hypocrisy. For example, the term was used by Marx and Engels to describe the elaborate system of 'false' logic used by the capitalists to justify their favored socio-economic positions. These writers would never have referred to 'communist doctrine' as an ideology. By the same token, it is common practice for non-communists to refer to communist doctrine as an ideology, thereby connoting something unsavory. In this sense a person would never use the term ideology to describe his own religious doctrine, though he might freely use it to describe another religious doctrine. Thus, the term is secular from the individual's standpoint. In recent times there has been a shift in the meaning of ideology in the direction of eliminating the negative connotation. Democratically oriented persons may now occasionally refer to belief in democracy and the rationale lying back of the belief as the 'democratic ideology'. When he does this he certainly imputes nothing but good and truth.

Newcomb speaks of ideologies as '. . . codifications of certain kinds of group norms' (1950, p. 274). The truth of an ideology may be defended even though there are no criteria by which its accuracy may be tested. Thus, ideology is intimately related to faith, in that an ideology must be accepted as faith.

From the standpoint of the individual, the term ideology may be used with a slightly different meaning. This involves personality structure and content. It would be accurate, for example, to speak of an 'authoritarian ideology' without implying adherence to a particular system, such as communism or fascism. This use refers to the individual's outlook upon self and society (i.e., other humans). Scales that have been developed for the assessment of authoritarian and nonauthoritarian personality characteristics may be used to describe individual social ideologies. From this standpoint, an individual's social ideology represents a holistic view of his self perception and his perception of society. In a sense it is a generalized, global attitude, virtually a 'philosophy of life', though not formally structured.

Judgment

This is either the process or the result of the process of classifying stimulus objects (including cognitive events) into categories. It is always comparative. In that many judgments are not ego-related, not all judgments can be classified as social attitudes. For example, one may judge one tree as taller than another. Such a judgment incorporates no ego-involvement, no affective property, and no 'barrier' or 'facilitation' character. On the other hand, one may judge a given person as better than another. Thus, to the extent that a judgment-produced perceptual set has ego-involvement, an affective property, and 'barrier' or 'facilitation' character it can be properly thought of as a type of attitude.

Opinion

An opinion is a tentative perceptual set toward points of view (cognitive organizations) or stimulus objects. An opinion is tentative in that the subject reserves the right to reverse himself and realizes that the cognitive organization or stimulus object he now perceives as a barrier may at a later time be viewed as a facilitation. Opinions play an important role in the thought process in that they represent cognitive summaries along the way. Ideas and constructs are organized during the constant process of cognitive exploration. Once such a summary emerges the individual may then 'stand back' and appraise it. To the extent that the appraisal is tentative, nonfixed, it is an opinion.

As with all these 'species terms', 'opinion' is often used loosely. Often it is used synonymously with the generic term 'attitude'. Public opinion polling, for example, samples attitudes of which only some are actually opinions. Some are well-fixed prejudices, ideologies, beliefs, values, and judgments. In general, additional information concerning attitude strength will reveal whether the opinion measured is actually an opinion or some other type of attitude.

The popular meaning attached to opinion may take any one of three meanings. First, it may refer to the individual's tentative set itself. Second, it may refer to a point of view or set in the abstract; that is, a possibility to which a person may or may not subscribe. Third, it may have a 'collective' meaning. This is to say that the term 'public opinion' means an attitudinal consensus at a given time which, it is supposed, may shift at a later time.

Value

The term *value* is used in many ways, though it is never unrelated to the attitude construct. Historically, there have been two basic theoretical approaches to the study of value. One rests upon the assumption that worth resides in the stimulus object, that the stimulus object has an intrinsic worth or importance which is unrelated to man, the user of the stimulus object. The other rests upon the assumption that stimulus objects do not have intrinsic worth, that an object's worth is only a function of the ways humans perceive it. According to this position, a given stimulus object could be of great worth to a person at a particular time, though at another time he might perceive it as a barrier. The ancient story of King Midas is evidence that this second position is much more in line with human behavior and experience than the first and that the distinction we are pointing out is not something new. The second view holds that the worth an individual ascribes to an object is its value for that individual. Thus, a given object has as many values as there are humans with varying worth ascriptions to perceive it.

Field theory has made much of the value concept. While field theory denies neither the existence nor the importance of stimulus objects, it insists upon assessing their significance properly. As we have pointed out, the individual's ascription of worth to a stimulus object is, to use field terms, assigning it a valence. Thus, for a given individual, a stimulus object with which the individual is familiar and for whom the stimulus object has significance, has a positive or negative valence. As the term is ordinarily used in psychology, this field theoretical interpretation may be applied to the individual's most important life goals.

In a broad psychological sense, Newcomb (1950) speaks of dominant frames of reference which tie together one's attitudes. Such frames of reference are guide lines or maps used to evaluate experience and behavior as being in line or out of line with life goals. When we include the goals it is proper to speak of these as 'value systems'. And Allport *et al.* (1951) have theorized that there are six possible life values: theoretical, economic, aesthetic, social, political, and religious. A person develops a personality structure and content which uses one or another of these 'life themes' as his dominant frame of reference. For example, the 'political personality' is preoccupied with social power, and evaluates stimulus objects predominantly from a power standpoint. Or, put differently, for such a person what is most important in life? In this case the answer would be: the attainment of power over others and the use of the stimulus objects about him for this purpose.

The value concept in contemporary psychology is quite broad and often loosely used. The fact that it is used so much should suggest, however, that it does have substance. For our purposes, we propose two uses. First, a *value* is an attitude which is dominated by the individual's interpretation of the stimulus object's worth to him in the light of his goals. Second, a *value system* is an individual's over-all life aspiration (what he really wants to achieve) which on the one hand gives direction to his behavior, and on the other hand is a frame of reference by which the worth of stimulus objects may be judged. In the value system sense, it is an elaborate and articulated organization of attitudes.

References

Allport, G. W., The historical background of modern social psychology. In Lindzey, G. (ed.). *Handbook of Social Psychology*. Reading, Mass.: Addison-Wesley Publishing Co., 1954.

Allport, G. W., Vernon, P. E., and Lindzey, G., *Study of values*. Boston: Houghton Mifflin Co., 1951.

Coutu, W., *Emergent human nature*. New York: Alfred A. K. Knopf, 1949.

Dunlap, K., *Religion: Its functions in human life*. New York: McGraw-Hill, 1946.

Krech, D., and Crutchfield, R. S., *Theory and problems of social psychology*. New York: McGraw-Hill, 1948.

Newcomb, T. M., *Social psychology*. New York: Dryden Press, 1950.

5 S. E. Asch

Attitudes as Cognitive Structures

Excerpts from: S. E. Asch, *Social Psychology*, Prentice-Hall, U.S.A., 1952.

An attitude contains a more or less coherent ordering of a variety of data. It sometimes makes sense, for example, to say that a person has a certain position on civil liberties, on public ownership, on the rights of minorities, or on a current political crisis. What we mean by this statement is that the variety of observations and arguments that he brings forward are in some measure unified and that they converge to make a case. They stand in an ordered relation to each other; they are distinguishably different from an aggregation of statements that happen to refer to the same problem. What the person says at one point is understandably connected with what he has stated earlier or will say later, in the same way that the parts of a story are sensibly connected. It is on this basis that we undertake to foretell how a person is likely to respond to a new development.

Our purpose here is to state two propositions about the cognitive aspect of attitudes: (1) An attitude is an organization of experiences and data with reference to an object. It is a structure of a hierarchical order, the parts of which function in accordance with their position in the whole. (2) At the same time a given attitude is a quasi-open structure functioning as part of a wider context. In the absence of concrete investigation the present discussion will be tentative, its aim being to point to problems of potential importance.

Earlier we said that an attitude has the character of a commitment to a policy. In this respect it represents a dynamic assessment of a given situation with reference to an end. One fundamental consequence of such an assessment is that certain facts become relevant, others less relevant and that certain data become crucial, others less important. For example, the decision to go away on vacation carries a host of consequences. It immediately orders a wide set of facts with reference to the given end. Certain tasks must be attended to in time; others are postponed; one may not undertake new obligations for the near future; and certain old plans have to be revised. The major decision introduces a consistent direction in the light of which numerous other decisions are settled.

This describes also, it seems to me, an aspect of the functioning of attitudes. The decision to fight the Axis powers carried as a necessary consequence the establishment of an allied command, the pooling of resources, the exchange of military information, and a military alliance with the Soviet Union. The decision that the Soviet Union is a potential enemy has dictated a revision of virtually every item of domestic and foreign policy, from the building of shelters to turning defeated enemies into allies.

This trend, so easily observable in situations demanding action, is also evident in attitudes whose relation to action is more complex. Language aptly refers to attitude as a perspective or a point of view, implying a certain unified way of looking at data. The statement that Negroes are lacking in industry, are mentally inferior, and are happy with their lot is not simply a set of three assertions that one individual happens to hold simultaneously. Were one to succeed in challenging one of them effectively, the others could not easily remain unaltered. When someone defends the system of capitalistic enterprise on the ground that it has raised living standards, that it promotes individual initiative and offers the best conditions for the expression and reward of talent, and that it is most compatible with the liberties of individuals, the strength of the position derives, it would seem, precisely from the mutual support that the various assertions offer one another. A particularly cogent illustration of the systematic interconnectedness of beliefs is furnished by the reactions of many nineteenth-century people to the doctrine of evolution. The surrender of the belief that God created them in their present form could not be confined to that particular datum. It created an upheaval of many other beliefs, even where the connections were not logically compelling. The study of attitudes must, it would seem, make the minimum assumption that a given view is relatively unified, consisting of interdependent parts in mutual relation.

If attitudes are structured cognitively definite consequences follow for investigation. It becomes necessary to describe their main lines of organization and the degree of structurization they possess. In so far as an attitude is part of a wider system, it cannot be understood in its own terms alone. It becomes necessary to understand the major directions or premises of the individual's outlook, the cleavages that may exist, and the functions of a given attitude within its context. Because it is a semi-autonomous system, we need to study its formation and change in accordance with conditions directly relevant to it. Because it is a dependent part of a wider system, it is necessary for us to see its place and function in the person's scheme of things, to see how it takes shape and changes in a medium of already functioning views. We may, for example, find that the formation of a given attitude will encounter resistance if it contradicts the wider system that tends to equilibrium, or that it will take shape to conform to the system. On the other hand, a change in a very cogent part may start a process that alters the system as a whole.

Interaction of Attitude with Fact

The significance of an attitude is to be found in the effects it exerts upon current experiences and the appraisal of new conditions. Generally an attitude functions as an orientation to and context for current events. It has some of the earmarks and functions of an hypothesis, being a systematization and ordering of old experience. It therefore relates present happenings to what we already know and believe. Most generally, attitudes sensitize us to events that we might otherwise overlook; they may also be responsible for the neglect of contemporary facts and for special interpretations of them.

A vital function of attitudes is to be found in their mode of interaction with facts. That there can be disagreement about facts is a matter of the greatest consequence. For facts have a special status; the world is built on them. It is therefore pertinent to ask: What forms of interaction take place between an existing attitude and a fact relevant to it? Concrete investigation of this question is unfortunately limited. What is needed is observation of reactions to facts that are compatible with one's established view and to facts that contradict it.

In the extreme instance the encounter of a contradictory fact can undermine an attitude and produce a movement in the opposite direction. Such changes occur with relative infrequency, but when they do occur they mark serious turning points in history and in personal life. There were convinced pacifists during the last war who under the pressure of events decided that they should take an active part in the struggle; this change was not the consequence of group pressure or other external forces. For a given datum to produce such a drastic change it must have a crucial bearing on the content of the attitude; this is why single data ordinarily do not suffice to topple an entire structure. It is more usual for contradictory facts to create doubt and thus pave the way for later change. Little may happen to the fixed view for the time being. The person may still speak as he has in the past, but he may become more curious and alert to ask questions and make new observations.

More frequently observation brings before us the resistance of attitudes to the encroachment of contradictory data. Then we observe their seeking character and their tendency to seize upon facts that will confirm them. Outstanding historical events, such as the signing of the Soviet-Nazi pact in 1939, provide dramatic instances. The reactions to this event were violently different; to some it proved the fundamental identity of the Nazi and Soviet régimes; others claimed that it was the only action the Russian government could take after the perfidy of the Western powers at Munich. In these reactions we see a clear-cut instance of an attitude functioning as the context and of the particular fact functioning as part. Instances of this kind permit us to observe the powerful trends toward the incorporation of a new datum into an existing view.

This result, it should be noted, is not usually achieved simply by ignoring data because they are unpleasant. An attitude more often alters the *interpretation* of facts in such a way that the contradiction is removed. In the absence of formal evidence we will mention only a few possibilities: (1) A fact may be rejected because its authenticity is questioned. Either one doubts the source or questions the fact on the ground that it conflicts with other, presumably more complete data. One may, for example, refuse to believe that the engaging young man one has just met belongs to a group one despises. (2) The meaning of a fact may be interpreted to reduce its threat to an existing view. The ways in which this is achieved vary. (a) A fact may be *segregated* on the ground that it is not relevant or that it is out-dated. If this happens the fact is accepted but the attitude remains unchanged. (b) A related reaction is to *limit the meaning* of the fact. In the extreme instance the fact is taken to be an exception. (c) A particularly significant reaction is to *select a meaning* for the fact to fit the given attitude. One possible meaning may be selected, or the fact may be placed in the context of other data harmonious with the attitude. The belief that Negroes are inferior intellectually fits neatly into an anti-Negro position. Or one can with very little exertion interpret intelligence as shrewdness and so furnish ostensible support for an existing point of view. One can observe much adroitness in the manipulation of meanings in the interests of an undisturbed outlook. (3) Equally significant are the effects of attitudes in prompting us to seek facts in accordance with them and to avoid those that might serve as a threat. Investigation will probably reveal other and more extreme reactions, such as the refusal to look at a fact, the failure to follow up its meaning, or the invention of facts on the spot.*

Attitude as Preconception

Psychologists have continually attempted to find a systematic place for attitude by equating it with one or another of the known psychological functions. Some have attempted to solve the problem by asserting that attitudes are learned responses, or conditioned emotional reactions. Others assimilated the operation of attitudes to a more particular effect of past experience. One of the effects of past experience is to form predispositions which decide the direction we will follow among possible alternatives when we subsequently face new conditions. It became evident early in psychological investigation that the action of an individual at a given moment was often not to be understood only in terms of the properties of the given stimulus-situation. A factor of great importance is how he is set or prepared for the given situation. We expect our neighbor, when he opens his mouth, to speak in English; we would be much surprised if he spoke to us in Latin. When we purchase an article we expect the clerk to wrap it, not to sing us an aria. We walk down the familiar street with full confidence that the grocery store is around the corner and that we will not be waylaid in broad daylight. We do not ordinarily think of all the strange possibilities that might happen; we are often not even aware of the expectations we do have. But this is all the more impressive an indication of the operation of sets; they function most reliably when they are not present to consciousness. In each of these instances we are set for a particular unfolding of events and quite unprepared for different possibilities. In this sense a mental set has some qualities of a preconception or a prejudgment. It seemed reasonable to conclude that attitudes are particularly enduring sets formed by past experience. This identification seemed to offer the hope of reducing complex social processes to those observed under simpler conditions.

There is a rough basis in observation for the view that attitudes are chronic mental sets or preconceptions. Often it appears that the work of evaluating and deciding is largely done before one examines a new situation.† Recently the identification of attitude

* Those who hold apparently the same views may also differ in their reactions to new facts. How persons deal with new and unexpected facts may indeed be a crucial test of the most decisive qualities of their attitudes – their narrowness or width, their openness or rigidity.

† For a number of interesting examples the reader is referred to O. Klineberg, *Social Psychology*. New York: Henry Holt, 1940. (See especially pp. 291–2 and 350–1.)

with preconception has been extended in a new direction. The view has gained currency that the decisive effect of attitudes is to distort perception, recall, and thinking or to function as a source of error. In what follows we shall examine the consequences of this assumption.

A recent investigation by Hammond (1948) starts with the proposal that the presence of an attitude can be detected and its strength estimated by measuring the distortion it exercises on judgment. Groups of individuals read a series of factual questions dealing with the important issues of United States relations with Russia and of labor-management problems. The following were typical statements: 'Average weekly wage of the war workers in 1945 was (1) $37, (2) $57.' 'Lend-lease accounted for (1) 14%, (2) 2% of Russia's war material.' The individuals were asked to select in each instance the more accurate of the two alternatives. Neither of the alternatives was correct; in fact, they were selected to deviate from the truth in opposed directions. Furthermore, the questions could not be answered accurately except by specifically informed persons. This was the reason for choosing the questions and the alternatives; 'the principal requirement (for selection of questions) was to eliminate reality, the truth of the matter, as a factor and thus *force the respondent into a choice of errors*.' (p. 40.) One of the groups consisted of employees in a labor organization; the other was composed of businessmen. They were selected on the assumption that they were likely to be biased in opposite directions on the given issues and that they would therefore diverge in their errors correspondingly.

The results indeed pointed clearly in the predicted directions. The businessmen judged the facts erroneously according to their general position, and so did the labor group. The findings seem to confirm the proposition that there is a tendency to accept those facts that support one's view and to reject those incompatible with it. Results similar to these obtained in other investigations have gradually become the ground for the assertion that the most significant function of attitudes is to restrict and bias the psychological field.

Although these results are of interest, they do not unambiguously support the conclusion that an attitude is usually a source of error. A clear interpretation of the exclusively quantitative data is difficult to reach. Shall we conclude that attitudes distorted recall? This would mean assuming what is by no means proven – that the correct information was previously available to the subjects. It is more probable that the judgments of the business and labor groups were consistent with the information at their disposal and that they had earlier arrived at different positions partly because of differences of information. The interpretation implies that attitudes arise when information is tainted. Are we to conclude that adequate knowledge is incompatible with having an attitude?

Returning to the main discussion, we may observe that there are a number of difficulties to the apparently innocuous identification of attitude with mental set. Sets usually have a poor cognitive and emotional content; their strength is proportionate to our lack of awareness of them. This is often not true of attitudes. Their objects may be highly conceptualized and complex, and increasing awareness may strengthen them. There is also the fact that sets, unlike attitudes, are easily disrupted by changed conditions. Finally, it is not helpful to refer one little-known process to another that, despite much study, is ill-understood.

Equating attitudes with preconception also incurs the risk of identifying them with bias and error. The consequence is to conclude that attitudes are stereotyped, irrational solutions of unsolvable problems. This is, in effect, to deny that anything constructive can take place in the functioning of attitudes or that there can be attitudes that strive toward understanding. It is also to assert that attitudes are, regardless of their content, psychologically identical. One may question whether psychologists actually wish to commit themselves to the view that the contemporaries of Zola who stood on his side in the defense of Dreyfus were blinded by prejudice just as were those who rioted in the streets of Paris against him and that those who fought Nazi Germany in the last war were on psychologically the same footing as their enemies. One wonders whether these assumptions do not betray a bias, whether they do not import into what presumes to be an examination of social actions a philosophy of the subjective nature of social processes.

The reduction of attitude to a particular psychological process such as preconception misses the problem that Shand saw, that of clarifying the qualities of order and consistency in social experience and action. It is inadequate for systematic reasons, since initial observation alone is sufficient to establish that attitude includes all psychological functions. The derivation of attitude from a particular function, although it has the appearance of simplicity, has the effect of suppressing the role of other functions, such as reasoning and the organization of emotional experiences. It encourages the belief that attitudes place no new questions of theory before psychology. It is at least a question whether we can pour social phenomena without residue into the old conceptual bottles. The danger is that the term attitude ceases to have clear meaning – that it becomes a synonym for learning or mental set, or for a vague and elastic mélange of operations.

Reference
Hammond, K. R., Measuring attitudes by error-choice: an indirect method. *J. Abn. Soc. Psych.*, 43, 38–48, 1948.

Part Two RESEARCH IN ATTITUDES

This second part of the book is subdivided into four sections:
(I) substantive research into attitude content; (II) research into
the origins and development of attitudes; (III) investigations of
attitude change; and (IV) studies of the relation between attitudes
and behaviour. A brief commentary introduces each section.

I Focus on Content

This section contains six content-centred examples of empirical research. The selections are chosen to be a typical cross-section of the social science literature in this field, but not largely, or not primarily, concerned with the dynamics and processes of attitudes. Ideas about foreigners (Himmelweit, Oppenheim and Vince), mothers' attitudes to child upbringing (Lynn and Gordon), political attitudes (Moskos and Bell), prejudice (Bettelheim and Janowitz), attitudes under conditions of unemployment (Jahoda, Lazarsfeld and Zeisel), and the relationship of certain attitudes with religious behaviour (Argyle) – these are the aspects of attitude on which attention was focused by the researchers involved. These excerpts and articles provide typical examples of valuable and interesting research whose focus was mainly on the attitudes themselves. One bias, however, we feel we should admit to: the selection for this section was as far as possible made from non-American sources. This was not because of any unfavourable attitude towards the United States on our part. On the contrary, it is indisputable that the large majority of the important work on attitudes has been carried out by American social scientists. This is reflected in the selections for the other sections of the book, where American sources dominate. In this section we have attempted to redress the balance a little.

6   H. T. Himmelweit, A. N. Oppenheim and P. Vince

The Influence of Television on Ideas About Foreigners*

Excerpt from: H.T. Himmelweit *et al.*, *Television and the Child*, Oxford U.P., London, 1958, pp. 253–6.

Television provides many opportunities for children to see how foreigners live and what their outlook and attitudes are. The BBC ran, at the time of testing, *Children's International Newsreel* and other types of programme designed to bring young viewers in contact with European countries. How far has television given children a better understanding of other people's ways of life ? How far has it made foreigners and foreign countries more attractive to them ?

We asked the children: *Suppose you could choose to be born again anywhere. Which country would you choose?* They were given two sentences to complete: *I would choose to be born in . . . I would choose this country because . . .* The question was deliberately worded so as to encourage children to name countries other than their own.

Television, we found, made viewers somewhat more interested in other countries; 51 % of the older children (as against 45 % of the controls) and 46 % of the younger viewers (as against 39 % of the controls) chose countries other than England. The difference, while consistent, was not, however, significant.

Of countries outside the Commonwealth, the United States received the highest mention by viewers and controls alike (about 18 %). There was a tendency for more viewers than controls to name European countries. This was especially so with the 10–11-year-olds (18 % as against 10 % of the controls; the figures for the 13–14-year-olds were 17 % and 12 % respectively). This greater interest probably reflected the greater familiarity with the life in these countries brought about by television programmes. The data from Norwich† showed no differences between future viewers and controls.

*This study also has relevance for the next section of the book, 'Focus on Origins', inasmuch as it deals with the effect of the medium of television on the formation of children's attitudes. – Eds.

†This and subsequent references to 'the Norwich data' or 'the Norwich children' represent an important and ingenious element of the over-all research design employed by Himmelweit *et al.* The main survey, of viewers

FOCUS ON CONTENT

The preference for European countries increased the longer children viewed. Twenty-one per cent among veteran viewers mentioned them, compared with 13% among the recent viewers.

We next compared the descriptions given by viewers and controls of different types of foreigners who had appeared on television in newsreels or plays. A sentence-completion test was used as follows: *Here is a list of different kinds of people. How would you describe them to a friend? Finish each sentence to show how you would tell your friend something about them – not what they look like, but what sort of people they really are.* The instructions were worded so as to avoid answers like 'Germans are people who live in Germany', and to encourage less stereotyped descriptions. Six groups of foreigners were included in the list. Two of these six were traditional 'out-groups', Jews and Negroes. Jews named as such occasionally feature in plays; Negroes are often seen in dance bands and variety shows. The French and the Americans were included as peoples towards whom most English people are generally well disposed. The remaining two, Russians and Germans, were peoples towards whom the general attitude might be neutral or hostile.

Answers were classified into four main categories to show whether: (1) children had gone beyond bare definition; (2) they referred to the way of life, the appearance, or the character of the people concerned; (3) the answers showed a neutral, non-evaluative, or a biased attitude; and (4) any descriptions given by viewers differed systematically from those given by the controls.

The Norwich data showed no difference between future viewers and controls.

As we expected any influence to be slight, we had to make our measuring instruments as sensitive as possible. Consequently in Norwich we worked out a change score for each child whereby the

---

and matched non-viewers, was carried out in four English cities – London, Portsmouth, Sunderland and Bristol. These cities were within television transmission areas before the study began. In Norwich, however, a new television transmitter was opened during the course of the research. This afforded the opportunity of a before-and-after study in Norwich. Children were first surveyed before television was available, and a year later a group of children whose families had since acquired sets were compared with a group whose families had not. Thus Himmelweit *et al.* were able to determine the extent to which 'future viewers' differed from children whose families turned out to be less inclined to acquire a television set. These findings could then be related back to the main survey results in the four other cities.

answers given in 1956 were compared with those given a year earlier – before television had come to the city (Table 1).

Table 1

Percentage of children in Norwich who changed from value judgements in 1955 to non-evaluative descriptions.

	13–14-year-olds		10–11-years-olds	
	v	c	v	c
Description of foreigners:	%	%	%	%
Negroes	6	4	13	5
Jews	19	10	16	7
Russians	34	10	24	3
Germans	46	27	22	18
French	31	20	16	8
Americans	13	14	19	9
Total cases	32	29	68	74

The analysis proved so time-consuming that while we coded all the Norwich cases, we coded only a smaller random sample from the main survey. The numbers were therefore relatively small and differences were not always statistically significant; nevertheless they were too consistent to have come about by chance; in each instance they showed difference between viewers and controls in line with the trend just noted.

This test showed that television influenced children's attitudes to foreigners in two ways. First, the Norwich children, after one year's viewing, made more objective and fewer evaluative statements. They would describe aspects of foreigners' lives rather than pass value judgements, even though the wording of the question encouraged the latter. For example, more children said that Jews are people who 'believe in God, not Christ' or that they are 'religious', than called them 'pleasant' or 'swindlers and misers'. More of them mentioned that Negroes are 'black people' or 'dark skinned', than that they are 'cunning' or 'unhappy'. Television seems to have produced in the child a more detached, objective attitude.

Secondly, in describing different sets of foreigners, the younger children were influenced by how the people had been presented on television. In the main survey more viewers than controls mentioned, for instance, that Jews were religious or carried out certain religious practices. This derives directly from television drama, for when Jews are identified in the plays as such there is usually some reference to their religious practices. More viewers than controls described the French as gay and witty, reflecting the fact that nearly all the French people they see on television are cabaret artists. Among younger children at least, more viewers than controls saw the Germans as arrogant and vicious – again, a reflection of television drama, where Germans are mainly presented in the role of Nazis (Table 2).

Table 2

Percentage of children who gave the following stereotyped views about foreigners.

	13–14-years-olds		10–11-year-olds	
	v	c	v	c
	%	%	%	%
French: gay, witty	14	8	6	1
Germans: vicious, arrogant	14	14	14	7
Jews: religious, practise their religion	14	9	11	7
Total cases	144	144	144	144

Viewers and controls gave the same stereotypes for Americans, Negroes, and Russians.

Horowitz (1936) has shown that attitudes to foreigners, especially 'out-groups', become more fixed and so less amenable to change as the child grows older. This matches our own findings, which show the influence of television to be more marked for the younger viewers than for adolescents.

Attitudes to foreigners in general

Next, in the list given to the older children, we included three statements with a bearing on xenophobia: *My own country is always right. You can't trust foreigners. We can learn a lot from foreign people.* They were asked for each statement to check one of three responses: *I agree, I disagree, I am not sure.*

We found differences in respect to one question out of the three. Significantly more viewers than controls disagreed with the statement *My own country is always right.*

A great deal of what we have examined in this chapter consisted in tracing the effects of a rather one-sided view of society on the child. Here, we have done the opposite – traced a broadening influence. The impact is limited, but nevertheless clearly discernible. The children we tested had seen BBC television only, where much thought is given to the presentation to children of the way of life of other countries.

If the children had had access to ITV only (which shows foreigners more often in the role of the criminal) the influence might well have been in the opposite direction, namely, that of increasing prejudice against specific 'out-groups'.

There is great scope here, through newsreels, and even more through drama, to acquaint children with the way of life of other countries and of other social groups.

Reference

Horowitz, E. L., The development of attitudes towards the Negro. *Arch. Psychol.*, 194, 34–5 (1936).

7 R. Lynn and I. E. Gordon

Maternal Attitudes to Child Socialization*

Reprinted from: R. Lynn and I. E. Gordon, *British Journal of Social and Clinical Psychology*, British Psychological Society, 1962, London, Vol. 1, pp. 52–5.

An important strand of evidence in our knowledge of the variables affecting the socialization of the child can be derived from the study of class differences in socializing techniques. It can be assumed, in the most general terms, that socialization is a function partly of inherited constitutional factors, and partly of environmental pressures. Hence any theory of the nature of these constitutional and environmental factors can and should be checked against social differences in them and the resultant degree of socialization which different classes attain.

The general feature of class differences in socialization which any theory of the socialization process must accommodate is that the middle class tends to be more socialized than the working class. This appears to be true both in the U.S.A. and in England. The American findings are substantial and have been summarized by Clausen (1957): 'The lower-class pattern of life . . . puts a high premium on physical gratification, on free expression of aggression, on spending and sharing. Cleanliness, respect for property, sexual control, educational achievement – all highly valued by middle-class Americans – are of less importance to the lower-class family.' Although far less work has been done in England it is likely that similar class differences exist; for example, delinquency is much more prevalent in the working class (Burt, 1935) and the working class is less educationally ambitious (Floud, Halsey and Martin, 1956).

A number of investigations have been carried out in an attempt to relate these class differences in socialization to differences in child-rearing practices. These studies have recently been reviewed by Bronfenbrenner (1958), who concludes that middle-class parents tend to use less physical punishment and rely more on

---

* This study, in its concern with methods of child socialization and its discussion of possible hereditary factors, has definite relevance for the next section of the book, 'Focus on Origins'. In particular, cf. Sanford's account of parental attitudes and family relationships in the development of authoritarianism. – Eds.

appeals to guilt and the threat of withdrawal of love. Bronfen-brenner also reviews some evidence indicating that the middle-class techniques of socialization are likely to be more effective, so that studies of family differences and class differences tend to reinforce each other.

Perhaps the most thorough investigation of this matter is that carried out by Sears, Maccoby & Levin (1957). In this study two correlated dimensions of maternal attitude towards aggression were found, namely punishment of aggression and permissiveness of aggression. Of these, the punishment of aggression factor seems relatively straightforward. It was found that a mother's punishment of her child's aggression was positively related to the amount of aggression the child displayed, and that working-class mothers made greater use of punishment, so that these class differences in child-rearing techniques do something to account for the class differences in socialization. On the other hand, the permissiveness factor does not seem to operate consistently, since maternal permissiveness was found to be positively related to the aggression of the child, and it might therefore be expected that working-class mothers would be more permissive than middle-class mothers. In fact, the reverse was found to be the case. These class differences in permissiveness throw some doubt on the finding of Sears and his associates, a doubt which is strengthened by Lynn's (1961) failure to confirm the finding among English families. It should be noted, however, that when the Sears sample was broken down into national groups, the British middle-class mothers emerged as less permissive than working-class mothers. This is, of course, the finding that would be expected from the theory that permissiveness encourages aggression, and if confirmed it would do something to strengthen the theory. Accordingly we have carried out the investigation described below to elucidate English class differences in mothers' attitudes to child rearing.

The Investigation

The sample of English mothers on whom the investigation was carried out was made up as follows. Forty-eight mothers (21 middle class and 27 working class) were obtained at parent–teachers' association meetings of two village schools in Devon. These mothers showed the same class differences as those reported by Sears, but in view of the possibility of bias in the sample a further investigation was made in the city of Exeter. Here middle- and working-class residential areas were selected and interviewers called at the houses; all mothers of children aged 4–18 years were asked to complete the questionnaire (described below) measuring attitudes to child-rearing. In this way a further 22 middle-class and 24 working-class mothers were obtained. The trend in this sample was in the same direction as that obtained from the parent–teacher associations and the two samples were therefore pooled.

The measuring instrument used consists of five scales drawn up and standardized by Sears and his colleagues. The scales take the form of remarks made by mothers about the behaviour of their 5-year-old children and the way they dealt with it. For example, the first item of the punishment of aggression scale runs: 'Yesterday Mark deliberately dumped a box of soap on the floor, and I decided the best way to handle it was to call off our afternoon walk to the playground.' The mother has to read these statements and indicate on a five-point scale how far she agrees or disagrees with the course of action taken. Three of Sears' scales were used in the present study, namely punishment of aggression, permissiveness of aggression, and permissiveness of immodesty.

The sample of mothers was divided into middle- and working-class on the basis of the husband's occupation as classified by the Registrar-General. Table 1 shows the mean scores of the middle- and working-class mothers and, for comparative purposes, of the American sample investigated by Sears.

All the mean differences between the social classes in England are statistically significant at the 0·05 level (using the 't' test). Of the differences between the total English sample and the American sample, the two differ significantly at the 0·05 level on the scales permissiveness of immodesty and permissiveness of aggression, but only differ significantly at the 0·10 level on the punishment of aggression scale.

Table 1

Mean scores and S.D.s of British middle-class and working-class and American mothers on scales assessing attitudes towards child socialization.

	Permissiveness of immodesty	Punishment of aggression	Permissiveness of aggression
British middle class	48·56 ± 7·46	42·44 ± 8·63	53·13 ± 6·59
British working class	40·88 ± 7·99	46·67 ± 6·98	49·61 ± 8·87
British total	44·55 ± 8·66	44·65 ± 8·07	51·30 ± 8·00
American total	54·65 ± 7·07	41·90 ± 7·31	60·13 ± 10·57

Discussion of Results

The results emerging from the study are as follows:

(1) In England, as in the U.S.A., middle-class mothers are less punitive than working-class mothers. This finding strengthens further the theory that there is a relation between maternal punitiveness and the aggression of the child.

(2) English middle-class mothers are also like American middle-class mothers in being more permissive of aggressive behaviour. This finding throws more doubt on the Sears finding that there is a relation between maternal permissiveness and the child's aggression.

(3) English mothers tend to be less permissive and more punitive than American mothers. Assuming that punitiveness is the more important factor, it would be expected from this finding that the English would be more aggressive and less well socialized in general than the Americans. While we do not know of any investigation explicitly designed to test this proposition, the available evidence makes us suspect that, if anything, it is the Americans who tend to be less well socialized than the English. For example, the number of murders per head of the population is considerably higher in America (Royal Commission on Capital Punishment, 1953); American school-children are less concerned about educational attainment (Sarnoff et al., 1958) and are educationally less forward (Pidgeon, 1958); and Americans have more extraverted behaviour patterns (Eysenck, 1959). We do not regard this evidence as more than suggestive, but it does present something of a challenge to the theory linking maternal punitiveness to the aggression of the child.

It is possible to explain this difficulty by considering hereditary factors. Aggression is related to Eysenck's personality dimension of extraversion (e.g. Eysenck, 1954), and individual differences in this dimension are determined to a considerable degree by inheritance (e.g. Shields, 1958). The fact that Americans are more extraverted than the English may therefore be due to the fact that they are genetically a more extraverted strain. When it is considered that Americans are descended from ancestors who have emigrated it seems not improbable that they are selected for some personality factor; and in view of the findings that people with extraverted characteristics are intolerant of monotonous stimuli (Petrie, Collins & Solomon, 1960) it seems not implausible that extraversion might be a factor in emigration. Such a hypothesis could, of course, easily be checked. Now it has been shown that extraverted mothers are less punitive towards their children than introverted mothers (Lynn, 1961) and this finding is consistent with the finding that American mothers are less punitive than English mothers. It is, therefore, suggested that the hereditary factor of extraversion accounts for both the non-punitiveness of American mothers and the aggressiveness of their children, and that the hereditary factor is a more important determinant of aggression than the mother's punitiveness.

We should like to express our gratitude to Professor R. R. Sears of Stanford University for lending us a copy of his maternal attitudes questionnaire; and to Mr David King, Mr Terence Dowling and Miss Ruth Carr for help in interviewing.

References

Bronfenbrenner, U., Socialization and social class through time and space. In *Readings in Social Psychology*, ed. Maccoby, E. E., Newcomb, T. M., and Hartley, E. L. New York: Henry Holt, 1958.

Burt, C., *The Subnormal Mind*. London: Oxford University Press, 1935.

Clausen, J. A., Social and psychological factors in narcotics addiction. *Law and Contemporary Problems*, 22, 34–51, 1957.

Eysenck, H. J., *The Psychology of Politics*. London: Methuen, 1954.

Eysenck, H. J., *Manual of the Maudsley Personality Inventory*. London: University Press, 1959.

Floud, J. E., Halsey, H. H., and Martin, F. M., *Social Class and Educational Opportunity*. London: Heinemann, 1956.

Lynn, R., Personality characteristics of the mothers of aggressive and unaggressive children. *J. genet. Psychol*. 99, 159–64, 1961.

Petrie, A., Collins, W., and Solomon, P., The tolerance for pain and sensory deprivation. *Amer. J. Psychol*. 73, 80–90, 1960.

Pidgeon, D. A., A comparative study of basic attainments. *Educ. Res.*, 1, 50–68, 1958.

Sarnoff, I., Lighthall, F., Waite, R., Davidson, K., and Sarason, S., A cross-cultural study of anxiety among American and English school children. *J. educ. Psychol*. 49, 129–36., 1958.

Sears, R. R., Maccoby, E. E., and Levin, H., *Patterns of Child Rearing*. Illinois: Evanston, 1957.

Shields, J., Twins brought up apart. *Eugen. Rev*. 50, 115–23, 1958.

8 C. C. Moskos and W. Bell

Attitudes Towards Democracy

Excerpt from: C. C. Moskos and W. Bell, *British Journal of Sociology*, Routledge, London, 1964, Vol. 15, Chapter 4, pp. 317–37.

The data reported here are from interviews with 111 top leaders in Jamaica, Trinidad and Tobago, British Guiana, and in Barbados, Grenada, and Dominica, a sample from the Little-Eight. These leaders were interviewed from August 1961, through April 1962, and included in each territory: the Premier, the most influential Cabinet members, top leaders of the opposition party(ies), heads of labour unions, wealthy merchants, large plantation owners, and newspaper editors. Also interviewed were leading members of the clergy, ethnic leaders, top educationists, leaders of voluntary organizations, prominent professionals, and high-ranking civil servants. In each of the territories, the leaders who were interviewed constituted, with a few exceptions, a systematically defined *universe* of the top national decision-makers.[1]

To locate such national leaders, a modified 'snow-ball' technique was used. Initially, persons in a cross-section of institutional sectors were selected who, on the basis of their formal roles or institutional positions, were likely to be top leaders. They were asked to identify individuals whom they considered to wield national influence. As the nominations of the national leaders accumulated, the most frequently mentioned persons were in turn asked to identify other influentials. In this way, the original positional approach gave way to a reputational approach, and the list of reputed leaders was increasingly refined. The same procedure was used in each of the territories, so that comparability between the units was insured. No leaders so selected refused to be interviewed, and when the field research had been completed, each leader had been questioned at some length about, among other things, the issues presented in this paper.

Although the data formally presented in this paper are limited to the interviews with the 111 top leaders, our thinking has been informed by observation, discussion with informants, additional and less systematic interviews, and reading a wide range of local newspapers and periodicals throughout several periods of field work and shorter trips to the West Indies from as early as 1956 (for one of the writers) to 1964.

55

Indicators of Democratic Beliefs

By democracy, we mean a political system 'in which public policies are made, on a majority basis, by representatives subject to effective popular control at periodic elections which are conducted on the principles of political equality and under conditions of political freedom'.[2] Operationally, we used two indicators of democratic beliefs. The first was similar to that used by Bell in his 1958 sample survey of democratic and undemocratic beliefs in Jamaica.[3] He used an Index of Political Cynicism used earlier by Charles R. Nixon and Dwaine Marvick[4] and classified Jamaican élites as either 'idealistic' or 'cynical' with respect to political democracy. The politically idealistic leaders, according to this Index, were those who had favourable judgments of the average Jamaican voter, while the politically cynical leaders were those who had unfavourable attitudes. The former were considered democratic and the latter undemocratic.[5]

In the present study the indicator similar to Bell's measure of political idealism or cynicism was based on the responses of the West Indian leaders to the question: 'Do you feel the typical (West Indian)* voter supports leaders who serve the long range interests of (the West Indies)?* That is, how competent do you feel the average (West Indian)* voter is?' The results were:

The West Indian electorate is:

	%
Competent	28
Incompetent	72
Total (111 cases)	100

The second indicator of democratic beliefs was based on the leaders' answers to the question, 'Do you think the democratic form of government is the best suited for (the West Indies)?', the referent being a British parliamentary type of government based on universal adult suffrage with guarantees for the maintenance of civil and minority rights. The percentage distribution of responses of the 111 West Indian leaders is as follows:

* The name of the territory appropriate to each respondent was inserted.

The democratic form of government is:

	%
Very suitable	50
Partially suitable	10
Unsuitable	40
Total (111 cases)	100

Given in Table 1 is a political typology based on the simultaneous responses to these two indicators of democratic attitudes.[6] Twenty-two per cent of the leaders were termed true 'democrats', that is, they thought that parliamentary democracy was very suitable for their home territories *and* that the voters were competent. The smallest group, 6%, were labelled 'authoritarian idealists', i.e. they had qualifications about the parliamentary form or believed it was unsuitable but held favourable attitudes towards the competency of the typical West Indian voter. 'Cynical parliamentarians', constituting 28% of the top West Indian leaders, were those who, while favouring a parliamentary system, thought that the average voter was incompetent. Finally, nearly half of the leaders were classified as 'authoritarians' because they neither believed in the suitability of the parliamentary form nor thought the typical voter was competent. One must conclude from these overall figures alone that the foundations of democracy as reflected in the beliefs and attitudes of the West Indian élite are somewhat shaky.

Table 1

A Political Typology of West Indian Leaders

Political Types	%
Democrats	22
Authoritarian idealists	6
Cynical parliamentarians	28
Authoritarians	44
Total	100
Number of Cases	(111)

Elaboration of the Meaning of the Political Types

(a) Relation to economic ideologies

The significance of the political types, as well as of the analysis to follow, can be enhanced if their import is made clear at the outset. The constructed political types have direct and obvious implications for the preferred nature of the political system and for the chances of the ideals of political democracy being at least striven for and perhaps to some degree achieved in fact. But the implications of these types are not confined to the nature or processes of the political system *per se*: they also bear on the broader questions of the desired outcomes or end results towards which political action is directed. To document this view we examine here the relationship between the political types and a major aspect of the West Indian leaders' long-range social philosophies: their economic ideologies.

We classified the West Indian leaders into five types according to their views on the proper role of the government in the economy of their territories: *reactionaries* – those who thought the state's role should be about what it was before the rise of the nationalist movements and should not extend beyond providing basic services such as a postal system, roads, police and fire protection; *conservatives* – those who wanted roughly to maintain the present situation, with the state in addition to providing basic services also being responsible for welfare schemes for the ill, aged, and unemployed, for public works, and for a general educational system, but with the reservation that taxation should be less discriminatory against the entrepreneurial class and that government should be less protective of labour union interests; *populists* – those who lacked long-term economic policies, and who were pragmatically concerned with immediate bread-and-butter issues, although accepting a belief in a market economy geared to the demands of labour unions or mass-based political organizations; *liberals* – those who wanted greater intervention of the government in the economy, but who did not foresee changes beyond the achievement of modern welfare capitalism; and *radicals* – those who advocated fundamental changes in the present system so that the state would become the major factor in determining local economic life, with the extreme radicals seeking the abolishment of all private property.

Reported in Table 2 is the relationship between economic ideologies and the political types. Truly democratic attitudes were most characteristic of liberals, 50% of whom were democrats, with most of the remainder being cynical parliamentarians. Almost the same proportion of populists, 46%, were democrats, but over one-third of them were authoritarians. The radicals were most evenly spread over the political types: 14% were democrats, 29% authoritarian idealists, 38% cynical parliamentarians, and 19% authoritarians. Over half of the conservatives and fully 95% of the reactionaries were authoritarians. Thus, excluding the radicals for the moment, there is a clear and strong relationship between the political types and economic ideologies, with the Right economic ideologists having more anti-democratic or authoritarian attitudes compared to the Left economic ideologists who have more democratic views. This is consistent with data we have reported elsewhere which show that opponents of the democratic revolution in the West Indies were those persons most out of step with the nationalist movements whose progressive policies were, in contrast to the rigidly stratified social system which then existed, supportive of political, economic, and social egalitarian principles.[7]

Table 2

Political Types by Economic Ideologies

Economic Ideologies	Percentage of West Indian Leaders who were					
	Democrats	Authoritarian Idealists	Cynical Parliamentarians	Authoritarians	Total per cent	Number of Cases
Radical	14	29	38	19	100	(21)
Liberal	50	4	42	4	100	(24)
Populist	46	0	18	36	100	(11)
Conservative	9	0	33	58	100	(33)
Reactionary	5	0	0	95	100	(22)

The tensions currently underlying West Indian society, however, are not to be understood solely as democratic and progressive forces combating non-democratic elements seeking to maintain their advantages or to restore the old order. For some West Indian leaders economic changes within the parliamentary system have been too superficial, as shown in the tapering-off of democratic attitudes among the radicals. Yet, unlike the opponents of parliamentary democracy on the Right, the radicals, among whom were found nearly all of the authoritarian idealists, had a greater faith in the political competency of the West Indian citizenry. While most of the non-democratic or authoritarian West Indian leaders were conservatives or reactionaries, there was also a tendency for some of the most egalitarian leaders to be authoritarians too, but for different reasons: they regarded parliamentary processes, as currently operating, as being unresponsive to popular needs, and blamed the parliamentary system for slowness in instituting radical reform. This is a growing sentiment which contains a challenge of great significance to democratic institutions and a potential threat to their survival.

(b) Revolutionaries and Counter-Revolutionaries

An additional elaboration of the meaning of the political types is found in the relationship between the types and attitudes towards the overthrow of the legally constituted government. Of course, advocacy of overthrow of a government is not in itself necessarily either democratic or anti-democratic. It depends. If the government in question is thwarting the control of ordinary citizens over their leaders, then such an overthrow might be inspired by democratic beliefs and attitudes. But if the government is pursuing democratic and progressive aims, then vehement opposition to it would be found among anti-democratic persons. Thus, advocates of overthrow of the government can be in this sense either revolutionary or counter-revolutionary.

Following the close of each formal interview, a time when rapport between the interviewer and respondent was generally highest, the West Indian leaders were queried about their views concerning the overthrow of the constitutionally elected governments of their territories. A total of 17% of the leaders indicated that they would either favour outright or acquiesce to a violent or illegal overthrow of the existing government, but there was considerable variation by political type:

Political Type	Percentage who condoned overthrow	Number of Cases
Democrats	0	(24)
Cynical parliamentarians	6	(31)
Authoritarian idealists	29	(7)
Authoritarians	33	(49)

Nearly all of the leaders who condoned overthrow of the government were either authoritarian idealists or out-and-out authoritarians. Different motives underlay such deep-seated opposition to the existing government: revolutionary as contrasted to counter-revolutionary sentiments. An examination of these diverse motives requires an indicator of the varying images of the good society held by the West Indian leaders, and we used the economic ideologies of the leaders given above as such an indicator.

The distribution was as follows:

Economic Ideologies	Percentage who condoned overthrow	Number of Cases
Radicals (revolutionary)	24	(21)
Liberals	0	(24)
Populists	9	(11)
Conservatives	12	(33)
Reactionaries (counter-revolutionary)	41	(22)

As might be expected, leaders having moderate economic ideologies were most likely to oppose overthrow of the constitutionally legitimate governments of their territories. All of the liberals as well as the large majority of the populists and conservatives supported orderly and stable government. The ideological extremists, particularly the Rightist variant (41% of the reactionaries), were the most hostile to the existing governments, but 24% of the radicals also condoned overthrow of the government.

These and other data indicate that counter-revolutionary more than revolutionary sentiments underlay the motives of the bitterest opponents of the existing governments. Furthermore, the deep-seated hostility of the reactionaries is some evidence of the basically progressive policies which the four emergent Caribbean nations have been implementing. At the same time, it is important to note that the undemocratic sentiments of the conservatives were not translated into advocacy of non-constitutional means. We suggest that while most of the West Indian reactionaries had withdrawn from active political participation (only 23% being high political activists overall), many of the conservatives sought to mitigate major changes in the *status quo* through involvement in the parliamentary system (46% engaging in high political activity). For the conservatives, the parliamentary system, though bringing on social change, was seen as the lesser of the two evils, the greater being contained in the potential threat of a radical-authoritarian regime.

61

That the efforts of the opponents of reform were perceived as at least somewhat successful by a few leaders is reflected in the fact that some radicals also advocated overthrow of the government. Whether or not the radical authoritarians will be able to find popular support in the future depends on the capacity of the West Indian democratic revolution to meet the rising social and economic aspirations that it has engendered. That is ... unless fairly substantial economic and social progress is achieved – including distributional reforms – under a democratic régime, the ranks of the authoritarian idealists may be markedly increased by egalitarian leaders who became disillusioned with the parliamentary system as an instrument of economic and social reform.

Differences by Territory

As reported in Table 3, the support for democracy was highest and authoritarian sentiment was lowest in Jamaica. There, experience with the modern democratic system is most mature of all the British territories in the West Indies – the franchise was extended

Table 3

Political Types by Territory

| Territory | Percentage of West Indian Leaders who were | | | | | |
	Demo-crats	Authoritarian Idealists	Cynical Parlia-mentarians	Authoritarians	Total per cent	Number of Cases
Jamaica	39	9	26	26	100	(23)
Trinidad	18	14	27	41	100	(22)
British Guiana	8	8	38	46	100	(13)
Little-Eight	19	2	26	53	100	(53)

to all Jamaican adults in 1944 compared to similar action in the other territories in the early 1950s – and a firm base in a two-party system exists, both parties – the liberal People's National Party and the more conservative Jamaica Labour Party – having each had some time at the helm of government. Probably, the longer experience of the Jamaican leaders in the give-and-take of parliamentary life and their witnessing of the electoral behaviour of the Jamaican citizenry for nearly two decades promoted a growing trust and faith in democratic processes. That is, the existence of a genuine parliamentary system well before full independence may be a major element in establishing the legitimacy of a democracy which extends into a post-independence period. Some support for this observation is given when we note that the relative number of Jamaican political idealists (i.e. democrats and authoritarian idealists) found in this 1961–2 study, 48%, was greater than the 42% of the Jamaican élites who could be termed idealistic in Bell's 1958 survey. Also, the fact that 65% of the Jamaican leaders in the 1961–2 study believed in the suitability of parliamentary democracy for Jamaica adds weight to the conclusion that on the average there has been growing support for democracy in Jamaica in the recent past.

In British Guiana, 38% of the leaders were cynical parliamentarians, the highest in the British Caribbean, and the number of democrats was the lowest. This reflects the internecine conflict which has marred political life in that territory in recent years: the two major political parties have come to be divided along the colony's social and racial cleavages. The communist-led People's Progressive Party draws upon the rural East Indians, and the socialist People's National Congress is supported by the urban Negroes, and a common response among Guianese leaders has been to praise the wisdom of their respective ethnic supporters and to denigrate the electoral competency of the opposite group.

In Trinidad, 18% of the leaders were democrats, 27% cynical parliamentarians, 14% authoritarian idealists, and 41% authoritarians. Thus, despite a communal cleavage in Trinidad similar to that of British Guiana (except that the relative number of East Indians and Negroes is reversed), there is a somewhat higher level of political idealism. This may reflect the partial success of the incumbent People's National Movement to consciously transcend racial lines. Trinidad offers itself as an example of a new nation where ethnic and racial cleavages have not resulted in breaking down parliamentary democracy, although such a breakdown remains a danger.

Among the leaders of the Little-Eight, authoritarian sentiments were highest. None the less, 45% of the leaders interviewed in the smaller islands were either democrats or cynical parliamentarians, and it should be remembered that the political development of the Little-Eight resembles that of the larger territories a decade or more ago. Although the term 'labour' is an indispensable appellation of political parties and the rhetoric of socialism is frequently used, most of the local political groups are personal vehicles with little ideology. An important exception to the low level of political party viability in the Little-Eight is Barbados; and it is more than mere coincidence that Barbados has enjoyed the largest measure of self-government over a longer period than any of the other smaller islands.

Social Correlates of the Political Types

Although we are dealing with four different emergent Caribbean nations, between which the *incidence* of the democratic attitudes varied, a similar pattern runs through all of them with respect to the correlates of democratic attitudes among their leaders. From partials not presented here, we found that individual configurations of attitudes, activities, and personal background characteristics relating to attitudes towards democracy were markedly similar from territory to territory. Thus we treat the West Indies as a whole and group the various territories together in the presentation of the following data.

Democrats and authoritarian idealists, as reported in Table 4, were most likely to be found among the younger leaders. The middle-aged were most likely to be cynical parliamentarians, and the oldest leaders were the most authoritarian. Also, virtually all of the authoritarian idealists were found among the youngest leaders. This finding contrasts somewhat with Bell's 1958 data which showed little variation in political idealism by age among the Jamaican élites.[8] This discrepancy may be due to the fact that this study only dealt with top West Indian leaders, while Bell's survey included many Jamaicans from the upper-middle ranks. Also Bell's survey was less representative of political and labour leaders, the group which constituted the largest number in the present study.

Although the data support a generally held view that ageing is positively related to conservatism (undemocratic sentiment is here regarded as conservative), the historical context of the West Indian experience suggests attention should be paid to more extrinsic factors. Rather than being concerned with age *per se*, we must also look to the values and ideas which are in circulation during a particular person's generation. It must be remembered that truly democratic forms of government are of recent origin in the West Indies. The younger West Indian leaders have had more of their lives shaped during a period when political democracy was a real alternative to either Crown Colony or limited franchise rule, and they have attained their maturity in a period during which democracy was actually operating in their territories.

Table 4

Political Types by Selected Social Characteristics

Selected Social Characteristics	Percentage of West Indian Leaders who were					
	Demo-crats	Authori-tarian Idealists	Cynical Parlia-mentarians	Authori-tarians	Total per cent	Number of Cases
Age						
55 and over	17	0	14	69	100	(36)
40 to 54	22	4	41	33	100	(58)
39 and under	30	30	10	30	100	(17)
Education						
College or higher	26	8	33	33	100	(36)
Secondary school	16	5	26	53	100	(57)
Elementary school	33	6	22	39	100	(18)
Wealth						
Wealthy	10	3	18	69	100	(39)
Not wealthy	28	8	33	31	100	(72)
Colour or ethnicity						
White	10	3	29	58	100	(38)
Light brown	25	5	10	60	100	(20)
East Indian and Chinese	8	8	42	42	100	(12)
Dark brown and black	34	10	32	24	100	(41)
Institutional sector						
Political or labour	36	13	30	21	100	(47)
Economic	9	0	18	73	100	(34)
Mass media	12	0	38	50	100	(8)
Civil service	12	0	76	12	100	(8)
Religious	0	0	14	86	100	(7)
Other	29	14	14	43	100	(7)

There was a tendency for cynical parliamentarianism to increase with level of education while the percentage of authoritarian idealists varied little by education. A more pronounced finding was the relatively high percentage of authoritarians among the West Indian leaders who had a secondary-school education only, while true democratic attitudes were most evident among leaders with either the most or least formal education. This association is in accord with Bell's earlier findings in which the least politically idealistic Jamaican élites were also in the middle educational levels. [9]

Two different factors account for this 'U'-shaped distribution. On the one hand, the percentage of persons with low educational levels who are democratic is evidence of the general finding: greater relative support for democracy among West Indian leaders of lower class origins (which is corroborated by findings reported above dealing with wealth, colour and ethnicity, and institutional sector). Thus, among some of the socio-economically disadvantaged sectors of society, democracy is perceived as advancing the welfare of the lower groups and is viewed with favour by the leaders with such backgrounds either because of class-interest or because of greater first-hand knowledge and empathy for the disadvantaged groups. On the other hand, the most highly educated leaders who favoured democracy relatively more than the middling educated leaders often seemed inconsistent with their class interest, *as narrowly conceived*, and reflected in their attitudes the enlightenment of a Western humanitarian ideology. They had usually been exposed to the latter during their higher education which, until the establishment of the University College of the West Indies in 1947 in Jamaica, meant an extended stay abroad, most often in the United Kingdom, the United States, or Canada.[10]

Wealth, an important variable in any society, also served to demarcate the West Indian political types. In this study, a person was termed wealthy if he owned a large home with a permanent household staff and had an income of such an amount and nature that he would probably be able to live close to his current standard of living even if he became incapacitated. As reported in Table 4, wealthy leaders were more likely to be authoritarians than the non-wealthy, and less likely to be any of the other three political types.

Dark brown and black leaders were most likely to be democrats and authoritarian idealists, the East Indians and Chinese most likely to be cynical parliamentarians, and light-brown and white-skinned leaders were most likely to be authoritarians. Again low social status is correlated with democratic attitudes.

66

Because wealth and colour are to some extent confounded in the West Indies, it is important to clarify their independent effects on the political types. From a table not shown here wealth appears more important than colour, especially for the authoritarians where nearly all of the total variation is accounted for by wealth and very little is accounted for by colour; for the democrats, the variation due to colour remains, although it is reduced more than that due to wealth.

The final social characteristic that is presented in Table 4 is the institutional sector in which the leaders exercised their national influence. Although some leaders engaged in several spheres of activity each leader was classified just once according to his primary function.

Democratic attitudes were most frequent among political and labour leaders and 'other' (e.g. voluntary organizations' heads, educationists) leaders. All of the authoritarian idealists also were in these same groups. Civil servants were the most likely to be cynical parliamentarians. Authoritarians were most prevalent among economic dominants and religious personages. In general, democrats were characteristically leaders of secular, mass-based organizations that were outgrowths of the modern West Indian awakening. Contrariwise, authoritarianism was most typical of those leaders who represented the established vested interests of West Indian society. Yet, it must be emphasized that the correlates between the institutional sectors and the political types, as with the other social background variables, were not perfect and there were many exceptions to the general pattern.

Causes of the Political Types

(a) The social distance hypothesis

From this brief presentation of some of the social correlates of the political types among West Indian leaders, we turn to a consideration of the underlying causes of democratic attitudes. Bell formulates three hypotheses from a *post factum* analysis of his data two of which we subject to test here.[11] The first is given below:

Hypothesis 1. Feelings of social distance towards the subordinate socio-economic-racial groups produce cynicism about political democracy.
Converse 1. Feelings of social nearness towards the subordinate socio-economic-racial groups produce idealism about political democracy.

The social correlates presented above, although somewhat confounded by other variables, tend to support this hypothesis and its
converse. That is, the most authoritarian leaders were economic
dominants, wealthy, and light skinned, those who typically would
be most distant from the masses in West Indian society, and the
most democratic leaders tended to be their opposites. The findings
that the intermediate educated were more authoritarian than
what would appear to be a more socially distant group, the highest
educated, seems to be inconsistent with the hypothesis. This
apparent exception is partially explained, however, by the fact
that wealthy West Indian leaders were more than twice as likely to
have only completed secondary school than be college graduates.

The social distance hypothesis can be directly tested by relating
views towards social inclusiveness – reduction of racial, religious,
or class distinctions between groups within a society – and the
political types. We constructed a measure of social inclusiveness
from attitudes of West Indian leaders towards reducing social
barriers within their territories as compared to increasing their
contact with persons outside of the West Indies. Leaders who
placed highest priority on eliminating internal social barriers were
termed 'social inclusivists'; conversely, persons who placed
secondary emphasis on reducing internal social barriers or who
favoured the perpetuation of such social distinctions within their
societies were designated 'social exclusivists'. As reported in
Table 5, inclusivists compared to exclusivists were much more
likely to be democrats, slightly more likely to be cynical parlia-

Table 5

Political Types by a Measure of Social Distance from the Masses

Feelings of Social Distance from the Masses	Percentage of West Indian Leaders who were					
	Demo-crats	Authoritarian Idealists	Cynical Parliamentarians	Authoritarians	Total per cent	Number of Cases
Social inclusivists (near)	39	15	31	15	100	(46)
Social exclusivists (distant)	9	0	26	65	100	(65)

mentarians, and much less likely to be authoritarians. All of the authoritarian idealists were social inclusivists. Thus, the hypothesis is supported.

The effect of social inclusiveness is particularly strong among those leaders who had a high opinion of the competency of the average West Indian voter; 54% of the social inclusivists were political idealists as compared to 9% of the social exclusivists. And it is the measure of idealism used here which most closely approximates the measure of democratic beliefs used by Bell in the 1958 survey.[12]

(b) *The powerlessness hypothesis*

Hypothesis 2. Feelings of powerlessness and the sense of losing relative power with respect to public affairs produce cynicism about political democracy.

Converse 2. Feelings of efficacy and the sense of gaining relative power with respect to public affairs produce idealism about political democracy.

During the transition to nationhood, tutelary democracies based on universal adult suffrage were established in the West Indies, with the tutelary aspects of the systems giving way as independence approached. Formal political power was transferred during this period, passing from the hands of Crown-appointed functionaries and their official and unofficial advisers among the economic dominants and other members of the local establishment into the hands of the leaders of the newly-formed mass-based organizations, the political parties and labour unions. Furthermore, the government was increasingly viewed as the instrument to bring about economic and social reforms. Thus, the transition to nationhood was also a transition from oligarchy to democracy and from *laissez-faire* to state intervention in the economy. Under such circumstances, the second hypothesis, stated above, is understandable.

The findings from the 1961–2 interviews with West Indian leaders generally support the hypothesis. Democratic sentiments were highest among the labour and political leaders, while economic dominants were more authoritarian. The greater likelihood of younger leaders being more democratic than older leaders might also be construed as being in accord with the powerlessness hypothesis, since these younger leaders were waxing while some of the older élites were waning.

A more direct measure of feelings of political efficacy was

obtained by classifying the West Indian leaders according to the amount of their political activity on the issue of national independence. If a leader engaged in open activity (e.g. pamphleteering, organizational work, speech-making) either *for or against* independence he was classified as high in political activity; all others were low political activists.

As shown in Table 6, West Indian leaders who were politically active were three times more likely to be democrats than were those who were politically passive. All of the authoritarian idealists were political activists. Cynical parliamentarianism was somewhat more characteristic of the political active than the passive élite. Passives in political affairs, on the other hand, were more than twice as likely as actives to be authoritarians.

Table 6

Political Types by a Measure of Political Power

	Percentage of West Indian Leaders who were					
Measure of Political Power	Democrats	Authoritarian Idealists	Cynical Parliamentarians	Authoritarians	Total per cent	Number of Cases
Politically active	31	11	32	26	100	(62)
Politically passive	10	0	22	68	100	(49)

(c) *Simultaneous effects of social distance and powerlessness*

Generally, feelings of social distance from the lower socio-economic-racial groups and a sense of losing power in public affairs in the West Indies during the last twenty years varied together and had similar effects on democratic attitudes. But they appear to have some independent effects on attitudes towards political democracy, as is shown in Table 7. For example, the percentage differences in political types between the extremes, using both social distance and powerlessness (politically active inclusivists vs. politically passive exclusivists), are generally higher than comparable differences shown by either variable alone in Tables 5 and 6, the difference in authoritarians among the politically active inclusivists compared to the politically passive exclusivists being the largest shown (66%).

Of further interest are the facts that all of the authoritarian idealists are politically active inclusivists and that with respect to the two extreme political types – democrats and authoritarians – social distance accounts for larger differences than does power-lessness.[13]

Table 7

Political Types by Measures of Social Distance and Political Power

Measures of Social Distance and Political Power	Percentage of West Indian Leaders who were					
	Democrats	Authoritarian Idealists	Cynical Parliamentarians	Authoritarians	Total per cent	Number of Cases
Politically active inclusivists	39	20	33	8	100	(36)
Politically passive inclusivists	40	0	20	40	100	(10)
Politically active exclusivists	19	0	31	50	100	(26)
Politically passive exclusivists	3	0	23	74	100	(39)

A Consequence of the Political Types

Although there is considerable interaction and some circularity of causation between social position and attitudes, and between some attitudes and others, it is often possible to determine the most likely direction of causation. Thus, the weight of our knowledge of recent developments in the West Indies, including the data presented here, leads to the conclusion that democratic attitudes were fostered as a result of social nearness to the masses and a sense of political efficacy, the latter in part reflecting the belief that the historical trends were moving towards democracy and reform, as they in fact were in the West Indies.

But the democratic attitudes themselves had further consequences: they resulted in favourable attitudes towards nationhood and promoted actions to bring about political independence from the United Kingdom. In the biographies of the West Indian leaders, Moskos finds considerable evidence of the time priority of democratic over nationalist attitudes and behaviours. That is, the nationalist leaders were democrats before they were nationalists.[14]

On the basis of both attitudes and activities, Moskos classified the West Indian leaders into three nationalist types: (1) true nationalists – those who favoured independence immediately; (2) acquiescing nationalists – those who temporized with respect to independence but were not firm supporters of the colonial system; and (3) colonialists – those who favoured the indefinite continuation of the colonial system. From Table 8, note that 79% of the democrats were true nationalists compared to only 8% of the authoritarians; conversely, none of the democrats were colonialists compared to 76% of the authoritarians. Cynical parliamentarians had an intermediate position on the question of political independence with 48% of them being acquiescing nationalists and 42% true nationalists. However, 100% of the authoritarian idealists were true nationalists, again reflecting the overwhelming change-leading proclivities of this group.

Table 8

Attitudes towards Political Independence by Political Types

Political Types	Percentage of West Indian Leaders who were			Total per cent	Number of Cases
	True Nationalists	Acquiescing Nationalists	Colonialists		
Democrats	79	21	0	100	(24)
Authoritarian idealists	100	0	0	100	(7)
Cynical parliamentarians	42	48	10	100	(31)
Authoritarians	8	16	76	100	(49)

The West Indian nationalist movements were organized within the liberal framework, with populist and radical principles being strong competitors. They were also inspired by democratic ideals, which along with the other rights of man, fraternity and especially equality, as Moskos shows elsewhere, propelled the nationalist leaders towards independence.[15] Thus, a democratic political system was not simply forced on the West Indians by the departing British, but it was an important part of the nationalist leaders' image of their own independent future.[16]

1. A detailed description and discussion of the selection of the top West Indian leaders, but not the particular data analysis reported here, are available in Charles C. Moskos, Jr, 'The Sociology of Political Independence: A Study of Influence, Social Structure and Ideology in the British West Indies', unpublished Ph.D. dissertation, University of California, Los Angeles, 1963; a revised version will soon appear in Wendell Bell, editor, *The Democratic Revolution in the West Indies: Studies in Nationalism, Leadership, and the Belief in Progress*, forthcoming. Additional findings from this study are reported in Charles C. Moskos, Jr, and Wendell Bell, 'West Indian Nationalism', *New Society*, No. 69, 23 January 1964, pp. 16–18; and Moskos and Bell, 'Emergent Caribbean Nations Face the Outside World', *Social Problems*, 12 (Summer, 1964), pp. 24–41.
2. Henry B. Mayo, *An Introduction to Democratic Theory*, New York: Oxford University Press, 1960, p. 70.
3. Wendell Bell, *Jamaican Leaders: Political Attitudes in a New Nation*, Berkeley and Los Angeles: University of California Press, 1964, Chapter V, 'Should Jamaica Have a Democratic Political System?' Although a few comparisons are made in this paper between the Jamaican results of the present study and Bell's earlier study, the two studies are not strictly comparable. Bell included middle ranks of leadership as well as upper, while the present study is confined to the *top* leaders. There are also differences in response rates and in procedures of collecting data: mail questionnaires vs. personal interviews.
4. Charles R. Nixon and Dwaine Marvick, 'Active Campaign Workers: A Study of Self-Recruited Élites', paper read at the annual meetings of the American Political Science Association, September, 1956; Dwaine Marvick, 'Active Campaign Workers: The Power Structures of Rival Parties', unpublished paper, University of California, Los Angeles, mimeographed; and Dwaine Marvick, 'The Middlemen of Politics', paper read at the annual meetings of the American Political Science Association, Washington, D.C., September 1962.
5. *Jamaican Leaders*, op. cit., pp. 108–9.
6. The second measure of democratic attitudes has been dichotomized in Table I by combining the 'partially suitable' and 'unsuitable' responses.
7. Moskos, op. cit.; and Moskos and Bell, 'West Indian Nationalism', op. cit.
8. *Jamaican Leaders*, op. cit.
9. ibid.
10. For a discussion of the ideological effects of the Jamaican educational system and an analysis of the function of higher education in changing attitudes in Jamaica, see James T. Duke, 'Equalitarianism Among Emergent Élites in a New Nation', unpublished Ph.D. dissertation, University of California, Los Angeles, 1963; soon to be published in Wendell Bell, editor, *The Democratic Revolution in the West Indies*, op. cit.
11. *Jamaican Leaders*, op. cit.

12. The social distance hypothesis was supported further when another measure of social nearness-distance was used based on the personal life styles of the West Indian leaders, e.g. their tastes concerning entertainment, language, and consumership. *West Indian* life styles (50 cases) were contrasted with the more socially distant Anglo-European life styles (61 cases). Those with West Indian life styles were more than twice as likely to be political idealists than were leaders with Anglo-European life styles.

13. Unfortunately, no data to test Bell's third hypothesis were collected in the 1961–2 survey. Accounting for the fact that political cynicism regarding political democracy developed not only among élites who opposed the political, economic, and social emergence of the lower classes that accompanied independence, but also among some élites who favoured, even agitated for, the changes that resulted in such an emergence, it was stated as follows: Among élites who favour progress, intolerance of recalcitrance (on the part of persons whom such progress is supposed to benefit) that is perceived to interfere with progress produces political cynicism.

14. 'The Sociology of Political Independence', in Bell, editor, *The Democratic Revolution in the West Indies*, op. cit.

15. ibid.

16. An important detail which relates to this point is in British Guiana where the two major political parties are split over the issue of proportional representation which has been proposed by the British government as a way of easing internal strife. However, both parties are nationalist and profess commitments to democracy, although one is Communist-led.

9 B. Bettelheim and M. Janowitz

Prejudice

Reprinted from: B. Bettelheim and M. Janowitz, *Scientific American*, U.S.A., 1950, pp. 3–5.

One of the central difficulties facing present-day society is the problem of how to deal with the dissatisfactions and aggressions which seem to be generated by man's close proximity to his fellow men. Since hostility is the force most disruptive to social living, the scientific analysis of group hostility should be one of the chief concerns of social scientists.

This article will report on a recent attempt to study the problem. Of the many tension areas within our society the particular one selected for our investigation was ethnic hostility – a polite term for racial prejudice. To learn whether hostility is actually the result of frustration, we needed a group of subjects with some common life experiences, and this we found in a sample group of Army veterans who had returned to civilian life. Since all had experienced comparable wartime deprivations, they offered an excellent opportunity to examine the hypothesis that the individual who suffers frustrations tries to restore his emotional balance by some form of hostile behavior. Our sample consisted of 150 former G.I.s who were residents of Chicago and represented all economic classes.

Through intensive interviews in which free association was always encouraged these men were sounded out on their attitudes toward Negroes, Jews and other ethnic minorities. The interviewers were psychiatrically trained social workers experienced in public-opinion surveying. The wide range of personal data sought required long interviews which took from four to seven hours and in several cases were carried on in two sessions. The veterans themselves were offered ample opportunity to express personal views on many issues and to recount their wartime experiences before the matter of ethnic minorities was first mentioned. The extensive contents of these case histories were then subjected to statistical and content analysis, which allowed us to make quantitative statements about the degree and type of ethnic hostility, as well as about feelings of deprivation, anxiety and a range of other psychological and sociological characteristics.

In general the analysis did not bear out the hypothesis that frustration necessarily generates dissatisfaction or hostility. Army experiences which seemed to involve objective hardship (e.g., combat, wounds, long service) did not in themselves appear to heighten dissatisfaction. For example, a 25-year-old infantry private first-class who had fought in North Africa, Italy and Germany, and who claimed, with some justification, that Army life had ruined his health, described his war experience as follows: 'I was a teletype operator in Africa for three or four months, and wasn't in combat then, but all the rest of the time I was laying wire in combat areas. We lost 80% of our company. I never thought I had a chance to come out of it alive. I came out lucky. I came out swell on money and passes. I didn't get any breaks, but to come back and be alive today is really swell.' Another typical response was that of a 30-year-old staff sergeant who had once been demoted: 'In my Army career I got a good break. I was made staff sergeant in 1942, only I was busted. But I made it back in another outfit. And I got to be mess sergeant, and mess sergeants eat good.'

On the other hand, a number of veterans whose experiences, objectively speaking, had been relatively free of hardship, felt that they had had bad breaks. A typical response in this group was the following: 'I wanted to get somewhere. But somebody else always got it. I deserved a rating and never got it. When they wanted somebody to repair something on a gun, I was always called because the other guy didn't know. That's why I never had no use for the Army. They never gave a rating to a person who should get one.'

Thus a man's evaluation of his Army career in retrospect was largely independent of the actual deprivations experienced and depended mainly on his emotional attitude toward this experience in particular, and, one may add, to life experiences in general.

Our main purpose was to find out how all this affected ethnic intolerance. On the basis of an exploratory study we found it possible to classify the veterans in four types according to the degree of intolerance or tolerance toward a specific ethnic group. With respect to their attitude toward Jews, for example, the four types were: (1) the intensely anti-Semitic, who spontaneously expressed a desire for restrictive action against the Jews even before the question was raised; (2) the outspokenly anti-Semitic, whose hostility toward the Jews emerged only on direct question; (3) the stereotyped anti-Semitic, who merely expressed various stereotyped notions about the Jews, some of which were not necessarily unfavorable from the interviewee's point of view; (4) the tolerant, who revealed no elaborately stereotyped beliefs about the Jews.

The attitudes of the 150 veterans toward Jews and Negroes, graded according to this scale, are summarized in charts. There was a considerable difference in tolerance toward Jews and Negroes, and the results showed that true ethnic tolerance, i.e. a tolerance which also included Negroes, was a rarity among these veterans.

Further analysis revealed that the men's actual Army experiences bore little relation to their attitude toward ethnic groups, nor was there any significant correlation between intolerance and age, education, religion, political affiliation, income, social status or even the subjects' preferences in newspapers, magazines or radio programs.

There was a close relation, however, between ethnic attitude and social mobility, i.e. a move up or down on the socio-economic scale, as compared with previous civilian employment, after the veteran was discharged from the Army. Ethnic hostility proved to be most highly concentrated in the downwardly mobile group, while the pattern was significantly reversed for those who had risen in social position. Those who had experienced no change were 'middle-of-the-roaders'. Over 70% of the stereotyped anti-Semites were found in this middle category; on the other hand, most of the same group were in the outspokenly anti-Negro category – a reflection of the fact that in this Northern urban industrial community it was 'normal' to have stereotyped opinions about the Jews, and to be outspoken in hostility toward the Negro.

It turned out that while the men's actual Army experiences showed no relation to intolerance, their subjective evaluations of those experiences definitely did. Those who felt they had had bad breaks in the Army were the most inclined to be hostile toward Jews and Negroes. A further study was made of the relation between intolerance and a readiness to submit in general to controls by society. If, by and large, an individual accepted social institutions, it seemed reasonable to assume that his acceptance implied a willingness to control his aggressive tendencies for the sake of society. Or, to put it another way, one might say that those men who felt that society was fulfilling its task in protecting them from unavoidable frustrations were also the ones who were willing in return to come to terms with society by controlling their aggressions.

Control, as a psychologist defines it, is the ability to store tension internally or to discharge it in socially constructive action rather than in unwarranted hostile action. There are three sources from which such control may come: (1) external or social pressure, (2) the superego, or the unconscious 'conscience', and (3) the ego, or rational self-control.

In actuality the three types of control are nearly always coexistent, and in any individual control will depend in varying degrees on all three. In the men studied, wherever control was present it was overwhelmingly the result of a combination of external and superego control, with the first dominant. Few men were also motivated significantly by rational self-control, and in even fewer was this dominant over superego or external control. Hence a study of external (i.e., societal) control was the only one that promised to allow insight into the correlation between a man's attitudes toward social control and the extent of his ethnic intolerance.

The analysis indicated that veterans who had stable religious convictions, regardless of the church they belonged to, tended to be the more tolerant. When the political party system was viewed as another norm-setting institution, a similar relationship of at least partial acceptance was found to be associated with tolerance. Whether the veteran was Democratic or Republican was in no way indicative of his attitude toward minorities. But the veteran who rejected or condemned both parties ('they're both crooks') tended to be the most hostile toward minorities.

To explore more fully this relationship between tolerance and control, the responses to other symbols of societal authority which signify external control of the individual also were investigated. The four institutions singled out as being most relevant were: the Veterans Administration, the political party system, the Federal government and the economic system, as defined by the subjects themselves. The analysis showed that only an insignificant percentage of the tolerant men rejected these institutions, while nearly half of the outspoken and intense anti-Semites did so. (This is in marked contrast to studies of certain types of college students, in whom radical rejection of authority is combined with liberalism toward minority groups.) In the case of the attitude toward the Negro, societal controls merely exercise a restraining influence; they do not suppress hostility but only make it less violent. The men who were strongly influenced by external controls were, in the majority, stereotyped and outspoken but not intense in their intolerance toward Negroes.

Thus it appears that in our society intolerance is related first to a lowering of social status, to feelings of frustration and insecurity. Next, the degree to which it finds open expression depends on the degree to which society approves or disapproves its expression. But the question remains: Why is ethnic hostility a favorite channel for discharging aggressive feelings?

Some of the reasons emerged, albeit indirectly, in an analysis of the stereotypes used by the veterans in describing minorities. With respect to the Jews, the composite pattern of stereotypes did not stress 'obnoxious' characteristics; the members of this sample of veterans, predominantly of the lower class and lower-middle class, did not often characterize Jews as pushy, over-bearing or loud. In the main the Jews were represented as a powerful, well-organized group which by inference threatened the subject. The most frequent assertion was that Jews were clannish, and that they helped one another. In the context in which this statement was made it almost invariably indicated that the veteran was decrying what he considered to be the unfair advantage in business and politics which accrued to the Jew who enjoyed greater social solidarity than himself.

On the other hand, the stereotypes used about the Negro stressed personally 'offensive' characteristics – his alleged dirtiness and immorality. The intolerant white described the Negro as a threat to the white man's economic and social status, maintaining that the Negro was 'forcing out the whites'.

This situation differs from that in Germany under the National Socialists. In Germany the National Socialists applied the whole list of stereotypes to the Jews; their anti-Semitic propaganda greatly emphasized the Jews' alleged dirtiness and lack of morality. In the U.S., where more ethnic minorities are available as possible targets, a tendency has emerged to separate the stereotypes into two sets and to assign them to separate minority groups. One set of stereotypes indicates feelings of anxiety over the Jews' supposed power. The other set indicates anxieties aroused by the Negroes' (and the Mexicans') assumed ability to permit themselves the enjoyment of primitive, socially frowned-upon forms of indulgence or gratification. The selection and use of stereotype seems to depend on the needs of the person applying them. It also appears that the minority that shows the greater difference from the majority in physical characteristics, such as skin color, is used for projecting anxieties associated with dirt and sex desires, while the minority that is more like the majority in appearance becomes a symbol for anxieties concerning over-powering control.

Had the veterans' contacts with Jews and Negroes in the Army affected their attitudes? Detailed analysis showed little apparent effect; their stereotypes of Jews they had met in the Army were largely just an extension of civilian concepts. A typical comment: 'There were only a few Jews in our outfit. One of them was a master sergeant. They did get up faster in rank and promotion, but we couldn't do anything about that. They would do favors for the officers and get promoted.'

Even when the veteran felt a personal attachment and respect for an individual Jew in his outfit, the stereotype remained: 'Oh, there was one Jew, Lieutenant Blank . . . almost forgot about him. He took pictures of me and a buddy of mine the day before he was killed. He was really white. At first I didn't like him and he knew it and picked on me at first, too. But then I changed my mind. He took care of his platoon all right. He saw to it that they had things they needed. They had cigarettes all the time when there weren't many around. That's the Jew in him – he was good at getting things like that. He'd do anything for his men and they'd do anything for him.'

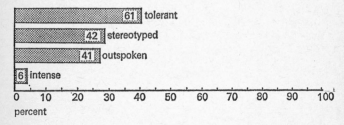

Attitudes toward Jews of the group studied were classified in four categories. The horizontal bars indicate the percentage of the group in each category. Numbers on the bars indicate the number of men in each category.

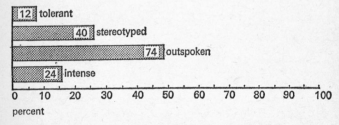

Attitudes toward Negroes were similarly classified. There were about the same number of stereotyped anti-Negro as stereotyped anti-Semitic expressions. There was a larger number of outspoken anti-Negro expressions.

These and many similar statements support the hypothesis that the individual's stereotypes are not only vitally needed defense mechanisms but are persistent, even under the impact of such immediate and realistic experiences as service with Jews and Negroes under conditions of war. Once a stereotype is formed, it is not easily changed by experience.

It seems reasonable to assume that as long as anxiety and insecurity persist as a root of intolerance, the effort to dispel stereotyped thinking or feelings of ethnic hostility by rational propaganda is at best a half-measure. On an individual level only greater personal integration combined with social and economic security seem to offer hope for better inter-ethnic relations. On the social level a change of climate is necessary. The veterans who accepted social controls and were more tolerant of other minorities were also less tolerant of the Negro, because discrimination against Negroes is more commonly condoned, both publicly and privately. This should lead, among other things, to additional efforts to change social practice in ways that will tangibly demonstrate that ethnic discrimination is contrary to the mores of society – a conviction which was very weak even among the more tolerant veterans.

10 M. Jahoda, P. F. Lazarsfeld and H. Zeisel

Attitudes Under Conditions of Unemployment*

Translated by M. E. Dasley
From: M. Jahoda et al., Die Arbeitslosen von Marienthal,
Verlag für Demoskopie, Allensbach, 1933, 2nd edn, 1960, pp. 47–65.

We began the inquiries in Marienthal by visiting 100 families to ask what particular requests they had for clothes in a collection we were organizing. During these visits we took the opportunity of gathering some information about the basic attitudes of the families through direct observation and conversation with them. Later when they collected the clothes, we asked some of them to tell us about their lives – a thing that most of them were only too willing to do. We also observed these people in many different situations: on our courses, at political meetings; we talked to them and about them. At all times the total information was recorded immediately. From this and from certain specialised sources (details of diet; questionnaires on how they spent their time, etc.) we constructed a detailed description of each family. Extracts of two such accounts of average families are reproduced here.

Family 366:

Husband, wife, 5 children – altogether 5·0 consumption units. Husband's unemployment allowance: 49 shillings; wife's allowance 22·4. shillings per fortnight. Daily income per consumption unit therefore: 1·02 shillings. Allotment holder.

From information obtained on visit: the flat, consisting of one small room and a large kitchen, is well kept. In spite of severely cramped conditions, there is nothing lying about. The children are clean and neat; the mother says she makes and mends all their clothes herself. In spite of this they have very few clothes. From the clothes collection the wife asks for a coat for her 14-year-old son. They had to sell their radio a few months

*This excerpt stems from a study of Marienthal, a small one-factory Austrian village whose population became totally unemployed with the closure of the factory in 1929 during the depression years. The study was conducted in 1931 and published in book form in 1932. A large quantity of the first edition fell victim to Hitler's book-burning. The excerpt is included here for two reasons: it implies a much wider interpretation of the concept of Attitude than is normally the case. Attitude in this study is approaching the idea of style of life. The second reason is that it approaches the assessment of attitudes with a variety of methods in their natural life setting. – Eds.

ago and can no longer afford a newspaper, as this is too expensive. She works very hard in the house, but sometimes her husband and children help.

From the husband's account: As long as he was working, things went well. He never let people impose on him and always stood up for his rights. However, he frequently had to change jobs. During the war he was in the army, and this was the worst time of all for him. Earlier he had been a band-master in his spare time and showed great enthusiasm for this. Occasionally he does this even now, but nowadays people have no money left for music. He often used to go to Vienna to listen to music; every Saturday evening he went out for a drink. Both these activities have now stopped, of course. He does not think that things will ever be better in Marienthal. The State is responsible for all this misery – it is the duty of the State, then, to maintain him. The general impression he makes is not a particularly discontented one. 'You can still go on living like this.'

From general conversation: 'It's easier for bachelors, they can emigrate ... but with a family? ...', 'I'd have liked the children to have a good education, but now you're lucky if you can give them enough to eat.' This man is described by the firm's engineer as a very well qualified worker.

From personal observation: He is a member of a political organization, but is not very politically aware. He often goes for walks and frequently plays cards in the Working Men's Club. His wife is an enthusiastic member of our course in design and has never missed a session. She even mends her husband's suits. The children's breakfast (bread and dripping) is always the same, whether before or after the day on which the assistance money is paid. One daughter who had been in service in various places, always comes back home because she feels happiest here. The family eats meat only once a week (horse meat stew).

From this information we can see how and to what extent they have cut down on basic needs: they do without a newspaper and a radio, they give up their trips to Vienna and visits to the pub: 'We can still live even like this,' comments the husband with indifference. But above all they save on food and on most essential articles of clothing. They also have to give up the idea of educating their children. As a result of all these measures of economy, however, they are able to maintain the physical health of their children and to run the household sensibly, as is seen, for instance, in their attempt to provide the children with regular nourishment (breakfast).

Another family:
Family 23.
Husband, wife, 3 children: In all 3·6 consumption units. Husband's

unemployment allowance 47·4 shillings. Wife's unemployment allowance 22·5 shillings per fortnight. Daily income therefore per consumption unit 1·38 shillings. Allotment holder.

From information obtained on visit: The flat consisting of one large room, kitchen and entrance hall is well kept. The children are clean and neatly dressed. At the clothes collection the wife asks for a jacket for her husband. She says she is unable to look for casual work as the children are too small. Her husband helps very little with the housework. She does not think that things will ever be any different in Marienthal, and has no plans for the future. But somehow or other they will manage to struggle on. Lunch, consisting of beans in sauce, was just being prepared.

From the husband's account: He wanted to become a butcher but his father would not let him. He said that if he could not be a butcher he would not do any training and upon leaving school went into a factory as an unskilled worker. During the war he was taken prisoner in Russia. 'I never had it so good as there.' He would have liked to stay there, 'but after all, you belong to your own country.' He has been living in Marienthal since 1921, and would like to go back to Russia. But he makes no attempt to achieve this end. 'We can manage for now,' he says.

From his wife's account: She had a bad time at home. She would dearly have liked to be a needlework teacher, but there was no question of this. Her first child was born when she was 17, but it soon died. Since then she worked in the factory until it closed down. She often quarrels with her husband because he does not bother about anything. Before he was out of work things were not so bad, but now he is hardly ever at home. She would so love to go out to enjoy herself occasionally. Sometimes she makes him stay at home, and goes off herself.

From general observations: The husband spends most of his time in the Men's club, reading newspapers and novels. He is always good-tempered and therefore popular with everyone. At one time he was often invited to socials at the pub, because he was so gay. At home his wife is boss, and always wants to know exactly how he spends his time.

From conversations with the wife: 'Somehow or other we'll manage; we can't all perish.'

Here too it is striking that they accept their fate with such calm. 'Somehow or other we'll manage,' says the wife, implying the possibility of reducing their needs and claims still further. This is the husband's feeling too, when he says 'We'll manage for now.' This family cuts down most of all on food, as does everyone else in Marienthal.

Closer examination reveals differences between these individual accounts which suggest that the attitudes vary considerably from one family to another. The two types of attitude we have already illustrated are representative of a middle group. Soon however we come across deviations from this which need closer analysis.

Let us begin with a deviation towards the positive:

Family 141:

Husband, wife, 2 children; in all 3·0 consumption units. Husband's unemployment allowance: 42·6 shillings, i.e., income of 1 shilling per consumption unit. Allotment holder and rabbit breeder.

Information obtained on visit: The flat, consisting of one room, w.c., kitchen, is neatly kept. The children give an impression of being tidy and well looked after. The wife apologizes for not having cleared up, although everything is very tidy. At the clothes collection she asks for something for her 9-year-old son. For lunch there is rabbit left over from Sunday.

From the husband's account: Right from his younger days he always held his own. During the war he refused promotion because he was a convinced opponent of warfare. He was taken prisoner by the Italians and learnt the language very easily. When he returned to Marienthal he married an old school friend. In the factory where he worked he was soon given a position of authority as shop steward, then Chairman of the Works Council. He has always played an active role in politics. His plans for the future are to take a course as a cutter, and later to open his own business in Vienna. He wants his son too to learn tailoring. He is a passionate reader. He would like to have emigrated to France, but his wife was opposed to this. Now he is glad that he did not go, because his colleagues who did, have had bad luck.

From conversation: He too finds the present situation quite bearable. As a political delegate he always has plenty to do because everyone comes to ask his advice; starvation is not all that imminent either. Both colleagues and superiors have always esteemed him highly and even now he is generally popular. His attitude is altogether a hopeful one.

From general observation: The wife visited the doctor regularly with her children, and followed his instructions strictly. She also makes use of all the other amenities provided in the village. They still have a number of good articles of clothing left over from better times; when necessary, the father himself alters these.

The two striking features of this account, as opposed to the two previous ones are: the great care with which the house is run and the atmosphere of contentment. There is no question of simply 'muddling through', but a fundamentally planned existence. The husband finds the present situation bearable, is full of hope and has a whole series of plans both for himself and for his son's education. Characteristic of this family is their ability to look forward to the future.

The picture is different again in the following families who differ from the middle group in a negative way. The negative attitude can take two different forms.

Family 363 is an example of one of these:

Husband, wife, 4 children; in all 4·2 consumption units. Wife's unemployment allowance recently stopped because apparently her husband could earn some money on the land. Present income therefore, nil. Rabbit breeder.

From the account of the visit: The flat, in a block, consisting of one room, kitchen and entrance, is in a terrible state. It is very dirty and untidy. The children and the adults have hardly anything to wear. The wife and children are very dirty. The whole place gives the impression of going to rack and ruin. There are many useless tatters of clothing lying about. The wife complains that her husband never helps her and is a nuisance to her. She asks for something warm from the clothes collection, not bothering to say for whom.

From the wife's account: Difficult early years; as soon as she left school she went to work in a factory. In 1925 she came to Marienthal. At first her marriage went well but now they are very unhappy; he is not entitled to any financial assistance because he has never been in regular employment. He never bothered about work but has always left everything to her. He often goes to the cinema; he 'barters' her belongings and tries to make some money that way; or he gossips and plays cards. She even has to chop the wood herself.

From conversation: 'I don't care about anything now'; 'I should be happy if I could put the children into care.'

From general observation: The household is particularly quarrelsome. The wife is not well liked. Her husband – a war casualty – is not a bad man, but simply incapable of doing anything. His wife is superior to him intellectually and takes advantage of this.

In this case we are dealing with a different attitude from that of the families described at the beginning of the chapter. They are no longer making any attempt to assess the relative importance of their needs, and to satisfy one at the expense of others. The impression is that they have let themselves go completely, they have nothing more to hang on to. Both the children and the flat – usually the last to be neglected – are in a bad state.

The attitude of family 467 is different again:

Family 467.

Husband, wife, 2 children; in all 3·0 consumption units. Husband's unemployment allowance: 42 shillings, i.e. daily income 1 shilling per consumption unit. Allotment holder.

From the account of the visit: The wife is very nervous, cries easily and seems terribly depressed. The flat, consisting of one room, w.c. and kitchen is kept beautifully clean. The whole family's clothes are neat and clean. From the clothes collection the husband asks for things for the children. He says that the worst of all is not being able to give the children anything. He is afraid that they will be retarded.

From the husband's account: He always expected a great deal from life, always wanted to get to the top, he was full of self-confidence and proud of his family. He studied and worked always successfully, so that at first when the slump came, he was convinced that nothing could happen to him. Even during the early months he believed that a man of his gifts could not fail. During the first year he wrote 130 applications for jobs, but had no replies. Now he can go on no longer. He tells how he stays in bed half the day to save breakfast and heating; he hardly ever goes out and is full of despair.

From conversation: 'It will never get better, only worse.' He wishes that everything would collapse. 'I would willingly bear anything if only the children could be spared.'

From general observation: There are still some good clothes left; the wife looks after the children very conscientiously and sends them regularly to a children's home. Her husband stays at home the whole day doing nothing at all. He has very little contact with other people in the village.

This family's attitude is characterised by great emphasis upon orderliness; in spite of the decrease in material goods, they try to run the household as well as before. But bound up with this sense of order is an unusual degree of expression of despair. Their sense of order distinguishes this family from the one just described; the mood of deep depression distinguishes them from the main group.

Even on first impression, the most frequently held attitude in Marienthal is that described in the first two accounts. An existence of hopeless indifference coupled with the view that after all nothing can be done about unemployment, and therefore a relatively calm frame of mind; even occasional sparks of happiness alongside a denial of the future which no longer plays a part even in phantasy – all this seemed to us best described by the term resignation. Even if this use of the word does not fully coincide with its everyday meaning which does not include the transitory image of contentment seen in some 'resigned' families, nevertheless there seemed to us to be no other word to characterise the reduced claims on life, the attitude towards life, devoid of all expectation. In all these families we found a very orderly household where children were well cared for and not in the least neglected. If from this picture we extract those criteria, which lead us to describe a family as resigned, then they are: restriction of all needs beyond those of the home but, at the same time, an ability to maintain the household, to look after the children and a feeling of relative well being.

The attitude presented by family 141 is clearly distinguished from this: the main impression of families like this is one of great activity. Their households are just as well run as those of the resigned families, but they have restricted their needs less, their horizon is broader, their energy greater. Again it was not easy to find an appropriate way of describing this behaviour. We finally chose the term 'unbroken' and set up the following criteria for this attitude: an ability to maintain the household and to care for the children, a feeling of well-being, activity, plans and hopes for the future, enjoyment of life, continuous attempts to get work.

The other two main groups can be described as 'broken'. Yet the differences between them are so great that we decided to take each one as a separate main group. For in the first case, the family failed in quite a different sphere from the second: with family 363 the weakness affected the household, in family 467 it affected mood and spirit.

Let us look first of all at all those who differ little from those described earlier in their outer mode of life, but whose subjective experience of life is quite different. These people are full of despair and this gives the group its name. Like the unbroken and resigned groups, these can keep their household in order, also look after their children. These main criteria then apply also to the despairing group. But in addition are the following criteria; despair, depression, hopelessness, a feeling that all effort is useless and therefore no further attempts to look for work, no attempts to improve their position; a tendency frequently to compare their lot unfavourably with the past.

The final group (family 363) differs from the three others in that they have given up any attempt to run their home. With an apathetic lethargy they let things take their own course without attempting to save anything from deterioration. We call this the apathetic group. The main characteristic of this group is their tendency to look on, devoid of energy and activity. The house and children are dirty and uncared for, they are not in a mood of despair, but just indolent. No plans are made, there is no hope, in running the home they are not concerned with satisfying basic needs, but spend irrationally. To this group belong those who drink. The family shows signs of disintegration and there is a great deal of quarrelling; this is frequently accompanied by begging and stealing. Not only are there no plans for the future, but none even for the following day or the next moment. The unemployment allowance is used up during the first few days with no thought of what will happen after that.

As one can see, it is typical of three of these four main groups to keep a sensible budget. From conversation with the women and the way in which they have kept a record of all their spending it emerges how constantly concerned they are with minute items of expenditure. But it is just as typical that even in this strict calculation there are again and again instances of rash spending. Whether we should interpret these as first signs of crumbling resistance or as the last reminiscence of former affluence cannot generally be determined. Let us give just a few examples of such episodes which were frequently encountered.

On many allotments, flowers are planted although people depend on their vegetables and potatoes; there are beds which could yield a crop of 80 kg. of potatoes, growing carnations, tulips, roses, harebells, pansies and dahlias. When asked why they do this, the answer is 'You cannot live by bread alone, you need something to cheer you up. It's so nice to have a vase of flowers indoors.'

One family whose insurance claims had expired a year ago and who use only saccharin in order to economise, one day bought a cardboard picture of Venice for 30 groschen* from a pedlar. Another family dependent only on emergency assistance bought very expensive black outfits for a funeral; a 50-year-old woman suddenly bought a pair of hair clippers on H.P.

Particularly often such episodes are connected with a helpless love for their children. Several typical examples are these:

A 12-year-old boy who turned up for school without a bite to eat the day before the allowances were paid, arrived the next day with a roll and sausage, two doughnuts and a bar of chocolate.

A street-vendor who sells picture-books and calendars says that the sale of picture books has not suffered nearly as much as that of calendars; in some cases he even has new customers, women who suddenly decide to buy a picture book as a present for a child.

* Groschen – Austrian coin.

89

Perhaps the first or the last example can be interpreted as a longing for some ray of happiness, and the other cases as symptoms of failing resistance. At any rate these examples are a reminder that even this very restricted way of life in Marienthal cannot always be brought down to a common denominator. In spite of this life in Marienthal is determined on the whole by those general characteristics which we have tried to highlight in the types of attitude described. Let us then turn again to our 4 groups and make a general survey of their distribution in Marienthal.

We studied 100 families in such detail that we were able to establish all the necessary facts for placing each one in one of the main groups. Examples of this can be seen in previous sections. These 100 families were described to us as being 'particularly worthy of consideration' at the beginning of our winter auxiliary campaign; of these:

16% were unbroken
48% resigned
11% in despair
25% apathetic. Total 100%

Later, during the course of our investigation, when we became better acquainted with the whole community we realised that in fact all the 'broken' families in Marienthal were included in our sample. From a total of 478 families 2·3% may be described as despairing, 5·3% as apathetic, roughly 8% have broken down under the stress of unemployment. The remainder probably belong to the 'resigned' and 'unbroken' groups in the same proportions as in our sample. This not only corresponds to our general impression but is also true in another connection: there are only slight variations in the way of life of these people and a large proportion of those families described as 'particularly worthy of consideration', represents the average in Marienthal: this was confirmed later when we were able to make an independent comparison. The 'unbroken' part of the community is therefore 3 parts resigned, one part unbroken, using the terms in exactly the same way as in our analysis above. If we include the apathetic and the despairing in the 'broken' group, then it would probably be true to say that all families in Marienthal are distributed amongst our main groups in the following way:

	%
Unbroken	23
Resigned	69
Broken	8
	100

Apart from the pressure of conditions generally there is probably another special reason why, at first, we found such a small number of families who had retained any hope of finding a way out. Probably a number of the most active and energetic inhabitants of Marienthal had already escaped the general fate of the village by leaving it, before we arrived.

The surrounding region was of little use for would-be emigrants; above all people hoped to emigrate permanently to Czechoslovakia or temporarily to Rumania. Since 1930 altogether 60 people had left. More skilled men could have settled in Rumania but no more could make up their minds to go. The people take this view: we became unemployed here; we'll wait here for things to get better – who knows what will happen to us elsewhere? This view was confirmed by the unfortunate experience of some who had emigrated to France.

Of particular interest here is the age of the emigrants. Of the 60 who left, only 13 were over 40; 47 were under 40 and 27 of these under 30. We can see then that a considerable proportion of the younger people in Marienthal – and probably the most energetic and capable – do not figure in our investigation at all because they had already left.

And in spite of this: if we are influenced by the direct impression gained through contact with the community, we feel that its whole way of life is determined more by an attitude of resignation than is at first suggested by the above figures. The lives of the unbroken and broken groups seem to be overshadowed by an impression of a totally resigned community, who, although they maintain some stability in the present, have lost all contact with the future.

This comes about because certain groups of the community, classified on a basis other than family membership, show the same characteristics as the resigned group. By this we mean children and young people. With them, the impression of resignation is all the more striking, because with these age groups one might expect anything but an attitude of resignation. We shall attempt to support this fact by a few data.

From the compositions that the children wrote on Christmas, we assessed their requests for Christmas presents on a uniform scale which was constructed with the help of experts, according to average prices. The average cost of Christmas presents they hoped for is seen in the following table.

| Children from Marienthal | 12 shillings |
| „   surrounding areas | 36   „ |

Moreover the children hardly dare to express even these modest wishes; many of the essays of the Marienthal children are typified by one characteristic: nearly a third of them are written in the subjunctive. These usually begin with an introductory sentence 'If my parents were not out of work – ' or something similar.

An 11-year-old boy writes:

'If my parents had any money, I should have asked for a violin, a suit, poster paints, a paint brush, a book, skates and a jacket.' 'I got a winter coat.'

A girl of the same age:

'I should have asked for a lot of presents if my parents had been in work. I didn't get anything: I only had a pair of glasses. I wanted an atlas and a pair of compasses.'

A 9-year-old boy:

'I would have loved a photograph album. I didn't get anything as my parents are out of work.'

Children who were not resigned before Christmas became so afterwards. For instead of happiness and surprises, Christmas brought many of the Marienthal children nothing but disappointment. This is shown by the difference between the presents they wanted and what they actually received.

	Surrounding areas	*Marienthal*
	%	%
More than they wanted	18	11
As much as they wanted	44	20
Less than they wanted	38	69
	100	100

Far more than half the children not living in Marienthal have their wishes fulfilled and only a third of them receive less than they expected. In Marienthal 69% of the children do not get what they hoped for. The difference between the present they asked for and what they actually received is greater in Marienthal than in surrounding areas, although they expect far less for Christmas than the other children.

Lack of long-term plans is a further characteristic of their basic attitude. This lack of ability to plan is drastically expressed in accounts of their life stories. 28 men and 29 women were questioned about their plans for the future. Only 15 indicated any sort of plans; most of them are thinking of moving away. With the exception of only one, however, they had not done anything to help realise these plans (cf. the above data on emigrants). In actual fact with them it is more a question of random wishes than concrete plans. The adults have no longer any plans for the future. How far this applies also to the younger people will be considered later.

The almost insuperable difficulties for individuals to better their lot makes this attitude an understandable one. As they themselves can do little to improve the general state of affairs the whole village succumbs to the general decline.

And again it is the children who set a particularly significant criterion. In the senior classes of the elementary school this essay title was set: 'Thoughts on unemployment'. What a difference between those children who had experienced unemployment in their own homes and those from surrounding areas! These too are familiar with unemployment. But while the Marienthal children accept it with hopeless resignation, the others express partly a deep satisfaction that they are not unemployed, and partly anxiety that they may one day be out of work. A 12-year-old boy from the region surrounding Marienthal, whose parents are farmers, writes:

'I have not yet thought about poverty and unemployment. I am glad that I have enough to eat.'

The son of a labourer from outside Marienthal writes:

'In most countries in Europe there is poverty and unemployment. In many rich families bread and scraps are thrown away and many a family would be grateful to us if they had something to eat each day. It is the same in all countries.'

The words 'grateful to us' express very clearly his own sense of well-being and the sharp distinction between him and all those whose lot is not so happy.

The Marienthal children on the other hand write from first-hand experience. A 12-year-old boy shows quite clearly how his imagination is already dominated by his experience of poverty. He writes:

'I should like to be an airman, a submarine captain, an Indian Chief and a mechanic. But I am afraid that it will be very difficult to get a good job.'

Of course a considerable number of children can only write a few disjointed childish sentences on the subject, regardless of whether their own family has been affected or not; this is our general experience with school essays.

The number of uninformative essays is in fact independent of whether they have experienced poverty; in one case it amounts to 47%, in the other 48%.

	Marienthal children	Others
	%	%
Not thought about it	16	28
Few sentences only	47	48
Own experience	37	2
Glad that parents still have work	—	16
Fear of unemployment	—	6
Total	100	100

The older the children, the more there are for whom unemployment is a personal problem, even if they themselves have not yet been affected by it. Typical of those 13- and 14-year-olds who have not yet been affected is a fear of the future that is expressed in the essay quoted above with the boy's many choices of career. There is also the fear of not getting a job. A 13-year-old girl writes:

'I should very much like to be a tailoress, but I'm afraid that I won't get a job at all or that I won't have anything to eat.'

The same attitude is found amongst young people who are not in an apprenticeship. For these we organised an essay competition with the topic: 'How do I imagine my future?'. Even from the poor response – only 15 essays came in, although the tempting prize was a new pair of trousers – it can be seen that interest in this question is very slight. This lack of plans can be seen more clearly from the type of answers given. Amongst the 15 were 5 written by young men in apprenticeships. There is a vast difference between their answers and those who have no work or apprenticeship. While the trainees all work out a personal plan for the future in connexion with the trade they are learning, the others write about general hopes for a better future; about Socialism 'where everyone will earn 300 shillings per month', about world revolution which will set the oppressed free; but unlike the trainees, they write nothing about their own personal future. Two typical representatives of each group are compared here. A 17-year-old tailor's apprentice writes:

'If I am to achieve happiness in life I should like to work as an assistant for two years after my apprenticeship, then to take a practical course in cutting, which I think promises success in the future. I then intend to find a job as a cutter in a firm. Later I should like to set up my own business.'

A 22-year-old, unemployed, wrote:

'In present day society I imagine my future as follows: In the present world-wide economic crisis where Capitalism is beginning to break down in all quarters, it cannot take much longer to shake off the yoke of capitalist reactionaries. I think that Capitalism will then soon collapse. The path of Socialism will then be paved; it would give me greatest pleasure to be able to work towards the establishment of Socialism.'

The problem of young people in Marienthal cannot be better illustrated than by describing the almost insuperable difficulties confronting young people who are unemployed. In Marienthal there are 131 young people (14–21), 62 boys and 69 girls. However, in spite of numerous attempts we did not succeed in making contact with them. We were able to observe two small political groups, the Young Socialist Workers and occasionally a group of German gymnasts; we were able to talk to them and work with them. But all the other young people – and that is the large majority – remained unapproachable, although a sports coach came out especially for the boys and a gym class was put on for the girls: they simply did not attend. They vanished completely and just 'knocked around together'. Even the leaders of the two political organizations agreed that their most difficult problem was to get hold of the young people.

In the children as well as the young people, an expression of resignation was very apparent. Since such an attitude is totally contrary to what we are accustomed to in children and young people, it is probably one reason why an attitude of resignation – in the sense that we have used in our analysis – seems to the outsider to be the fundamental attitude in Marienthal.

11 M. Argyle

The Attitudes of Religious People

Excerpt from: M. Argyle, *Religious Behaviour*, Routledge, London, 1958.

[. . . .]

Political Attitudes

Political attitudes may be defined by the way a person votes or says he votes. Alternatively, attitude scales can be constructed which differentiate between Radicals and Conservatives – they include items on such subjects as private enterprise and economic security.

Religious people are more conservative in politics than non-religious people. Table 1 gives the results of a British survey and shows the very low percentage of people with no religion who vote Conservative.

Table 1

Denomination and Voting, Great Britain 1951

	Conservative	Labour	Liberal
Church of England	45	37	8
Nonconformist	27·5	40·5	18
R.C.	33	51	6
Scottish Church	43·5	37	7·5
Other	33	35·5	15
None	17	54	6

(From Eysenck, 1954, p. 21)

British and American surveys show that Protestants tend to vote Conservative more than Catholics, and that Jews support left-wing parties: Centers (1951) found a correlation of ·36 between Protestantism and Republicanism in America. This is probably partly due to class differences, since Catholics have a higher working-class composition in both countries. However, a number of American studies show that Protestants are still more Republican with social class held constant (cf. Lipset *et al.*, 1954, p. 1140). Table 2 shows this for Lazarsfeld's study (1944) of Erie County.

96

Table 2

Denomination, Voting and Social Class, Erie County 1944

	Protestant	Catholic
Av+	76	29
Av	66	25
Av−	54	23
Very poor	43	14

(Percentage of the denomination voting Republican; from Lazarsfeld, 1944)

Centers (op. cit.) found a correlation of ·36 between Protestantism and Republican voting, and ·19 between Protestantism and social class – showing that class differences between denominations are only a partial explanation.

These results using voting as a criterion of political attitude are paralleled by investigations using attitude scales – where radical opinions are generally defined as those favouring communism and birth control and being opposed to war. Such studies agree with the others in finding that religious people are more conservative (e.g. Carlson, 1934). However, it has been found in a number of American studies that Catholics* hold more conservative attitudes than Protestants, and Protestants than Jews (Sappenfield, 1942), although the voting statistics show Protestants as most conservative. The explanation may be that Catholics vote Democrat as the result of an historical tradition: the Irish and German immigrants in the second half of the last century settled in the cities and the Democratic party was favourably inclined towards them, as well as having more influence among the urban population. (Lubell, 1956.) English Catholics similarly contain many Irish who are traditionally opposed to the Tories. Lipset (op. cit. p. 1140) shows that members of religious minority groups often support left-wing parties. It seems likely that Catholics have an intrinsically right-wing attitude, but they may vote for left-wing parties in America and Great Britain for one of the reasons mentioned. Jews have left-wing votes and attitudes, and in America this is quite inconsistent with their class position.

Finally there is some evidence that religious people are less interested in politics. Ringer and Glock (1955) found that parish-

* It should be noted that these scales include items on sexual ethics and other matters on which Catholic teaching is 'conservative'; items on drinking and gambling might produce different results (Nowlan, 1957).

ioners most committed to the church were least willing to allow the priest to participate in politics. Similar findings are reported later on the relation between religious activity and concern over social issues. Part of the explanation may lie in the inverse pattern of relations between religious and political interests and the age-sex variables: women are more concerned with religion, men with politics; young and old people are most active in religion, the age group 35–55 in politics (Lipset, loc. cit.).

Summary

Religious people are more conservative and are less interested in politics than other people. Catholics have more conservative attitudes, but in Britain and America support left-wing parties: this is partly due to class differences. Protestants support right-wing parties, Jews support the left and have radical attitudes.

Racial Prejudice

Several American surveys have found that religious people are more prejudiced against Jews and Negroes, as shown by attitude scales on racial attitudes. Table 3 shows the scores on scales of ethnocentrism for 1,332 people studied in the 'Authoritarian Personality' investigations in California.

Some investigators have not obtained these results. Chein for instance found a correlation between prejudice and church attendance, but when he analysed denominations separately the correlation was reversed; his Catholics were more prejudiced than

Table 3

Ethnocentrism and Religion

Catholics	4·21
Major Prot. Denom.	3·89
Minor Prot. Sects	2·49 (n=23)
Unitarians	1·99 (n=23)
No denom.	2·71
Church attenders	3·96
Non-attenders	2·87
Religion important	180·7
Religion unimportant	115·4

(From Adorno *et al.*, 1950, pp. 210–17)

his Protestants, the Protestants than the Jews, and since the Catholics attended church more often, this created a spurious overall correlation between attendance and prejudice (cf. Harding, *et al.*, 1954, p. 1039). Similarly, Prothro and Jensen (1950) found small positive correlations of ·05 and ·09 between favourable attitudes to the church and towards Negroes and Jews respectively; correlations were computed separately for six colleges which were denominationally fairly pure. Parry (1949) found that non-church-going Protestants were more prejudiced than church-going Protestants, and Allport (1954) found less prejudice in a group of twenty fervent Catholics than in twenty 'who seemed more influenced by the political and social aspects of religious activity' (p. 452). However many investigations show that atheists and agnostics are less prejudiced – this is shown in Table 3 and was found in Ross's study (1950) of 2,000 Y.M.C.A. members. It seems possible that there may be a curvilinear relation between religious activity and prejudice: out-and-out atheists and agnostics are less prejudiced than church members who never go to church, while more frequent attenders are also less prejudiced. It is not the genuinely devout who are prejudiced but the conventionally religious.

Turning now to denominational differences, it has often been found that Catholics are the most prejudiced, members of the major Protestant bodies slightly less so. This was found in the Authoritarian Personality research, where it also emerged that members of small sects were very low in prejudice, though only twenty-three such people were tested. Chein, as reported above, found Catholics, Protestants and Jews to be prejudiced in that order, while Allport and Kramer (1946) in a study of 437 students found 71% of Catholics in the most prejudiced half, compared with 62% of Protestants, 22% of Jews and 27% of those with no religious upbringing. It will be noticed that the Catholic-Protestant difference is slight, and it has occasionally been found that Catholics are *less* prejudiced (cf. Harding, *et al.*, 1954). Spoerl (1951) and Parry (1949) found that members of different denominations were prejudiced towards different groups: generally speaking Catholics are prejudiced towards Negroes and orientals, Protestants towards Jews and working-class minority groups, while Jews are prejudiced towards white majority groups.

Although there is evidence that members of the Catholic church in America tend to be slightly more prejudiced than other people, it should be noted that the leaders of this church have been prominent in opposing racial segregation both in the U.S.A. and in South Africa.

Summary

Regular and devout church attenders tend to be less prejudiced than non-attending members, though religious people in general are more prejudiced than non-religious people. Catholics are most prejudiced, closely followed by the major Protestant denominations; Jews and sect members are the least prejudiced.

Suggestibility

As several investigations have now shown, suggestibility is not a single trait, but is composed of a number of relatively independent elements. Eysenck (1947) experimented with a variety of different test situations and concluded that there were at least three types – (1) Primary (or psychomotor) suggestibility, in which people carry out a motor movement, upon repeated suggestion by the experimenter but without conscious participation by the agent, (2) Secondary suggestibility, in which people will perceive or remember the thing suggested, and (3) Prestige suggestion, in which people change their opinion after being told that a prestige person holds a different one.

There is considerable evidence that religious conservatives are high on prestige suggestibility. Symington (1935) studied 612 people using a comprehensive test of orthodoxy of belief. There was clear evidence from the questionnaire answers that the conservatives were more dependent on group opinion – for example the liberals reported that they disliked being told what to do, and gave evidence of facing the facts squarely before forming an opinion. Dreger (1952) studied thirty people from each extreme of liberalism and conservatism out of an initial group of 490, the groups being carefully equated for other variables. Various scores from the Thematic Apperception Test and the Rorschach indicated that conservatives had a greater need for dependence than the liberals. Finally the fact that authoritarians are more religious, combined with Hoffman's finding (1953) that they are more affected by social influence, points to the same conclusion.

Supplementary evidence comes from investigations of self-confidence and inferiority feelings. Janis (1954) found that subjects who were low on ratings of self-esteem – including depression and inhibition of aggression – were more influenced by written propaganda. Neurotic, particularly obsessional, people were less influenced. A number of studies show that Catholics and other religious conservatives are lacking in self-confidence and self-esteem. Symington's conservatives (1935) considered that there were more things wrong with them on the Pressey test. Several studies of Catholic theological students and novices show them to be submissive and to have inferiority feelings on various personality tests or self-ratings (e.g. McCarthy, 1942).

There is evidence on primary suggestibility from a variety of religious groups, in every case showing that religious people are more suggestible in this sense too. Howells (1928) gave a series of psychomotor tests to fifty extreme radicals and the same number of conservatives. Five tests of psychomotor suggestibility all showed the conservatives to be the more suggestible. Sinclair (1928) obtained similar results comparing fifty students who did have marked mystical experiences with fifty at the other extreme. Primary suggestibility seems to be particularly strong amongst members of revivalist and evangelical bodies. As reported in another section (pp. 52–3), many people at early revivals showed signs of twitching and jerking before finally collapsing; this is primary suggestibility and may be a particular trait of revivalist audiences. Some of them go to hospital in states of 'religious excitement', a form of hysteria (p. 106). Coe (1916) studied 100 people who had been converted, and found that those who had been converted 'suddenly', i.e. at revivals, produced motor automatisms more frequently under hypnosis. Brown and Lowe (1951) tested a large number of students on the Minnesota Multiphasic Personality Inventory (MMPI) and found that a group of Bible students – who would be extreme Protestants – scored high on hysteria. Janet and others thought that hysterics were particularly prone to primary suggestibility. Eysenck (1947) found that while neurotics in general were thus suggestible, hysterics were no more so than other neurotics; however, he agrees that the impersonal suggestions which were used might have been less effective for hysterics than face-to-face suggestions (p. 190).

Summary

Religious conservatives are subject to prestige suggestion. Various religious groups have been found to be high on primary suggestibility, but this is probably most true of extreme Protestants.

Authoritarianism*

A number of investigators have drawn up questionnaires containing miscellaneous political, religious and other items, and have studied the statistical relations between these items. In particular

* For an account of the syndrome of authoritarianism and its genesis, see the next article by Sanford. – Eds.

they have arrived at two or more 'factors' which between them will stand for the original items, and from which an individual's score on any particular items can be predicted. Ferguson (1944) did a series of such factor analyses, and one of his factors he called 'humanitarianism': this was measured by scales measuring attitudes towards war, capital punishment and the treatment of criminals – these three correlating closely with one another. His second factor was called 'religionism', which will be discussed later.

The next study to be considered is that of Adorno and others (1950) on the Authoritarian Personality, which was mentioned above in connexion with racial prejudice. Attitude scales were developed for Anti-Semitism, Ethnocentrism and for Political and Economic Conservatism: these correlated to the extent of ·43–·76. From these a further scale, the F-scale, was developed which would measure the basic personality mechanisms underlying the previous tendencies without referring directly to them. This scale correlated with the others to the extent of ·53–·73 and was taken as a measure of 'authoritarianism'. There has been a lot of research on this dimension and it is now clear that it is by no means a pure factor, but rather a combination of several tendencies. The F-scale measures the opposite of Ferguson's humanitarianism (Eysenck, 1954, p. 238), as can be seen by comparison of the items in the two scales.

Eysenck (1944) factor analysed 700 replies to a thirty-two-item questionnnaire. As shown in Figure 7, he obtained factors of Radicalism-Conservatism and of tough- and tender-mindedness. Inspection of the items in the various quadrants however shows that the fourth quadrant contains the orthodox conservative religious views corresponding to Ferguson's religionism factor, while the second quadrant contains items on evolution and sex representing the opposite pole of the religionism factor. Similarly, the first and third quadrants correspond to humanitarianism. As Eysenck says, 'when the results . . . are compared with Ferguson's analysis, it will be found that agreement is striking with respect to the actual position of the items, but that his two main factors . . . are rotated from R(adicalism) and T(ough-minded) through an angle of 45°.' (1953, p. 233.)

In Eysenck's and Ferguson's analyses, religionism and authoritarianism (or humanitarianism) are shown at right angles – i.e. as statistically independent. However, as shown previously, authoritarianism is considerably higher for religious people, and in particular for Catholics, though certain Protestant sects are low

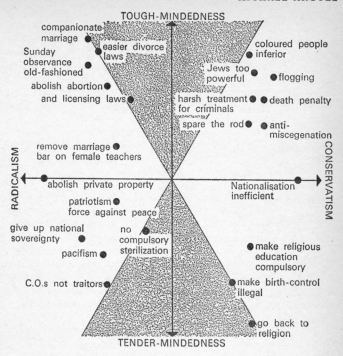

Figure 7 Eysenck's R and T factors.

on it. Similarly, Kirkpatrick (1949) made a careful study of the correlation between religionism and humanitarianism, including an analysis of a stratified sample of 215 individuals, and found a correlation of − ·24. Such variations in the results are presumably due to different definitions of the dimensions being considered. The general relations between authoritarianism, political conservatism and religionism may be represented as in Figure 8.

If *authoritarianism* is measured in a way which makes it more like political conservatism, then there is a closer correlation with religion. If *religionism* is defined in a way which stresses orthodoxy of belief and church membership rather than church attendance, it will lie in the 'A' position in Figure 8, and be associated with authoritarianism, political conservatism and prejudice. If religionism is defined by church attendance and other measures of genuine

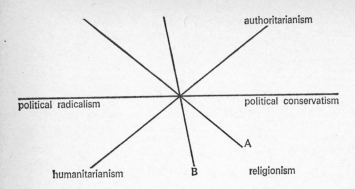

Figure 8 Religion and Authoritarianism

religious involvement, it will lie in position 'B', and may be associated with low race prejudice, liberal rather than conservative views in politics, and low scores on authoritarianism. Religionism A is stronger for Catholics and other religious conservatives, Religionism B for Unitarians, Jews and other religious liberals. This fits in with the fact that Catholics are higher on authoritarianism than Protestants, and Protestants higher than Jews (p. 84; Lipset, 1953).

Another phase of the Adorno project studied the personality variables associated with authoritarianism. The results of a series of clinical interviews with people at the extremes of the dimension show that authoritarians (i) have greater repression of unacceptable tendencies in themselves, (ii) project these impulses on to others, who may be seen as hostile and threatening, (iii) show a higher degree of conformity, (iv) are more concerned with power than love in dealing with other people and (v) have a rigid kind of personality. The tendency of authoritarians to use projection (ii) as a defence mechanism will be referred to in the theoretical section of the book. Their conformity and tendency to submit to social pressures (iii) will be used to account for the hierarchical structure of the Catholic church.

A related personality variable is that of punitiveness: people are said to be extrapunitive if they react to frustration by aggression directed outwards, intropunitive if the aggression is directed inwards, and impunitive if they do not react aggressively at all. This aspect of personality is often measured by means of the Rosenzweig Picture-Frustration test (1946), a projection test in

104

which reactions to various forms of frustration are expressed: the test has been found to correlate with overt measures of aggression. It would be expected that authoritarians would be extrapunitive, in view of their hostility towards out-groups and their weak internalization of a superego (pp. 159–60). Sanford (1950) gave tests for both dimensions to 1,000 subjects and found that the authoritarians reacted extrapunitively unless the frustrating person was powerful, in which case they were intropunitive; the humanitarians on the other hand responded impunitively. King and Funkenstein (1957) found that religious conservatives and those whose fathers were stern disciplinarians (two correlates of authoritarianism) had the same cardiovascular stress reaction that is found when anger is directed outwards.

Summary

Authoritarianism is higher for religious people in general, particularly for Catholics and other religious conservatives, though it is probably low for Unitarians, Jews and members of minor sects.

References
Adorno, T. W., *et al.*, *The Authoritarian Personality*. New York: Harper, 1950.
Allport, G. W., *The Nature of Prejudice*. Cambridge, Mass.: Addison-Wesley, 1954.
Allport, G. W., and Kramer, B. M., Some roots of prejudice. *J. Psych.*, **22**, 9–39, 1946.
Brown, D. G., and Lowe, W. L., Religious beliefs and personality characteristics of college students. *J. Social Psych.*, **33**, 103–29. 1951.
Carlson, H. B., Attitudes of undergraduate students. *J. Social Psych.*, **5**, 202–12, 1934.
Centers, R., *The Psychology of Social Classes*. Princeton Univ. Press, 1949.
Coe, G. A., *The Psychology of Religion*. University of Chicago Press, 1916.
Dreger, R. M., Some personality correlates of religious attitudes as determined by projective techniques. *Psych. Monogr.*, **66**, No. 3, 1952.
Eysenck, H. J., General social attitudes. *J. Social Psych.*, **19**, 207–27, 1944.
Eysenck, H. J., *Dimensions of Personality*. London: Kegan Paul, 1947.
Eysenck, H. J., *The Structure of Human Personality*. London: Methuen, 1953.
Eysenck, H. J., *Psychology of Politics*. London: Routledge, 1954.
Ferguson, L. W., Socio-psychological correlates of the primary attitude scales. I. Religionism. II. Humanitarianism. *J. Social Psych.*, **19**, 81–98, 1944.
Harding, J., *et al.*, Prejudice and ethnic relations. Chapter 27 in Lindzey, ed., 1954.
Hoffman, M. L., Some psychodynamic factors in compulsive conformity. *J. Abnorm. Soc. Psych.*, **48**, 383–93, 1953
Howells, T. H., A comparative study of those who accept as against those who reject religious authority. *Univ. Ia. Stud. Char.*, **2**, No. 2, 1928.

Janis, I. L., Personality correlates of susceptibility to persuasion. *J. Pers.*, **22,** 504–18, 1954.

King, S. H., and Funkenstein, D. H., Religious practice and cardiovascular reactions during stress. *J. Abnorm. Soc. Psych.*, **55,** 135–7, 1957.

Kirkpatrick, C., Religion and humanitarianism: a study of institutional implications. *Psych. Monogr.*, **63,** No. 9, 1949.

Lazarsfeld, P. F. *et al.*, *The People's Choice*. New York: Duell, Sloan and Pearce, 1944.

Lindzey, G. (ed.), *Handbook of Social Psychology*. Cambridge, Mass.: Addison-Wesley, 1954.

Lipset, S. M., Opinion formation in a crisis situation. *Public Opinion Quarterly*, **17,** 20–46, 1953.

Lipset, S. M. *et al.*, The psychology of voting: an analysis of political behaviour. Chap. 30 in Lindzey, 1954.

Lubell, S., *Revolt of the Moderates*. New York: Harper, 1956.

McCarthy, T. J., Personality traits of seminarians. *Stud. Psych. Cath. Univ. Amer.*, **5,** No. 4, 1942.

Nowlan, E. H., The picture of the 'Catholic' which emerges from attitude tests. *Lumen Vitae*, **12,** 275–85, 1957.

Parry, H. J., Protestants, Catholics and prejudice. *Int. J. Op. Att. Res.*, **3,** 205–13, 1949.

Prothro, E. T., and Jensen, J. A., Interrelations of religious and ethnic attitudes in selected southern populations. *J. Social Psych.*, **32,** 45–49, 1950.

Ringer, B. J., and Glock, C. Y., The political role of the church as defined by its parishioners. *Public Opinion Quarterly*, **18,** 337–47, 1955.

Rosenzweig, S., The picture-association method and its application in a study of reaction to frustration. *J. Pers.*, **14,** 3–23, 1945.

Ross, M. G., *Religious Beliefs of Youth*. New York: Association Press, 1950.

Sanford, F. H., *Authoritarianism and Leadership*. Philadelphia: Inst. for Research in Hum. Relat., 1950.

Sappenfield, B. R., The attitudes of Catholic, Protestant and Jewish students. *J. Social Psych.*, **16,** 173–97, 1942.

Sinclair, R. D., A comparative study of those who report the experience of the divine presence and those who do not. *Univ. Ia. Stud. Char.*, **2,** No. 3, 1928.

Spoerl, D. T., Some aspects of prejudice as affected by religion and education. *J. Social Psych.*, **33,** 69–76, 1951.

Symington, T. A., *Religious Liberals and Conservatives*. Teach. Coll. Contr. Educ. No. 640, 1935.

II Focus on Origins

What gives rise to a certain attitude or complex of attitudes, how and why does it develop? Empirical research on the origins, development, or formation of attitudes is not plentiful: this is one area which is much in need of further systematic investigation.* A quest for the sources of attitudes, moreover, can be interpreted and approached in several different ways. The three selections here represent different approaches to the sources of attitudes. Nevitt Sanford's account of authoritarianism and its genesis, which is built on many years of systematic research, interprets attitudinal structure as deeply rooted in personality dynamics and development. Sanford also provides a clear descriptive formulation of characteristic syndromes of the authoritarian personality which will be useful to students unfamiliar with the literature on authoritarianism. Leonard Bloom summarizes and appraises Jean Piaget's research and theory on the development of moral attitudes. Piaget's is a theory of 'stages' in development, but at the same time one which strongly emphasizes the social determinants of ethical attitudes and 'conscience'. Mervin B. Freedman stresses changes in the cultural climate of American society in his report of a study demonstrating some fascinating differences in attitudes and values between separate age-groups. Freedman concludes that cultural changes seem to be accompanied by changes in personality structure as well as by changes in attitudes.

* However, for other articles in this book which are relevant to this section the reader may consult the excerpt from Himmelweit, Oppenheim and Vince and the article by Lynn and Gordon, both in the previous section; and the article by Siegel and Siegel in the next section on attitude change. – Eds.

12   R. N. Sanford

The Genesis of Authoritarianism

Excerpt from: R. N. Sanford, *Psychology of Personality*, J. L. McCary (ed.), Logos Press, U.S.A., 1959, pp. 305–12.

The major hypothesis guiding our investigations into the origins of authoritarianism was that such central structures of personality had their beginnings in experiences of early childhood. It must be granted, however, that the evidence on this was of a rather indirect sort: it was limited to what our subjects *said* about their childhoods. Naturally such retrospective accounts were distorted by the subjects' contemporary outlook. Nevertheless, it was possible to make reasonable inferences about what actually happened. Sometimes the reference was to more or less objective events or circumstances which the subject apparently had no reason to invent or magnify; sometimes, with knowledge of common modes of distortion, one could, so to speak, read between the lines and arrive at a reasonably convincing picture of the childhood in question. By taking the many differences between the reports of subjects scoring high and those scoring low on the F and E scales* and considering these in the light of contemporary knowledge and theory of personality development, it was possible to put together a plausible account.

It may be helpful at this point to sketch very briefly the contrasting accounts of childhood by high- and low-authoritarian subjects. High-authoritarian men more often described their fathers as distant and stern, while the 'lows' tended to describe him as relaxed and mild. High-authoritarian women characteristically saw the father of their childhoods as hard-working and serious, while low-scoring women more often perceived him as intellectual and easy-going. The mother of high-scoring subjects, both male and female, was more often said to be kind, self-sacrificing and submissive, while the mother of low-scoring subjects was more often described as warm, sociable and understanding. High-scoring men tended to accent the mother's moral restrictiveness, low-scoring men her intellectual and aesthetic interests. High-scoring women more often described their mothers

* For some details of the development of the F (fascism) scale and the E (ethnocentrism) scale, see the previous excerpt from Argyle. – Eds.

as models of morality, restricting and fearsome, while low-scoring women were more often able to offer realistic criticism of their mothers.

In general, high scorers gave a less differentiated picture of their parents than did the lows. The tendency of the former was to offer a somewhat stereotyped and idealized picture at the beginning of the interview but to allow negative features to make their appearances when there was questioning about details; while the latter more often undertook an objective appraisal with good and bad features mentioned in their place.

When it came to the matter of the relations between the parents, the tendency of the high scorers was to deny any conflict, the lows usually describing some conflict in more or less realistic terms. High-scoring men usually described their homes as being dominated by the father, low-scoring men more often described homes in which there was general orientation toward the mother.

Discipline in the families of the more authoritarian men and women was characterized in their accounts by relatively harsh application of rules, in accordance with conventional values; and this discipline was commonly experienced as threatening or traumatic or even overwhelming. In the families of subjects low on authoritarianism, on the other hand, discipline was more often for the violation of principles, and the parents more often made an effort to explain the issues to the child, thus enabling him to assimilate the discipline.

In view of the more authoritarian subject's obvious inclination to put as good a face as possible upon his family and his childhood situation, we were inclined to assume that such negative features as appeared in his account were probably to be taken more or less at their face value; that is, to believe that the high-authoritarians came, for the most part, from homes in which a rather stern and distant father dominated a submissive and long-suffering but morally restrictive mother, and in which discipline was an attempt to apply conventionally approved rules rather than an effort to further general values in accordance with the perceived needs of the child.

This view of the matter seems to be in accordance with the findings of a recent quantitative study by Harris et al.[6] These workers showed that the parents of prejudiced children tended in their answers to a questionnaire to emphasize obedience, strict control, the inculcation of fear and the like significantly more than did the parents of relatively unprejudiced children.

The real need here, of course, is for longitudinal studies in which development of trends in children are observed against a background of actual events and practices in the home. The closest to this ideal so far would appear to be the work of Frenkel-Brunswik and her associates. These workers have measured prejudice in children as young as 10 years and have obtained information on family background, handling of discipline, and childhood events by means of visits to the home and extensive interviews with the parents: Frenkel-Brunswik writes,[3] [p. 236]:

A preliminary inspection of the data supports the assumption made in *The Authoritarian Personality* that warmer, closer and more affectionate interpersonal relationships prevail in the homes of the unprejudiced children; the conclusions concerning the importance of strictness, rigidity, punitiveness, rejection vs. acceptance of the child seem to be borne out by data from the children themselves . . .

In the home with the orientation toward rigid conformity, on the other hand, actual maintenance of discipline is often based upon the expectation of a quick learning of external, rigid and superficial rules which are bound to be beyond the comprehension of the child. Family relationships are characterized by fearful subservience to the demands of the parents and by an early suppression of impulses not acceptable to the adults.

In this picture of parents and their discipline are very probably the major sources of the most essential features of the authoritarian personality syndrome, the superego's failure to become integrated with the ego, and certain crucial shortcomings in the ego's development. Discipline that is strict and rigid and, from the child's point of view, unjust or unreasonable may be submitted to, but it will not be genuinely accepted, in the sense that the child will eventually apply it to himself in the absence of external figures of authority. There also is good reason to believe that authoritarian discipline, of the sort described above, acts directly to prevent the best ego development. Where the child is not allowed to question anything, to participate in decisions affecting him, nor to feel that his own will counts for something, the stunting of the ego is a pretty direct consequence. It is for this reason that, when it comes to talking with parents about the prevention of authoritarianism and ethnocentrism in children, the recommendation is: 'Treat the child with respect – especially after he is about two years old and begins to show signs of having a will of his own.' This has nothing to do with permissiveness, nor does it work against the maintenance of high standards. Naturally the parent has to put certain things across; but, if he is to get acceptance and not mere submission, he must at least recognize that he is dealing with another human being.

General Formulation of the Authoritarian Personality Syndrome*

It seems worth while, now, to attempt a formulation in hypothetical terms of the over-all F-pattern, a formulation that seems to order most of the statistical facts and clinical observations made, which may, it is hoped, serve as a guide to further research.

A very strict and punitive superego is behind the inability to admit blame or to bear guilt found in the F-syndrome. It is this inability that makes it necessary for the subject to put blame onto others who may then be hated in the way that he would hate himself were he to become conscious of his own impulses. This superego is not integrated with the ego but stands much of the time in opposition to it. Indeed, the ego would get rid of it altogether if it could. And sometimes it almost succeeds. It is this state of affairs that permits one to speak of the superego in the F-syndrome as rigid. It either works in a total, all-out fashion, when one may observe strict adherence to conventional standards, strict obedience to the authorities of the moment accompanied by feelings of self-pity, or it works apparently not at all, as in a high school sorority initiation, or in the riots of sailors in San Francisco on V-J Day, or in children in an authoritarian classroom when the teacher is away. These examples show the great importance of external agencies, be they authority figures or the social groups of the moment. Wishing to be free of the punitive superego, the individual is always ready to exchange it for a suitable external agency of control; and if this external agency offers gratification of id needs at the same time, as in the crowd where anything goes because 'everybody is doing it', or, as in the case of the authoritarian leader who says, 'there is your enemy', then the way is open to generally regressive behavior.

The key notion here is the failure of the superego to become integrated with the ego. It is quite likely that the chief opponent of authoritarianism in the personality is an internalized superego that *is* genuinely integrated with the ego. Yet it must be admitted that something very similar to what has just been said about superego functioning in the F-syndrome has been put forward in

---

* Those unfamiliar with the literature on authoritarianism will find the following account of the syndrome helpful with references to authoritarianism and the F-scale in other contributions to this book; in particular those by Argyle, Freedman, and Siegel and Siegel. – Eds.

psychoanalytic writings as a theory of superego functioning in general. Indeed, there is some justification for Fromm's [5] allegation that the Freudian superego is an 'authoritarian superego'. Insofar as the Freudian superego is limited to that which is built up through 'identification with the aggressor', as described by Anna Freud [4] in particular, Fromm is quite right. But Freud had many other things to say about the superego, and probably never did arrive at a theory which satisfied him.

The interesting theoretical question here concerns the role of identification with the aggressor in the genesis of the superego in the authoritarian structure. On first view, this formulation seems made to order for what is known of the F-syndrome. The individual manages his ambivalent feelings toward his punitive parent by identifying himself with that parent, by actually internalizing the punitiveness, now receiving masochistic satisfaction through submission to parent figures and sadistic gratification through the punishment of others. The question here is whether, or to what extent, this 'authoritarian superego' is truly *inside* the personality. There is much to be said for the view elsewhere [7] that the superego in the authoritarian pattern derives from infantile projections and introjections, that through failures in ego development it remains as an unconscious source of extreme anxiety, and that it is in order to escape this anxiety or in the hope of getting rid of its source that the individual must seek and have an authority.

The underlying drives that have loomed largest in these discussions, as they did in the research, are aggression, dependence, submission, passivity and homosexuality. Not only were these drives hypothesized in order to explain the interconnectedness of surface manifestations, but clinical studies also provided a mass of evidence that these were the crucial motivating forces in the more authoritarian subjects. Whether one speaks of id tendencies here depends upon his definition of that concept. One is inclined to say that these are id tendencies, for, though they have undoubtedly been in considerable part built up through experience, they are certainly primitive, impulsive, childish and alien to the ego. The important thing is that these drives were repressed in childhood, and hence were no longer accessible to the maturing effects of experience. It is for this reason that the subject acts as if any expression of dependence were the equivalent of a total descent into infantilism, as if any show of hostility against the parents were a giveaway of the wish to destroy them altogether. Given drives which are felt to have such potency, it is natural that anxiety should frequently be acute and that extreme measures for warding it off should have to be taken.

113

But subjects who are relatively free of authoritarianism also have to deal with aggression against parents, with dependence, passivity and homosexual trends. Indeed, there is nothing to indicate that these tendencies are less strong in them than in the more authoritarian subjects; the difference lies in the way these tendencies are managed. This is a matter of ego functioning. Because of the various failures in this department, such as the extreme narrowness of consciousness, rigidity of functioning, and use of primitive mechanisms of defense, that distinguish the more authoritarian subjects, there is justification for speaking of their greater ego weakness. But the weakness of the ego cannot be considered apart from the size of the task that it has to perform. There is in the authoritarian pattern the picture of an ego that is in constant danger of being overwhelmed either by emotional impulses from within or authoritative demands from without. In these circumstances it must devote itself to its last-ditch defenses, so to speak, being in no position to undertake any forward movements. When one asks what is crucially determining in this pattern, he finds himself accenting now the underlying impulses, now the demands and threats, now the ego weakness itself. However he looks at it, he perceives a single structure, the several features of which are mutually dependent.

The Historical Matrix of Authoritarianism

The above accounts of the genesis of authoritarianism in the individual personality put the emphasis upon early experiences in the family. Now it is necessary to ask what makes parents behave in the ways that apparently promote authoritarianism in their children? It will not do merely to say they are authoritarian themselves, thus pushing things back indefinitely into the past. One must consider that family life, within which personality develops, is constantly under the impact of various complex social and historical factors. In what times and places, under what general sociological conditions, or what conditions of cultural change, or stability, is the development of authoritarian personalities favored or discouraged? This is a critically important matter about which there is very little exact knowledge.

Very much has, of course, been written about the importance of German institutions, or perhaps better, the breaking up of certain institutions – in the genesis of authoritarian and fascist personalities before and during the time of Hitler; but there is much here that remains mysterious. And it is not so easy to carry over knowledge of the German case so that it helps to explain the incidence of authoritarian personality in the United States. The kind of research that is called for is well exemplified in the work of Bjork-lund and Israel,[2] who relate modal personality and family structure to other aspects of the social process, such as growing industrialization and urbanization; and that being undertaken by the Institute for Social Research at Oslo in which authoritarianism, among other things, is being studied in seven different nations.

When it is said that authoritarian personality structure has its genesis in family life that, in its turn, goes forward under the influence of social conditions and processes, one means that the attitudes and practices of parents with respect to their children may be responses to stimuli of the moment. Such stimuli might arouse or set in motion such beliefs and policies as those found by Harris *et al.*[6] in the parents of prejudiced children. It is easy to imagine, for example, middle-class parents, who have climbed rapidly, and who have been made to feel insecure with respect to their new-found status, directing toward their children precisely that type of desperate, unreasonable control that has seemed to be most important in the genesis of the authoritarian syndrome. For that matter, one can understand such parental behavior resulting from a loss of status and of self-respect, as was so common in Germany in the aftermath of World War I.

References
1. Adorno, T., Frenkel-Brunswik, E., Levinson, D., and Sanford, R. N., *The Authoritarian Personality*. New York: Harper, 1950.
2. Bjorklund, E., and Israel, J., The Authoritarian Ideology of Upbringing. Mimeographed. Sociologiska Institutionen, Uppsala, Sweden, 1951.
3. Frenkel-Brunswik, E., Further Explorations by a Contributor. In *Studies in the Scope and Method of the Authoritarian Personality*, R. Christie and M. Jahoda, eds., Glencoe, Ill.: Free Press, 1954.
4. Freud, A., The Ego and the Mechanisms of Defence. New York: International Universities Press, 1946.
5. Fromm, E., *Man for Himself*. New York: Rinehart, 1947.
6. Harris, D. B., Gough, H. G., and Martin, W. E., Children's Ethnic Attitudes: II. Relationship to parental beliefs concerning child training. *Child Development*, **21**, 169–81, 1950.
7. Sanford, R. N., The dynamics of identification. *Psych. Rev.*, **62**, 106–18, 1955.

Piaget's Theory of the Development of Moral Judgment

Excerpt from: L. Bloom, *Journal of Genetic Psychology*, Journal Press, U.S.A., 1959, Vol. 95, pp. 3–12.

Of particular interest to the student of child and social psychology is the nature of the child's moral development, and one of the pioneers in the scientific study of these motives of children was Jean Piaget. He had no place for *a priori* moralizing about the child's notions of right and wrong, and without allegiance to any school of psychology, he used empirical methods that permitted the repetition and testing of his enquiries, and the verification, rejection, or modification of his hypotheses.

Piaget's classic research, *The Moral Judgment of the Child*,[12] appeared in England in 1932, and is based upon a simple situation, natural and familiar to the child subjects of the investigations: a game of marbles played in working-class districts of Geneva and Neuchâtel. This close regard for what activity the child finds natural is an integral part of the early method of Piaget. He claims to have discerned a tendency in children to think of laws and rules in the most factual and literal way. The child is not concerned that he is only playing a game, but follows the letter of the law rigidly. There is an unquestioning acceptance of the logic and justice of a moral rule, even though the reflecting adult might think the rule is harsh, unjust, inappropriate, arbitrary or foolish. The rule is part of the given world and can no more be changed than the tides can be meddled with or the rhythm of the seasons altered. This 'moral realism' is more typical of the younger child; as the child grows older he becomes more flexible and more imaginative.

Piaget next discusses 'cooperation and the development of the idea of justice'. He asserts that the child's notions of fairness and justice are independent of adult precept and influence, requiring 'nothing more for (their) development than the mutual respect and solidarity which holds among children themselves'. Gradually, a predominantly retributive and equalitarian justice is replaced by more rational and objective considerations.

Piaget claims that children pass through four successive stages in their play. In the *motor and individual* stage, the child plays individually and as his feelings and motor habits dictate. He tosses blocks about the room, he rattles pebbles in a tin, and collective rules are irrelevant to him. It is indeed difficult to distinguish in this behavior a game with rules in contrast with inchoate exploration of the physical world.

Next the *egocentric* stage, between two to five years onwards, in which the child first receives from outside himself the example of definite codes of rules. There is now a pattern to his playing. The child imitates the example of the rules that he notices, but he still continues largely to play by himself, not troubling too much to find other children with whom to play, and without trying to establish spontaneously his own conventions and rules. He plays egocentrically, in a parallel fashion; all can win the games, no one bothers to define the rules, but they are followed as far as they are recognized.

Between the ages of seven and eight years the stage of *incipient cooperation* appears. The aims of competing and winning become important, and children are much concerned with clear definitions of the rule and protocol. But even now they are not entirely clear about the rules, and if they are asked individually to define rules they may give contradictory accounts.

At about 11 to 12 the child becomes concerned with the *codification of rules* and the details of play are well known by the whole group and carefully observed by its members.

These findings suggest the hypothesis that to very young children 'a rule is sacred because it is traditional; for the older ones it depends on mutual agreement'. Piaget continues to argue that for children from five to eight 'social life and individual life are one', and the gradual diminution of conformity that takes place as the child grows is a correlate of increasingly clear and definite structuring of his personality. In effect agreeing with Kurt Lewin, he writes that 'childish egocentrism is in its essence an inability to differentiate between ego and the social environment'. However, as the child becomes less subject to the supervision of elders and adults, as he takes part in more social groups and social situations, and as he becomes physically and emotionally like older children and adults, we see his awe diminishing and his individuality asserting itself.

Extending the child's attitudes to the rules of the game to his attitude to rules in general, Piaget shows that the responsibility for the breach of a rule is not judged after taking motives into account, but according to the results of the behavior. A child judges as naughtier another who accidentally breaks three cups, than one who deliberately smashes one. It would be interesting to refer this back to games and to ask, for example, if children regard as more serious the fault of a child who 'loses' the game by two goals by his justifiable lack of skill, or one who loses it by one goal as a result of his deliberate inattention. Older children are less prone to judge naughtiness by the amount of 'damage' done, and are correspondingly more ready to consider the offender's motives. The young child absorbs and adopts the adult way of looking at lies and damage, and because adult responses are often harsh and literal the child adopts harsh and literal notions of responsibility. Adults tend to present to the child cut-and-dried obligations before he is sufficiently mature emotionally and socially to assimilate them intelligently, i.e. to apply them to relevant situations; the child fails to understand the principles (if any) behind the obligations and the offences and cannot generalize to analogous situations. Instead the obligations become 'ritual necessities', 'taboos' and an 'ineffectual deduction from the words spoken by adults'. This is re-enforced by memory and experience: thought lags behind action, and once the child has experienced a dramatic situation of adult constraint he will continue to judge according to that earlier situation though it is no longer appropriate.

Similar considerations apply to lies. Not until Piaget questioned children of about 10 to 11 did he find evidence that children believed that to tell a lie you must tell an intentional falsehood. This shows 'how completely external to the child's own mind the interdiction of lying still remains in the early stages'. Thus: 'when a material action is too closely attached to the lie the child has a certain difficulty in dissociating the lie so far as it is psychological action from the actual results of the concomitant external act'.

In sharp contrast with his views of the origins of moral realism Piaget holds the child's ideas of justice to be largely independent of the example of the adult. This contrasts too with the views of psychoanalysis on the moral development of the child. He distinguishes three periods in this development: (*a*) Lasting to seven or eight in which justice is subordinated to adult authority; (*b*) between about eight and 11, which is the stage of progressive equalitarianism; (*c*) from about 11 or 12 during which equalitarian justice is tempered by considerations of equity. In the first stage every punishment is accepted 'as perfectly legitimate, as necessary, and even as constituting the essence of morality; if lying were not punished one would be allowed to tell lies'. In the second stage punishment becomes do-as-you-would-be-done-by, equality increases, good behavior begins to be sought for its own sake independently of reward or punishment. Piaget does not, however, analyse the 'reward' of adult approval and general benignity. How does the child learn to distinguish good from bad behavior unless there are 'rewards' and 'punishments', in situations in which he can recognize the appropriateness of the one or the other? In the last stage the child takes into account the circumstances of each case individually, and no longer are the same law and the same punishment applicable to all children in the same way.

Piaget was strongly influenced by the sociologist Emile Durkheim, and he concludes with some socio-psychological observations on child morality. There are, he argues, two types: the inflexible and group-enforced as distinct from the objective and autonomous, analogous to the fundamental types of social relationship posited by Durkheim in his *On the Division of Labour in Society*. Essentially: ethics and morality can only be explained by reference to social organizations, and changes in morality can only be understood by referring to changes in social structure and socially sanctioned values. Morality presupposes rules and laws transcending the individual; out of individual action emerges a code of morality explicable *sui generis* without reference to the personal wishes, goals, hopes, and acts of individuals. Child morality stems either from adult or from child constraint, and in either case the morality that emerges is social. Coupled with the behavioral conformity of the child and adult to a moral code is a subjective feeling of constraint, which is the root of the sense of guilt or shame, remorse, right and wrong, conscience. These subjective feelings, too, are the result of social values and pressure and not the contrary.

Piaget, despite his acute awareness of the power and autonomy of social determinants of behavior, is sharply critical of the exclusively social explanations of child psychology. Piaget argues that because there are two networks of social relations for children there are two types of child morality. There is the morality that arises from the network of child relationships among themselves, and that which arises from the relationships of adults to children. The child not only lives by the code of rules that the adults enforce, but by that enforced by his fellows. Though both these codes are social they reflect two quite different types of authority: that due to unilateral respect (e.g. the attitude of the younger to the older child) and that due to mutual respect, and restraint is different in these two types. As contemporary society is tending to adopt the rule of cooperation in place of the rule of naked constraint, so in education coercion is giving way to 'the habit of internal discipline, of mutual respect and of "self-government".'

In evaluating Piaget's contribution, it is tempting to confine the criticism to his inadequate sampling, lack of controls, haphazard reporting, and presentation. It must be admitted that his work shows these technical defects, but these objections in themselves would not completely fault Piaget's original and highly stimulating work. More serious objections lie in his apparent oblivion to the part that cultural and class factors may play in determining the child's judgements. These ignored factors may affect both the content of the child's beliefs, and the psychological processes of their development. Liu[10] found that native-born American children raised in America showed much greater severity of moral judgement and much less subtlety of analysis than Chinese-born Americans raised in America, and he considered that these marked differences were the result of the great intimacy of the Chinese-American family and the Confucian philosophy which encourages consideration of moral questions. Harrower[5] found that English middle-class children showed much more temperate and flexible moral judgements than their working-class peers, and that both groups made fewer retributive and immature judgements than Piaget's sample. Other investigators such as Ball,[2] MacRae,[11] Himmelweit,[6] Havighurst and Taba report similarly that Piaget's findings need to be modified to allow for class and cultural differences.

A further complication is that Piaget nowhere suggests the psychological dynamics of the learning of moral judgements; why it is, for example, that at one time the child learns from his peers and at another from adults. Piaget's discussions of the learning are essentially in a rather old-fashioned behavioristic stimulus-response framework, with the stimulus being social pressure in one form or another. The subtlety of the interrelationships between children and between children and adults is nowhere suggested, and from the Piaget and Durkheim point of view it is difficult to understand how a child might ever develop moral judgements that are not accepted by or acceptable to his group. How can we explain, understand, and help the anti-social child, who resists or for other reasons does not follow the lines of conduct and thought that his society provides? Who is not 'constrained' like his fellows? It may be that by adult standards, his moral judgement is of a higher ethical quality than that of his peers, he may for example show a gentleness and forgivingness that is not to be expected from his age group, or he may commit anti-social behavior. The child does not learn moral judgement in the somewhat mechanical fashion that Piaget implies, but will only learn spontaneously and fruitfully if his personal relationships with his peers and adults are emotionally satisfactory to him, for it has been amply demonstrated by now that the child's emotional development (of which his moral judgement is one major aspect) depends upon the child's having adult models from whom he introjects his moral attitudes. He may simulate a group-sanctioned moral code, but so may a slave simulate what his masters desire him to. Unless he has learned to trust and to expect justice and morality from the adult world in very young childhood, he will not learn to make the conscious and active moral judgements that are most worthy of men.

The content of moral judgement is largely learned from the norms that society has developed, but since Piaget wrote his book, we have begun to consider in more detail the differences between children and adults in their mode or manner of making moral judgements. We are concerned more with such personality differences as rigidity and flexibility in making judgements than in specific manifestations of moral judgement, and in this too we see a reason to consider that the Piaget-behavioristic approach is inadequate to answer problems that are significant to modern child and social psychology. The *quality* of the emotional responses of the child to matters of conscience (or more mundane problems such as the rules of a game of marbles, which are often of gravest import to a child), severity of super-ego or laxness, gentleness or stringency and the like are emotional variables that mediate between social demands and ordinances, and are no less a result of personal relationships than of social constraint – a constraint that some children are ignorant of, and others acutely sensitive to, while yet others grudgingly capitulate with feelings of resentment, and others joyfully accept.

Piaget at once overestimates and underestimates the cognitive element in child behavior. He overestimates it in his reliance upon the questionnaire technique to give valid and reliable information about the child's behavior in the vagaries of everyday situations. He underestimates it in the implicit and questionable assumption that there are fundamental differences in the modes of thought of adults as compared with children. We are nowhere told the intelligence range of the sample that Piaget questioned in terms of results on a standard intelligence test, of which plenty existed in 1932. It is arguable that *IQ* is very directly connected with the child's ability to make conceptual judgements and enter into subtle conversations with erudite psychologists, and if Piaget's sample was of children of lower intelligence it is not unexpected that many of their judgements seem crude by adult standards, illogical and undifferentiated. There is a mixture of logic and irrationality in both children and adults, but it cannot be assumed *a priori* that logic or irrationality are more typical of one 'stage' than another. We have to equate the problems and situations for the intellectual capacity and experience of the individual, which does not tacitly admit that there are different stages in the capacity for logical thought: the child thinks both logically and illogically, but about many different things from those that the adult considers. This is largely a function of the different size and content of the child's phenomenal world. Take an adult outside his common experience and he too is prone to think irrationally. In this book as in his others, Piaget seems to have an implicit opinion that the complexity of child thought is much less than other child psychologists would think to be the case. A consideration of the verbal behavior of the child suggests that the child is from a very early age capable of quite complicated and adequate thought processes and differentiation, using by the age of eight all parts of speech and a very large vocabulary which suggests that he is capable of employing the higher mental processes if in a rudimentary form. We cannot but feel, therefore, that some of Piaget's results are due to his questioning children of lower *IQ*, or that he failed to obtain from them answers as well differentiated as children of their age could reasonably give.

The problems that Piaget touched upon in this enquiry were singularly important to children, and though Piaget is a skillful, sensitive, and thorough interviewer, it may be that if the questions were presented differently, e.g., indirectly, the responses would have differed. It is possible that the results of later investigators which contradict those of Piaget are due to this factor of uncertainty. Piaget, too, ignores the child's use of gesture and expression to convey his meaning. A child may reply 'Yes', sardonically, doubtfully, as a full agreement . . . ; we are rarely told of the circumstance surrounding the answers that would permit to decide for ourselves precisely what the child meant. It is remarkable that so few children gave qualifications in their answers; if children are not as rigid as Piaget occasionally suggests it seems highly probable that their answers would often begin with a phrase like: 'It all depends . . .'

Modern psychology is much concerned with 'stages' in development, but we cannot legitimately assume that there are clear-cut stages through which the child moves (effortlessly?), without conflict and doubt, unerringly absorbing the crystal-clear moral and social precepts and codes of rules that are presented to him by his fellows or by the adults with whom he has a significant relationship. Piaget's system can incorporate the data from other cultures and social classes; this is a straight-forward problem of expressing development in general terms that can be demonstrated by different contents. For Piaget, as for the Freudians, it is arguable that the processes of development are the same the world over, because the bio-psychological problems of maturation are the same for all people; it is the social and outward expression of basic problems of maturation that differ. This consideration only requires Piaget to adapt his theory to take account of local factors. But Piaget does not consider to what extent the child's moral development and judgement is affected by conflict in moral codes and between them. To what extent can the child recognize and comprehend such conflicts? To what degree is the child unable to develop as an adequate and healthy moral being because of the riven nature of the world he is living in, or because of an inability or lack of opportunity to form the emotional attachments which are basic to emotional-moral development, making it (and other social-personal development) meaningful and relevant?

Conflicts in the child's moral world may come from differences between his adult companions' and his child fellows' values, or from conflict among the adults from whom he is learning. Adult conflict and confusion may come from conflict in the social world reflected in the uncertainty of his adult mentors, but it may also come from the inadequacy of the adults to understand or to manipulate the world for their emotional satisfaction: they may be intellectually or emotionally unable to present to the child an accurate picture or model, because they are themselves unable to recognize it. This lack of attention to conflict in the child's world of moral (and other) judgements is perhaps derived from Piaget's tendency to emphasize the intellectual and logical aspects of thinking, which became more marked in his later work. This change in approach has been neatly summed up by James Anthony. Piaget's 'happy animistic child, chatting so unselfconsciously and charmingly on the mountains of the Salève or by the shores of Lake Geneva, has been transformed into a mathematical automaton, a cybernetic machine, with, as Piaget proudly proclaims, a negative feedback, the only one of its kind in developmental psychology'. Piaget's early work paralleled in the field of cognition Freud's work in the field of the affective life. His early research was marked with a sensitivity which converted the verbal interview technique (despite its many drawbacks) into a subtle and useful instrument of investigation. It is possible that had Piaget continued to perfect his observations, he would have been led to appreciate the conflictual and affective factors in child life, and with his interests in sociology and psychology, he would have contributed much to a more precise factual definition of the parts played by social and psychological, and affective and cognitive factors in child behavior.

References
1. Anthony, J., The system makers: Piaget and Freud. *Brit. J. Med. Psychol.*, **30**, Part 4, 1–12, 1957.
2. Ball, A., A test of group conformity in the moral judgments of children. *Brit. J. Educ. Psychol.*, **25**, 129–30, 1955.
3. Berlyne, D. E., Recent developments in Piaget's work. *Brit. J. Educ. Psychol.*, **27**, 1–12, 1957.
4. Brown, A. W., *et al.*, Influence of affectional family relationships on character development. *J. Abn. & Soc. Psychol.*, **42**, 422–28, 1947.
5. Harrower, M. R., Social status and the moral development of the child. *Brit. J. Educ. Psychol.*, **4**, 75–95, 1934.
6. Himmelweit, H. T. A study of the attitudes, value systems, and behaviour of young adolescents belonging to different social status groups. *Bull. Brit. Psychol. Soc.*, **20**, 7, 1953.
7. Inhelder, B., Developmental psychology. In *Annual Review of Psychology*. Palo Alto, Calif.: Annual Reviews, 1957.
8. ————., Criteria of the stages of mental development. In *Discussions on Child Development* (J. M. Tanner and B. Inhelder, *Eds.*). London: Tavistock, 1956.
9. Isaacs, N., The significance of Piaget. *Bull. Brit. Psychol. Soc.*, **34**, 67, 1958.
10. Liu, C. H., The influence of cultural background on the moral judgment of the child. Ph.D. Dissertation, Columbia University, 1950.
11. Macrae, D. J., A test of Piaget's theories of moral development. *J. Abn. & Soc. Psychol.*, **49**, 14–18, 1949.
12. Piaget, J., The Moral Judgment of the Child. London: Kegan Paul, 1932.

14 M. B. Freedman

Changes in Attitudes and Values Over Six Decades

Reprinted from: M. B. Freedman, *Journal of Social Issues*, Society for the Psychological Study of Social Issues, U.S.A., 1961, Vol. 17, Chapter 1, pp. 19–28.

Changes in the climate of American opinion and in the character structure of Americans are a never-ending object of interest and curiosity for observers of our social scene. In the last century such observers were likely to be men of letters, if not actually literary men proper. Tocqueville, Mark Twain, Henry James come to mind as a few examples. In recent years, since the first World War and particularly in the last generation, this function has been assumed increasingly by social scientists. They and the critics rather than the creative writers have been the ones to tell us what is going on in American life. Lionel Trilling sees in this phenomenon indication of the decline of the novel. For example, it is difficult to think of a novel that tells us as much about what it is like to be a woman today, as *The Bostonians* (James, 1945) tells us about what it was like to be a feminist in 1875 or thereabouts. For the former kind of information one is likely to read Simone de Beauvoir or Margaret Mead. Be that as it may, those social scientists who have devoted themselves in recent years to complex analysis of the American social scene have received considerable attention. They have been widely read, and they have had considerable influence. Of late the publications of some social scientists, philosophers and theologians with social scientific interests, and thoughtful people who might be described as on the fringes of social science, for example, in the publishing business, have received the kind of attention formerly reserved for major works of fiction alone.

For the most part, analysts of long-term trends in American culture have had to operate without the benefit of what we now regard as indispensable material to a proper study of people or social events, that is, interviews, questionnaires, planned observation, and the like. Such techniques were little utilized prior to the '30's, and only since the end of World War II has any sizable and complex body of data been built up systematically in the social sciences. Let me interject that by social science in this context I mean the newer ones – cultural anthropology, psychology, sociology – and I exclude those with a long tradition, for example, history and economics. Which is not to say, however, that systematic and reliable data bearing on long-past events are completely and forever unavailable. Considering the importance of the topic there is a considerable burden upon research workers in the social sciences to contribute what they can to the body of knowledge about changes in American culture and character.

The activities of the Mellon Foundation at Vassar College (Sanford, 1956) have provided such an opportunity. As part of the general research program some opinions and attitudes of Vassar alumnae of various periods going back as far as the Class of 1904 have been explored (Freedman, 1959). The Mellon Foundation is a research venture into the mysteries of personality development during the college years. Attention has been centered on current students, but studies of alumnae have occupied a prominent place in the scheme of things. Alumnae groups have been studied by a variety of methods – test, questionnaire, interview, and assessment devices.

One of the instruments used to measure the kinds of changes that take place in current students has been the California Public Opinion Survey – the 60-item questionnaire containing the familiar F and E Scales, consisting of 32 and 20 items respectively, and the 8 item PEC Scale (Adorno et al., 1950). The questionnaire is administered with the standard instructions. Respondents to each item may select any position from plus to minus three to indicate their degree of agreement or disagreement with the sentiment expressed. No zero or neutral response is permissible. The F Scale was, of course, developed as a measure of authoritarianism,* a personality syndrome which has yet to be defined with precision, but which nevertheless is predictive of behaviour in a variety of situations. Among many traits which have been subsumed under the rubric of authoritarianism are compulsiveness, rigidity, intolerance of ambiguity, punitive morality, submission to power, conventionality, cynicism, and anti-intraception. The E Scale is a measure of the related phenomenon of ethnocentrism, the disposition to glorifying ingroups, family, country, social class, and the like, while attributing negative qualities to outgroups, for example, Negroes or foreigners. The PEC Scale, that is, Political Economic Conservatism, has been found to possess little reliability as a scale, chiefly because of its brevity, and in our studies no attempt has been

---

* For an account of the syndrome of authoritarianism and its genesis, see the first contribution to this section, by Sanford. – Eds.

made to deal with *PEC* scores as such. The items of the scale have been utilized for their individual contributions, however.

In order to obtain data on alumnae comparable to those available for current students the California Public Opinion Survey was included among the tests and questionnaires administered to the alumnae groups that we studied. This paper is concerned with comparisons among the various alumnae groups and with comparisons between the alumnae groups and current students on the *F* and *E* Scales. Some comparisons using individual items will also be reported.

Samples

The Classes and numbers involved are:

1. Eighty-five members of the Class of 1904, almost the entire class of surviving alumnae.

2. Forty-three members of the Class of 1914, tested at a class reunion. How representative these women are of their entire class is, of course, an open question. As we shall see shortly, however, alumnae who attend reunions appear to yield test results much like those obtained from alumnae who do not attend reunions but who respond to invitations by mail to cooperate in a scientific survey.

3. Seventy-three alumnae of the Classes of 1921–'24. Sixteen were tested at a reunion. The remaining 57 are members of the Class of 1923 who responded to mail invitations to participate. The two separate means differ by only 0·01 of a point, the standard deviations differing by 3·09, an insignificant amount.

4. Fifty members of the Classes of 1929–'35 who participated in a three-day assessment study at Vassar College.

5. Seventy-seven alumnae of the Classes of 1940–'43. Thirty were tested at a class reunion, the remaining 47 being members of the Class of 1943 who responded by mail. The additional 34 returns yielded a mean 4·67 points greater and a standard deviation 4·29 points lower, neither difference approaching significance.

6. Finally, 200 members of the Class of 1956, chosen at random from a total sample of 378, the latter figure comprising almost the total graduating class.

The returns of the Classes of 1929–'35 were obtained four years ago. The Class of 1956 was tested shortly before graduation. The remaining returns have been obtained within the last two years.

Before reporting our results some attention to the general nature of the samples is in order. First, of course, we are dealing only with women – and with the kind of women who go to colleges like Vassar – highly intelligent women of relatively favored socio-economic backgrounds. Not much is known about the nature of possible changes in the backgrounds or characteristics of women who have gone to college in various periods of this century. We do possess knowledge that now as compared to the early years of the century Vassar has fewer students whose parents are clergymen, teachers, or in literary professions. The percentage of professional versus business backgrounds has not changed, but the nature of the professions has. Now law and medicine are more heavily represented. Since 1930 more foreign students and members of minority groups, particularly Jews, have been accepted as students. The proportion of such students is still fairly low, however. Considering everything I am of the opinion that our samples possess a degree of homogeneity of background that would seldom be found in studies designed to cover so wide an age range.

It should be noted that our samples of alumnae are confined to women who are members, although not necessarily active ones, of the alumnae association. Those graduates who have maintained no contact with the college in recent years are not represented. Sixty to 70% of the alumnae to whom letters were sent responded by completing and returning the tests, and, of course, the extent to which the results of the non-respondents may differ from those reported in this paper is unknown.

Results

Table 1 presents the means and standard deviations on the F Scale for each of the above-mentioned groups.

Table 1

Means and Standard Deviations on the F Scale

Class(es)	N	$\bar{x}$	S.D.
1904	85	121·14	35·84
1914	43	99·53	33·99
1921–'24	73	100·96	28·86
1929–'35	50	87·98	22·15
1940–'43	77	87·56	24·44
1956	200	95·09	23·87

Several trends are immediately apparent. The Class of 1904 is easily significantly higher according to the t test than any other group. Nineteen hundred and fourteen and the early '20's are paired with the next highest means, the means of the two groups being less than a point apart. The mean for 1914 differs from that of the '30's at the ·06 level of significance and from the '40's at the ·05 level. The '30's and the '40's are the groups with the lowest means, 87·98 and 87·56 respectively. For the Class of 1956 we have a mean of 95·09, which differs from that of the '40's at the ·03 level of significance and from the '30's at the ·05 level. Nineteen hundred and fifty-six is, of course, significantly lower than 1904 but not lower than 1914 or the early '20's. Thus, although the mean of 1956 differs from that of the early '20's, the level of significance is only ·12.

In short, we find 1904 to be the highest on the F Scale, 1914 and the '20's paired as the next highest, and the early '30's and 40's lowest of all because of the significant rise for the Class of 1956. Probably this is as good a time as any to say that I think that these results mean something. I do not consider them to be largely the product of a tendency to agree with fatuous and bombastic statements – a matter of response set, in short. Recent work by Brown and Datta (1959), Webster (1958), and Christie, Havel, and Seidenberg (1958) demonstrates that authoritarianism cannot be explained by acquiescence. Thus, for a sample of Vassar students, a highly reliable and experimentally independent measure of response set (KR 21 = ·93) correlates only ·26 with the F Scale (Webster, Freedman, and Sanford, 1957).

An interesting finding is the discovery that the earlier groups are likely to adopt more extreme positions in response to individual items. Chi square tests of the significance of the difference for proportions demonstrate that 1904 and 1914 differ significantly from the early '20's and subsequent groups in their use of 'three' responses. Later groups adopt more moderate positions. They are

Table 2

Means and Standard Deviations on the E Scale

Class(es)	N	$\bar{x}$	S.D.
1904	85	64·30	27·58
1914	43	47·86	23·41
1921–'24	73	48·92	21·37
1929–'35	50	44·36	17·03
1940–'43	77	41·70	16·45
1956	200	44·70	17·97

more likely to respond with a 'one' or a 'two'. This finding lends support to the notion that as compared to earlier periods in our history, the recent American scene has been characterized by less fixity or greater flexibility of opinion – or perhaps, greater conformity or homogeneity of opinion.

As one would anticipate, and as Table 2 indicates, results for the E Scale display a similar pattern. Nineteen hundred and four is highest of all, significantly higher than 1914 and 1921–'24 at the ·01 level.

The means of 1929–'35 and 1940–'43 differ from the mean of the early '20's at the ·17 and ·02 levels of significance respectively. Unlike the situation with the F Scale, however, there is no significant rise on E for 1956.

Discussion

How do we account for the fact that alumnae of some classes and decades differ widely from others in the kind of general outlook measured by these scales? Is it due to chronological age, that is, a matter of experience rather unique to a time of life? Is it a function of childhood conditioning, a predisposition to a particular quality of outlook in adulthood as a consequence of having been a child at a certain period of American life? To what extent is current outlook a reflection of the influence of schooling, chiefly perhaps, college experience? It is difficult, of course, to attempt answers to such questions. As the psychoanalysts say about complex intrapsychic phenomena, the attitudes measured by the statements of the California Public Opinion Survey are likely to be overdetermined.

We do, however, possess some leads. First, I am inclined to rule out chronological age as a cogent explanatory factor. While on such a basis one could account for differences between groups of women widely separated in age, this hardly explains the large differences that are found between members of adjacent decades, for example, 1904 compared to 1914, or 1921–'24 compared to 1929–'35. Why should women averaging 74 years at the time of testing respond differently from women who are 66 on the average, or why should women of 47 at the time of testing differ from those who are 43?

The matter of the contribution of childhood experience to test scores in later life is, of course, one on which little empirical information can be brought directly to bear. My general view of the matter would be that at least in recent times, American culture has not been an authoritarian one. So I should be of the opinion that only a minority of individuals would have undergone the kinds of childhood experiences delineated in *The Authoritarian Personality* (Adorno *et al.*, 1950), experiences which would be expected to lead to rigid fixation upon authoritarian sentiments. To put this in another way, I should be inclined to think of most individuals who express authoritarian views as open to new experience and the possibility of change. And in educated people I believe that the period of greatest change in general social outlook is likely to be the college years.* Events at large on the national or international scene often have considerable influence upon the attitudes of college students, as we shall see shortly, when we consider the individual items of the California Public Opinion Survey.

In short, I consider experiences of the college years to be a major source of the variations in attitudes by decade which we observe. Increasing liberalization of social outlook in American culture during the years of this century has in general been reflected in comparable changes in college students (although perhaps in the last few years this trend has been reversed in some respects). And these changes have apparently persisted after college.

Results obtained with current students support this theory. Incoming freshman classes at Vassar yield means on F ranging from 115 to 118 with a standard deviation of about 25. Means for graduating seniors cluster around 95 with a standard deviation of about 24. Some evidence that the sentiments expressed by seniors persist with but little change is provided in Table 3. It may be seen

Table 3

Means and Standard Deviations on the F and E Scales for Alumnae Who Were Tested as Seniors

Scale	Class	N	Date of Retest	Seniors	Alumnae
F	1955	74	1959	x̄ 91·16	x̄ 93·62
				SD 23·36	SD 24·60
F	1956	79	1959	x̄ 99·34	x̄ 96·14
				SD 21·94	SD 22·00
E	1955	74	1959	x̄ 44·69	x̄ 45·37
				SD 15·49	SD 17·23
E	1956	79	1959	x̄ 45·56	x̄ 44·84
				SD 17·76	SD 14·87

* For an empirical study of social factors in changing the attitudes of college students, see the article by Siegel and Siegel in the next section on attitude change. – Eds.

that when alumnae who were given the *F* and *E* Scales as seniors are retested three and four years later, there is very little change. At least for a period of three or four years after graduation, the alumnae seem to be adhering rather closely to the views expressed as seniors.

But perhaps study of the individual items provides the most support for the notion that the tenor of the times at which the alumnae were in college is intimately related to the attitudes they now display. In the discussion to follow the significance of the difference between groups for scores on individual items has been calculated using the chi square technique, utilizing two by four tables rather than two by six tables. The 'two' and 'three' response categories at each extreme have been combined, because in the smaller samples of alumnae expected frequencies in the 'three' cells fall below acceptable levels for calculation of chi square.

Consider the item, 'What this country needs most, more than laws and political programs, is a few courageous, tireless, devoted leaders in whom the people can put their faith.' As Table 4 indicates, the '40's is the only group in which the majority, 57%, reject this view of leadership. Although only the differences between the '40's and the '20's and the Class of 1904 are significant, the trend seems rather clear. In a similar vein the early '40's is the group most emphatic in rejecting the notion that, 'Obedience and respect for authority are the most important virtues that children should learn,' with 77% responding negatively. In comparison with the '40's the differences are significant for 1904, 1914, and 1956, and P= ·19 for the Classes of 1921–'24.

The Classes of 1940–'43 respond most negatively to the statement that, 'Now that a new world organization is set up, America must be sure that she loses none of her independence and complete power as a sovereign nation,' with 82% of the group expressing disapproval of the sentiment expressed. Here the early '40's differ significantly from 1904 and 1956, with the difference from 1921–'24 falling at the ·08 level of significance. In the case of the item, 'Human nature being what it is, there will always be war and conflict,' the early '40's are closest to 1914 and 1904 in expressing disapproval. Forty-seven per cent of the Class of 1914 reject the item, 44% of '04, and 37% of 1940–'43, with the remaining groups expressing disapproval by smaller margins.

The above comparisons and the fact that the Classes of 1940–'43 have the lowest *E* Scale score of any group would seem to reflect the attitudes of the years just prior to and during World War II in the United States: optimistic views of man's potential and of post-war

Table 4

Percentages of Rejection of Selected Items of the Public Opinion Survey

Item	Class(es):	1904 N=85	1914 N=43	1921– '24 N=73	1929– '35 N=50	1940– '43 N=77	1956 N=200
What this country needs most, more than laws and political programs, is a few courageous, tireless, devoted leaders in whom the people can put their faith.		17	49	32	42	57	44
Obedience and respect for authority are the most important virtues that children should learn.		35	49	62	70	77	51
Now that a new world organization is set up, America must be sure that she loses none of her independence and complete power as a sovereign nation.		34	72	66	75	82	58
Human nature being what it is, there will always be war and conflict.		44	47	21	32	37	30
It is only natural and right for each person to think that his family is better than any other.		62	65	78	66	69	52
Some day it will probably be shown that astrology can explain a lot of things.		81	87	78	94	94	80
Science has its place, but there are many important things that can never possibly be understood by the human mind.		29	58	37	53	42	39

society, fervent internationalism, alertness to the possibility and dangers of dictatorship or authoritarian rule, and the like.

As a sidelight it is interesting to note that the generally liberal position of the alumnae of the early '40's in social and broadly political matters is not accompanied by anything approaching

133

economic liberalism or radicalism. Vassar alumnae in general are quite conservative in economic affairs, but even in this conservative company the alumnae of the early '40's are distinguished by the fixity of their position. Thus, 92% of the group reject the statement that, 'It is up to the government to make sure that everyone has a secure job and a good standard of living.' The majority of alumnae of the early '30's oppose this idea also, but as one would expect, by a reduced majority, that is, 72%.

Similarly, it is likely that the views of current students may to a considerable extent be regarded as reflections or functions of certain large-scale trends in American life. Turning again to the item, 'Obedience and respect for authority are the most important virtues that children should learn,' we find that only 51% of the Class of 1956 reject this item, in comparison with 77% for the Classes of 1940–'43 and 70% for the Classes of 1929–'35, with $P < 0.001$ and $= 0.17$, respectively. One has to go back to 1914 and 1904 to find smaller percentages of rejection than that of 1956, 49% and 35% respectively. 'It is only natural and right for each person to think that his family is better than any other.' Table 4 indicates that the Class of 1956 rejects this statement by the smallest majority of any group. P is significant for the difference between 1956 and the early '20's, $= 0.08$ for the difference between 1956 and the Classes of 1929–'35, and $= 0.07$ for the difference between 1956 and 1940–'43.

'Some day it will probably be shown that astrology can explain a lot of things.' Eighty per cent of the Class of 1956 disagree as compared with 78% for the early '20's. The margin of disagreement is greater for all other groups. $P = 0.08$ for the difference between 1956 and 1914.

In general I believe that we may see in the above comparisons of the Class of 1956 with the other groups some of the smugness and the attachment to the status quo which is characteristic of many segments of American society today. Similarly we may discern some of the irrationality, the phony kind of romanticism, perhaps, that has become prominent in our current life, as witness our recent shallow religious revivals.

If we consider the Public Opinion Survey, particularly the F Scale, in its more purely psychological aspects, that is, if we think of it as telling us something about the nature of the personality, as a clue to the way in which inner impulses are handled, and as an index of the amount of self-insight possessed by the subject, the conclusion seems obvious that social and individual psychological processes parallel one another rather closely. Changes in American society and culture seem to be accompanied by changes in individual personality structure as well as by changes of opinion and attitude.

References

Adorno, T. W., Frenkel-Brunswik, E., Levinson, D. J., and Sanford, R. N., *The Authoritarian Personality*. New York: Harper, 1950.

Brown, Donald R., and Datta, Lois-Ellin., Authoritarianism, verbal ability, and response set. *Journal of Abnormal and Social Psychology*, **58**, 131–4, 1959.

Christie, Richard, Havel, Joan, and Seidenberg, Bernard, Is the F scale irreversible? *Journal of Abnormal and Social Psychology*, **56**, 143–58, 1958.

Freedman, Mervin B., A half-century of Vassar opinion. *Vassar Alumnae Magazine*, **44**, 3–6, 1959.

James, Henry, *The Bostonians*. New York: Dial, 1945.

Sanford, Nevitt (Editor), Personality development during the college years. *Journal of Social Issues*, **12**, 3–72, 1956.

Webster, Harold, Correcting personality scales for response sets or suppression effects. *Psychological Bulletin*, **55**, 62–4, 1958.

Webster, Harold, Freedman, Mervin, and Sanford, Nevitt, Research manual for VC attitude inventory and VC figure preference test. Vassar College, Mary Conover Mellon Foundation, 1957.

III Focus on Change

Attitude change and the complementary topics of social influence and persuasibility have been the major focus of attitude research and theory during the last two decades. Definite advances have been and continue to be made. Of special note are the increasing sophistication of research design on the one hand, and the elegance and ingenuity of the theoretical models under development, on the other.* The first important programme of continuous empirical study of persuasion and attitude change was initiated and directed for many years by Carl Hovland at Yale University; thus we begin our selections for this section with a summary by Hovland and his colleagues of their enterprising experimental work. The excerpt in which Herbert Kelman makes valuable theoretical distinctions among processes of social influence is included here rather than in the later section on theory because it is specifically concerned with the topic of attitude change. William J. McGuire, refreshingly turning our attention to the problem of why attitudes do *not* always change when subjected to persuasive communications, reports on a number of his own ingenious experiments. Alberta and Sidney Siegel present a neat example of a field study, or 'natural social experiment', on changes in attitudes: they base their work on explicit social psychological theory of the effects of membership and reference groups on attitudes and values. Finally, one of the studies of 'brainwashing' or 'thought reform': not, in this instance, one of the well-known accounts of the persuasive techniques used against prisoners-of-war in Korea, but a report of the attempted thought reform of native

* The contributions on attitude theory by Zajonc and by Sarnoff, in Part Three, section 1 of this book, both deal with theories whose major focus of convenience is on the area of attitude change. Indeed, in the last two decades theories of attitude organization have very largely grown out of empirical work on persuasion and attitude change. Thus the contributions of Zajonc and Sarnoff are very relevant to the present section, and may be read in conjunction with it. So also may the article by Janis and King, which appears in the next section, 'Focus on Behaviour', and the article by Hovland in the final section of the book, on attitude methodology. – Eds.

Chinese intellectuals. These Chinese refugees were interviewed in Hong Kong by Robert J. Lifton, and the resulting account full of human interest, is necessarily a more clinical and impressionistic document than the controlled studies which constitute the large majority of the research literature.

15 C. I. Hovland, I. L. Janis and H. H. Kelley

A Summary of Experimental Studies of Opinion Change*

Excerpt from: C. I. Hovland *et al.*, *Communication and Persuasion*, Yale Univ. Press, 1953.

Most of the results can be viewed as specifying the effects of a communication according to the nature of (1) the communicator (*who* says it), (2) the communication (*what* is said), and (3) the audience (*to whom* it is said). Within each of these three areas selected topics have been investigated, primarily by controlled experimental studies on classroom audiences. We shall indicate the generalizations which are beginning to emerge, but again remind the reader that a great deal of replication and systematic variation, both in our own and in other cultures, will be required before comprehensive propositions can be conclusively established.

A. The Communicator

Several of our studies analyze the effects upon opinion of varying the expertness and trustworthiness of the communicator. In the experiment by Hovland and Weiss[2] identical newspaper and magazine articles were attributed to various high credibility sources (like Robert Oppenheimer) in one group and to low credibility sources (like *Pravda*) in another. The results of this and supplementary investigations[1, 11, 16] indicated:

(1) Communications attributed to low credibility sources tended to be considered more biased and unfair in presentation than identical ones attributed to high credibility sources.

(2) High credibility sources had a substantially greater immediate effect on the audience's *opinions* than low credibility sources.

(3) The effects on opinion were not the result of differences in the amount of attention or comprehension, since information tests reveal equally good learning of what was said regardless of the credibility of the communicator; variations in source credibility seem to influence primarily the audience's motivation to accept the conclusions advocated.

* This excerpt comprises a summary of a research programme which applied controlled experimental methods to the study of basic processes in persuasion and attitude change. Further details of the experiments cited here are to be found in earlier chapters of Hovland, Janis & Kelley. – Eds.

(4) The positive effect of the high credibility sources and the negative effect of the low credibility sources tended to disappear after a period of several weeks.

B. The Communication

When a communicator attempts to persuade people to adopt his conclusions he usually employs arguments and appeals which function as incentives. Among the major classes of such incentives are (*a*) substantiating arguments, which may lead the audience to judge the conclusion as 'true' or 'correct'; (*b*) 'positive' appeals, which call attention to the rewards to be gained from acceptance; and (*c*) 'negative' appeals, including fear-arousing contents, which depict the unpleasant consequences of failure to accept the conclusion.

Some of our experimental studies highlight the ways in which symbols operate as effective incentives, while others stress factors involved in the effective organization of arguments.

1. *Fear appeals.* One way a communication can reinforce the acceptance of new beliefs is to arouse and then alleviate emotional tension. When an emotional appeal is successful, it may be assumed that the communication not only produces strong emotional reactions but also insures that emotional tension will be reduced at the time the recommended belief is rehearsed. When a communication relies on fear appeals, its effectiveness in arousing emotional tension depends upon such factors as explicitness, source, and prior communication experiences. The content usually is directed toward depicting a state of affairs in which the goals, security, or values of the audience are threatened.

Some of the factors which determine whether or not a fear-arousing communication will be effective were investigated in an experiment by Janis and Feshbach.[4] The study involved the arousal of fear by depicting potential dangers to which the audience might be exposed. Three different forms of an illustrated lecture on dental hygiene, representing three different intensities of fear appeal, were given to high school students. It was found that the strong appeal produced greater emotional tension than the moderate appeal, which in turn produced greater tension than did the minimal appeal. However, the greatest change in conformity to the communicator's recommendations was produced by the minimal appeal. The strong appeal failed to produce any significant change in dental hygiene practices and was less effective than the minimal appeal in producing resistance to counterpropaganda.

These findings suggest that the use of strong fear appeals will interfere with the over-all effectiveness of a persuasive communication if such appeals evoke a high degree of emotional tension without adequately providing for reassurance. The evidence is consistent with the following two hypotheses:

a. The use of a strong fear appeal, as against a milder one, increases the likelihood that the audience will be left in a state of emotional tension which is not fully relieved when the reassuring recommendations contained in the communication are rehearsed.

b. When fear is strongly aroused but not fully relieved by the reassurances contained in a persuasive communication, the audience will become motivated to ignore or to minimize the importance of the threat.

2. *Salience of group norms.* Various types of communication content having to do with group norms may function as powerful incentives for the acceptance or rejection of new opinions. Some inferences about relevant types of content can be drawn from the discussion of predispositional factors underlying conformity to group norms. For instance, communications which call attention to group membership may prompt the individual to take account of group norms in forming his opinion on a given issue. This effect has been described as the 'salience' of the group.

A study by Kelley [8] sought to ascertain whether the salience of group membership has any direct effect upon the resistance to change of group-anchored attitudes. The principal subjects were Catholic students in a public high school and in a nondenominational college. Students of other religious faiths were also included for purposes of comparison. During the regular class sessions, when the salience of any particular religious affiliation could be expected to be low, some of the students received reading material intended to heighten the salience of Catholic Church membership and others received unrelated 'neutral' material. The students were then given statements intended to modify their opinions in a direction away from Catholic norms. For the high school students, when salience of the church was high, the Catholics tended to show greater resistance to change than when salience was low. Thus the findings suggest that the use of contents which arouse awareness of a reference group can have a marked effect on the audience's tendency to accept or reject the recommended opinion. The absence of a similar effect for the college students, however, raises some question as to whether the phenomenon is a general one or occurs only for persons who are strongly attached to a group but have relatively little understanding of its norms.

Preliminary evidence was also obtained on the retention of

opinion changes produced under high and low salience. Under the particular conditions investigated, the low salience sample continued to show more effect at the time of a delayed test. This problem should be investigated further, particularly under conditions where, as suggested by various theoretical considerations, the retention of change produced under high salience is likely to be superior.

3. *Conclusion drawing*. A recurrent problem in preparing communications is whether to state the conclusion explicitly or to leave it to be drawn by the audience. There are theoretical considerations favoring each alternative. A study to determine the effectiveness of conclusion drawing with respect to a typical social issue was conducted by Hovland and Mandell.[1] Two groups of college students listened to a transcribed talk on 'Devaluation of Currency'. In one group the appropriate conclusion was drawn by the speaker while in the other group the conclusion was left up to the audience. Under the conditions of this experiment, conclusion drawing by the communicator produced significantly more opinion change. The following general hypothesis is suggested: In communications which deal with complicated issues, it is generally more effective to state the conclusion explicitly than to rely upon the audience to draw its own conclusions. With less complex issues, however, one would expect more members of the audience to be able to derive the appropriate conclusion independently. Similarly the superiority of conclusion drawing by the communicator would be expected to be less pronounced with more intelligent persons than with less intelligent – although within the narrow range of ability represented by college students in this experiment, no such relationship was found.

The extent to which the topic produces 'ego involvement' might also be a factor that determines the relative effectiveness of explicit conclusion drawing. On topics where the individual is less inclined to be dependent upon experts and more likely to resist the influence of others, implicit treatment may be more effective. This may be characteristic of problems discussed in psychotherapy, for which 'nondirective' techniques are frequently advocated. Conditions under which implicit presentation is more effective with mass communications remain to be investigated.

4. *Preparation for future experiences*. Special problems arise in planning the content of a communication when the task is that of preparing an individual or an audience for some future event or communication. As yet, little is known about the conditions under which preparatory communications diminish or augment

the psychological impact of later events. When people have been given reassuring or optimistic communications beforehand, are they less likely to develop pessimistic attitudes in response to subsequent 'bad' news? What types of preparatory communications will mitigate the effects of subsequent experiences of failure or disappointment? Such problems not only are of practical importance but also involve a number of general theoretical issues concerning the way in which persuasive communications can predispose an audience to interpret and react to subsequent life experiences.

Three experiments on the effects of preparatory communications have been undertaken in our research program. One of these was the study by Lumsdaine and Janis[14] on the effectiveness of different types of content in preparing individuals to resist the influence of subsequent counterpropaganda. Two versions of a recorded radio program were used, in both of which the commentator advocated the view that it would be at least five years before Russia could produce A-bombs in quantity. One group of high school subjects received a one-sided version, which presented only the arguments that supported the speaker's conclusion. Another group was given a two-sided version, which contained the same arguments and the same conclusion but in addition discussed the main arguments on the opposite side of the question. Half the subjects in each group were subsequently given a second communication in which a different speaker advocated an opinion opposed to that presented in the initial communication.

Under conditions where there was no exposure to counterpropaganda, the two versions were found to be about equally effective in modifying opinion. But for the subjects subsequently exposed to the counterpropaganda, the two-sided version proved to be markedly more effective in producing sustained opinion change. It appears that when a two-sided presentation is used the hearer is led to the recommended opinion in a context which takes account of opposing arguments. In this way he is given an advance basis for ignoring or discounting the opposing arguments and is thus 'inoculated' against subsequent communications which advocate a contradictory point of view.

A second experiment, which used some of the same subjects as in the preceding experiment, was carried out by Janis, Lumsdaine, and Gladstone.[7] The opportunity to study the effects of a preparatory communication arose unexpectedly when President Truman announced that an atomic explosion had occurred in Russia. It was possible to observe the effects of an 'optimistic' communication in preparing the audience for an unfavorable news event, inasmuch as the subjects had been exposed three months earlier to the radio program (described above) which took the position that Russia would be unable to produce large numbers of A-bombs for many years to come. Following the President's announcement, those subjects who had received the optimistic program were compared with an equivalent control group which had not. It was found that the control subjects were much more likely to develop the expectation that Russia would soon have a large supply of A-bombs and that war would be imminent. Thus preparatory communication produced resistance to the impact of the subsequent news event. The findings are consistent with the hypothesis that once a belief is modified by an effective communication there will be a tendency for the newly acquired opinions to interfere with the subsequent acquisition of any incompatible opinions.

A third type of problem concerns the use of communications to prepare individuals for experiences of failure. Subsequent events become especially important whenever a communication makes use of incentives which involve predictions about the future (e.g. statements to the effect that acceptance of the recommended opinion will lead to successful attainment of some specific goal). If the predictions are contradicted by subsequent events, or if the individual acts upon these predictions and experiences failure, the degree of acceptance will tend to be markedly reduced. Whenever new beliefs are likely to be followed by initial experiences of failure it may be necessary for the communicator to prepare the audience for such results, by apprising them of the possibility of subsequent failure in such a way that failures will be discounted and produce minimal frustration. A preliminary investigation by Janis and Herz,[5] the results of which became available while the present volume was in preparation, indicates the role of prior communications in 'inoculating' individuals for failure experiences. Their findings suggest that preparatory communications may teach the individual to anticipate that he will ultimately be rewarded if he 'sticks with' the communicator's recommendations, and give him a basis for discounting failures, so that he will be less likely to experience frustration or to interpret subsequent failures as a sign that he is behaving incorrectly.

C. The Audience

It is generally recognized that people will react differently to the same social pressures: incentives can function adequately only insofar as the individual has the necessary motivational predispositions. By taking account of such factors it should be possible to arrive at a more comprehensive set of general principles for predicting opinion changes.

1. *Group conformity motives.* Some of the most important predispositions are those related to the groups in which the person holds membership. During the past decade there has been increasing research into the development of norms within groups and the degree of conformity to them exhibited by various members (e.g.[15]). Some of the evidence from these studies suggests that persons who are most highly motivated to maintain their membership tend to be most susceptible to influence by other members within the group.

The discussion of group membership factors in the present volume has dealt primarily with the resistance that group members offer to communications which advocate views contrary to the group's norms. Kelley and Volkart[9] investigated the resistance to change of group-anchored attitudes as a function of the members' valuation of the group. Boy Scouts' attitudes toward camping and woodcraft activities were studied both before and after a speech by an outside adult who criticized the Scouts' emphasis upon these activities and recommended instead various activities in the city. The amount of change induced by this counternorm communication was studied in relation to an index of how much each Scout valued his membership in the troop. Under conditions where opinions were expressed privately, boys who most highly valued their membership were least influenced by the communication. Thus, the findings support the general hypothesis that persons who are most strongly motivated to retain their membership in a group will be most resistant to communications contrary to the standards of that group.

2. *Individual differences in persuasibility.* In addition to the motives stemming from group membership there are other sources of individual differences in responsiveness to communications. For example, prior research has indicated that differences in mental ability may affect the extent to which the individual is susceptible to persuasion. But there is a complex relationship involved: persons with higher intellectual ability would be expected to be able to learn what is presented more readily and to draw appropriate inferences more effectively; but they are also likely to be more critical in accepting arguments and conclusions than persons with lesser ability.

Differences in persuasibility associated with motivational

aspects of personality would also be anticipated. Relevant data are provided in a study by Janis.[3] On the basis of the degree of change following three communications, subjects (undergraduates) were divided into categories of high, moderate, and low persuasibility. Personality data were obtained from detailed clinical reports on a small number of subjects who received psychological counseling, and from a personality inventory given to a larger group of subjects.

Both sets of data provided evidence in support of the hypothesis that persons with low self-esteem are predisposed to be highly influenced by persuasive communications. Students who manifested social inadequacy, inhibition of aggression, and depressive tendencies showed the greatest opinion change.

A second hypothesis suggested by the results is that persons with acute psychoneurotic symptoms are predisposed to be resistant to persuasive communications. The students who were most resistant to change had come for counseling largely because of acute neurotic symptoms similar to those of patients diagnosed as having obsessional neurosis, hysteria, or anxiety neurosis. The hypothesis was supported by the personality inventory results: students who remained relatively uninfluenced had higher scores than others on items indicative of neurotic anxiety and obsessional symptoms.

D. Response Factors

In all of our studies we have been concerned with the *effects* of communications, and hence with the responses of the audience. But in several investigations special aspects of response have been analyzed. One set of problems has to do with the effects of active participation, and another with the duration of the changes in response produced by persuasive communication.

1. *Active participation*

It frequently happens that an individual is induced to conform overtly before he has come to accept a norm or belief as his own. In the socialization of the child and in situations of entering a new community or social group, verbal conformity to normative beliefs is often required. In most cases these beliefs are eventually internalized; in many cases they are not. It would be important to investigate the factors leading to these alternative outcomes.

Janis and King[6] designed an experiment* to test the following hypothesis: When exposure to the same persuasive communication

---

* The full report of this study by Janis and King is included in the next section, 'Focus on Behaviour'. – Eds.

is held constant, individuals who are required to verbalize the communication aloud to others will tend to be more influenced than those who are passively exposed. The experiment involved the comparison of opinion changes in two experimental groups of college students: (1) 'active participants' who were induced to play a role which required them to deliver a talk in a group situation and (2) 'passive controls' who merely read and listened to the same communication.

The findings, based on three different communications concerning expectations about the future, support the conclusion that spoken agreement induced by role playing tends to increase the effectiveness of persuasive communication. The investigators then proceeded to explore the possible psychological mechanisms underlying the gain from active participation. Two suggestive leads emerged: (1) the amount of opinion change occurring with active participation may depend upon the amount of improvisation, i.e. the extent to which the main points are reformulated and illustrative examples are inserted or additional arguments invented; (2) the amount of opinion change is a function of the degree to which the individual feels satisfied with his performance in giving the talk.

A second experiment by King and Janis[12], using a more ego-involving topic, was designed to determine whether either of the two factors suggested by the first experiment is critical in producing participation effects. To test the effects of improvisation, some subjects were required to present the talk without a script, after having read it silently, while others were permitted to read directly from the script. Experimental variations were introduced in order to produce varying degrees of satisfaction and dissatisfaction with respect to the individual's speaking performance. The results consistently indicate that the amount of opinion change produced through active participation is dependent upon the amount of improvisation but is not related to the amount of satisfaction. Improvised role playing could be viewed as a technique whereby the individual is stimulated to make the communication as effective as possible, devising exactly the kind of arguments, illustrations, and motivating appeals that are most likely to be convincing to himself.

Further data on verbal conformity were obtained by Kelman[10] in an experiment in which various types of incentives were compared. Immediately after hearing a talk, school children were asked to write essays on the issue in question. Three experimental variations were introduced by offering different incentives for writing essays conforming to the communicator's position: the control group was offered no special incentive; a second group (high incentive) was told that every student who conformed would receive a prize: a third group (low incentive) was told that every student who conformed would be eligible for the prize but that only a few would receive it. The results showed the control group to have the lowest and the high incentive group the highest degree of conformity. The amount of opinion change, however, did not vary directly with the degree of conformity: significantly more change was found in the low incentive group than in either of the other two groups. The essays produced under the low incentive condition were found to be of superior quality and to contain a higher frequency of new arguments. The findings provide additional support for the improvisation hypothesis and suggest that the effects of active participation depend upon whether the act of overt conformity is accompanied by inner responses of a supporting or of an interfering nature.

It seems likely that under certain conditions role playing and other means of producing verbal conformity may *interfere* with acceptance. This is suggested by some of the incidental findings in the experimental studies. For instance, Kelman observed signs of resentment among subjects who were given a strong incentive to conform. In the Janis and King experiment, it was noted that a group of subjects who experienced dissatisfaction with their role-playing performance showed significantly less opinion change than the passive controls who did not engage in role playing. Systematic exploration is needed to discover the conditions under which active participation has negative or boomerang effects.

2. *Duration of effects*

Prior research has indicated considerable variability in the extent to which changes in opinion produced by communication are maintained over time. Several of our studies have been concerned with the paradoxical increase in opinion change which sometimes appears after a lapse of time (the 'sleeper effect'). The study by Hovland and Weiss[2] suggests one possible explanation of the effect. They found that when a low credibility communicator presented the communication very small initial changes in opinion were obtained. But after a delay of four weeks the 'negative prestige' tended to disappear while the conclusion was still remembered. This could account for the increased opinion change in the direction advocated in the communication. Their analysis suggests that people may initially resist accepting material presented by a low credibility source, but after a period they may no longer associate the conclusion with the source. This dissociation tendency would be maximal when the communication contains arguments and evidence which can be evaluated on their own merits and are likely to be recalled without bringing the source to mind. However, when the source and content are intimately related the tendency to dissociate them should be much less.

This line of reasoning would suggest that the sleeper effect will occur only when cues as to the source are absent. The effect should disappear if the audience is reminded of a low credibility source at the time of later testing. A study to test this prediction was carried out by Kelman and Hovland.[11] Separate experimental groups were exposed to the same talk on juvenile delinquency, preceded by an introduction in which either 'positive' or 'negative' characteristics were attributed to the speaker. Three weeks later, at the time of a follow-up test, the source was 'reinstated' for half the subjects by reminding them who the speaker had been. The results showed that the positive communicator had the greatest initial effect and the negative communicator the smallest initial effect on the subjects' opinions. Subsequently, under nonreinstatement conditions, there was a decline in agreement with the positive speaker and an increase in agreement with the negative, as was found in the Hovland and Weiss study. Reinstatement of the source, however, increased the extent of agreement with the positive communicator and decreased the agreement with the negative. The reinstated sources produced effects approximately equal to those obtained at the time of the initial communication.

These experiments indicate, then, that delayed effects can be explained by the absence of the communicator as a cue for acceptance or rejection. However, the evidence fails to support the hypothesis that the opinion changes over time are a function of simple *forgetting* of the source. The critical difference seems to be contingent upon whether or not the source and the content are recalled at the same time. If the audience is reminded of the source, there is relatively little change over time. But normally there seems to be a tendency to dissociate the content from the source and consequently the positive (or negative) influence of the source declines with time.

References
1. Hovland, C. I., and Mandell, W., An experimental comparison of conclusion-drawing by the communicator and by the audience. *J. Abnorm. Soc. Psychol.*, **47**, 581–8, 1952.
2. Hovland, C. I., and Weiss, W., The influence of source credibility on communication effectiveness. *Publ. Opin. Quart.*, **15**, 635–50, 1951.

3. Janis, I. L., Personality correlates of susceptibility to persuasion. *J. Personal*, **22,** 504–18, 1954.

4. Janis, I. L., and Feshbach, S., Effects of fear-arousing communications. *J. Abnorm. Soc. Psychol.*, **48,** 78–92, 1953.

5. Janis, I. L., and Herz, M., The influence of preparatory communications on subsequent reactions to failure. (In preparation.)

6. Janis, I. L., and King, B. T., The influence of role-playing on opinion-change. *J. Abnorm. Soc. Psychol.* **49,** 211–18, 1954.

7. Janis, I. L., Lumsdaine, A. A., and Gladstone, A. I., Effects of preparatory communications on reactions to a subsequent news event. *Publ. Opin. Quart.*, **15,** 487–518, 1951.

8. Kelley, H. H., Salience of membership and resistance to change of group-anchored attitudes. *Hum. Rel.*, **8,** 275–89, 1955.

9. Kelley, H. H., and Volkart, E. H., The resistance to change of group-anchored attitudes. *Am. Soc. Rev.*, **17,** 453–65, 1952.

10. Kelman, H. C., Attitude change as a function of response restriction. *Hum. Rel.*, **6,** 185–214, 1953.

11. Kelman, H. C., and Hovland, C. I., 'Reinstatement' of the communicator in delayed measurement of opinion change. *J. Abnorm. Soc. Psychol.*, **48,** 327–35, 1953.

12. King, B. T., and Janis, I. L., Comparison of the effectiveness of improvised versus non-improvised role playing in producing opinion changes. *Hum. Rel.*, **9,** 177–86, 1956.

13. Kurtz, K. H., and Hovland, C. I., The effect of verbalization during observation of stimulus objects upon accuracy of recognition and recall. *J. Exp. Psychol.*, **45,** 157–64, 1953.

14. Lumsdaine, A. A., and Janis, I. L., Resistance to 'counterpropaganda' produced by a one-sided versus a two-sided 'propaganda' presentation. *Publ. Opin. Quart.* **17,** 311–18, 1953.

15. Sherif, M. A., A preliminary study of inter-group relations. In J. H. Rohrer and M. Sherif, eds. *Social psychology at the crossroads*. New York, Harper, pp. 388–424, 1951.

16. Weiss, W., A 'sleeper' effect in opinion change. *J. Abnorm. Soc. Psychol.*, **48,** 173–80, 1953.

16 H. C. Kelman

Three Processes of Social Influence

Excerpt from: H. C. Kelman, *Public Opinion Quarterly*, Princeton, U.S.A., 1961, Vol. 25, pp. 57–78.

Social influence has been a central area of concern for experimental social psychology almost since its beginnings. Three general research traditions in this area can be distinguished: (1) the study of social influences on judgments, stemming from the earlier work on prestige suggestion;[1] (2) the study of social influences arising from small-group interaction;[2] and (3) the study of social influences arising from persuasive communications.[3] In recent years, there has been a considerable convergence between these three traditions, going hand in hand with an increased interest in developing general principles of social influence and socially induced behavior change.

One result of these developments has been that many investigators found it necessary to make qualitative distinctions between different types of influence. In some cases, these distinctions arose primarily out of the observation that social influence may have qualitatively different effects, that it may produce different kinds of change. For example, under some conditions it may result in mere public conformity – in superficial changes on a verbal or overt level without accompanying changes in belief; in other situations it may result in private acceptance – in a change that is more general, more durable, more integrated with the person's own values.[4] Other investigators found it necessary to make distinctions because they observed that influence may occur for different reasons, that it may arise out of different motivations and orientations. For example, under some conditions influence may be primarily informational – the subject may conform to the influencing person or group because he views him as a source of valid information; in other situations influence may be primarily normative – the subject may conform in order to meet the positive expectations of the influencing person or group.[5]

My own work can be viewed in the general context that I have outlined here. I started out with the distinction between public conformity and private acceptance, and tried to establish some of the distinct determinants of each. I became dissatisfied with this dichotomy as I began to look at important examples of social influence that could not be encompassed by it. I was especially impressed with the accounts of ideological conversion of the 'true believer' variety, and with the recent accounts of 'brainwashing', particularly the Chinese Communist methods of 'thought reform'.[6] It is apparent that these experiences do not simply involve public conformity, but that indeed they produce a change in underlying beliefs. But it is equally apparent that they do not produce what we would usually consider private acceptance – changes that are in some sense integrated with the person's own value system and that have become independent of the external source. Rather, they seem to produce new beliefs that are isolated from the rest of the person's values and that are highly dependent on external support.

These considerations eventually led me to distinguish three processes of social influence, each characterized by a distinct set of antecedent and a distinct set of consequent conditions. I have called these processes *compliance*, *identification*, and *internalization*.[7]

Three Processes of Social Influence

Compliance can be said to occur when an individual accepts influence from another person or from a group because he hopes to achieve a favorable reaction from the other. He may be interested in attaining certain specific rewards or in avoiding certain specific punishments that the influencing agent controls. For example, an individual may make a special effort to express only 'correct' opinions in order to gain admission into a particular group or social set, or in order to avoid being fired from his government job. Or, the individual may be concerned with gaining approval or avoiding disapproval from the influencing agent in a more general way. For example, some individuals may compulsively try to say the expected thing in all situations and please everyone with whom they come in contact, out of a disproportionate need for favorable responses from others of a direct and immediate kind. In any event, when the individual complies, he does what the agent wants him to do – or what he thinks the agent wants him to do – because he sees this as a way of achieving a desired response from him. He does not adopt the induced behavior – for example, a particular opinion response – because he believes in its content, but because it is instrumental in the production of a satisfying social effect. What the individual learns, essentially, is to say or do the expected thing in special situations, regardless of what his private beliefs may be. Opinions adopted through compliance should be expressed only when the person's behavior is observable by the influencing agent.

Identification can be said to occur when an individual adopts behavior derived from another person or a group because this behavior is associated with a satisfying self-defining relationship to this person or group. By a self-defining relationship I mean a role relationship that forms a part of the person's self-image. Accepting influence through identification, then, is a way of establishing or maintaining the desired relationship to the other, and the self-definition that is anchored in this relationship.

The relationship that an individual tries to establish or maintain through identification may take different forms. It may take the form of classical identification, that is, of a relationship in which the individual takes over all or part of the role of the influencing agent. To the extent to which such a relationship exists, the individual defines his own role in terms of the role of the other. He attempts to be like or actually to *be* the other person. By saying what the other says, doing what he does, believing what he believes, the individual maintains this relationship and the satisfying self-definition that it provides him. An influencing agent who is likely to be an attractive object for such a relationship is one who occupies a role desired by the individual – who possesses those characteristics that the individual himself lacks – such as control in a situation in which the individual is helpless, direction in a situation in which he is disoriented, or belongingness in a situation in which he is isolated.

The behavior of the brainwashed prisoner in Communist China provides one example of this type of identification. By adopting the attitudes and beliefs of the prison authorities – including *their* evaluation of *him* – he attempts to regain his identity, which has been subjected to severe threats. But this kind of identification does not occur only in such severe crisis situations. It can also be observed, for example, in the context of socialization of children, where the taking over of parental attitudes and actions is a normal, and probably essential, part of personality development. The more or less conscious efforts involved when an individual learns to play a desired occupational role and imitates an appropriate role model would also exemplify this process. Here, of course, the individual is much more selective in the attitudes and actions he takes over from the other person. What is at stake is not his basic sense of identity or the stability of his self-concept, but rather his more limited 'professional identity'.

The self-defining relationship that an individual tries to establish or maintain through identification may also take the form of a reciprocal role relationship – that is, of a relationship in which the roles of the two parties are defined with reference to one another. An individual may be involved in a reciprocal relationship with another specific individual, as in a friendship relationship between two people. Or he may enact a social role which is defined with reference to another (reciprocal) role, as in the relationship between patient and doctor. A reciprocal role relationship can be maintained only if the participants have mutually shared expectations of one another's behavior. Thus, if an individual finds a particular relationship satisfying, he will tend to behave in such a way as to meet the expectations of the other. In other words, he will tend to behave in line with the requirements of this particular relationship. This should be true regardless of whether the other is watching or not: quite apart from the reactions of the other, it is important to the individual's own self-concept to meet the expectations of his friendship role, for example, or those of his occupational role.

Thus, the acceptance of influence through identification should take place when the person sees the induced behavior as relevant to and required by a reciprocal role relationship in which he is a participant. Acceptance of influence based on a reciprocal role relationship is similar to that involved in classical identification in that it is a way of establishing or maintaining a satisfying self-defining relationship to another. The nature of the relationship differs, of course. In one case it is a relationship of identity; in the other, one of reciprocity. In the case of reciprocal role relationships the individual is not identifying with the other in the sense of taking over *his* identity, but in the sense of emphatically reacting in terms of the other person's expectation, feelings, or needs.

Identification may also serve to maintain an individual's relationship to a group in which his self-definition is anchored. Such a relationship may have elements of classical identification as well as of reciprocal roles: to maintain his self-definition as a group member an individual, typically, has to model his behavior along particular lines and has to meet the expectations of his fellow members. An example of identification with a group would be the member of the Communist Party who derives strength and a sense of identity from his self-definition as part of the vanguard of the proletarian revolution and as an agent of historical destiny. A similar process, but at a low degree of intensity, is probably involved in many of the conventions that people acquire as part of their socialization into a particular group.

Identification is similar to compliance in that the individual does not adopt the induced behavior because its content *per se* is intrinsically satisfying. Identification differs from compliance, however, in that the individual actually believes in the opinions and actions that he adopts. The behavior is accepted both publicly and privately, and its manifestation does not depend on observability by the influencing agent. It does depend, however, on the role that an individual takes at any given moment in time. Only when the appropriate role is activated – only when the individual is acting within the relationship upon which the identification is based – will the induced opinions be expressed. The individual is not primarily concerned with pleasing the other, with giving him what he wants (as in compliance), but he is concerned with meeting the other's expectations for his own role performance. Thus, opinions adopted through identification do remain tied to the external source and dependent on social support. They are not integrated with the individual's value system, but rather tend to be isolated from the rest of his values – to remain encapsulated.

Finally, *internalization* can be said to occur when an individual accepts influence because the induced behavior is congruent with his value system. It is the content of the induced behavior that is intrinsically rewarding here. The individual adopts it because he finds it useful for the solution of a problem, or because it is congenial to his own orientation, or because it is demanded by his own values – in short, because he perceives it as inherently conducive to the maximization of his values. The characteristics of the influencing agent do play an important role in internalization, but the crucial dimension here – as we shall see below – is the agent's credibility, that is, his relation to the content.

The most obvious examples of internalization are those that involve the evaluation and acceptance of induced behavior on rational grounds. A person may adopt the recommendations of an expert, for example, because he finds them relevant to his own problems and congruent with his own values. Typically, when internalization is involved, he will not accept these recommendations *in toto* but modify them to some degree so that they will fit his own unique situation. Or a visitor to a foreign country may be challenged by the different patterns of behavior to which he is exposed, and he may decide to adopt them (again, selectively and in modified form) because he finds them more in keeping with his own values than the patterns in his home country. I am not implying, of course, that internalization is always involved in the situations mentioned. One would speak of internalization only if acceptance of influence took the particular form that I described.

Internalization, however, does not necessarily involve the adoption of induced behavior on rational grounds. I would not want to equate internalization with rationality, even though the description of the process has decidedly rationalist overtones. For example, I would characterize as internalization the adoption of beliefs because of their congruence with a value system that is basically *irrational*. Thus, an authoritarian individual may adopt certain racist attitudes because they fit into his paranoid, irrational view of the world. Presumably, what is involved here is internalization, since it is the content of the induced behavior and its relation to the person's value system that is satisfying. Similarly, it should be noted that congruence with a person's value system does not necessarily imply logical consistency. Behavior would be congruent, if in some way or other, it fitted into the person's value system, if it seemed to belong there and be demanded by it.

It follows from this conception that behavior adopted through internalization is in some way – rational or otherwise – integrated with the individual's existing values. It becomes part of a personal system, as distinguished from a system of social-role expectations. Such behavior gradually becomes independent of the external source. Its manifestation depends neither on observability by the influencing agent nor on the activation of the relevant role, but on the extent to which the underlying values have been made relevant by the issues under consideration. This does not mean that the individual will invariably express internalized opinions, regardless of the social situation. In any specific situation, he has to choose among competing values in the face of a variety of situational requirements. It does mean, however, that these opinions will at least enter into competition with other alternatives whenever they are relevant in content.

It should be stressed that the three processes are not mutually exclusive. While they have been defined in terms of pure cases, they do not generally occur in pure form in real-life situations. The examples that have been given are, at best, situations in which a particular process predominates and determines the central features of the interaction.

Antecedents and Consequents of the Three Processes

For each of the three processes, a distinct set of antecedents and a distinct set of consequents have been proposed. These are summarized in the table below. First, with respect to the antecedents of the three processes, it should be noted that no systematic quantitative differences between them are hypothesized. The probability of each process is presented as a function of the same three determinants: the importance of the induction for the individual's goal achievement, the power of the influencing agent, and the prepotency of the induced response. For each process, the magnitude of these determinants may vary over the entire range: each may be based on

Summary of the Distinction between the Three Processes

	Compliance	Identification	Internalization
Antecedents:			
1. Basis for the *importance of the induction*	Concern with social effect of behavior	Concern with social anchorage of behavior	Concern with value congruence of behavior
2. Source of *power of the influencing agent*	Means control	Attractiveness	Credibility
3. Manner of achieving *prepotency of the induced response*	Limitation of choice behavior	Delineation of role requirements	Reorganization of means-ends framework
Consequents:			
1. Conditions of performance of induced response	Surveillance by influencing agent	Salience of relationship to agent	Relevance of values to issue
2. Conditions of change and extinction of induced response	Changed perception of conditions for social rewards	Changed perception of conditions for satisfying self-defining relationships	Changed perception of conditions for value maximization
3. Type of behavior system in which induced response is embedded	External demands of a specific setting	Expectations defining a specific role	Person's value system

157

an induction with varying degrees of importance, on an influencing agent with varying degrees of power, and so on. The processes differ only in terms of the *qualitative* form that these determinants take. They differ, as can be seen in the table, in terms of the *basis* for the importance of the induction, the *source* of the influencing agent's power, and the *manner* of achieving prepotency of the induced response.

1. The processes can be distinguished in terms of the basis for the importance of the induction, that is, in terms of the nature of the motivational system that is activated in the influence situation. What is it about the influence situation that makes it important, that makes it relevant to the individual's goals? What are the primary concerns that the individual brings to the situation or that are aroused by it? The differences between the three processes in this respect are implicit in the descriptions of the processes given above: (a) To the extent that the individual is concerned – for whatever reason – with the *social effect* of his behavior, influence will tend to take the form of compliance. (b) To the extent that he is concerned with the *social anchorage* of his behavior, influence will tend to take the form of identification. (c) To the extent that he is concerned with the *value congruence* of his behavior (rational or otherwise), influence will tend to take the form of internalization.

2. A difference between the three processes in terms of the source of the influencing agent's power is hypothesized. (a) To the extent that the agent's power is based on his *means control*, influence will tend to take the form of compliance. An agent possesses means control if he is in a position to supply or withhold means needed by the individual for the achievement of his goals. The perception of means control may depend on the agent's *actual* control over specific rewards and punishment, or on his *potential* control, which would be related to his position in the social structure (his status, authority, or general prestige). (b) To the extent that the agent's power is based on his *attractiveness*, influence will tend to take the form of identification. An agent is attractive if he occupies a role which the individual himself desires [8] or if he occupies a role reciprocal to one the individual wants to establish or maintain. The term 'attractiveness', as used here, does not refer to the possession of qualities that make a person likeable, but rather to the possession of qualities on the part of the agent that make a continued relationship to him particularly desirable. In other words, an agent is attractive when the individual is able to derive satisfaction from a self-definition with reference to him. (c) To the extent that the agent's power is based on his *credibility*, influence will tend

to take the form of internalization. An agent possesses credibility is his statements are considered truthful and valid, and hence worthy of serious consideration. Hovland, Janis and Kelley[9] distinguish two bases for credibility: expertness and trustworthiness. In other words, an agent may be perceived as possessing credibility because he is likely to *know* the truth, or because he is likely to *tell* the truth. Trustworthiness, in turn, may be related to over-all respect, likemindedness, and lack of vested interest.

3. It is proposed that the three processes differ in terms of the way in which prepotency is achieved. (a) To the extent that the induced response becomes prepotent – that is, becomes a 'distinguished path' relative to alternative response possibilities – because the individual's choice behavior is limited, influence will tend to take the form of compliance. This may happen if the individual is pressured into the induced response, or if alternative responses are blocked. The induced response thus becomes prepotent because it is, essentially, the only response permitted: the individual sees himself as having no choice and as being restricted to this particular alternative. (b) To the extent that the induced response becomes prepotent because the requirements of a particular role are delineated, influence will tend to take the form of identification. This may happen if the situation is defined in terms of a particular role relationship and the demands of that role are more or less clearly specified; for instance, if this role is made especially salient and the expectation deriving from it dominates the field. Or it may happen if alternative roles are made ineffective because the situation is ambiguous and consensual validation is lacking. The induced response thus becomes prepotent because it is one of the few alternatives available to the individual: his choice behavior may be unrestricted, but his opportunity for selecting alternative responses is limited by the fact that he is operating exclusively from the point of view of a particular role system. (c) Finally, to the extent that the induced response becomes prepotent because there has been a reorganization in the individual's conception of means-ends relationships, influence will tend to take the form of internalization. This may happen if the implications of the induced response for certain important values – implications of which the individual had been unaware heretofore – are brought out, or if the advantages of the induced response as a path to the individual's goals, compared to the various alternatives that are available, are made apparent. The induced response thus becomes prepotent because it has taken on a new meaning: as the relationships between various means and ends become restructured, it

emerges as the preferred course of action in terms of the person's own values.

Depending, then, on the nature of these three antecedents, the influence process will take the form of compliance, identification, or internalization. Each of these corresponds to a characteristic pattern of internal responses – thoughts and feelings – in which the individual engages as he accepts influence. The resulting changes will, in turn, be different for the three processes, as indicated in the second half of the table. Here, again, it is assumed that there are no systematic quantitative differences between the processes, but rather qualitative variations in the subsequent histories of behavior adopted through each process.

1. It is proposed that the processes differ in terms of the subsequent conditions under which the induced response will be performed or expressed. (a) When an individual adopts an induced response through compliance, he tends to perform it only under conditions of *surveillance* by the influencing agent. These conditions are met if the agent is physically present, or if he is likely to find out about the individual's actions. (b) When an individual adopts an induced response through identification, he tends to perform it only under conditions of *salience* of his relationship to the agent. That is, the occurrence of the behavior will depend on the extent to which the person's relationship to the agent has been engaged in the situation. Somehow this relationship has to be brought into focus and the individual has to be acting within the particular role that is involved in the identification. This does not necessarily mean, however, that he is consciously aware of the relationship; the role can be activated without such awareness. (c) When an individual adopts an induced response through internalization, he tends to perform it under conditions of *relevance of the values* that were initially involved in the influence situation. The behavior will tend to occur whenever these values are activated by the issues under consideration in a given situation, quite regardless of surveillance or salience of the influencing agent. This does not mean, of course, that the behavior will occur every time it becomes relevant. It may be out-competed by other responses in certain situations. The probability of occurrence with a given degree of issue relevance will depend on the strength of the internalized behavior.

2. It is hypothesized that responses adopted through the three processes will differ in terms of the conditions under which they will subsequently be abandoned or changed. (a) A response adopted through compliance will be abandoned if it is no longer

perceived as the best path toward the attainment of social rewards. (b) A response adopted through identification will be abandoned if it is no longer perceived as the best path toward the maintenance or establishment of satisfying self-defining relationships. (c) A response adopted through internalization will be abandoned if it is no longer perceived as the best path toward the maximization of the individual's values.

3. Finally, it is hypothesized that responses adopted through the three processes will differ from each other along certain qualitative dimensions. These can best be summarized, perhaps, by referring to the type of behavior system in which the induced response is embedded. (a) Behavior adopted through compliance is part of a system of external demands that characterize a specific setting. In other words, it is part of the rules of conduct that an individual learns in order to get along in a particular situation or series of situations. The behavior tends to be related to the person's values only in an instrumental rather than an intrinsic way. As long as opinions, for example, remain at that level, the individual will tend to regard them as not really representative of his true beliefs. (b) Behavior adopted through identification is part of a system of expectations defining a particular role – whether this is the role of the other which he is taking over, or a role reciprocal to the other's. This behavior will be regarded by the person as representing himself, and may in fact form an important aspect of himself. It will tend to be isolated, however, from the rest of the person's values – to have little interplay with them. In extreme cases, the system in which the induced response is embedded may be encapsulated and function almost like a foreign body within the person. The induced responses here will be relatively inflexible and stereotyped. (c) Behavior adopted through internalization is part of an internal system. It is fitted into the person's basic framework of values and is congruent with it. This does not imply complete consistency: the degree of consistency can vary for different individuals and different areas of behavior. It does mean, however, that there is some interplay between the new beliefs and the rest of the person's values. The new behavior can serve to modify existing beliefs and can in turn be modified by them. As a result of this interaction, behavior adopted through internalization will tend to be relatively idiosyncratic, flexible, complex, and differentiated.

References

1. See, for example, S. E. Asch, *Social Psychology*, New York, Prentice-Hall, 1952.

2. See, for example, D. Cartwright and A. Zander, editors, *Group Dynamics*, Evanston, Ill., Row, Peterson, 1953.

3. See, for example, C. I. Hovland, I. L. Janis, and H. H. Kelley, *Communication and Persuasion*, New Haven, Yale University Press, 1953.

4. See, for example, L. Festinger, 'An Analysis of Compliant Behavior', in M. Sherif and M. O. Wilson, editors, *Group Relations at the Cross-roads*, New York, Harper, pp. 232–56, 1953; H. C. Kelman, 'Attitude Change as a Function of Response Restriction', *Human Relations*, Vol. 6, pp. 185–214, 1953; J. R. P. French, Jr., and B. Raven, 'The Bases of Social Power', in D. Cartwright, editor, *Studies in Social Power*, Ann Arbor, Mich., Institute for Social Research, pp. 150–67, 1959; and Marie Jahoda, 'Conformity and Independence', *Human Relations*, Vol. 12, pp. 99–120, 1959.

5. See, for example, M. Deutsch and H. B. Gerard, 'A Study of Normative and Informational Social Influence upon Individual Judgment', *Journal of Abnormal and Social Psychology*, Vol. 51, pp. 629–36, 1955; J. W. Thibaut and L. Strickland, 'Psychological Set and Social Conformity', *Journal of Personality*, Vol. 25, pp. 115–29, 1956; and J. M. Jackson and H. D. Saltzstein, 'The Effect of Person-Group Relationships on Conformity Processes', *Journal of Abnormal and Social Psychology*, Vol. 57, pp. 17–24, 1958.

6. For instance, R. J. Lifton, '"Thought Reform" of Western Civilians in Chinese Communist Prisons', *Psychiatry*, Vol. 19, pp. 173–95, 1956.

7. A detailed description of these processes and the experimental work based on them will be contained in a forthcoming book, *Social Influence and Personal Belief: A Theoretical and Experimental Approach to the Study of Behavior Change*, to be published by John Wiley & Sons.

8. This is similar to John Whiting's conception of 'Status Envy' as a basis for identification. See J. W. M. Whiting, 'Sorcery, Sin, and the Super-ego', in M. R. Jones, editor, *Nebraska Symposium on Motivation*, Lincoln, University of Nebraska Press, pp. 174–95, 1959.

9. Op. cit., p. 21.

17 W. J. McGuire

Inducing Resistance to Persuasion

Excerpt from: W. J. McGuire, *Advances in Experimental Social Psychology*, L. Berkowitz (ed.), Academic Press, U.S.A., 1965, pp. 200–21.

The Inoculation Approach

A. *Use of Cultural Truisms*

McGuire's series of experiments on inducing resistance to persuasion stems from a biological analogy, whence the term 'inoculation theory'. In the biological situation, the person is typically made resistant to some attacking virus by pre-exposure to a weakened dose of the virus. This mild dose stimulates his defenses so that he will be better able to overcome any massive viral attack to which he is later exposed, but is not so strong that this pre-exposure will itself cause the disease. Alternatively, biological resistance can be augmented by supportive therapy such as adequate rest, good diet, and vitamin supplements. Inoculation is likely to be superior to supportive therapy to the extent that the person has previously been brought up in a germ-free environment. It is a seeming paradox that individuals raised aseptically tend to appear vigorously healthy (even without supportive therapy) but are highly vulnerable when suddenly exposed to massive doses of the disease virus.

Since the experimenter wished to make heuristic use of the inoculation analogy in deriving hypotheses about producing resistance to persuasion, he chose to deal as far as possible with beliefs that had been maintained in a 'germ-free' ideological environment, that is, beliefs that the person has seldom, if ever, heard attacked. Nearly all beliefs should be of this sort, according to the selective-avoidance postulate, which implies that a person avoids dissonant information wherever possible. While this has been widely accepted (Festinger, 1957; Klapper, 1949, 1960), the empirical evidence for it is not clear-cut (Steiner, 1962). Hence, to be more certain that the beliefs used in these experiments met the conditions of inoculation theory, 'cultural truisms' were used as the beliefs to be made resistant to persuasive attacks. 'Cultural truisms' are beliefs that are so widely shared within the person's social milieu that he would not have heard them attacked, and

163

indeed, would doubt that an attack were possible. Beliefs maintained in so monolithic an ideological environment would approximate, as regards inoculation theory, the health status of an organism raised in a germ-free environment.

After much pretesting (which showed that cultural truisms were rarer in our college samples than had been expected), one area was finally found that abounded in almost unanimously accepted propositions, namely, health beliefs. Upwards of 75% of the student samples checked '15' on a 15-point scale to indicate their agreement with propositions like: 'It's a good idea to brush your teeth after every meal if at all possible'; 'Mental illness is not contagious'; 'The effects of penicillin have been, almost without exception, of great benefit to mankind'; 'Everyone should get a yearly chest X-ray to detect any signs of TB at an early stage'. These truisms (which, as shown below, proved quite vulnerable when exposed to massive attacks without prior 'immunizing' treatment) were used, in the experiments described below, as the beliefs to be made resistant to persuasion by procedures derived by analogy from biological inoculation.

B. Basic Assumptions and Relevant Variables

1. *Underlying Assumptions.* McGuire's version of the inoculation theory assumes that pretreatments designed to make truisms resistant to subsequent persuasive attacks will be effective to the extent that they overcome two basic difficulties: one, the believer is unpracticed in defending his belief; and two, he is unmotivated to undertake the necessary practice. He is unpracticed because he has never been called upon to defend the truism. He is unmotivated to start practicing because he regards the belief as unassailable.

It follows that any prior treatment designed to improve the believer's defenses must motivate him to develop a defense of a truism whose validity he regards as obvious. Motivation can be supplied by making him aware of the vulnerability of the truism. That is, to be effective the prior defense of a truism presumably should be threatening rather than reassuring about the belief. An obvious way of threatening him is by pre-exposure to weakened forms of the attacking arguments.

It also follows that supplying motivation alone is inadequate for an effective defense. Because of the believer's lack of prior practice, he may not be able to bolster his belief sufficiently unless he is given careful guidance in developing defensive material; or, if he is required to develop such material on his own initiative, he must at least be given considerable time to do so.

From this background of assumptions, we derive a number of predictions about the relative immunizing effectiveness of various kinds of prior defenses. The three basic variables which are involved in most of these predictions are described first. The derivation of the specific predictions involving them is taken up in the later sections of this chapter which present the separate experiments.

2. *The Defensive Variables.* The first of these three variables is the amount of threat contained in the defenses. Two basic types of defenses were used which differed in amount of threat: 'supportive' and 'refutational'. The supportive defense was nonthreatening; it consisted of giving the believer various arguments in support of the truism. The refutational defense was more threatening; instead of positively supporting the truism, it mentioned several arguments attacking the belief, and then proceeded to refute these attacking arguments. The experimenter reasoned that this pre-exposure would be threatening enough to be defense-stimulating, but not so strong as to overwhelm the truism.

These refutational defenses, considered in relation to the subsequent attacks, were one of two types. Either they mentioned and refuted the very arguments against the truism that were to be used in the subsequent attacks, or they mentioned and refuted arguments different from the ones to be used in the attacks. This refutational-same vs. refutational-different defensive variation is useful in determining whether any increased resistance to persuasion derives from the generalized motivational effect of the threatening mention of the arguments against the truism (as required by inoculation theory), or whether it stems from the useful defensive material provided directly by the refutations.

A second defensive variable that was manipulated in many of the experimenter's inoculation studies was the amount of unguided, active participation in the defense required of the believer. Two levels of this variable were generally used: a relatively passive condition, in which the believer read a defensive essay that had been prepared for him, and an active condition, in which the believer wrote such an essay. This variable was relevant to both of the assumed difficulties in immunizing cultural truisms: the believer's lack of practice and his lack of motivation.

A third variable manipulated in several of the experiments was the interval between the defense and attack. This time period ranged from a few minutes to a maximum of one week. Here the primary concern was the interaction between time and the other variables. The theoretical relevance of these three variables will be discussed later, along with the description of the experiments that tested the predictions in which they were involved.

A number of additional variables were manipulated to clarify certain theoretical ambiguities in one or another of the studies described below, but they are described later in the chapter with the experiment where they were employed.

General Experimental Procedure

The basic procedures were quite similar from experiment to experiment in the series reported below. Hence, for economy of exposition the general methodological paradigm will be described at the outset. Then, in describing each individual experiment, its method will need to be described only in so far as it departs in important ways from this general paradigm.

The experiments involved two sessions, the first devoted to the defenses; the second, to the strong attacks and to measuring the resultant belief levels. The interval between the two sessions varied from a few minutes to 7 days. The subjects were usually college students enrolled in introductory psychology courses at large state universities who were fulfilling a course requirement that they participate in a certain number of hours of psychological experiments. The present studies were usually represented to them as studies of verbal skills. The issues being defended and attacked were the health truisms described above.

A. First (Defensive) Session

The subjects were told the experimenter was studying the relation between reading and writing skills in the two-session experiments. In the first 50-minute session the subject actually participated in several defensive conditions, e.g. he might receive an active-refutational, passive-refutational, active-supportive, and passive-supportive defense, each defense dealing with a different truism.

An active refutational defense consisted of a sheet of paper on which was listed a truism – e.g. 'Everyone should brush his teeth after every meal if at all possible'. Then would come a one-sentence argument against this truism – e.g. 'Too frequent brushing tends to damage the gums and expose the vulnerable parts of the teeth to decay' – and the instructions to use the white space below to write a paragraph refuting this argument against the truism. Halfway down the page came another argument against the truism and instructions to refute it in the space following. The passive-refutational defense stated the truism and the two arguments against it in an introductory paragraph; then followed two further paragraphs, each refuting one of these arguments. The active and passive supportive defenses were analogous to the refutational in format, except that instead of arguments against the truism, they cited two arguments supporting it, and then (in the active condition) asked the subject to write paragraphs defending these supportive arguments, or (in the passive condition) presented two such defensive paragraphs for him to read. In the passive defenses, to substantiate the subterfuge that we were studying reading skills, the subject was asked to pick out and underline the crucial clause in each paragraph.

In some of the experiments, the subject filled out an opinionnaire on the truisms after completing these defenses, so we could measure the direct strengthening effects of the defenses prior to the attacks. More typically, no opinionnaire was administered until the end of the second session, and the direct strengthening effect was determined by including defense-only, no-attack conditions in the design.

B. Second (Attacking) Session

Immediately after (or 2 or 7 days after this defensive session) followed a 50-minute second session devoted to attacks on the truisms and administration of an opinionnaire to determine final belief levels on the truisms. The attacks all had the form of a three-paragraph essay (similar in format to the passive defenses). The first paragraph stated the truism, remarked that some informed people were beginning to question its validity, and mentioned two attacking arguments. Each of the next two paragraphs developed in detail one of these attacking arguments. For those conditions in which a refutational defense had been given, half were followed by an attack using the same arguments against the truism as had been refuted in the prior defense (constituting it a 'refutational-same' defense); the other half were followed by attacks using quite different arguments against the truism from those that had been refuted in the defense (constituting a 'refutational-different' defense). The designs typically had each subject furnish control data on a 'defense-only' and a 'neither-defense-nor-attack' truism. The specific truisms were, of course, rotated around the conditions from subject to subject.

After reading (and underlining the crucial clause in) the attacking messages, the subject filled out some personality tests (introduced to substantiate the claim that the experiment was investigating personality correlates of verbal skills). He then filled out the opinionnaire on the truisms, purportedly to determine if the subject's feelings about the topics had any effect on his ability to utilize his verbal skills in the reading and writing 'tests'. The opinionnaire consisted of four statements dealing with each truism. The subject was called upon to check off his agreement with the statement on a scale from one to 15. The direction of the statement was varied, so that sometimes 15 represented complete acceptance of the truism, and sometimes complete rejection. However, in the results reported below, to make reading easier, the appropriate responses are reversed so that the 15 score always represents complete acceptance of the truism and a one score complete rejection of it.

After completing the opinionnaire, the subject replied to standardized questions probing his actual perception of the experiment. Finally, the true purpose of the experiment was revealed to him, and the various deceits used and the reasons for employing them were explained. Approximately 3 months later a follow-up letter was sent to him, reminding him that the argumentative material he had dealt with had been selected solely for experimental purposes and that the arguments were not necessarily true. More detailed information on the materials, designs, etc., are given in the original published reports of the experiments cited in the paragraphs that follow.

Supportive vs. Refutational Defenses

A series of experiments were carried out to test the hypothesis that defenses of truisms are effective to the extent that they contain threatening mention of arguments against the truism. These studies, in which the experimenter manipulated the extent to which the defenses mentioned arguments supporting the truism vs. arguments attacking the truism, are described in the present section. The first study showed that defenses which present arguments supporting the truism are less effective in conferring resistance to subsequent strong attack than are refutational-same defenses (which ignore arguments positively supporting the truism but do mention and refute the same arguments against the belief as are to be used in the subsequent attack). The second experiment demonstrated that a refutational defense is almost as effective when it refutes arguments against the truisms which are different from those to be used in the later attack as when it refutes the very same arguments used in the attack.

A third study illustrated that, when combined with the threatening refutational defense, the supportive defense gains an efficacy that it lacks when used alone. In the fourth study, it was demonstrated that an extrinsic threat (forewarning of the impending attack) prior to the defenses, enhances their immunizing effectiveness, especially that of the otherwise not-threatening supportive defense. Conversely, a fifth study showed that a prior reassurance (feedback that one's peers also agree with the truism) decreases the effectiveness of the defenses. A sixth study revealed that the immunizing efficacy of the refutational defense derives at least as much from the threatening prior mention of the attacking arguments as from the reassuring earlier refutations of the attacking arguments which had been mentioned. Each of these studies is described in more detail, together with additional findings of interest, in the paragraphs below.

A. Supportive vs. Refutational-Same Study

1. *Experimental Conditions.* In a first experiment (McGuire and Papageorgis, 1961), each of 130 students read a defensive essay on one truism and wrote a defensive essay on another in a regular meeting of his freshman English course. Two days later, he read messages attacking these two truisms and also a third, non-defended truism. On a fourth truism he received neither defense nor attack (the four specific truisms being rotated around the four conditions from student to student). He then filled out an opinionnaire measuring his beliefs on all four truisms.

For 66 of the students, each defensive essay was supportive, mentioning four arguments supporting the truism and then presenting a paragraph substantiating each argument (in the reading, passive condition), or then asking the student to write a substantiating paragraph for each argument (in the writing, active condition). For the other 64 students, each defensive essay was refutational, ignoring supportive arguments and mentioning four arguments against the truism and then presenting a paragraph refuting each (in the passive condition), or then calling upon the student to write a refuting paragraph against each argument (in the active condition). The passive-condition subjects were allowed 5 minutes to read each of the 1000-word essays; the active-condition subjects were allowed 10 minutes to write each essay. The attacks 2 days later consisted of 1000-word essays to be read, each mentioning four arguments against the belief and then presenting a paragraph substantiating each argument.

2. *Immunizing Effectiveness.* As Table 1 shows, the more threatening, refutational defense was clearly superior to the supportive defense in conferring resistance to the subsequent attacks. The

attacks, when not preceded by a defense, reduced adherence to the truisms from 12·62 to 6·64 on the 15-point scale. When the refutational defense preceded the attacks, the mean belief score was reduced only to 10·33, which is significantly ($p < 0.001$) higher than in the attack-only condition. The supportive defenses were much less successful in inducing resistance. In the supportive defense conditions, the mean belief score after the attacks was 7·39, which is not only significantly ($p < 0.001$) lower than in the refutational-defense treatment, but is not even significantly higher than the no-defense, attack-only condition ($p = 0.16$). Hence the supportive defense is not only much less effective than the refutational in conferring resistance, but has not clearly been shown to be effective at all.

Table 1

Mean Belief Levels after Attacks* Preceded by Refutational–Same vs. Supportive Defenses†‡

Type of participation	Refutational defense then attack	Supportive defense then attack	Refute minus support
Passive reading	11·51 (35)§	7·47 (32)	+4·04
Reading and underlining	11·13 (31)	7·63 (32)	+3·50
Writing from outline	9·19 (31)	7·94 (32)	+1·25
Writing without guidance	9·46 (35)	6·53 (32)	+2·93
Weighted mean	10·33 (132)	7·39 (128)	+2·94

* Control levels: neither attack nor defense = 12·62 ($N = 130$); attack only (with no prior defense) = 6·64 ($N = 130$).
† 15·00 indicates complete adherence to the truism; 1·00 indicates complete disagreement.
‡ Data from McGuire and Papageorgis (1961).
§ Numbers in parentheses give the number of cases on which cell means were based.

3. *Direct Strengthening Effect.* In this experiment, the subjects completed the opinionnaire not only at the end of the second session, but also at the end of the first session. Comparing each subject's two responses provides a measure of the direct strengthening effects of the various defenses (as opposed to their conferred resistance to the later attacks). In terms of this criterion, the supportive defenses apparently were superior to the refutational. Immediately after the supportive defenses, the mean belief score was $14·34$; immediately after the refutational, it was $13·91$ ($p = 0·10$ for the difference). Furthermore, while the refutational defense was superior to the supportive one in all four participation conditions as regards resistance conferral (see Table 1), the supportive defense was superior in producing a direct strengthening effect. This type of reversal was found repeatedly in the present series of experiments: the defenses which left the beliefs seemingly strongest tended to be the defenses which conferred the least resistance to subsequent attacks. This reversal, called the 'paper tiger' phenomenon, shows the peril of assuming the immunizing effectiveness of a defense to be a direct function of its apparent strengthening effect, and is in accord with the inoculation theory.

B. Refutational-Same vs. -Different

1. *Hypotheses.* A later experiment by Papageorgis and McGuire (1961) compared the resistance-conferring efficacy of the refutational defense when the later attacks used arguments which differed from those mentioned and refuted in the defense, with their efficacy when the later attacks used the same arguments used in the defense. If, as implied by the inoculation theory, the refutational defense derives immunizing efficacy from the motivation-stimulating threatening mention of arguments against the truism, then its effectiveness should be general and manifested even against attacks using novel arguments. On the other hand, if the refutational defense gains its effectiveness solely from the refutation rather than the mention of the arguments, the resistance it confers should be more specific to attacks by the same arguments that had been refuted.

2. *Procedure.* The study designed to distinguish between these two explanations employed only refutational defenses, since the hypotheses did not concern the supportive defenses. Also, only passive (reading) defenses were employed, since the relevance of the active defenses (even of the refutational type) to the predictions is less clear; the amount of refutational material received was more under

the subject's control than the experimenter's in the active condition. Alternative forms of the passive refutational defense were made up for each truism. Each form employed a different pair of arguments against the truism, the defensive message first mentioning and then refuting this pair in a 600-word essay. Correspondingly, there were two forms of the message attacking each truism, each form mentioning and then corroborating one of these pairs of attacking arguments. A crossover design was used so that each given pair of arguments refuted in a defense was followed by an attack using the same arguments for half the subjects, and by one using the different pair of arguments for the other half. A total of 73 summer school students served in the two sessions, defensive and attacking, which were separated by a one-week interval.

3. *Results.* Once again the attacks proved very damaging to the truisms when they were not preceded by a defense. In the attack-only condition, the mean belief level went down to 5·73 on the 15-point scale as compared to a mean of 13·23 in the neither-defense-nor-attack control condition, a drop significant at well above the 0·001 level. The refutational defenses did confer appreciable resistance to the attack: When the attack had been preceded by the refutational-same defense, the mean belief level was 9·25; after one preceded by the refutational-different defense, it was 8·70. Each of these means in the defense-and-attack conditions is significantly higher than the 5·73 mean in the attack-only condition, and they are not significantly different from one another. These outcomes tend to conform to inoculation theory, since the refutational defense confers resistance even to novel attacks. Indeed, the resistance to novel attacks that was produced is not significantly less than the resistance to attacks by the very same arguments that were refuted.

In a further attempt to identify the mechanisms underlying the resistance-conferral by the refutational defense, two additional variables were measured at the end of the second (attacking) session. One of these was a semantic-differential-type scale designed to measure the perceived quality and credibility of the arguments used in the attack. The attacks were seen as significantly ($p < 0.05$) less credible when preceded by a refutational defense (whether the defense was refutational-same or refutational-different) than when not preceded by any defense. A second post-attack test called upon the person to write down as many arguments as he could in support of the truism. The inoculation theory prediction was that the motivational stimulation from the threatening refutational defense would result in the believer's accumulating more supportive material for the truism during the week following the attack. However, although there was a slight tendency for the subjects who had received the refutational defense to think up more supportive arguments than those who had received no defense, the difference was not significant ($0.20 > p > 0.10$).

C. Combinational Effects

1. *Hypotheses and Method.* A third experiment (McGuire, 1961b) like the second, used passive (reading) defenses only and compared the immunizing efficacy of combinations of supportive and refutational defenses with that of single defenses. In keeping with inoculation theory, the experimenter attributed the ineffectiveness of the supportive defense (found in McGuire and Papageorgis (1961) described above) to the believer's lack of motivation to assimilate its arguments; the supporting statements seemed to belabor the obvious. The refutational defense did supply some motivation by its threatening mention of arguments against the truism, but did not, in the case of the refutational-different defense, supply any specifically useful material to the unpracticed subject for acting on this induced motivation to bolster the truism. Hence, it was predicted that the supportive and refutational defenses used together would confer more resistance than the sum of their individual effects. It was further predicted that this 'whole greater than the sum of its parts' effect would be more pronounced when the supportive defense was added to refutational-different than when added to refutational-same defenses.

One hundred and sixty-two students enrolled in introductory college courses were used to test these predictions. They received supportive-only, refutational-only, or supportive-plus-refutational defenses on different truisms. In the cases of refutational defenses, half were refutational-same, and half refutational-different. The attacking session followed immediately after the defensive.

2. *Results.* Both of the combination predictions were confirmed. When used alone, neither the refutational-different nor the supportive defenses conferred significant resistance to the immediate attacks. When used in combination, they produced considerable ($p < 0.01$) resistance. Also confirmed was the prediction that the combination with the supportive defense would be especially effective for the refutational-different defense; there was a significant interaction ($p < 0.01$) in the predicted direction between the refutational-only vs. refutational-plus-supportive variable and

the -same vs. -different variable. The refutational-different defense profited more from the addition of the supportive defense as regards producing resistance to an immediate post-defense attack. These and other findings of the study under discussion are described more fully elsewhere (McGuire, 1961b).

D. Added Threats and Reassurances

1. *Theory.* According to the inoculation theory, prior defenses lose effectiveness in making truisms resistant to persuasion because the believer is over-confident and therefore unmotivated to assimilate the defenses adequately. This motivational deficit is particularly pronounced in the case of the supportive defense, while the refutational defense does contain an intrinsic threat – mention of attacking arguments – which arouses some motivation. If this theoretical analysis is correct, it follows that any intrinsic threat to the truism (e.g. a forewarning that it will be attacked), presented to the believer before the defense material, should increase his motivation to assimilate the material and hence enhance its immunizing effectiveness. This extrinsic threat should be especially beneficial to the supportive defense which is particularly needful of such additional motivation. Conversely, a predefense reassurance that the truisms were indeed beyond controversy (e.g. by feedback that everyone in the believer's group agreed with them) should actually decrease the effectiveness of the defenses by further depressing the already inadequate motivation to assimilate these defenses. To test these derivations, two experiments were carried out, one manipulating extrinsic threats, the other, extrinsic reassurance.

2. *Extrinsic Threat Manipulation.* In the first of these two studies (McGuire and Papageorgis, 1962), each of the 96 subjects received supportive, refutational-same, and refutational-different defenses of three truisms and no defense of a fourth belief. All the defenses were of the passive (reading) type. Then the subjects were given four attacking messages, one aimed at each of the truisms. Finally, their opinions regarding each truism were measured.

For half the subjects the experiment was introduced in the usual way, as a verbal skills test dealing with health topics, and no mention was made of the fact that the truisms would be attacked in the later reading passages. The 48 subjects so instructed constituted the 'no-forewarning' condition. The other 48 subjects, those in the 'forewarning' condition, received a quite different rationale for the experiment. They were told the experimenter was measuring how persuasible they were by asking them to read attacks on four health truisms which they took for granted. Before they read the attacks, they also were informed, they would be allowed to read defenses of some of those beliefs.

3. *Results.* The forewarning of attack did indeed enhance the immunizing effectiveness of the defenses, as shown in Table 2. It can be calculated from the scores in Table 2 that after the defenses and attacks in the forewarning condition, the mean belief level was 11·67, and in the no-forewarning condition it was only 10·93, a difference significant above the 0·05 level. Also as predicted, this enhancement due to the threatening forewarnings is greater for the supportive than the refutational defense, the interaction being significant at the 0·05 level.

There are several possible explanations for these results, however. For example, the higher means in the forewarning conditions after defenses and attacks might not be due to the hypothesized enhancement of the defenses caused by the increased motivation which the threat produced, but rather could stem from a direct reduction in the impact of the attack due to its identification as such by the forewarning. The means in the attack-only control condition shown in Table 2 rule out this alternative interpretation; when not preceded by a defense the attacks are at least as effective in the

Table 2

Final Belief Levels with and without Forewarning before the Defenses*†

Foreknow-ledge of attack prior to defense	Attack-only (no prior defense)	Defense and attack conditions			
		Supportive defense	Refut.-same defense	Refut.-diff. defense	Neither defense nor attack
Yes	9·95 (24)‡	12·09 (48)	11·79 (48)	11·12 (48)	12·52 (24)
No	10·23 (24)	10·11 (48)	11·68 (48)	10·98 (48)	13·20 (24)
Combined	10·09 (48)	11·10 (96)	11·73 (96)	11·05 (96)	12·86 (48)

* 15·00 indicates complete adherence to the truism.
† Data from McGuire and Papageorgis (1962).
‡ Numbers in parentheses give the number of cases on which cell means were based.

forewarning as in the non-forewarning conditions. Further evidence along these lines is presented in the original publication.

4. *Extrinsic Reassurance Manipulation.* In the second of these two studies (Anderson, 1962), each of 96 subjects received a pattern of defenses and attacks similar to that in the forewarning study described above. However, in this study, instead of a threatening forewarning manipulation, there was a reassuring feedback prior to the defenses. At the beginning of the group-administered defensive session, all the subjects were asked to give their opinions on a series of health truisms, including the four crucial ones. By a subterfuge, 48 subjects were then given feedback which indicated that the other subjects had almost unanimously agreed that the four crucial beliefs were true beyond a doubt. These 'high reassurance' subjects received no feedback on the 'filler' truisms. The other 48 subjects (who constituted the 'low reassurance' condition) received no feedback regarding the crucial truisms, although they did receive reassuring feedback regarding four filler truisms.

5. *Results.* The outcome of this study is shown in Table 3. The final belief levels in the three defense-and-attack conditions combined was 10·63 in the reassurance condition and 11·53 in the

Table 3

Final Belief Levels with and without Reassuring Feedback before the Defenses*†

Reassuring feedback of group agreement	Attack-only (no prior defense)	Defense and attack conditions			Neither defense nor attack
		Supportive defense	Refut.-same defense	Refut.-diff. defense	
Yes	10·20 (24)‡	9·58 (48)	11·52 (48)	10·80 (48)	12·40 (24)
No	10·74 (24)	11·06 (48)	12·12 (48)	11·41 (48)	12·68 (24)
Combined	10·47 (48)	10·32 (96)	11·82 (96)	11·10 (96)	12·54 (48)

* 15·00 indicates complete adherence to the truism.
† Data from Anderson (1962).
‡ Numbers in parentheses give the number of cases on which cell means were based.

no-reassurance condition, a difference significant at the 0·01 level. Hence, as predicted on the basis of inoculation theory, reassurance prior to the defenses actually lessens their immunizing effectiveness. That the effect is produced via the defenses (rather than through any direct effect of the reassurance manipulation upon the attacks) is shown by the fact that the difference between the high and low reassurance groups in the attack-only conditions is trivial.

The predicted interaction of reassurance and type of defense was not found in this study. It can be seen in Table 3 that the reassurance reduced the effectiveness of the supportive defense more than that of the refutational defenses. However, this trend is significantly only at the 0·20 level.

E. Independent Manipulation of Threat and Reassurance

1. *Theory and Method.* Yet another investigation sought to determine whether the immunizing efficacy of the refutational defense derives, as predicted from inoculation theory, from their threatening components. A final experiment (McGuire, 1963a) in this series utilized independent manipulation of the two components of the refutational defenses: namely, the threatening component (mention in the first paragraph of some arguments attacking the truism); and the reassuring component (refutations of these attacking arguments in the later paragraphs). To isolate the separate effects of these two components, they were manipulated orthogonally in the present experiment. Specifically, half of the refutational defenses were 'high threat', mentioning four arguments attacking the truisms; and half were 'low threat', mentioning two such arguments. Each of these types was further dichotomized so that half were 'high reassurance' defenses, in which two of the

Table 4A

Number of Counterarguments Presented in the Various Refutational Defense Conditions

| | Threat | |
Reassurance	High threat	Low threat
High reassurance	4 mentioned 2 refuted	2 mentioned 2 refuted
Low reassurance	4 mentioned 0 refuted	2 mentioned 0 refuted

mentioned attacking arguments were refuted; and half were 'low reassurance' defenses, which refuted none of the mentioned arguments. The design is sketched in Table 4A.

A total of 288 subjects served in this study, participating in a defensive and an attacking session separated by 2 days. All the defenses were of the 'passive' type, requiring of the subject only that he read the prepared refutational-defense messages.

2. *Results.* The outcome, shown in Table 4B, indicates that both the threatening and the reassuring components of the refutational defenses contributed to their resistance to attack. As regards reassurance, the superiority of high reassurance over low is significant at the 0.05 level ($F = 4.85$); in the case of the threat variable the superiority of high threat over low is significant at the 0.01 level ($F = 13.52$).

Table 4B

Final Belief Levels after Attacks Preceded by Defenses Involving Varying Numbers of Counterarguments*†

| Reassurance | Threat | | Overall |
	High	Low	
High	11·07	10·54	10·75
	(96)‡	(144)	(240)
Low	10·97	9·75	10·23
	(96)	(144)	(240)
Overall	11·02	10·14	10·49
	(192)	(288)	(480)

* 15·00 indicates complete adherence to the truism.
† Data from McGuire (1963a).
‡ Numbers in parentheses give the number of cases on which cell means were based.

These results confirm the inoculation theory prediction that the more threatening defense will be more effective in making truisms resistant to subsequent attacks. The theory did not rule out the possibility that other components of the refutational defense also would contribute to resistance to persuasion, any more than Boyle's law implies the invalidity of Charles's law. Hence, the finding that reassurance promotes resistance is not necessarily in conflict with

178

inoculation theory. The experimenter's conjecture is that if the reassurance comes from the threat, the believer's confidence in the truisms is increased and his tendency not to heed the defenses is augmented. If, on the other hand, the reassurance comes after the threat has already stimulated the believer's motivation to assimilate the defense, then it will heighten resistance to attack. Further study should clarify this point.

Effects of Active Participation in the Defense

A. Theory

A second series of hypotheses derived from the inoculation notion dealt with the effects of requiring the believer to participate actively, without guidance, in the prior defense of the truisms. Our initial analysis of the resistance of cultural truisms to attack assumed that because these truisms had been maintained in an ideologically 'germ-free' environment, there would be two deficits making it difficult to utilize prior defense to make them resistant to persuasion. First, there would be a practice deficit: since the believer would seldom if ever have been called upon to defend the truism, he would not find it easy to do so unless he was carefully guided in the defense. Second, there would be a motivational deficit: because the believer would be too confident of the validity of these supposedly obvious and unassailable truisms, he would be little motivated to assimilate defensive material that was presented to him.

It follows that this 'active participation in the defense' variable is relevant in opposite ways to both the practice and the motivational deficits of the truisms. With regard to the deficit in prior practice, the active (writing) defensive condition is more disadvantageous than the passive (reading) condition, since it imposes more demands upon the believer to summon up bolstering material from his inadequate cognitive repertory. He will tend to perform the writing task poorly and, consequently, the active defensive session tends to be unproductive and wasted. In contrast, the passive defense makes relatively little demand on the believer's prior preparation; he has only to read the presented defensive material. Hence, his lack of practice is no great handicap. In the case of the motivational deficit, on the other hand, the active condition is at less of a disadvantage than the passive, since the very poorness of the believer's performance at the essay-writing task should bring home to him how inadequately based is his confidence in the truism. This should motivate him to correct this state of affairs.

179

Since the theoretical analysis indicates that the two processes touched off by this active-passive manipulation have opposite effects on the dependent variable (conferred resistance), the experimenter might seem to be left in a sorry state for making predictions. Such is not the case, however. Predictions can be made regarding interaction effects between this activity variable and other variables which tend to intensify the advantages or disadvantages of active participation with respect to conferring resistance.

B. Effects of Requiring Participation

1. *Theory and Method.* The first experiment designed to test the effect on conferred resistance of manipulating the amount of unguided, active participation in the defense varied this participation over four levels. The highest degree of unguided participation was called 'unguided writing'. It consisted of giving the subjects a sheet of paper headed by a statement of the truism and telling him that he had 20 minutes to write an essay defending the truism. Subjects were assigned either to a supportive-defense condition by being told that their essays should be restricted to presenting arguments positively supporting the truism, or to a refutational-defense condition by being told that their essays should mention and then refute possible arguments against the truism. They were told that their essays would be scored for argumentative skill and relevance, but were given no further guidance.

A slightly less demanding condition, called 'guided writing' was the same as above, except that the sheets headed by the truisms also listed arguments that could be used in writing the essay. The people in the supportive-defense condition were given one-sentence synopses of each of four arguments supporting the truisms. Those in the refutational defense conditions were given four pairs of sentences, each pair consisting of a statement of an argument attacking the truism, and a statement suggesting a refutation of that argument.

Still less demanding was the 'reading and underlining condition'. Here each subject received a mimeographed, defensive essay about 1000 words long to read. In the supportive condition the first paragraph mentioned four arguments supporting the truism, and then followed four paragraphs, each developing more fully one of the supporting arguments. In the refutational condition the first paragraph mentioned four arguments attacking the beliefs, and then followed four paragraphs, each refuting one of these attacking arguments. The subjects in this reading condition were instructed that they would have 5 minutes to read and to underline in each paragraph the shortest clause that contained the gist of the whole paragraph. They were told they would be scored on the basis of their accuracy at this task and their ability to answer a later series of reading comprehension questions.

The least demanding participation condition, called 'passive reading', was the same as the reading and underlining condition, except that the underlining task was omitted so that the subject had simply to read the paragraph passively during the 5 minutes and prepare for the later reading comprehension questions.

In this experiment (McGuire and Papageorgis, 1961), each of the 130 subjects served in two defensive conditions in the first session: a writing defense on one truism and a reading defense on another. All the refutational defenses were of the refutational-same type. In the second session 2 days later, each received attacks on the two defended truisms and also an attack on a third, undefended truism (to yield an attack-only control score), and no attack on still a fourth truism (to yield a neither-defense-nor-attack control score). The four specific truisms were rotated around these four conditions from subject to subject. Beliefs were measured at the ends of both the first and second sessions.

While there are, as described above, both beneficial and detrimental effects to be expected from requiring active participation in the defense, it is possible under the experimental conditions obtaining here to make a main order prediction: the detrimental effects are likely to be dominant so that the active-participation requirement will probably have the net effect of interfering with the immunizing effectiveness of the defense. The reason is that the relative disadvantage of the active conditions (their being too demanding for the unpracticed subject) is likely to be fully operative, while their relative advantage (supplying motivation to take part seriously in the defense) is somewhat obviated by the moderate degree of such motivation established by the present conditions, even in the passive group. As the previously described series of experiments showed, the refutational defense, even in the passive condition, contains a motivation-stimulating threat to the belief. In addition, the reading-comprehension instructions also motivate these college student subjects to address themselves seriously to assimilating these defensive essays, even though the essays seem to belabor the obvious.

The above reasoning enables the experimenter to make predictions regarding both main effects and interactions in this study. Forced-compliance studies (Kelman, 1953; King and Janis, 1956;

Brehm and Cohen, 1962) usually find that active participation in the defense of a belief opposing one's own views generally augments the amount of internalized attitude change. However, in the present case of defending already accepted truisms, the opposite is predicted: namely, the greater the active participation requirement, the less the conferred resistance to subsequent attacks.

The above considerations also give rise to the interaction prediction: the superiority of the passive over the active defense will be more pronounced with the refutational defence than with the supportive. As pointed out in the analysis of the experimental conditions, whatever advantage the active condition might offer – its motivation-inducing threat – is lost in the case of the refutational defense because here even the passive condition offers two sources of motivation to assimilate the defense: the mention of the threatening, attacking arguments which are to be refuted, and the achievement motivation to do well, produced by the announcement of the reading comprehension test.

2. *Main Effect Results*. The outcome of this experiment has already been presented in Table 1, which shows the final belief scores in the eight defense-and-attack conditions (i.e., four levels of active participation for the supportive and for the refutational defenses) and in the attack-only and neither-defense-nor-attack control conditions. As Table 1 shows, the main effect prediction is confirmed; over the four levels of increasing participation there is a steady decline in immunizing effectiveness. With regard to the main manipulation of this variable, reading vs. writing, the superiority of the former is significant at the 0.001 level. (Also noteworthy is the finding of the same consistent trend over the four conditions in the direct strengthening effects of the defense, as shown by the mean belief levels at the end of the first session. The superiority of reading over writing in this regard reached the 0.05 level of significance, despite the low ceiling restraining any further increase in the pre-attack means.) This immunizing superiority of reading over writing is especially striking considering that the time allowed for the writing defense (20 minutes) was four times that allowed for the reading.

3. *Interaction Result*. The interaction prediction is also confirmed by the results. While the reading defense was superior to the writing for both supportive and refutational defenses, reading was only slightly superior to writing for the supportive defense (7·56 vs. 7·23) but considerably superior for the refutational defense (11·33

vs. 9·33). This interaction was significant at the 0·05 level. Several subsequent studies (McGuire, 1963a,c) confirmed both the main and the interaction effects reported here. However, they showed in addition that the sizable superiority of reading over writing for the refutational-same defense, which was demonstrated in this study, does not hold also for the refutational-different defense. Indeed, the superiority of reading over writing tends to be even less for the refutational-different defense than for the supportive defense. The next section discusses this lack of superiority with the refutational-different defense which can be derived from the inoculation theory.

C. Active and Passive Combinational Effects

1. *Theory.* In the case of refutational defenses, the inoculation theory has implications regarding the advisability of using double defenses, active plus passive (i.e. having the subject both read and write a refutational essay defending the truism), as compared with using just one of these. The implications follow from the same assumptions that were used to derive the previous predictions. The refutational-same defense presumably owes its efficacy to two factors. The first is its mild, motivating threat to the truism, due to its mentioning arguments attacking the truism and from demonstrating to the believer (especially in the active defense condition) how poorly prepared he is to defend the truism. The second immunizing source is the refutational material which is useful in resisting subsequent attacks that employ the same attacking arguments that had been refuted. This refutational material, however, is less useful against attacks employing novel arguments. Hence, the refutational-same defense derives its efficacy from both components, the threatening mention and the reassuring refutation of attacking arguments. But the refutational-different derives its efficacy mainly from the first component. From this now-familiar analysis, two interaction predictions follow.

The first prediction deals solely with the single defenses and involves an interaction between the active vs. passive variable and the refutational-same vs. -different variable. As discussed above, the active defense more effectively supplies the threatening motivational component and the passive better supplies the reassuring refutational content. Stringing together these various assumptions into a polysyllogism, we can derive the conclusion that for refutational-same defenses, the passive defense will be superior to the active, but for the refutational-different defenses, the active will be superior to the passive.

183

The second prediction, dealing with an interaction between the single vs. double variable and the refutational-same vs. -different variable, is reached through reasoning very similar to the above. The attacking arguments are refuted less well in the single defense and, hence, the single defense supplies the motivation-inducing threatening component more effectively, while the double (active plus passive) defense more effectively supplies the reassuring refutational content. By again stringing together a polysyllogism of assumptions, we derive the following prediction: for refutational-same defenses, the double defense will be superior to the single, but for the refutational-different defense the single will be superior to the double.

2. *Method.* To test these two hypotheses within a single design, we used six refutational defense conditions: active-only, passive-only and active-plus-passive, each of these three being further dichotomized into refutational-same and refutational-different. (No supportive defenses were used in this study.) The second session, in which the usual attacking essays were presented, came 2 days later. There were also attack-only and neither-defense-nor-attack control conditions. A total of 168 college students served in both sessions, each furnishing data for four different conditions. Further details regarding the method can be found in McGuire (1961a).

When the double defenses (active plus passive) were used, the order in which they came was counterbalanced, so that half the subjects first wrote a refutational essay and then read an already prepared one; the other half read such an essay before they wrote their own. In the results reported below, both orders are combined, since the effect of order turned out to be trivial. It should be at least mentioned here, however, that this null effect of order is embarrassing to inoculation theory; on the basis of the same assumptions used throughout these studies, this theory yields a number of predictions regarding order effects. Yet in neither of the two studies designed to test order-effect predictions (McGuire, 1961a,b) were these predictions confirmed. The two studies cited discuss these embarrassing results more fully.

3. *Results.* The prediction regarding the single-defense condition was confirmed, at least in a weak, interaction reformulation. As seen in Table 5, the passive defense is superior to the active for the refutational-same defense, but the reverse is true for the refutational-different defense. Considering the refutational-same

184

and -different conditions separately, the superiority of the passive over the active for the refutational-same defense is significant at the 0·08 level (two-tails), which tends to corroborate the result of the McGuire and Papageorgis (1961) study reported in the previous section; while the predicted reversal for the refutational-different defense, the superiority of the active over the passive, attains the 0·13 level of significance. Combining these two reverse trends, the predicted interaction is significant at the 0·02 level.

Table 5

Final Belief Levels after Combinations of Active and Passive Refutational Defenses and Attacks*†

| Type of attack | Participation in defense | | | |
	Active only	Passive only	Active, then passive	Passive, then active
None	12·94 (48)‡	12·75 (48)	12·57 (24)	13·37 (24)
Same counterarguments	10·66 (48)	11·47 (48)	12·15 (48)	12·18 (48)
Different counterarguments	11·42 (48)	10·62 (48)	10·92 (48)	10·71 (48)

*Control levels: neither-defense-nor-attack = 12·78 (N = 96); attack-only = 8·60 (N = 48).
† 15·00 indicates complete adherence to the truism.
‡ Numbers in parentheses give the number of cases on which cell means were based.

The second prediction regarding the single vs. double defense is also confirmed in its interaction formulation by the present study, as seen in Table 5. For the refutational-same condition, the double defense is sizably superior to the single, the final means being 12·17 and 11·02, respectively, a difference significant at the 0·01 level. For the refutational-different defense, the double is only slightly superior to the single, the means being 10·82, and 11·06, respectively. This predicted interaction effect is significant at the 0·01 level.

References
Anderson, L. R., M.A. Thesis, University of Illinois, Urbana, Illinois, 1962.
Brehm, J. W., and Cohen, A. R., *Explorations in Cognitive Dissonance.* Wiley, New York, 1962.

185

Festinger, L., *A Theory of Cognitive Dissonance*. Row, Peterson, Evanston, Illinois, 1957.

Kelman, H. C., *Human Relations*, **6**, 185–214, 1953.

King, B. T., and Janis, L., *Human Relations*, **9**, 177–86, 1956.

Klapper, J. T., 'Effects of the Mass Media'. Bureau of Applied Social Research, Columbia University (mimeo), New York, 1949.

Klapper, J. T., *Effects of Mass Communication*. Free Press, Glencoe, Illinois, 1960.

McGuire, W. J., *J. Abnorm. Soc. Psych.*, **63**, 326–32, 1961a.

McGuire, W. J., *Sociometry*, **24**, 184–97, 1961b.

McGuire, W. J., Threat and reassurance as factors in conferring resistance to persuasion. (In preparation.) 1963a.

McGuire, W. J., Cross-issue generalization of conferred resistance to persuasion. Unpublished manuscript. 1963c.

McGuire, W. J., and Papageorgis, D., *J. Abnorm. Soc. Psych.*, **62**, 327–37, 1961.

McGuire, W. J., and Papageorgis, D., *Public Opinion Quarterly*, **26**, 24–34, 1962.

Papageorgis, D., and McGuire, W. J., *J. Abnorm. Soc. Psych.*, **62**, 475–81, 1961.

Steiner, I. D., *J. Abnorm. Soc. Psych.*, **65**, 266–7, 1962.

18   A. E. Siegel and S. Siegel

Reference Groups, Membership Groups and
Attitude Change*

Reprinted from: A. E. Siegel and S. Siegel, *Journal of Abnormal and Social Psychology*, American Psychological Association, U.S.A., 1957, Vol. 55, pp. 360–4.

In social psychological theory, it has long been recognized that an individual's *membership groups* have an important influence on the values and attitudes he holds. More recently, attention has also been given to the influence of his *reference groups*: the groups in which he aspires to attain or maintain membership. In a given area, membership groups and reference groups may or may not be identical. They are identical when the person aspires to *maintain* membership in the group of which he is a part; they are disparate when the group in which the individual aspires to *attain* membership is one in which he is not a member. It has been widely asserted that both membership and reference groups affect the attitudes held by the individual.[4]

The present study is an examination of the attitude changes which occur over time when reference groups and membership groups are identical and when they are disparate. The study takes advantage of a field experiment which occurred in the social context of the lives of the subjects, concerning events considered vital by them. The subjects were not aware that their membership and reference groups were of research interest; in fact, they did not know that the relevant information about these was available to the investigators.

The field experiment permitted a test of the general hypothesis that both the amount and the direction of a person's attitude change over time depends on the attitude norms of his membership group (whether or not that group is chosen by him) and on the attitude norms of his reference group.

This hypothesis is tested with subjects who shared a common

* The investigation reported in this article and the theory which gave rise to the hypotheses are of relevance to the previous section of the book, 'Focus on Origins'. In particular, Siegel and Siegel, in studying attitude change in college students in a natural setting, reveal a part of the process which Freedman, in his study of six decades, attempts to see in broader perspective. – Eds.

reference group at the time of the initial assessment of attitudes. They were then randomly assigned to alternative membership groups, some being assigned to the chosen group and others to a nonchosen group. Attitudes were reassessed after a year of experience in these alternative membership groups with divergent attitude norms. During the course of the year, some subjects came to take the imposed (initially nonpreferred) membership group as their reference group. Attitude change after the year was examined in terms of the membership group and reference group identifications of the subjects at that time.

The Field Experiment

The Ss of this study were women students at a large private coeducational university. The study was initiated shortly before the end of their freshman year, when they all lived in the same large freshman dormitory to which they had been assigned upon entering the university. At this university, all women move to new housing for their sophomore year. Several types of housing are available to them: a large dormitory, a medium-sized dormitory, several very small houses which share common dining facilities, and a number of former sorority houses which have been operated by the university since sororities were banished from the campus. These latter are located among the fraternity houses on Fraternity Row, and therefore known as 'Row houses'. Although the Row houses are lower in physical comfort than most of the other residences for women, students consider them higher in social status. This observation was confirmed by a poll of students (5, p. 205), in which over 90% of the respondents stated that Row houses for women were higher in social status than non-Row houses, the remaining few disclaiming any information concerning status differences among women's residences.

In the spring of each year, a 'drawing' is held for housing for the subsequent year. All freshmen must participate in this drawing, and any other student who wishes to change her residence may participate. It is conducted by the office of the Dean of Women, in cooperation with woman student leaders. Any participant's ballot is understood to be secret. The woman uses the ballot to rank the houses in the order of her preference. After submitting this ballot, she draws a number from the hopper. The rank of that number determines the likelihood that her preference will be satisfied.

In research reported earlier,[5] a random sample was drawn from the population of freshman women at this university, several tests were administered to the Ss in that sample, and (unknown to the Ss) their housing preferences for the forthcoming sophomore year were observed by the investigator. The Ss were characterized as 'high status oriented' if they listed a Row house as their first choice, and were characterized as 'low status oriented' if they listed a non-Row house as their first choice. The hypothesis under test, drawn from reference group theory and from theoretical formulations concerning authoritarianism, was that high status orientation is a correlate of authoritarianism. The hypothesis was confirmed: freshman women who listed a Row house as their first choice for residence scored significantly higher on the average in authoritarianism, as measured by the E-F scale[1, 2] than did women who listed a non-Row house as their first choice. The present study is a continuation of the one described, and uses as its Ss only those members of the original sample who were 'high status oriented', i.e. preferred to live in a Row house for the sopho-more year. In the initial study,[5] of the 95 Ss whose housing choices were listed, 39 were 'high status oriented', i.e. demonstrated that the Row was their reference group by giving a Row house as their first choice in the drawing. Of this group, 28 were available to serve as Ss for the follow-up or 'change' study which is the topic of the present paper. These women form a homogeneous subsample in that at the conclusion of their freshman year they shared a com-mon membership group (the freshman dormitory) and a common reference group (the Row). These Ss, however, had divergent experiences during their sophomore year: nine were Row resid-ents during that year (having drawn sufficiently small numbers in the housing drawing to enable them to be assigned to the group of their choice) and the other 19 lived in non-Row houses during that year (having drawn numbers too large to enable them to be assigned to the housing group of their choice).

E-F scores were obtained from each of the 28 Ss in the course of a large-scale testing program administered to most of the women students at the university. Anonymity was guaranteed to the Ss, but a coding procedure permitted the investigators to identify each respondent and thereby to isolate the Ss and compare each S's second E-F score with her first.

To prevent the Ss from knowing that they were participating in a follow-up study, several procedures were utilized: (a) many persons who had not served in the earlier study were included in the second sample, (b) the testing was introduced as being part of a nation-wide study to establish norms, (c) the test administrators were different persons from those who had administered the initial tests, (d) Ss who informed the test administrator that they had already taken the 'Public Opinion Questionnaire' (E-F scale) were casually told that this did not disqualify them from participating in the current study.

The Ss had no hint that the research was in any way related to their housing arrangements. Testing was conducted in classrooms as well as in residence, and all procedures and instructions were specifically designed to avoid any arousal of the salience of the housing groups in the frame of reference of the research.

The annual housing drawing was conducted three weeks after the sophomore-year testing, and, as usual, each woman's housing ballot was understood to be secret. In this drawing, each S had the opportunity to change her membership group, although a residence move is not required at the end of the sophomore year as it is at the end of the freshman year. If an S participated in this drawing, the house which she listed as her first choice on the ballot was identified by the investigators as her reference group. If she did not, it was evident that the house in which she was currently a member was the one in which she chose to continue to live, i.e. was her reference group. With the information on each S's residence choice at the end of her freshman year, her assigned residence for her sophomore year, and her residence choice at the end of her sophomore year, it was possible to classify the subjects in three categories:

A. Women ($n = 9$) who had gained assignment to live on the Row during their sophomore year and who did not attempt to draw out of the Row at the end of that year;
B. Women ($n = 11$) who had not gained assignment to a Row house for the sophomore year and who drew for a Row house again after living in a non-Row house during the sophomore year; and
C. Women ($n = 8$) who had not gained assignment to a Row house for the sophomore year, and who chose to remain in a non-Row house after living in one during the sophomore year.

For all three groups of Ss, as we have pointed out, membership group (freshman dormitory) and reference group (Row house) were common at the end of the freshman year. For Group A, membership and reference groups were identical throughout the sophomore year. For Group B, membership and reference groups were disparate throughout the sophomore year. For Group C, membership and reference groups were initially disparate during the sophomore year but became identical because of a change in reference groups.

As will be demonstrated, the Row and the non-Row social groups differ in attitude norms, with Row residents being generally more authoritarian than non-Row residents. From social psychological theory concerning the influence of group norms on individuals' attitudes, it would be predicted that the different group identifications during the sophomore year of the three groups of Ss would result in differential attitude change. Those who gained admittance to a Row house for the sophomore year (Group A) would be expected to show the least change in authoritarianism, for they spent that year in a social context which reinforced their initial attitudes. Group C Ss would be expected to show the greatest change in authoritarianism, a change associated not only with their membership in a group (the non-Row group) which is typically low in authoritarianism, but also with their shift in reference groups, from Row to non-Row, i.e. from a group normatively higher in authoritarianism to a group normatively lower. The extent of attitude change in the Ss in Group B would be expected to be intermediate, due to the conflicting influences of the imposed membership group (non-Row) and of the unchanged reference group (Row). The research hypothesis, then, is that between the time of the freshman-year testing and the sophomore-year testing, the extent of change in authoritarianism will be least in Group A, greater in Group B, and greatest in Group C. That is, in extent of attitude change, Group A < Group B < Group C.

Results

Group norms

From the data collected in the large-scale testing program, it was possible to determine the group norms for authoritarian attitudes among the Row and the non-Row women at the university. The E-F scale was administered to all available Row residents ($n = 303$) and to a random sample of residents of non-Row houses ($n = 101$). These Ss were sophomores, juniors, and seniors. The mean E-F score of the Row women was 90, while the mean E-F score of the non-Row was 81. The E-F scores of the two groups were demonstrated to differ at the $p < 0.001$ level ($\chi^2 = 11.1$) by the median test (6, pp. 111–116), a non-parametric test, the data for which are shown in Table 1.

Attitude change

The central hypothesis of this study is that attitude change will occur differentially in Groups A, B, and C, and that it will occur in the direction which would be predicted from knowledge of the group norms among Row and non-Row residents in general. The

Table 1

Frequencies of E-F Scores Above and Below Common Median for Row and Non-Row Residents

	Residents of Non-Row Houses	Residents of Row Houses	
Above Median	36	166	202
Below Median	65	137	202
Total	101	303	404

28 Ss of this study had a mean E-F score of 102 at the end of their freshman year. The data reported above concerning authoritarianism norms for all women residing on campus would lead to the prediction that in general the Ss would show a reduction in authoritarianism during the sophomore year but that this reduction would be differential in the three groups; from the knowledge that Row residents generally are higher in authoritarianism than non-Row residents, the prediction based on social group theory would be that Group A would show the smallest reduction in authoritarianism scores, Group B would show a larger reduction, and Group C would show the largest reduction. The data which permit a test of this hypothesis are given in Table 2. The Jonckheere test,[3] a nonparametric k-sample test which tests the null hypothesis that the three groups are from the same population against the alternative hypothesis that they are from different populations which are ordered in a specified way, was used with these data. By that test, the hypothesis is confirmed at the $p < 0.025$ level.

Discussion

Substantively, the present study provides experimental verification of certain assertions in social group theory, demonstrating that attitude change over time is related to the group identification of the person – both his membership group identification and his reference group identification. The hypothesis that extent of attitude change would be different in the three subgroups of Ss, depending on their respective membership group and reference group identifications, is confirmed at the $p < 0.025$ level; in extent of change in authoritarianism, Group A < Group B < Group C, as predicted.

192

Table 2

Freshman-Year and Sophomore-Year E-F Scores of Subjects

Group	E-F Score End of Freshman Year	End of Sophomore Year	Difference
A	108	125	−17
	70	78	−8
	106	107	−1
	92	92	0
	80	78	2
	104	102	2
	143	138	5
	110	92	18
	114	80	34
B	76	117	−41
	105	107	−2
	88	82	6
	109	97	12
	98	83	15
	112	94	18
	101	82	19
	114	93	21
	104	81	23
	116	91	25
	101	74	27
C	121	126	−5
	87	79	8
	105	95	10
	97	81	16
	96	78	18
	108	73	35
	114	77	37
	88	49	39

Another way of looking at the data may serve to highlight the influence of membership groups and reference groups. At the end of the freshman year, the Ss in Groups A, B, and C shared the same membership group and the same reference group. During the sophomore year, the Ss in Group A shared one membership group while those in Groups B and C together shared another. From membership group theory, it would be predicted that the extent of

193

attitude change would be greater among the latter Ss. This hypothesis is supported by the data (in Table 2): by the Mann-Whitney test (6, pp. 116–127), the change scores of these two sets of Ss (Group A versus Groups B and C together) differ in the predicted direction at the $p < 0.025$ level. This finding illustrates the influence of *membership* groups on attitude change. On the other hand, at the conclusion of the sophomore year, the Ss in Groups A and B shared a common reference group while those in Group C had come to share another. From reference group theory, it would be predicted that attitude change would be more extensive among the subjects who had changed reference groups (Group C) than among those who had not. This hypothesis is also supported by the data (in Table 2): by the Mann-Whitney test, the change scores of these two sets of Ss (Groups A and B together versus Group C) differ in the predicted direction at the $p < 0.05$ level. This finding illustrates the influence of *reference* groups on attitude change. Any inference from this mode of analysis (as contrasted with the main analysis of the data, by the Jonckheere test) must be qualified because of the nonindependence of the data on which the two Mann-Whitney tests are made, but it is mentioned here to clarify the role which membership and reference groups play in influencing attitude change.

The findings may also contribute to our understanding of processes affecting attitude change. The imposition of a membership group does have some effect on an individual's attitudes, even when the imposed group is not accepted by the individual as his reference group. This relationship is shown in the case of Group B. If the person comes to accept the imposed group as his reference group, as was the case with the Ss in Group C, then the change in his attitudes toward the level of the group norm is even more pronounced.

Methodologically, the study has certain features which may deserve brief mention. First, the study demonstrates that it is possible operationally to define the concept of reference group. The act of voting by secret ballot for the group in which one would like to live constitutes clear behavioral specification of one's reference group, and it is an act whose conceptual meaning can be so directly inferred that there is no problem of reliability of judgment in its categorization by the investigator. Second, the study demonstrates that a field study can be conducted which contains the critical feature of an experiment that is usually lacking in naturalistic situations: randomization. The determination of whether or not a woman student would be assigned to the living group of her choice was based on a random event: the size of the number she drew from the hopper. This fact satisfied the requirement that the treatment condition be randomized, and permitted sharper inferences than can usually be drawn from field studies. Third, the test behavior on which the conclusions of this study were based occurred in a context in which the salience of membership and reference groups was *not* aroused and in which no external sanctions from the relevant groups were operative. This feature of the design permitted the interpretation that the E-F scores represented the Ss' internalized attitudes (4, p. 218). Finally, the use of a paper-and-pencil measure of attitude and thus of attitude change, rather than the use of some more behavioral measure, is a deficiency of the present study. Moreover, the measure which was used suffers from a well-known circularity, based on the occurrence of pseudo-low scores (1, pp. 771; 5, pp. 221–222).

Summary

In the social context of the lives of the subjects, and in a natural social experiment which provided randomization of the relevant condition effects, the influence of both membership and reference groups on attitude change was assessed. All subjects shared a common reference group at the start of the period of the study. When divergent membership groups with disparate attitude norms were socially imposed on the basis of a random event, attitude change in the subjects over time was a function of the normative attitudes of both imposed membership groups and the individuals' reference groups. The greatest attitude change occurred in subjects who came to take the imposed, initially nonpreferred, membership group as their reference group.

References

1. Adorno, T. W., Frenkel-Brunswick, Else, Levinson, D. J., and Sanford, R. N., *The authoritarian personality*. New York: Harper, 1950.
2. Gough, H. G., Studies of social intolerance: I. Some psychological and sociological correlates of anti-Semitism. *J. Soc. Psychol.*, **33**, 237–46, 1951.
3. Jonckheere, A. R., A distribution-free k-sample test against ordered alternatives. *Biometrika*, **41**, 133–45, 1954.
4. Sherif, M., and Sherif, Carolyn W., *Groups in harmony and tension*. New York: Harper, 1953.
5. Siegel, S., Certain determinants and correlates of authoritarianism. *Genet. Psychol. Monogr.*, **49**, 187–229, 1954.
6. Siegel, S., *Nonparametric statistics for the behavioral sciences*. New York: McGraw-Hill, 1956.

19   R. J. Lifton

Thought Reform of Chinese Intellectuals

Excerpts from: R. J. Lifton, *Journal of Social Issues*, Society for the
Psychological Study of Social Issues, U.S.A., 1957, Vol. 13, pp. 5–20.

The Chinese Communist program of *Szu Hsiang Kai Tsao* or
'thought reform' is unique both as a social experiment and as a
laboratory for cross-cultural psychiatric study. Applied to Westerners and Chinese, to professors, students, and peasants, it combines
a remarkably widespread dissemination with impressive emotional
force and depth.

It is a subject which has received much attention in this country
(under the popular term 'brainwashing') when involving such
groups as American prisoners of war and other incarcerated
Westerners. But there has been surprisingly little systematic
psychological investigation of the thought reform procedures
which the Chinese have employed with their own people, particularly with their intellectuals.

The most intensive of these all-Chinese thought reform programs
for intellectuals is that conducted in the 'revolutionary colleges' –
set up all over China immediately after the Communist takeover.
These were particularly active between 1948 and 1952, when they
represented an ideological hard core for the entire thought reform
movement, an extreme model for reform efforts throughout the
population. Their techniques – which I will here attempt to
describe and interpret – can give us a key to the understanding
of all Chinese thought reform programs, whether applied to
Chinese intellectuals, United Nations prisoners of war, or
Western missionaries.

The material is drawn from seventeen months of psychiatric
research into the overall problem of thought reform, which I
conducted in the British Crown colony of Hong Kong from February 1954 to June 1955. I interviewed twenty-five Westerners* and
fifteen Chinese intellectuals who had experienced some type of
thought reform on the Chinese mainland prior to fleeing to Hong
Kong. Some of the Chinese, whose interview data contributed to
this paper, were seen for as many as eighty hours over the entire
seventeen-month period, others for just a few sessions. But where-

* Results of this work with Westerners have been presented elsewhere.[7, 8]

ever possible I sought to work intensively with relatively few subjects, rather than superficially with many.

I conducted most of the interviews through an interpreter; only in a few cases was this unnecessary, when the subject had a fluent knowledge of English through exposure to a Westernized education. I will not discuss here the rather interesting ramifications of this three-way communication system, but I found that when I was able to work with a subject over a long period of time, a meaningful relationship could be established and reliable material obtained. Shorter-term contacts – because of the language and cultural barriers, and the stresses of the Hong Kong political atmosphere – were apt to be much less productive, and at times even misleading. I was also able to obtain useful information through talks with a few Chinese who had been on the 'reforming' end of the process, in faculty and Communist Party positions. Personal interviews were always the major focus of the work, but I supplemented these through study of relevant documents and Chinese cultural material. And even more invaluable was the constant advice and collaboration offered to me by numerous scholars, Chinese and Western, in the China field. It is my hope in this paper and in future work – through applying a psychiatric perspective to East Asian cultural problems – to be able to make some contribution in return.

The Revolutionary College

Who attends a revolutionary college? Students are drawn from many divergent sources: former KMT officials and affiliates, teachers who had been associated with the old régime, Communist cadres who had demonstrated significant 'errors' in their work or thoughts, party members who had spent long periods of time in KMT areas, students returning from the West, and finally, arbitrarily selected groups of university instructors or recent graduates. Many in these groups came in response to thinly veiled coercion – the strong 'suggestion' that they attend; but others actively sought admission on a voluntary basis, in order to try to fit in with the requirements of the new régime, or at least to find out what was expected of them.

The college itself is tightly organized along Communist principles of 'democratic centralism'. One center may contain as many as 4,000 students, subdivided into sections of about 1,000 each, then classes of 100–200 each, and finally into six- to ten-man groups. The president of the institution may be a well known scholar serving as a figurehead; technically below him in rank are a vice-president and the section heads, who are likely to be Communist Party members, and exert the real authority at the center. Under their supervision are the class heads, each of whom works with three special cadres.

These cadres, usually long-standing and dedicated party workers, play a central role in the thought reform process; they are the connecting link between the faculty and the students, and it is they who perform the day-to-day leg work of the reform process. The three cadres of each class may be designated according to function: the executive cadre, concerned essentially with courses of study; the organizing cadre, most intimately involved with the structure and function of the small group and the attitudes of the individual students who make them up; and the advisory cadre – the only one of the three who may be a woman – offering counsel on personal and ideological problems which come up during this arduous experience.

I have divided the six-month reform course into three stages, which represent the successive psychological climates to which the student is exposed as he is guided along the path of his symbolic death and rebirth: The Great Togetherness, The Closing in of the Milieu, and Submission and Rebirth.

The Great Togetherness: Group Identification

New students approach the course with a varying mixture of curiosity, enthusiasm and apprehension. When a group of them arrives, their first impression is likely to be a favorable one. They encounter an atmosphere which is austere, but friendly – an open area of low-slung wooden buildings (frequently converted from military barracks) which serve as living quarters and class rooms – old students and cadres greeting them warmly, showing them around, speaking glowingly of the virtues of the Revolutionary College, of the Communist movement, of the new hope for the future. Then, after a warm welcoming speech from the president of the college, they are organized into ten-man study groups. And for a period of from a few days to two weeks they are told to 'just get to know each other'.

Students are surprised by this free and enthusiastic atmosphere; some among the older ones may remain wary, but most are caught up in a feeling of camaraderie. Within the small groups they vent their widely-shared hostility towards the old régime – an important stimulus to the thought reform process. There is a frank exchange of feeling and ideas, past and present, as they discuss their background experiences, and hopes and fears for the future[1]

There is an air of optimism, a feeling of being in the same boat, a high *esprit de corps*.

Next, through a series of 'thought mobilization' lectures and discussions, the philosophy and rationale of the program are impressed upon the individual student: the 'old society' was evil and corrupt; this was so because it was dominated by the 'exploiting classes' – the landowners and the bourgeoisie; most intellectuals come from these 'exploiting classes' (or from the closely related petit-bourgeoisie) and therefore retain 'evil remnants' of their origins and of the old régime; each must now rid himself of these 'ideological poisons' in order to become a 'new man' in the 'new society'. In this way, he is told, the 'ideology of all classes' can be brought into harmony with 'objective material conditions'.[1] Mao Tse-tung is frequently quoted in his references to 'diseases in thought and politics' which require 'an attitude of "saving men by curing their diseases"'.[2]

At this time, and throughout the program, *thought reform is presented to the student as a morally uplifting, harmonizing, and therapeutic experience*.

Then the formal courses begin – the first usually entitled The History of the Development of Society (to be later followed by Lenin on the State and Materialistic Dialects, History of the Chinese Revolution, Theory of the New Democracy, and Field Study – visits to old Communist workshops and industrial centers). The subject matter is introduced by a two- to six-hour lecture delivered by a leading Communist theorist. This is followed by the interminable *hsueh hsi* or study sessions within the ten-man group, where the real work of thought reform takes place. Discussion of the lecture material is led by the group leader who has been elected by its members – usually because of his superior knowledge of Marxism. At this point he encourages a spirited exchange of all views, and takes no side when there is disagreement. The other students realize that the group leader is making daily reports to a cadre or to the class head, but the full significance of these is not yet appreciated; they may be viewed as simply a necessary organizational procedure. Most students retain a feeling of pulling together toward a common goal in a group crusading spirit.

The Closing in of the Milieu: The Period of Emotional Conflict

About four to six weeks from the beginning of thought reform – at about the time of the completion of the first course – a change begins to develop in the atmosphere. With the submission of the first 'thought summary' (these must be prepared after each course) there is a shift in emphasis from the intellectual and ideological to the personal and the emotional. The student begins to find that he, rather than the Communist doctrine, is the object of study. A pattern of criticism, self-criticism, and confession develops – pursued with increasing intensity throughout the remainder of the course.

Now the group leader is no longer 'neutral'; acting upon instructions from above, he begins to 'lean to one side', to support the 'progressive elements', to apply stronger pressures in the direction of reform. He and the 'activists' who begin to emerge take the lead in setting the tone for the group. The descriptions of past and present attitudes which the student so freely gave during the first two weeks of the course now come back to haunt him. Not only his ideas, but his underlying motivations are carefully scrutinized. Failure to achieve the correct 'materialistic viewpoint', 'proletarian standpoint', and 'dialectical methodology' is pointed out, and the causes for this deficiency are carefully analyzed.

Criticisms cover every phase of past and present thought and behavior; they not only 'nip in the bud' the slightest show of unorthodoxy or non-conformity, but they also point up 'false progressives' – students who outwardly express the 'correct' views without true depth of feeling. Group members are constantly on the look-out for indications in others of lack of real involvement in the process. Each must demonstrate the genuineness of his reform through continuous personal enthusiasm and active participation in the criticism of his fellow students. In this way he can avoid being rebuked for 'failure to combine theory with practice'.

Standard criticisms repeatedly driven home include: 'individualism' – placing personal interests above those of 'the people' – probably the most emphasized of all; 'subjectivism' – applying a personal viewpoint to a problem rather than a 'scientific' Marxist approach; 'objectivism' – undue detachment, viewing oneself 'above class distinction', or 'posing as a spectator of the new China'; 'sentimentalism' – allowing one's attachment to family or friends to interfere with reform needs, therefore 'carrying about an ideological burden' (usually associated with reluctance to denounce family members or friends allegedly associated with the 'exploiting classes'). And in addition: 'deviationism', 'opportunism', 'dogmatism', 'reflecting exploiting class ideology', 'overly technical viewpoint', 'bureaucratism', 'individual heroism', 'revisionism', 'departmentalism', 'sectarianism', 'idealism', and 'pro-American outlook'.

The student is required to accept these criticisms gratefully when they are offered. But more than this, he is expected both to anticipate and expand upon them through the even more important device of *self-criticism*. He must correctly analyze his own thoughts and actions, and review his past life – family, educational, and social – in order to uncover the source of his difficulties. And the resulting insights are always expressed within the Communist jargon – corrupt 'ruling class' and 'bourgeois' influence derived from his specific class origin.

The criticism and self-criticism process is also extended into every aspect of daily life, always with a highly moralistic tone. Under attack here are the 'bourgeois' or 'ruling class' characteristics of pride, conceit, greed, competitiveness, dishonesty, boastfulness, and rudeness. Relationships with the opposite sex are discussed and evaluated, solely in terms of their effects upon the individual's progress in reform. Where a 'backward' girl friend is thought to be impeding his progress, a student may be advised to break off a liaison; but if both are 'progressive', or if one is thought to be aiding the other's progress, the relationship will be condoned. Sexual contacts are, on the whole, discouraged, as it is felt that they drain energies from the thought reform process.

The student must, within the small group, *confess* all the evils of his past life. Political and moral considerations here become inextricably merged; but especially emphasized are any 'reactionary' affiliations with the old régime or with its student organizations. Each student develops a running confession, supplemented by material from his self-criticisms and 'thought summaries'; its content becomes widely known to students, cadres and class heads, and it serves as a continuous indicator of his progress in reform.

Most are caught up in the universal *confession compulsion* which sweeps the environment: students vie to outdo each other in the frankness, completeness, and luridness of their individual confessions; one group challenges another to match its collective confessions; personal confession is the major topic of discussion at small group meetings, large student gatherings, informal talks with cadres, and in articles in wall newspapers. Everywhere one encounters the question: 'Have you made your full confession?'

Confession tensions are brought to a head through a mass, prearranged, revival-like gathering where a student with a particularly evil past is given the opportunity to redeem himself. Before hundreds, or even thousands, of fellow students he presents a lurid description of his past sins: political work with the Nationalists, anti-Communist activities, stealing money from his company, violating his neighbor's daughter. He expresses relief at 'washing away all of my sins', and gratitude toward the government for allowing him to 'become a new man'.

As the months pass 'progressives' and 'activists' take increasing leadership, aided by group manipulations by cadres and class heads. Where a group leader is not sufficiently effective, if his reports to the class head are not considered satisfactory, or where there is a general 'lagging behind' in a particular group – a re-shuffling of groups is engineered from above. The weak group becomes reinforced by the addition of one or two 'activists', and the former group leader, in his new group, is reduced to the level of an ordinary student. Although group leaders may still be elected by the students, these shifts can insure that this position is always held by one considered 'progressive' and 'reliable'.

At the same time 'backward elements' – students with suspicious backgrounds, whose confessions are not considered thorough enough, who do not demonstrate adequate enthusiasm in reforming themselves and criticizing others, whose *attitudes* are found wanting – are singled out for further attention. Such a student becomes the target for relentless criticism in his group; and during odd hours he is approached by other students and cadres in attempts to persuade him to mend his ways. Should he fail to respond, friendliness gives way to veiled threats, and he may be called in to receive an official admonition from a class head. As a last resort, he may be subjected to the ultimate humility of a mass 'struggle' meeting: in ritualistic form, he is publicly denounced by faculty members, cadres, and fellow students – his deficiencies reiterated and laid bare. It becomes quite clear that his future in Communist China is indeed precarious, and the ceremony serves as a grim warning for other students of questionable standing.

In response to all of these pressures no student can avoid experiencing some degree of fear, anxiety, and conflict. Each is disturbed over what he may be hiding, worried about how he may come out of this ordeal. Some, recalling either stories they have heard or personal experiences, find revived in their minds images of the extreme measures used by the Communists in dealing with their enemies. All are extremely fearful of the consequences of being considered a 'reactionary'.

Students who show signs of emotional disturbance are encouraged to seek help by talking over their 'thought problem' with the advisory cadre, in order to resolve whatever conflicts exist. Many experience psychosomatic expressions of their problems – fatigue, insomnia, loss of appetite, vague aches and pains, or gastro-intestinal symptoms. Should they take their complaints to the college doctor, they are apt to encounter a reform-oriented and psychologically-sophisticated reply: 'There is nothing wrong with your body. It must be your thoughts that are sick. You will feel better when you have solved your problems and completed your reform.' And, indeed, most students are in a state of painful inner tension; relief is badly needed.

Submission and 'Rebirth'

The last stage – that of the over-all thought summary or final confession – supplies each student with a means of resolving his conflicts. It is ushered in by a mass meeting at which high Communist officials and faculty members emphasize the importance of the final thought summary as the crystallization of the entire course. Group sessions over the next two or three days are devoted exclusively to discussions of the form this summary is to take. It is to be a life history, beginning two generations back, and extending through the reform experience. It must, with candor and thoroughness, describe the historical development of one's thoughts, and the relationship of these to actions. It is also to include a detailed analysis of the personal effects of thought reform.

The summary may be from five to twenty-five thousand Chinese characters (roughly equivalent numerically to English words) and require about ten days of preparation. Each student then must read his summary to the group, where it is subjected to more prolonged and penetrating criticism. He may be kept under fire for several days of detailed discussion and painful revision – as every group member is considered responsible for the approval of each confession presented, and all may even have to place their signatures upon it.

The confession is the student's final opportunity to bring out anything he has previously held back, as well as to elaborate upon everything he has already said. It always includes a detailed analysis of class origin. And in almost every case its central feature is the denunciation of the father – both as a symbol of the exploiting classes, and as an individual. The student usually finds the recitation of his father's personal, political, and economic abuses to be the most painful part of his entire thought reform. He may require endless prodding, persuasion, and indirect threats before he is able to take this crucial step. But he has little choice, and he almost invariably complies.

The confession ends with an emphasis on personal liabilities which still remain, attitudes in need of further reform – and the solemn resolve to continue attempts at self-improvement, and to devotedly serve the régime in the future. When his confession is approved, the student experiences great emotional relief. He has weathered the thought reform ordeal, renounced his past, and established an organic bond between himself and the government. His confession will accompany him throughout his future career as a permanent part of his personal record.

It is no wonder that this period of the final thought summary is frequently referred to as 'taking a bath'. It is the symbolic submission to the régime, and at the same time the expression of individual rebirth into the Chinese Communist community.

Psychological Principles

What are the most important psychological principles of this thought reform process as it bears down upon the Chinese intellectual? These could be expressed from many points of view, but I will here briefly discuss the five general areas which I consider to be of greatest significance. The analysis must be derived, of course, from the manner in which I see the process through my own Western eyes. I make no claim that the Chinese Communists would themselves view it in the same fashion; indeed, we can be quite sure that their theoretical frame of reference is related to Marxist doctrine and practice, and would hardly include these psychiatric categories.

Milieu Control

Thought reform creates what is probably the most profoundly controlled and manipulated group environment that has ever existed. During the *hsueh hsi* sessions which take up most of the student's waking hours, his every action, thought, and attitude may be noted by the group leader and reported to a cadre or a faculty member – who may in turn use this knowledge to specify new approaches to be used upon the individual student or upon the group as a whole. And during after-hours there is little relief: since it is considered the duty of each student to help others in their reform, and to make known to the authorities any relevant information, even casual conversations may be reported back.

Little spontaneity of expression can exist, as the student can never be certain that anything he says will not be made use of to bring further pressures to bear against him. He is living in a virtually airtight communication system: he does not leave it, no outside or contradictory ideas come through to him, and he never has the opportunity to weigh objectively a thought or attitude. He is involved in a vast drama in three acts (the three stages described), directed from above in a predetermined sequence, and performed again with a new cast of characters during each six months reform course.

The milieu quickly imposes its values and its language – and the student must live, think, and phrase his ideas solely within this ethical code and semantic vernacular. His environment is so mobilized that it will psychologically support him only if he meets its standards, and will quickly and thoroughly undermine him when he fails to do so. More and more, there is a blending of external and internal milieux, as his own attitudes and beliefs become identical with those of his outer environment.

It is this quality of *milieu control* which gives the thought reform program its awesome effect upon the individual. It is similar to what George Orwell so brilliantly envisioned in his novel, *Nineteen-Eighty-Four*. Orwell – in a Western conception – saw milieu control accomplished through mechanical means, such as the two-way 'telescreen'. But the Chinese have done it through a *human recording and transmitting* apparatus, extending their control more deeply into the student's innermost world. This human form of milieu control, practiced throughout China on a less intensive basis, explains how the Communists are able to maintain such tight reins over their sprawling population without benefit of an advanced mechanical communication system.

Guilt, Shame and Confession

In its stress upon past evils and its demand for confession and reform, thought reform exerts a continuous pressure upon the student toward experiencing a *sense of guilt* – feelings of sinfulness and expectations of punishment. But perhaps an even more potent weapon among Chinese is that of shame.* The 'backward' student or non-conformist is criticized, harassed, rejected, publicly disgraced – a pariah cast out by his fellows. In his loss of 'face' – of social recognition, prestige, and of self-esteem – he cannot help but experience feelings of personal humiliation, of failing to meet the standards of the prevailing group. On the other hand, in

* In this paper I will make no attempt to explore the many important questions which thought reform raises in regard to psychiatric theory – such as the significance of the occurrence of guilt and shame in Chinese culture. The fact that both emotions are effectively employed in the process would tend to add support to Singer's criticisms of the concept of guilt and shame cultures, in which China is customarily placed in the 'shame' category (9). It is true, however, that the sense of shame is the more important sanction in this all-Chinese application of thought reform. For further understanding, it is necessary to compare the inner meanings of these emotions to individual Chinese and Western subjects, which I intend to do in later publications.

complying – informing on others, allowing himself to be publicly exposed, and especially in criticizing his father – he may find that his actions are in conflict with his previous ethical and behavioral standards, and this also leads to feelings of guilt and shame. Either way, as guilt and shame mount within, he may come to feel that his fear and conflicts – in fact all of his emotional pain – are caused by his own evil and worthlessness. He begins to believe that he is deserving of any punishment or rejection which the group may impose, and that he is really in need of reform.

Thus, thought reform plays upon susceptibilities to these two disturbing emotions developed in the student over the course of his lifetime. He can, and indeed he must, find relief through the pre-scribed confession method. Through critically laying himself bare, he finds both an outlet for the pressure valves of guilt and shame, and a means of regaining standing in his environment. The con-fession becomes an inner compulsion, and at the same time a useful and necessary adaptive device. It may contain gross exaggerations, and omit special individual secrets; but it is nonetheless a symbolic expression of atonement and redemption – an act of self-surrender in making one's peace with a demanding milieu.

Group Analysis and Sanction

The *hsueh hsi* or small study group is the vehicle for all thought reform pressures. And in a group-oriented culture like the Chinese – where so much emphasis has always been placed upon group harmony rather than individualistic achievement – this greatly en-hances the effectiveness of the program.

The group has at its disposal a set of psychological principles attributing all personality traits to class origin. Although this has questionable theoretical validity in our eyes, it can be effectively made use of for the purpose of reform. The group also employs approaches which resemble some of those we use in our own psy-chiatric work: depth interpretations, emphasis upon inner feelings, viewing early life influences as important factors in shaping the adult personality, and requiring the person under 'treatment' to bring out most of his own material.

Thought reform manipulations make use of mutual hostilities–as long as these can be harnessed to promote the reform process. He who has been sharply criticized is likely in turn to throw the book at his critic – although this is technically not the 'correct' attitude to show. It is only when these animosities become so marked that they interfere with reform that the authorities will intervene–sometimes through transferring one of the combatants into a different group.

In addition, the group adds a highly-charged morality and an absolute doctrinal authority for the 'correctness' of any solution or point of view. It is difficult indeed for the individual student to stand up to this multi-dimensional approach. He is bound to begin to feel – when he disagrees, meets criticisms, fails to comply, or even has an 'incorrect' thought – that this must be his personal problem; it is he who must give way and 'change'.

Emotional Appeals

Thought reform does not consist entirely of painful experiences; it contains many meaningful psychological satisfactions as well. To an intellectual who had been disaffected from the former régime, dissatisfied and highly confused in his status, thought reform offers much to fill this emotional vacuum. Despite his conflicts, he experiences the 'great togetherness' I have already mentioned – in small groups, in the Communist movement, and in the binding emotions of nationalism. He undergoes the emotional catharsis of personal confession, the relief of saying the unsaid, of holding nothing back. He attains the rewards of self-surrender, of giving up his individual struggles, merging with an all-powerful force, and thereby sharing its strength. And finally – perhaps most important of all – he shares the powerful bond of participation in a great 'moral crusade' – reforming himself, reforming others around him, reforming society, joining in the 'struggle for peace', 'the brotherhood of man', and 'the great Communist future'.

The Shift in Role Behavior and in Personal Identity

Chinese culture and particularly the Chinese family have traditionally emphasized the concept of proper roles: they have concretized specific patterns of behavior which are developed in the individual largely through the expectations and demands of others. For instance, in Chinese life the role of the husband, the wife, the elder brother, the younger brother, the father, the mother, and the daughter have always been clearly typed and well defined. But during the revolutionary ferment of the first half of the twentieth century, many of these patterns came under sharp criticism by vanguard intellectual groups. [5, 6] And in the years prior to the Communist take-over the social and political confusion placed additional strains upon the intellectual in his attempts to reconcile old roles with new ideas – in his concept of who and what he was, or his sense of inner identity. [3, 4] He was torn between such identities as the filial son, the rebellious reformer, and the uninvolved cynic. The Communists seek to resolve this dilemma in each student by supplying a common identity – that of the zealous adherent of the new régime. Of the three former identities, the second (the rebellious reformer) can be made quite compatible with thought reform, the third (the uninvolved cynic) can be easily undermined, but the first (the filial son) has the deepest emotional roots, and stands most in the way of the reform process.

Thus, one of thought reform's major goals is a highly significant shift in role behavior and personal identity – from the filial son or daughter to the enthusiastic participant in the Communist movement. It is dramatically symbolized in the student's denunciation of his father: he must renounce the symbol of the old order and the mainspring of his former identity before he can accomplish his personal upheaval. And he is expected to bring the same 'correct behavior' and loyalty to his new set of allegiances. This is particularly true for younger students, those in their post-adolescence or early adulthood; this is normally a period of *identity crisis*[3] – a time when the individual is most susceptible to ideological or religious conversion – and it has been very much the case with the young Chinese intellectual. The break with his family and his past is his symbolic death – the mystical union with The Government and The People, his rebirth.

Adding up all five of these psychological categories, thought reform bears certain resemblances to emotional experiences with which we are more familiar. In its zeal to 'save souls', its emphasis upon guilt and shame, its demand for atonement, recantation, and reform, it resembles an induced religious conversion. In its analytic procedures and its 'therapeutic' emphasis, it is a coercive form of psychotherapy – unique in *supplying both the disease and the cure*. Through all of these techniques it harnesses the most powerful human emotions in the total manipulation of the individual.

Does this type of 'thought reform' succeed? Do these psychological pressures achieve their aims? Here, we cannot do more than speculate, as the cases at our disposal are only the 'failures' – those who fled. But from their composite descriptions, we may delineate three types of responses: the zealous 'converts', who are the most successful products – particularly among the young; the resistors who felt suffocated by the process, some of whom break away; and the great majority of students, the in-between group – partially convinced, but essentially concerned with adapting themselves to this great stress, and assuring their future under the new régime. Some people in the first and third groups may feel 'purified' and helped by the process, despite the pain they have experienced. On the other hand, some of my subjects who defected had originally been extremely sympathetic to the régime – with them the process had a reverse effect.

The question of belief in abstract theoretical ideas is not the most important one; what counts psychologically is the individual's need to find an identity and a way of life under these existing pressures. He can do this only through some degree of 'reform' – whether from the depths of his soul, in mere outward compliance, or, like most, somewhere in-between.

On the whole, we can say that thought reform seems to develop in most students intellectual and emotional responses which are useful to the Communist régime. *These responses continue to be supported and demanded by the general environment of Communist China long after the course has been completed, and this is a crucial factor in the program's effectiveness.* Thought reform thus accelerates the process by which Marxist doctrine and ethics become the major 'realities' open to the Chinese intellectuals in their struggles to attain harmony with their outer world.

References
1. Ai Ssu-ch'i, On Problems of Ideological Reform. *Hsueh Hsi*, January 1, 1951, *III*, No. 7.
2. Brandt, Conrad, Schwartz, Benjamin, and Fairbank, John K., Correcting Unorthodox Tendencies in Learning, the Party and Literature and Art, *A Documentary History of Chinese Communism*. Cambridge, Massachusetts: Harvard University Press, 392, 1952.
3. Erikson, Erik H., The Problem of Ego Identity. *Journal of the American Psychoanalytic Association*, **4**, 56, 1956.
4. Erikson, Erik H., On the Sense of Inner Identity. *Health and Human Relations*. New York: The Blackstone Co., 1953.
5. Kiang, Wen-Han., *The Chinese Student Movement*. Morningside Heights, New York: Kings Crown Press, 1948.
6. Lang, Olga., *Chinese Family and Society*. New Haven: Yale University Press, 1946.
7. Lifton, Robert J., Chinese Communist 'Thought Reform': The Assault upon Identity and Belief. Presented before the Annual Meeting of the American Psychiatric Association, Chicago, Illinois, May 1956.
8. Lifton, Robert J., 'Thought Reform' of Western Civilians in Chinese Communist Prisons. *Psychiatry*, **19**, 173–95, 1956.
9. Piers, Gerhart, and Singer, Milton B., *Shame and Guilt*. Springfield, Illinois: Charles C. Thomas, 1953.

IV Focus on Behaviour

From time to time the argument is heard that there is little point in studying verbally expressed attitudes in themselves, since we do not know to what extent these may be reflected in the relevant actions or behaviour. The few available empirical studies of the relationship between attitudes and behaviour suggest that the criticism has some justification. It is dangerous to assume that a knowledge of attitudes is in itself predictive of behavioural consequences in specific situations. This does not mean, however, that social scientists should renounce the study of attitudes. What it does imply is a need for theoretical models which do justice to the complexities of the relationships between attitudes and behaviour, and for theory-guided investigations of these relationships. There are some indications in the current literature of attempts towards these ends, but by no means enough, considering the importance of the issue.* DeFleur and Westie, in the first article of this section, comment on the 'paucity of investigations of the overt-action correlates' of verbally expressed attitudes, and themselves report a study of attitude 'salience', an individual's readiness to translate his attitude into overt action in specific social contexts. Janis and King examine experimentally the influence of behaviour on attitudes – striking because their hypothesis that 'saying is believing' reverses what is usually assumed to be the causal direction of the relationship. By experimental intervention in a

* Contributions in other parts of the book are also of interest for this section. Zajonc's review of theories in the next section includes Festinger's dissonance theory, which attempts to take account of discrepancies between private beliefs and public behaviour. The theoretical excerpt from Sarnoff also separates private from public attitudes; and the article by Cook and Selltiz in the final section of the book also touches on the issue. – Eds.

natural group setting, and with the illumination of individual case study materials, Raymond L. Gorden shows how a person's definition of the social situation in which he finds himself influences his public expression of his private opinions.

20 M. L. DeFleur and F. R. Westie

Verbal Attitudes and Overt Acts

Reprinted from: M. L. DeFleur and F. R. Westie, *American Sociological Review*, American Sociological Association, U.S.A., 1958, Vol. 23, pp. 667–73.

In the face of the steady stream of studies of the verbal dimension of attitudinal behavior, the paucity of investigations of the overt-action correlates of such verbal behavior is indeed striking. Those who have conducted attitude research are not surprised by this one-sided emphasis: overt acceptance-avoidance acts are extremely difficult to isolate and measure. One source of this difficulty lies in the fact that few, if any, standardized situations or instruments have been developed enabling the investigator to quantify, on a positive-negative continuum, an acceptance or avoidance act for a set of subjects, with other conditions held constant.[1]

The present paper reports an attempt to develop an instrument which can readily be used in an interview situation for measuring the 'salience' of a person's attitudinal orientations. It also explores the use of reference groups by subjects whose attitudinal salience is being measured. The term *salience* can be defined as the readiness of an individual to translate his (previously expressed verbal) attitude into overt action in relation to the attitude object. The relationship between inner conviction and overt behavior has frequently been discussed in connection with the validity of measures of verbal attitudes. In a thorough summary of the literature, Green[2] comments on this view of attitude measurement validity, pointing out that the validity of an attitude scale is actually the extent to which it truly represents behavior within a particular *attitude universe*. He distinguishes between a verbal attitude universe, from which attitude scale items are drawn, and an action attitude universe, consisting of a variety of overt behavior forms regarding the attitude object. Validity in the measure-mean of an attitude is the problem of determining the degree to which it measures behavior within its appropriate universe; it is not necessarily a problem of determining the extent to which it predicts behavior from one universe to another. In line with this view, the purpose of the present study is not to develop a device for 'validating' other attitude instruments. Its aim rather is to provide a simple device which can be used as an 'action opportunity' for a subject to give public and overt testimony of his acceptance or rejection of a Negro in a specific action context.

Studies of Inconsistency

Earlier studies indicate that a person's verbal acceptance or rejection of minority groups may be quite unrelated to what he actually does or would do in overt interaction situations. For example, in company with a couple from China, LaPiere[3] made an extensive tour of the Pacific Coast and transcontinental United States during which they were accommodated by over 250 restaurants, hotels, and similar establishments. Refusal of service by virtue of the racial characteristics of the Chinese occurred only once. But when LaPiere sent each establishment a letter and questionnaire requesting a statement of its policy regarding accommodating Chinese clients, over 90% of the replies noted that they adhered to a policy of non-acceptance of such minority group members. In these cases, the overt act reversed the stated intention.

In a more recent study of overt behavior or action attitudes by Lohman and Reitzes[4] 151 residents of an urban neighbourhood were located who were also members of a particular labor union. Two conflicting norms regarding behavior toward Negroes prevailed in these two collectivities. The urban neighborhood was predominantly white and was resisting Negro penetration; a property owners' association (of which the subjects were members) had been organized for this purpose. In this behavioral area, that is, with respect to having a Negro for a neighbor, the subjects uniformly acted in an anti-Negro manner. However, the 151 subjects also belonged to a labor union with a clear and well-implemented policy of granting Negroes complete equality on the job. Here, then, with the same subjects and the same attitude object, were two seemingly opposite action forms. An explanation of this situation in terms of individual verbal attitudes would be inadequate. The authors show that each of the formal organizations (the union and property owners' association) provided the individual with a set of well-formulated reasons and justifications for his actions in each of these spheres. Clearly, action attitudes may be determined to a considerable degree by the extent to which the individual is actually or psychologically involved in social systems providing him with norms and beliefs which he can use as guides to action when *specific* action opportunities arise.

In studying attitude salience, then, it may be predicted that individuals faced with the necessity of making an action decision with regard to Negroes will partially determine the direction of this action by consideration of the norms and policies of social groups which are meaningful to them. Ordinarily, we do not expect subjects to be involved in such well-defined groups, with clearly specified policies regarding action toward Negroes, as those studied by Lohman and Reitzes. Norms and guides to action in more ordinary situations are more likely to be derived from family, friends, or other persons used as reference groups. For this reason, the present paper includes a probe into the reference groups invoked in an action decision made by subjects regarding public involvement with Negroes.

In the larger program of experiments, of which the present report is a part, the subjects were studied from the standpoint of the relationship between three dimensions of their attitudinal behavior: verbal, autonomic-physiological, and overt. There were three phases to this research: attitude testing, a laboratory session in which the subjects' autonomic-physiological responses to race stimuli were recorded, and a post-laboratory interview. This paper, however, is concerned only with the relationship between the verbal and overt dimensions and draws its data largely from the post-laboratory interview.

The Summated Differences Scales[5] were administered to 250 students in introductory sociology classes. From the 250 cases, two smaller groups were selected for more intensive study. The distribution of total scores was determined, and from those scoring in the top quartile (indicating the greatest verbal rejection of Negroes) 23 subjects were selected on the basis of eight criteria (noted below). These individuals were carefully matched, by the method of frequency distribution control, with 23 subjects scoring in the lowest quartile (indicating the least verbal rejection of Negroes). The matching process reduced the size of the original group substantially, but 46 subjects were thus carefully selected for their similarity on eight characteristics of their social background. The frequency distributions of the groups were matched according to age, sex (half of each group was male), marital status, religion, social class, social mobility experience, residential history, and previous contact with Negroes. For convenience, we refer to that group showing the greatest verbal rejection of Negroes as the 'prejudiced group', and their counterparts at the opposite end of the verbal scales as the 'unprejudiced group'.

Method

After each subject had completed a laboratory session in which his autonomic responses to race relations stimuli were recorded,[6] he was conducted to an interview room where a variety of questions, devices, and situations were presented to him regarding his feelings about Negroes. Shortly before the end of this hour-long post-laboratory interview the subject was presented with what may be called an 'overt action opportunity'. In the laboratory session, and in earlier phases of the interview, each subject had viewed a number of colored photographic slides showing interracial pairings of males and females. Some of these slides portrayed a well-dressed, good-looking, young Negro man paired with a good-looking, well-dressed, young white woman. Others showed a white man similarly paired with a Negro woman. The background for all of the slides consisted of a table, a lamp, and a window with a drapery, giving an effect not unlike that of a living room or possibly a dormitory lounge. The persons in the photographs were seated beside each other in separate chairs, and were looking at one another with pleasant expressions. The photographer and models had been instructed to strive for a portrayal of cordiality, but not romance.[7] Each of the 46 subjects had given projective interpretations of 'what was happening' in these pictures.

To present the overt action opportunity, the interviewer told each subject that another set of such slides was needed for further research. The subject was first asked if he (or she) would be willing to be photographed with a Negro person of the opposite sex, a request which elicited a wide variety of responses, as well as considerable hesitation in many cases. A number indicated willingness, but others refused categorically to be so photographed. Then, regardless of his (or her) stated position, the subject was presented with a mimeographed form and informed that this was 'a standard *photograph release agreement*, which is necessary in any situation where a photograph of an individual is to be used in any manner'. The photograph release agreement contained a graded series of 'uses' to which the photograph would be put (see Figure 1), ranging from laboratory experiments, such as they had just experienced, to a nationwide publicity campaign advocating racial integration. They were to sign their name to each 'use' which they would permit.[8]

In American society, the affixing of one's signature to a document is a particularly significant act. The signing of checks, contracts, agreements, and the like is clearly understood to indicate a binding obligation on the part of the signer to abide by the

The directors of the experiment you just participated in need more photographs like you saw on the screen (with Negroes and whites posed together). If you will volunteer to pose for such photographs, please indicate the conditions under which you will allow these pictures to be used by signing the 'releases' below. You may sign *some of them, all of them,* or *none of them as you see fit.* (It is standard practice to obtain such a signed release for any kind of photograph which is to be used for some purpose.)

If you are not interested in participating in this phase of the study, you are absolutely free to do as you wish. If you do not want to commit yourself in any way on this matter, it is perfectly all right and we will respect your decision. Whatever you do, your decision will be held in the strictest confidence.

I will pose for a photograph (of the same type as in the experiment) with a Negro person of the opposite sex with the following restrictions on its use:

1. I will allow this photograph to be used in laboratory experiments where it will be seen only by professional sociologists.

    Signed..

2. I will allow this photograph to be published in a technical journal read only by professional sociologists.

    Signed..

3. I will allow this photograph to be shown to a few dozen University students in a laboratory situation.

    Signed..

4. I will allow this photograph to be shown to hundreds of University students as a teaching aid in Sociology classes.

    Signed..

5. I will allow this photograph to be published in the *Student Newspaper* as part of a publicity report on this research.

    Signed..

6. I will allow this photograph to be published in my home town newspaper as part of a publicity report on this research.

    Signed..

7. I will allow this photograph to be used in a nation-wide publicity campaign *advocating racial integration.*

    Signed..

Figure 1 Photograph authorization.

provisions of the document. The signing of the document in the present study took on additional significance due to the involvement of the racial variable.

The problem of the validity and reliability of this device as a measure of the salience of a subject's attitude toward Negroes can be only partially answered at present. Various approaches to establishing the validity of measuring instruments have been discussed in the literature.[9] The question of acceptable criteria of validity for a particular instrument has received many answers, and the entire issue is currently a controversial one. Such validating techniques as the 'known groups' method are unacceptable for measures of salience because the evidence for validity rests upon comparisons of groups on the basis of known *verbal* attitudes. Correlating the instrument with other measures of overt acceptance-avoidance acts would be a useful method, but no standardized instruments exist for such a task.

If the items in an instrument are a reasonably good representation of the items characterizing the attitudinal universe, many investigators would say that the scale is valid by definition, that is, it has *face validity*. The term *intrinsic validity* has been used by Gulliksen to describe this situation.[10] A method which he suggests for at least a preliminary approach to validating an instrument is to employ a group of 'experts' to evaluate the items selected for a measuring device.

In a modified version of Gulliksen's procedure, the series of 'photograph usages' was submitted in random order to eight judges, who were sociologists of faculty status. The judges were asked to rate the usages, ranking first the use to which they felt the prejudiced person would least object. There was almost complete agreement among their rankings: only one judge reversed the order of a single adjacent pair in the 618 pair-judgments. In the eyes of presumably competent specialists, then, the items of the instrument represent an ordered sample of acts which prejudiced persons would object to in regularly increasing degrees.

The items in the instrument were designed and arranged so that they represent a cumulative series, thereby providing an obvious possibility for scaling. This was not undertaken, however, with the present version of the instrument due to the relatively small number of scale items and subjects. Nevertheless, the response patterns show almost complete transitivity: in only three of the 46 cases were there irregularities in the cumulative feature of the instrument. (In these three instances subjects did not sign an item lower on the scale, selecting one with a higher rank.) This pattern is a rough indication that the reproducibility would be rather good if the items were to be scaled. Such evidence of transitivity, of course, gives only a partial answer to the question of reliability, just as the judgments of experts meet only partially the validity problem.

The subjects uniformly perceived the behavioral situation posed for them as a highly realistic request, and many clearly exhibited discomfort at being caught in a dilemma. Wishing to cooperate with the interviewer, they nevertheless preferred to be uninvolved in a photograph with a Negro of opposite sex. There were a few, of course, who were quite willing to sign the agreement and did so without hesitation.

Verbal Prejudice and Overt Acts

The purpose of creating this situation was to provide the subjects opportunity to give public and overt testimony of their acceptance or rejection of Negroes. But the data so obtained also allow a test of the hypothesis that individuals with negative or positive verbal attitudes will act in accord with those attitudes in an overt situation.

The results of the photographic release agreement and its relationship to the verbally elicited attitudinal category of the subjects are given in Table 1. Subjects were classified as falling above or below the mean level of endorsement. The distribution was such that the mean and median fell at identical points.

Table 1

Relationship between Race Attitudes and Level of Signed Agreement to Be Photographed with Negro

Signed Level of Agreement	Subject Attitude	
	Prejudiced	Unprejudiced
Below $\overline{X}$	18	9
Above $\overline{X}$	5	14

Chi square $= 7 \cdot 264$
$p < 0 \cdot 01$

In this situation, there was clearly a greater tendency for the prejudiced persons than the unprejudiced to avoid being photographed with a Negro. The relationship is significant, suggesting some correspondence in this case between attitudes measured by verbal scales and an acceptance-avoidance act toward the attitude object. In spite of the statistical significance, however, there were some prejudiced persons who signed the agreement without hesitation at the highest level, as well as some unprejudiced persons who were not willing to sign at any level. Thus, the relationship between these verbal and overt attitudinal dimensions, while significant, is not a simple one-to-one correspondence. These findings are consistent with much of the earlier research, some of which is described above. The factors which account for this seeming inconsistency need careful exploration.

One possibility of explaining the inconsistency in the present study is to assume that prejudiced subjects who signed at the higher levels and unprejudiced persons who refused to sign were misclassified by the original measurement of verbal attitudes. But this explanation is suspect due to the fact that the individuals used as subjects represent the extremes (upper and lower quartiles) of the verbal attitude distribution. While this does not eliminate the possibility of error, of course, it reduces it considerably. The inadequacy of an explanation on the basis of error alone is also suggested by the distribution in Table 1. Fourteen of forty-six subjects (almost one-third) show behavior patterns in opposition to their verbally elicited attitudes – this is too large a proportion to attribute to measurement errors. The latter, moreover, theoretically are cancelled out by errors in the opposite direction.

The lack of a straight-line relationship between verbal attitudes and overt action behavior more likely may be explained in terms of some sort of social involvement of the subject in a system of social constraints, preventing him from acting (overtly) in the direction of his convictions, or otherwise 'legitimizing' certain behavioral patterns. These channelizing influences on behavior have received theoretical attention in terms of such concepts as 'reference groups', 'other directedness', and 'significant others'.

Reference Groups

Reference groups were cited earlier as possibly an important influence upon the direction of behavior of individuals confronted with action opportunities regarding attitude objects. This possibility accounts for our hypothesis that the act of signing the photograph agreement involves a conscious consideration of reference groups. Thus the subjects were asked, immediately following their response to the document, 'Was there any particular person or group of people (other than the interviewer) who came to mind when you decided to sign (or refused to sign) this document? That is, are there people who you felt would approve or disapprove?' (Since the entire interview was recorded on tape for later study, it was possible to examine carefully the responses to this question.) The majority of the subjects needed little or no prompting for presumably they had certain key groups or individuals clearly in mind when they made their decisions.

Sixty reference groups were identified as being influential in the decision-making of the 46 subjects regarding the signing of the photographic release. Nearly three-fourths of them ($71·8\%$) invoked some type of reference group when faced with this problem, while the remaining fourth ($28·2\%$) apparently made an 'inner-directed' decision. Perhaps significantly, *all* of those who did cite a reference group mentioned some type of peer group, while only a third referred to the family. In all cases the subjects were able to state whether these groups would approve or disapprove of their posing for such a photograph.

Riesman (among others) has discussed the peer group as an important source for behavioral cues and has described the 'other-directed' personality, presumably on the increase in American middle-class society, as a type for which the peer group operates as a predominant director of behavior.[11] Earlier research, for example the Bennington study,[12] has shown that campus groups function as important influences on attitudes. The present findings are consistent with these conclusions.

In summary, verbally expressed attitudes were significantly related to the direction of the action taken by subjects regarding being photographed with a Negro of the opposite sex. On the other hand, a third of the subjects behaved in a manner quite inconsistent with that which might be expected from their verbal attitudes. Whatever the direction of this action, however, it was a *peer-directed* decision for the majority, with the subjects making significant use of their beliefs concerning possible approval or disapproval of reference groups as guides for behavior.

Conclusions

The present findings have at least two implications for further research. First, in order to analyze the relationship between the verbal and action dimensions of attitudes, it may be necessary to add to attitude scales a systematic categorization of the system of social constraints within which individual behavior ordinarily takes place. Thus, analysis of the beliefs of an individual about the attitudes, norms, and values held by his reference groups, significant others, voluntary organizations, peer groups, and the like may be essential for better prediction of individual lines of action with the use of verbal scales. This would represent a more distinctly sociological approach.

Second, a systematic development of standardized *overt action opportunities* may be necessary before an individual can be accurately classified on a positive-negative continuum, concerning a particular attitude object. That is, standardized opportunities for subjects to make overt acceptance-avoidance acts may provide quantitative assessment of the *salience* of attitudes by classifying overt non-verbal action toward an attitude object. The photograph authorization reported here is a crude attempt to classify such action. Further studies of salience could be based on overt action opportunities in small group settings. For example, individuals could be observed and their behavior categorized when given actual opportunities, say, for physical contact with a Negro, to be seen in public with a Negro in primary group settings, or to use physical facilities used by Negroes. Such behavioral settings could provide standardized ways of measuring the action attitudes of subjects placed in such contexts. They could also provide methods for validating measuring instruments such as the one described in this paper.

Methods which require elaborate or cumbersome physical facilities would have limited utility in the practical measurement of attitude salience. Measuring instruments such as the photograph authorization have the advantage of portability. If it can be shown that these measures correlate highly with overt action in standardized small group behavioral situations, their validity can be established more firmly.

Further advances in the prediction of overt behavior from attitude measuring instruments may require both systematic measures of the social anchorages of individual psychological orientations and careful studies of their translation into overt social action. These would probably help to clarify the often perplexing relationship between the verbal and overt action dimensions of attitudinal phenomena.

References and Notes

1. There have been several attempts to develop *hypothetical situations tests* as measures of what subjects thought they might do in hypothetical situations which were described to them. Such statements of belief are not conceptually different from other forms of verbal behavior with which verbal attitudes are measured. See, e.g. A. C. Rosander, 'An Attitude Scale Based Upon Behavior Situations', *Journal of Social Psychology*, 8 (Febru-

ary, 1937), pp. 3–15. Also: C. Robert Pace, 'A Situations Test to Measure Social Political-Economic Attitudes', *Journal of Social Psychology*, 10 (August 1930), pp. 331–44.

2. Bert F. Green, 'Attitude Measurement', in Gardner Lindzey, editor, *Handbook of Social Psychology*, Cambridge, Mass.: Addison-Wesley, 1954, Vol. I, Chapter 9.

3. Richard T. LaPiere, 'Attitudes vs. Actions', *Social Forces*, 13 (December, 1934), pp. 230–7.

4. Joseph D. Lohman and Dietrich C. Reitzes, 'Deliberately Organized Groups and Racial Behavior', *American Sociological Review*, 19 (June, 1954), pp. 342–8.

5. This device employs the principle of eliciting a response to a white person of a given occupational status and then, many pages later, a response to a Negro of the same occupational status, each portrayed in the same hypothetical relationship with the respondent. Numerical differences between the responses to whites and to Negroes are then summed. For example, in one item the respondent is asked to respond (from 'strongly agree' to 'strongly disagree' in five possible categories) to the statement 'I believe I would be willing to have a *Negro Doctor* have his hair cut at the same barber shop in which I have mine cut.' Later, after approximately 200 items have been interposed, he is asked to respond to the statement, 'I believe I would be willing to have a *White Doctor* have his hair cut at the barber shop where I have mine cut.' Thus, a respondent may 'strongly disagree' to one of these propositions and 'agree' to the other. The wide separation between the white and Negro of identical occupation by interposing a great many items provides a concealment factor. The ability of the respondent to remember how he responded earlier is greatly reduced by this control. The difference between the responses is given a numerical value indicating differential acceptance of the white and Negro of the same occupational status in this particular relationship with the respondent. A total of eight occupational categories are involved and a large variety of activities. In all, over 500 responses are elicited from a given subject. The respondent's total score is simply the summated numerical differences between his responses to whites and Negroes of similar occupation in a variety of relationships with the respondent. The total score indicates the extent to which the respondent regards Negroes as objects to be accepted or rejected as compared to whites.

The reliability coefficients of the scales were derived through testing and retesting 99 undergraduate students of Indiana University. The time interval between the test and retest was five weeks. The reliability coefficients were as follows:

Scale I	Residential:	$r = 0.95$
Scale II	Position:	$r = 0.95$
Scale III	Interpersonal-Physical:	$r = 0.80$
Scale IV	Interpersonal-Social:	$r = 0.87$
Combined Scores:		$r = 0.96$

For a detailed discussion of this device, see Frank R. Westie, 'A Technique for the Measurement of Race Attitudes', *American Sociological Review*, 18 (February, 1953), pp. 73–8.

6. These autonomic responses to racial stimuli are described in some detail in a paper forthcoming in the *Journal of Abnormal and Social Psychology*. Briefly, they consist of galvanic skin responses and changes in finger blood volume occurring when prejudiced and unprejudiced subjects viewed photo-

graphic slides portraying Negroes and whites of both sexes shown singly and in all possible pairs. The results indicate that attitudinal responses include changes in the autonomic system which differ for types of subjects classified as prejudiced and unprejudiced.

7. This effort to avoid romantic and sexual connotations was made so that the slides could be used as projective devices in another phase of the research. In spite of these efforts, female subjects tended to 'see' these situations as romantic.

8. In all cases, it was emphasized to the subject that he was free to terminate his participation in the experiment at any time. He was told that he could do so without prejudice on the part of the interviewer, and that he would remain anonymous in this decision. No subject took advantage of this opportunity.

9. See, e.g. Harold Gulliksen, 'Intrinsic Validity', *The American Psychologist*, 5 (October 1950), pp. 511–17.

10. ibid.

11. David Riesman, *The Lonely Crowd*, New Haven: Yale University Press, 1950, *passim*.

12. Theodore M. Newcomb, 'Attitude Development as a Function of Reference Groups: The Bennington Study', reprinted in E. E. Maccoby, T. M. Newcomb, and E. L. Hartley, editors, *Readings in Social Psychology*, New York: Henry Holt, 1958, pp. 265–75.

21 I. L. Janis and B. T. King

The Influence of Role-Playing on Opinion Change*

Reprinted from: I. L. Janis and B. T. King, *Journal of Abnormal and Social Psychology*, American Psychological Assoc., U.S.A., 1954, Vol. 49, pp. 211–18.

In many everyday situations, people are induced to play social roles in which they express ideas that are not necessarily in accord with their private convictions. That certain types of role-playing experiences can facilitate changes in personal opinions has been suggested by various impressionistic observations (e.g. Myers[8]). In recent years, psychodramatic techniques which involve role-playing have been developed for use in adult education programs, leadership training, employee counseling, and psychotherapy ([1],[5], [6],[7],[9]). The usual procedure consists of having persons in a group play specified roles in a simulated life situation. One of the main values of this role-playing device, according to its proponents, is that it has a corrective influence on various beliefs and attitudes which underlie chronic difficulties in human relations (cf. Maier[6]).

As yet little is known about the conditions under which role-playing leads to actual changes in personal opinions. The present experiment was designed to investigate the effects of one type of demand that is frequently made upon a person when he is induced to play a social role, namely, the requirement that he overtly verbalize to others various opinions which may not correspond to his inner convictions.

As a preliminary step in exploring the effects of role-playing, one of the present authors interviewed a group of collegiate debaters who, as members of an organized team, repeatedly were required to play a role in which they publicly expressed views that did not correspond to their personal opinions. Most of the debaters reported that they frequently ended up by accepting the conclusions which they had been arbitrarily assigned to defend. Myers'[8] impressionistic account of the improvement in morale attitudes produced by participation in an Army public-speaking course points to the same phenomenon and suggests that attitude

*This is a study of the way in which behaviour may affect attitudes. As such, it is also relevant to the previous section of the book, on attitude change. The investigation was in fact part of the Yale University programme of research summarized in the excerpt from Hovland, Janis and Kelley. – Eds.

changes may occur even when role-playing is artificially induced. If true, it would appear that 'saying is believing' – that overtly expressing an opinion in conformity to social demands will influence the individual's private opinion. Consequently, it seemed worth while to attempt to investigate the effects of this type of role-playing in a more controlled laboratory situation where, if the alleged gain from role-playing occurs, it might be possible to isolate the critical factors and to explore systematically the mediating mechanisms.

The role-playing effects described above have not as yet been verified by systematic research. If verified, they would still remain open to a variety of alternative explanations. For instance, inducing the individual to play a role in which he must advocate publicly a given position might guarantee exposure to one set of arguments to the exclusion of others. An alternative possibility, however, is that even when exposed to the same persuasive communications, people who are required to verbalize the content to others will tend to be more influenced than those who are only passively exposed. In order to test this hypothesis, the present experiment was designed so that communication exposure would be held constant by comparing the opinion changes of active participants and passive controls who were exposed to the same communications.

Method and Procedures

An initial questionnaire, which was administered as an opinion survey in a large classroom of male college students, contained a series of questions concerning expectations about the future. Included in this 'before' questionnaire were the following key opinion items, which dealt with the subject matter of the three communications to which the experimental groups were subsequently exposed:

Item A: During the past year a number of movie theaters were forced to go out of business as the result of television competition and other recent developments. At the present time there are about 18,000 movie theaters remaining. How many commercial movie theaters do you think will be in business three years from now?

Item B: What is your personal estimate about the *total supply of meat that will be available for the civilian population* of the United States during the year 1953? (. . . —% of what it is at present.)

Item C: How many years do you think it will be before a *completely effective* cure for the common cold is discovered?

The experimental sessions were held approximately four weeks after the initial questionnaire had been filled out, and were represented as being part of a research project designed to develop a new aptitude test for assessing oral speaking ability. The subjects (Ss) were asked to give an informal talk based on an outline prepared by the experimenters (Es) which stated the conclusion and summarized the main arguments to be presented. The arguments were logically relevant but highly biased in that they played up and interpreted 'evidence' supporting only one side of the issue. Each active participant was instructed to play the role of a sincere advocate of the given point of view, while two others, who were present at the same experimental session, listened to his talk and read the prepared outline. Each S delivered one of the communications and was passively exposed to the other two. In order to prevent selective attention effects, the active participant was not told what the topic of his talk would be until his turn came to present it. He was given about three minutes to look over the prepared outline, during which time the others (passive controls) also were requested to study duplicate copies of the same outline so as to be prepared for judging the adequacy of the speaker's performance. After the first talk was over, another S was selected to present the second communication, and then the remaining S presented the third communication, the same procedures being followed in each case.

Immediately after the last talk was finished, Ss were given the 'after' questionnaire, much of which was devoted to rating the performance of each speaker. The key opinion items were included among numerous filler items, all of which were introduced as questions designed to provide information about the student's interests and opinions concerning the three topics so as to enable the investigators to select the most appropriate topic for future applications of the oral speaking test.

In all three communications, the conclusions specified an opinion estimate which was numerically *lower* than that given by any of the students on the 'before' test. Thus, all active participants were required to argue in favor of an extreme position which differed from their initial beliefs. The influence of each communication could readily be observed

Table 1

Schema of the Experimental Conditions

	Group A (N = 31)	Group B (N = 29)	Group C (N = 30)
Communication A: movie theaters	active participants	passive controls	passive controls
Communication B: meat supply	passive controls	active participants	passive controls
Communication C: cold cure	passive controls	passive controls	active participants

by noting the degree to which the students in each group *lowered* the opinion estimates on the 'after' test.

The basic schema of the experiment is shown in Table 1. In each row of the table which represents exposure to a given communication, there is one group of active participants and two contrasting groups which, when combined, form the group of passive controls. In effect, the experimental treatments were repeated with different communication contents, providing three separate instances of active versus passive exposure, although the same *S*s were used throughout.

In order to obtain some information for checking on selective attention effects, a variation of the passive control condition (not represented in the table) was introduced into the experiment by using a small supplementary group who listened and took notes on all three talks. In addition, base-line data for assessing the effectiveness of the communications were obtained from a comparable group of 'pure' controls who were not exposed to any of the communications.

Results and Discussion

Effects of Active Participation

Initially, on each of the three key items in the precommunication questionnaire, the difference between the active participation group and the passive control group was nonsignificant. The opinion changes observed after exposure to the three communications are shown in Table 2.* The results indicate that in the case of two of the three communications (A and B), the active participants were more influenced than the passive controls. For both communications, the differences in net sizable change are statistically reliable, and the differences in net (slight or sizable) changes, although non-reliable, are in the expected direction.

In the case of the third communication (C), the two groups showed approximately the same amount of opinion change. But additional findings (based on confidence ratings given by each *S* immediately after answering the key opinion questions) indicate

---

* The table does not include the data on the 'pure' (unexposed) control group. The net changes for this group were approximately zero in the case of all three key items, and the corresponding net changes for the active participants and the passive controls (shown in the last rows of the table) were significantly greater (*p*'s range from 0·10 down to < 0·01). Hence, all three communications had a significant effect on the opinions of those who were either actively or passively exposed to them.

The probability values reported throughout this paper are based on one tail of the theoretical distribution. Whenever intergroup comparisons were made with respect to the net percentage who changed by a given amount, the reliability of the difference was tested by the formula presented in Hovland, Lumsdaine, and Sheffield (3, p. 321).

that the active participants who presented Communication C, like those who presented the other two communications, expressed a higher level of *confidence* in their postcommunication estimates than did the corresponding passive controls. Table 3 shows the net changes in confidence ratings for each of the three communications in terms of a breakdown that takes account of the direction and magnitude of opinion change. The breakdown was necessary inasmuch as a successful communication would be expected to increase the confidence only of those who changed their opinions in the direction advocated by the communication. The net change in confidence shown for each subgroup is based on a comparison of pre- and postcommunication ratings given by each S, and was computed by subtracting the percentage who showed a decrease in confidence from the percentage who showed an increase in confidence. In general, the findings in Table 3 reveal a consistent pattern for all three communications: in every instance, active participation tended to have at least a slight positive effect with respect to increasing the confidence of those whose opinion estimates were influenced by the communication. The results indicate that active participation resulted in a significant gain on confidence particularly among those students whose opinion estimates were markedly influenced by Communication C.* This finding is especially striking in view of the fact that the opinion change results for Communication C (Table 2) failed to show any gain from active participation.

* For the entire group of active participants who were exposed to Communication C, there was a net increase in confidence of 37%; the corresponding net increase for the entire group of passive controls was only $13\frac{1}{2}$%. This difference was due entirely to the marked gain in confidence manifested by those students in the active group who had changed their opinion estimates in the direction advocated by the communication. The results in the first row of the table indicate that, among the students whose opinion estimates were uninfluenced by Communication C, the active participants showed a small net decrease in confidence which was equal to that shown by the passive controls. The next row of Table 3 indicates that, among those students who decreased their opinion estimates by at least one-half year or more after exposure to Communication C, the active participants showed a greater net increase in confidence than the passive controls; the difference of 31% approaches statistical significance ($p = 0.07$). Finally, the last row of the table shows that an even greater difference in confidence changes emerges when the comparison is limited to those students who decreased their opinion estimates by five years or more. (The $49\frac{1}{2}$% difference is reliable at beyond the 0.05 confidence level.) Further analysis of the subgroup data indicated that the differences shown in this table could not be attributed to statistical artifacts arising from initial differences between the various subgroups.

Table 2

Comparison of Active Participants with Passive Controls on Amount of Change in Opinion Estimates

Changes in Opinion Estimates†	Communication A: (Movie Theaters)		Communication B: (Meat Shortage)		Communication C: (Cold Cure)	
	Active Participants (N = 31)	Passive Controls (N = 57)*	Active Participants (N = 29)	Passive Controls (N = 57)	Active Participants (N = 30)	Passive Controls (N = 53)
	%	%	%	%	%	%
Sizable increase	0	2	0	2	7	6
Slight increase	3	9	7	14	10	9
No change	23	20	24	16	13	19
Slight decrease	29	46	27½	49	23	15
Sizable decrease	45	23	41½	19	47	51
Total	100	100	100	100	100	100
Net change (% increase minus % decrease)	−71	−58	−62	−52	−53	−51
Slight or sizable change						
Sizable change	−45	−21	−41½	−17	−40	−45
p	0·01		0·01		>0·30	

*The number of cases in each passive control group is slightly smaller than expected from the N's shown in Table 1 because the data from a few cases were inadequate and hence were eliminated from the analysis (e.g. the individual failed to give an answer to the particular question).

†The 'net change' (slight or sizable) is defined as the percentage changing in the direction advocated by the communication minus the percentage changing in the opposite direction. The 'net sizable change' in the case of Communication A refers to the difference in the percentages who lowered and raised their estimate by 5,000 (movie theaters) or more. For Communication B, a sizable change was 5 (years) or more; for Communication C it was 25 (per cent) or more.

Table 3

Comparison of Active Participants with Passive Controls on Amount of Change in Confidence

Subgroup Breakdown According to Changes in Opinion Estimates	Net Change in Confidence (per cent increase minus per cent decrease)					
	Communication A		Communication B		Communication C	
	Active Participants	Passive Controls	Active Participants	Passive Controls	Active Participants	Passive Controls
1. *Uninfluenced:* opinion estimates increased or unchanged	−12% (N = 8)	−5% (N = 18)	0% (N = 9)	+6% (N = 18)	−11% (N = 9)	−11% (N = 18)
2. *Influenced:* opinion estimates slightly or sizably decreased	+9% (N = 23)	−10% (N = 39)	−20% (N = 20)	+5% (N = 39)	+57% (N = 21)	+26% (N = 35)
Gain from active participation	+19%		+15%		+31%	
3. *Highly influenced:* opinion estimates sizably decreased	−7% (N = 14)	−38% (N = 13)	+25% (N = 12)	0% (N = 11)	+64½% (N = 14)	+15% (N = 27)
Gain from active participation	+31%		+25%		+49½%	

Insofar as confidence ratings can be regarded as indicators of the degree of conviction with which the new opinions are held, the positive findings based on the opinion change data for Communications A and B are partially confirmed by the confidence change data based on Communication C. Thus, the data based on all three communications contribute evidence that the effectiveness of the communications (as manifested by opinion changes or by confidence changes) tended to be augmented by active participation.

Although Ss were not told what their topic would be until they were about to begin giving the talk, it is possible that the ego-involving task of presenting one of the talks may have given rise to emotional excitement or other interfering reactions which could have had the effect of reducing the Ss' responsiveness when passively exposed to the other two communications. This possibility appears extremely improbable, however, in the light of supplementary control observations:

1. Some of the passive controls had been exposed to the communications *before* giving their own talk, while others were passively exposed *after* having given their own talk. Nonsignificant differences were found in the amount of opinion change shown under these two conditions.

2. The results from the passive controls were 'replicated' by the results from an independent group of 16 students who did not give an oral presentation, but who were asked to follow the prepared outline carefully and to note down the main arguments given by each of the three speakers. Despite the fact that their notes were fairly complete and indicated a relatively high degree of attention to the content of all three communications, these supplementary controls displayed approximately the same amount of opinion change as the original group of passive controls.*

Observations pertinent to explanatory hypotheses

Many different types of speculative hypotheses could be put forth to account for the facilitating effects of active participation, postulating a gain in attention and learning from overtly rehearsing

---

* It is conceivable, of course, that the activity of taking notes on the talks might have interfered with responsiveness to the persuasive content of the communications. While this possibility cannot be excluded, it seems implausible inasmuch as our Ss were college students who had had considerable practice in taking notes during lectures. Educational research on the effects of note taking indicates that this form of activity generally has a beneficial rather than a detrimental effect on the student's ability to absorb the content of an oral communication.[2]

the communication, or a gain in comprehension from reformulating the arguments in one's own words, or a gain in motivation from playing the role of communicator, etc. Some supplementary observations were made for the purpose of exploring various factors which might provide leads to the key mediating mechanisms. Although far from conclusive, the evidence derived from these observations provides a preliminary basis for selecting explanatory hypotheses which warrant further experimental analysis.

The findings based on the supplementary controls (who were required to take notes on the three talks) suggest that variation in attention level probably was not a crucial factor that could explain the participation effects observed in the present experiment. More promising clues were discovered by taking account of differences in the types of reactions evoked by the three communications. We have seen that in the case of Communications A and B, a clear-cut gain from active participation was manifested by changes in opinion estimates; but, in the case of Communication C, opinion estimates were unaffected, the gain being manifested only in the form of increased confidence. With a view to discovering some differentiating factor, we examined the available evidence bearing on the question of why active participation might be more effective under certain stimulus conditions (represented by Communications A and B) than under other conditions (represented by Communication C).

The first step in this inquiry was to examine E's notes on: (a) the active Ss' behavior while giving their talks, and (b) Ss' statements in the informal interviews conducted at the end of each experimental session. These observations provide two suggestive leads:

1. The active participants who presented Communication C seemed to engage in *less improvisation* than those who presented the other two communications. The Communication C group appeared to adhere much more closely to the prepared outline, making little attempt to reformulate the main points, to insert illustrative examples, or to invent additional arguments.

2. Active participants in the Communication C group seemed to experience much more difficulty than the other groups in presenting their talks. During their performance they appeared to be more hesitant and tense. Afterwards, they expressed many more complaints about the task, claiming that their topic was more difficult to present than either of the other two. In general, these subjects seemed *less satisfied* with their performance than those who presented the other two topics.

The first observation suggests that mere repetition of a persuasive communication may have little or no effect as compared with an improvised restatement. This observation is in line with some suggestive findings from an opinion change study by Kelman[4] in which seventh-grade students were given a communication, and, immediately afterwards, were offered various incentives to write essays in support of the communicator's position. Kelman observed that the essays written by the group which showed the greatest amount of opinion change tended to be longer, to include more improvisation, and to be of better over-all quality (as rated by several judges) than the essays written by the other experimental groups.

Reformulating and elaborating on the communication might be a critical factor in producing the gain from active participation, perhaps because the communicatee is stimulated to think of the kinds of arguments, illustrations, and motivating appeals that he regards as most convincing. The importance of the improvisation factor in relation to participation effects could not be investigated further with the data at hand from the present experiment, but is currently being studied by the present authors in another experiment that is specifically designed to compare the effects of different types of active participation.

With respect to the second observation, it should be noted that there may have been an objective basis for the greater dissatisfaction experienced on Communication C because of the greater amount of unfamiliar technical material it contained. The 'cold cure' outline referred to a great many technical details concerning the cold virus, antibiotics, allergic reactions, and antihistamines. Many of these details were probably unfamiliar to Ss, and consequently it may have been difficult for them to 'spell out' the implications of the arguments. In contrast, the outlines for the other two topics contained very little technical material, relying mainly on arguments that were likely to be quite familiar to college students.

Systematic evidence relevant to Ss' *perception* of the difficulty of presenting each communication was obtained by making use of the self-rating schedule which each student filled out after exposure to the three communications. Table 4 shows the percentage in each experimental group who rated their own performance as adequate or satisfactory on each of six self-appraisal items.

The most comprehensive question was the following: 'What is your over-all rating of the informal talk given by this speaker – how good a job do you think he did in presenting his material? ____ Excellent; ____ Very Good; ____ Satisfactory; ____ Poor; ____ Very Poor.'

Table 4

Self-Ratings of Active Participants in Each Experimental Group

Self-Rating Response	Experimental Groups (Active Participants)		
	Communication A: (Movie) ($N = 31$)	Communication B: (Meat Supply) ($N = 29$)	Communication C: (Cold Cure) ($N = 30$)
	%	%	%
1. *Over-all performance* was at least 'satisfactory'	94	83	63
2. Rarely or never spoke in a *monotonous* tone of voice	64	76	53
3. Rarely or never *incoherent* in presenting arguments	74	83	57
4. No *distortions* or *misinterpretations* of arguments in the prepared outline	32	52	13
5. No *omissions* of any of the main arguments	74	72	70
6. Succeeded in giving the impression of being '*sincere*'	52	52	43
Combined rating on all six items:— five or more favourable self-ratings	39	52	13

The percentage who rated themselves as 'satisfactory' or better (shown in the first row of the table) was significantly lower for the group who presented Communication C than for the groups who presented Communications A and B ($p = 0.002$ and 0.04, respectively). On the remaining five items, each of which dealt with a specific aspect of the speaker's performance, the Communication C group also tended to rate themselves lower than did the other two groups. (On the combined rating, based on all six items, the percentage differences are statistically significant at beyond the 0.05 confidence level.) The findings consistently indicate that the students in the Communication C group felt less satisfied with their oral speaking performance than did those in the other two groups. Since the group differences in self-ratings tend to parallel the group differences in amount of gain from active participation, the results suggest that *satisfaction with one's own performance* may be a critical factor that determines the magnitude of participation effects.

235

Further evidence which supports this hypothesis was obtained from an analysis of individual opinion changes, comparing active participants with high and low self-ratings for each of the three communications. For example, among the active participants who presented Communication C, there were 18 students whose self-ratings were comparatively 'high' (three to six favorable responses), and 12 cases whose self-ratings were predominantly 'low' (zero, one, or two favorable responses); 55% of the 'highs' as against only 17% of the 'lows' showed a sizable net opinion change in the direction advocated by the communications ($p = 0.05$). In general, the comparisons based on all three communications consistently indicate that a greater amount of opinion change occurred among those active participants who rated their oral speaking performance as satisfactory or better. Active participants who felt that they performed poorly, on the other hand, failed to show any more opinion change than the passive controls, and, in the case of Communication C, showed markedly less change than the passive controls ($p = 0.07$).

During the experimental sessions there were no apparent sources of external social rewards from the environment. Since the others present remained silent, the active participant had no opportunity to know how they were reacting to his talk, except possibly by subtle signs from their facial expressions or from their bodily movements. But even in the absence of any external cues to social approval, it seems probable that *anticipations* concerning such approval would occur if the individual felt that he was performing well, as expressed in his self-ratings. Thus, expectations of favorable audience reactions may have occurred less frequently among Ss who were required to perform the relatively difficult task of presenting the unfamiliar technical material in Communication C than among those who were required to perform the less difficult task of presenting Communication A or B. The increase in opinion change produced by role-playing might be mediated by the individual's sense of achievement or his elated feelings about the adequacy of his oral performance. One hypothesis that would follow from this assumption is that when a person conforms outwardly to social demands by playing a role which requires him to advocate a given opinion, he will begin to believe what he is saying if he is made to feel that he says it well.

Although the above hypothesis is suggested by the supplementary correlational findings, it will obviously remain open to question until tested by more precise methods. One cannot be certain that the responses used to assess 'satisfaction' represent a separate variable which is causally related to opinion changes. Acceptance of the communication might be a common factor which inclines those who are most influenced to perceive themselves as having performed well, in which case the self-ratings might merely reflect the same thing as the measures of opinion change. Moreover, even if the two variables can be varied and measured independently, the possibility remains that the observed relationship may be due to some third variable, such as amount of improvisation.

As was noted earlier, the group of active participants who showed the least amount of opinion change not only expressed a low degree of satisfaction but also displayed a relative absence of improvisation in their oral performances. Either the 'satisfaction' factor or the 'improvisation' factor might prove to be a critical mediating variable. Before drawing a definite conclusion, it is necessary to investigate each factor experimentally – for instance, by giving the Ss 'expert' performance ratings which raise or lower their feelings of satisfaction, and by using instructions which increase or decrease the amount of improvisation. These methods are currently being employed in our further research on the effects of role-playing.

There is another important problem which arises from the findings in the present experiment and which also requires systematic investigation: Does social role-playing facilitate the internalization of externally imposed value judgments, mores, and taboos? The persuasive communications used in this study dealt with relatively impersonal beliefs about the future, and the main findings show that acceptance of opinions of this sort was markedly increased by experimentally induced role-playing. It remains problematical, however, whether active participation also influences the acceptance of opinions and attitudes that are more directly tied up with daily life activities, interpersonal relationships, and emotionally charged dilemmas.

Obviously, it is unsafe to generalize widely from a single exploratory study based on the opinion changes of college students produced in a somewhat artificial test situation. Nevertheless, the present experiment provides preliminary evidence indicating that verbal conformity elicited by role-playing can significantly influence the acceptance of new beliefs. Under certain specifiable conditions which await further investigation, it seems to be true that 'saying is believing'.

Summary and Conclusions

The experiment was designed to determine whether or not overt verbalization, induced by role-playing, facilitates opinion change. Male college students were assigned at random to two main experimental groups: (*a*) active participants, who, with the aid of a prepared outline, played the role of a sincere advocate of the given point of view, and (*b*) passive controls, who silently read and listened to the same communication. In the experimental sessions, three different communications were used, each of which argued in favor of a specific conclusion concerning expected future events and was presented by a different active participant. Opinion measures obtained at the end of the session were compared with the 'before' measures obtained about one month earlier.

In general, the active participants tended to be more influenced by the communications than were the passive controls. In the case of two of the communications the active participants showed significantly more opinion change than the passive controls. In the case of the third communication, both groups showed approximately the same amount of opinion change, but active participation, nevertheless, tended to increase the level of confidence of those whose opinion estimates were influenced by the communication. The main findings, together with various methodological checks, support the hypothesis that overt verbalization induced by role-playing tends to augment the effectiveness of a persuasive communication.

Additional observations were analyzed in order to explore possible mediating factors underlying the gain in opinion change due to active participation. From behavioral records and interviews, two suggestive leads emerged. In those cases where role-playing produced a marked increase in opinion change: (*a*) the individual displayed a relatively great amount of improvisation in his talk, and (*b*) he felt comparatively well satisfied with his oral speaking performance. The first factor suggests that the gain from role-playing may occur primarily because the active participant tends to be impressed by his own cogent arguments, clarifying illustrations, and convincing appeals which he is stimulated to think up in order to do a good job of 'selling' the idea to others. The second factor suggests an alternative explanation in terms of the rewarding effects of the individual's sense of achievement or feelings of satisfaction with his performance in the role of active participant. Additional evidence pertinent to the second factor, based on a self-rating questionnaire which the *S*s filled out immediately after giving the talk, consistently indicated that the greatest amount of opinion change occurred among those active participants who felt that their oral speaking performance was satisfactory. Both the 'improvisation' factor and the 'satisfaction' factor warrant further investigation.

References
1. Bavelas, A., Role-playing and management training. *Sociatry*, **1**, 183–91, 1947.
2. Crawford, C. E., Some experimental studies of the results of college note taking. *J. educ. Res.*, **12**, 379–86, 1925.
3. Hovland, C. I., Lumsdaine, A. A., and Sheffield, F. D. *Experiments on mass communication*. Princeton: Princeton University Press, 1949.
4. Kelman, H. C., Attitude change as a function of response restriction. *Hum. Relat.*, in press.
5. Lippitt, R., The psychodrama in leadership training. *Sociometry*, **6**, 286–92, 1943.
6. Maier, N. R. F., *Principles of human relations*. New York: Wiley, 1952.
7. Moreno, J. L., *Psychodrama*. Vol. 1, New York: Beacon House, 1946.
8. Myers, G. C., Control of conduct by suggestion: an experiment in americanization. *J. appl. Psychol.*, **5**, 26–31, 1921.
9. Zander, A., and Lippitt, R., Reality-practice as educational method. *Sociometry*, **7**, 129–51, 1944.

22 R. L. Gorden

Attitude and the Definition of the Situation

Reprinted from: R. L. Gorden, *American Sociological Review*, American
Sociological Assoc., U.S.A., 1952, Vol. 17, pp. 50–8.

The main purpose of this study is to explore the relationships between a person's *private opinion* and his *definition of the situation* and
how they affect his expression of *public opinion* in a social situation.

The pursuit of this objective is divided into two phases. The first
is an experimental study in which the only aspect of the individual's
definition of the situation under consideration is his *estimate of the
group opinion*. This part of the study describes the extent to which
each individual alters his private opinion to conform to his estimation of the group opinion when asked to express his opinion in
that group. The second phase of the study uses case materials to
gain insight into the reasons for the behavior of the extreme conformists and nonconformists. In this material, other aspects of
each person's definition of the situation are considered in addition
to his estimate of the group opinion.

In order to observe the dynamic interplay between each person's
private opinion and his *definition of the situation* which interact to
develop his expression of *public opinion*, it is necessary to study a
group (*a*) in which there is a wide range of private opinions, (*b*)
where the members of the group are so intimately acquainted as to
have a clear definition of the situation with respect to the particular
subject upon which they are asked to express themselves, and (*c*)
where there is variation in the *definition of the situation* from person
to person resulting from differences in each person's background,
the nature of his connection with the group, and his role and status
in the group.

Description of the Group Studied

The study began by participant observation of a group of 36
members of a co-operative living project. Because of turnover in
membership and individuals taking vacations during some phase
of the collection of data, complete data were collected on only 24
of the members.

About half of the members were students and the rest worked in
a variety of professions, semi-professions, and vocations ranging

from college instructor to waitress. All but one person had some college education. The ages ranged from 21 to 35 years. Half were males and half were females. These people lived in a large, single-family residence which had four floors and seven bathrooms.

The household tasks were shared and all the members ate the evening meal in the common dining room. According to another study by the writer, some of the more important forces bringing the people into the co-op were (a) a common interest in the co-operative movement, (b) economical housing, (c) a desire for primary association with other minority groups, (d) a desire to meet members of the opposite sex, and (e) a desire to be in an atmosphere where members of minority groups can relax and be treated as equals.

Although the group was composed of a wide variety of cultural backgrounds, there was one common denominator; namely, all the members belonged to a minority group. The group included seven Negroes, nine Jews, of whom only two attended religious services (Reformed), five members of Catholic background, of whom only two considered themselves in good standing with the church, and three pacifists. Of the three married couples living in the house, two were interracial marriages.

The political affiliation and beliefs in the group can best be characterized by the following categories: Democrats, 15; ex-Progressives, 14; Socialists, 4; Communist, 1; Republican, 1. The seven Negroes were all Democrats and were noticeably more conservative than the Caucasians. This is mainly because the Negroes were trying to achieve a higher status than their parents. The Caucasians, on the other hand, tended to be rebellious against the 'bourgeois' standards of their parents.

In the opinion of the writer, this group is heterogeneous enough to offer wide variations in attitude toward Russia and, at the same time, the members are sufficiently identified with the group to be influenced by a rather clear conception of the norms of the group.

The Experimental Situation

Opinion on Russia was chosen for this study because it is a subject with emotional content, a subject toward which this group holds a wide range of feelings, and a subject upon which the sanctioned range of expression of public opinion is narrowing.

The writer was a regular member of the co-op group for a period of months and was able to collect data from observation and non-directive interviewing before the experimental phase of the study was begun.

Three types of data relating to the experimental study were collected. First, each individual recorded his *private opinion* on Russia on a Likert-type attitude scale in a situation where the respondent was assured complete anonymity. Second, in a manner described in detail later, he was asked to express his opinion on each of these items in the presence of his fellow co-op members. These responses are referred to as his *public opinion*. Third, by a method also described later, he was asked to make an estimate of the opinion of the group on each of these same items. These responses are hereafter referred to as his *estimate of group opinion*, which is the only aspect of his *definition of the situation* which is obtained in the experimental situation. Other aspects of his definition are dealt with later in the case study material. Thus we have, from each individual, three types of responses to each of 12 items dealing with Russia. An item-for-item comparison of the three responses can thus be made for each individual, since the 'anonymous' questionnaires were secretly identifiable.

For the experiment the 24 members were divided into two subgroups matched according to race, occupational status, sex, and rank order of the total score on their *private opinion*. The two groups were interviewed simultaneously in different rooms. Two interviewers worked with each group. In one group both interviewers were co-op members. In the other group one was a co-op member and the other was an 'outsider' representing a nationally known opinion research organization. This procedure was used in an effort to detect any effect the interviewer himself might have on the responses in the group situation. A comparison of the responses received by each interviewer, and subsequent interviews with the respondents 'after the study was completed', indicated that the respondents in general felt that all the interviewers were objective, neutral, and uncritical in comparison with the others who were listening to their responses.

The experiment had been proposed to the group as a scientific study of a new public opinion polling technique. At a regular house meeting, the group voted unanimously to cooperate with the writer in this study.

The following interviewing technique was used. The group was told that the interviewers would make a statement regarding Russia, and the respondent was to say to what extent he agreed or disagreed with the statement, using the five possible replies indicated on a card which was going to be handed to him. The group was also told that the members should listen to the replies of the others so that they could be prepared to estimate the group opinion.

At this point in the design of the study, an important question of methodology presented itself – When and how can each individual's most valid estimate of the group opinion be obtained? A pretest with another group seemed to indicate that an individual's awareness of the discrepancy between his private opinion and his conception of the opinions of a given group of people was not as acute at any time *before* actually making a statement on a controversial subject as it became when the physical act of speaking occurred. Some individuals reported a growing awareness *during* the utterance of their statements, which caused them to alter the wording in order to soften the impact on the group. Other individuals testified that, although they would change the wording of a statement which they had strongly endorsed before, they did not sense an acute emotional reaction until *after* the statement was finished.

Since it was impossible to interrupt the person during his statement in this experiment, it was decided that the respondent should give his estimate of the group opinion on each item, immediately *after* his statement on *each item*, by indicating on a check-chart his estimate of the group opinion. It was suggested in the directions to each respondent that this could be done most accurately by comparing the direction and degree of the feeling of the group in relation to his own feeling on that particular item and then quickly checking his first impression.

There were many indications of the effect of the group pressure on the individual other than his choice of response. After the directions were given to the group, there were definite symptoms of tension and awareness of the group pressure. It is the writer's belief that each one felt that it was a bit awkward to appear to be too interested in the opinions of the group and so made an effort to be busy, thus easing his own tension as well as that of the person being interviewed. This conviction is based on such observations as the following:

Case 2, a person who had the most anti-Russian score on both the anonymous response and the group response, came into the group, whispered to her husband, and left. He also left to set the table for dinner. After a while the interviewer went after him and told him it would take only a minute. He consented reluctantly because, he explained, he was busy. After his own interview, however, he had time to remain in the group until the last interview was completed.

Case 8 sat on one end of a couch with a Penguin Book in his hand, opened to page 38. Twenty-two minutes later he was on the same page.

Five of the respondents who usually speak in normal voices replied almost inaudibly to the interviewer, whose ear was approximately three feet from the respondent. In these cases the interviewer would pretend not to have heard, and in a clear, matter-of-fact voice audible to the rest of the group ask, 'You said agree? Was that strongly or moderately? Strongly? Thank you'.

In two cases where the person felt that the group strongly disagreed with his statement, the interviewer and the respondent had the following exchange.

Respondent: (in an almost inaudible voice) Agree strongly.
Interviewer: Did you say agree or disagree?
Respondent: Agree.
Interviewer: Was that strongly or moderately?
Respondent: Moderately.
Interviewer: Moderately? Thank you.

It appears that each thought better of his first response and changed from strongly to moderately, which was nearer to his conception of the group norms. The general atmosphere of the group had a lack of spontaneity and a stiff sort of nonchalance.

Analysis of Data

There are some general relationships between the three scores, which are consistent for the group. Analysis of the relationship between *private opinion* and *estimate of group opinion* indicates a marked tendency for the individual to estimate correctly the *direction* of the median opinion of the group (as indicated by the aggregate private opinion) in relation to his own private opinion.*

From Table 1 we see that those whose opinions were more pro-Russian on the *private opinion* scale tended correctly to estimate the group opinion as being more anti-Russian than their own.† It can be said that 20 of the 24 people were correct in their estimate in regard to the general direction of the group opinion.

There is another general relationship found between the individual's *private opinion* and his *estimate of the group opinion*. Those who are pro-Russian on the private opinion scale tend to estimate the opinion of the group as being more pro-Russian than it actually is, and *vice versa*, as shown in Table 2. Thus, although the estimate of the direction of the group mean from the individual's private

* Anonymous opinion is divided into pro- and anti-Russian by the median.
† Group opinion was obtained from the median score on the aggregate of private opinions.

Table 1

Distribution of Respondents by Their Private Opinions on Russia and the Direction of Their Estimate of the Group Opinion in Relation to Their Own Private Opinions

Individual's Private Opinion	Direction of Estimate of Group Opinion		Total
	More Pro-Russian	More Anti-Russian	
Pro-Russian	2	10	12
Anti-Russian	10	2	12
Total	12	12	24

Table 2

Distribution of Respondents by Their Private Opinions on Russia and Their Accuracy in Estimating Mean Opinion of the Group

Individual's Private Opinion	Accuracy of Estimate of Group Opinion		Total
	Too Pro-Russian	Too Anti-Russian	
Pro-Russian	10	2	12
Anti-Russian	2	10	12
Total	12	12	24

opinion is correct, the conception of the absolute position of the group appears to be influenced by the individual's own feeling, as well as by the actual group opinion.

It can be similarly demonstrated that there is a positive relationship between the anonymous opinion and the opinion expressed in the group, as may be seen from Table 3.

Table 3

Distribution of Respondents by Their Private Opinions on Russia and Their Public Opinions on Russia

Private Opinion	Public Opinion		Total
	Pro-Russian	Anti-Russian	
Pro-Russian	11	1	12
Anti-Russian	1	11	12
Total	12	12	24

Tables 1, 2 and 3 show that in general each person can correctly estimate whether the group is either more or less pro-Russian than himself, but he usually does not realize that the amount of this difference is as great as it is. Also, in general, there are no individuals who shift from the 'pro' category on their *private* opinion to the 'anti' category on their *public* opinion or *vice versa*.

This rather crude analysis does not, however, demonstrate the shifts of lesser magnitude. In order to reveal these smaller changes we must compare each person's total score for the three types of responses. Since there are 12 items with five-point responses, the possible range of the total scores is from 12 to 60, with 60 representing the extreme pro-Russian score.

In 13 cases the expression of *public opinion*, as indicated by *total scores* in the group situation, more closely approximated the person's conception of the group norms than did his *private opinion*. In eight cases the expression in the group is further from their conception of group norms than is their expression in the anonymous situation. In three cases there was no change in the total score from the anonymous to the group situation.

This might suggest that in general the person's expression of opinion regarding Russia is influenced by his conception of how others regard Russia. This appears to be a plausible enough result, but the eight cases whose attitudes were counter to their conceptions of the group, and the three who indicated no influence by the group, must be studied in comparison with the 13 cases who conformed to the group.

It is necessary at this time to point out that the comparison of these three total scores for each person is used only for a rough group comparison, and that there are certain meaningful differences that are hidden in the total scores. For example, we shall compare the actual responses on the separate items by Case 2 with those by Case 23, which in terms of total scores appear very similar. Thus in Table 4 we see that, although in both cases the *total* score was practically the same in columns *II* and *III*, there are a number of disagreements in the individual items (see items 4, 6, 8, and 10) in Case 2, and no discrepancy in Case 23.

Table 4

A Comparison of the Responses of Two Individuals on Each Item in the Three Scores

Item Number	Case 2			Case 23		
	I Private Opinion	*II* Estimate of Group	*III* Public Opinion	*I* Private Opinion	*II* Estimate of Group	*III* Public Opinion
1	1	2	2	1	2	2
2	2	1	1	3	1	1
3	4	4	4	3	3	3
4	2	4	2	2	2	2
5	2	1	1	2	4	4
6	4	1	5	3	4	4
7	2	5	5	1	2	2
8	1	5	1	2	2	2
9	3	2	2	4	4	4
10	4	2	4	4	4	4
11	2	4	4	4	4	4
12	5	5	5	4	5	5
Total	32	36	36	33	37	37

In Case 2 the person resisted his conception of the group norms to the extent of six points in the pro-Russian direction (items 4 and 8), and also resisted to the extent of six points in the anti-Russian direction (items 6 and 10), making the total score the same. On the other hand, Case 23 on each item conformed to her conceptions of the group norms even though it meant becoming more pro-Russian on items 1, 5, 6, 7, and 12, and more anti-Russian on item 2. Thus we see the inadequacy of total scores for describing the individual variation in relationship to his conception of the group norm.

These two cases are discussed because they afford the most clear contrast with respect to the degree to which individual variations are concealed by total scores. In no other case was the inconsistency as great as in Case 2.

In order to avoid such deception and in order to sharpen our analysis, we shall use the following four terms to describe the possible relationships between the three types of responses:

Agreement will indicate the extent to which the person's private opinion coincides with his estimate of the group opinion.

Conformity will indicate the degree to which the person alters his private opinion to conform more closely to his conception of the group norms when speaking in the group.

Resistance will indicate the extent to which a person retains his original private opinion despite his conception of the group as being different.

Reaction will be used to describe the situation where a person in effect reverses the direction of his private opinion in order to be different from the group.

The frequency of each of these modes of adjustment for each individual is shown in Table 5. A comparison of column *A* with any of the other columns is not valid, because the figures in column *A* represent the number of *items* out of the 12 where the individual's responses indicated no differences between his private opinion and his conception of the group opinion. However, a comparison of columns *B*, *C*, and *D* is meaningful, since the figures in each of these columns represent the total number of *degrees* of a given type of response for the 12 items. Therefore, inspection of Table 5 allows us to compare individuals with respect to the *proportion* of conformity, resistance, or reaction. However, the total of columns *B*, *C*, and *D* for any one case is limited by the number of items, indicated in column *A*, where there was agreement between the person's private opinion and his estimate of the group opinion. Only when the individual's private opinion differs from his estimate of the group opinion can we record the effect of his conception of the group opinion on his expression of public opinion. The totals of columns *B*, *C*, and *D* indicate that, for the group as a whole, conformity was the predominant mode of adjustment to the discrepancy between the person's private opinion and his estimate of the group opinion.

Since the reliability of these responses is unknown, no attempt is made to explain why each individual had a particular proportion of conformity, resistance, or reaction. Instead, it would seem more prudent to select only the extreme conformists and the extreme nonconformists and explore the case study materials in an attempt to explain these contrasting patterns of adjustment.

The degree of conformity was determined by the formula $B - (C + D)$, where the letters refer to the columns in Table 5. The conformists chosen were those with the two highest scores on this

Table 5

The Degree of Agreement, Conformity, Resistance, and Reaction by Individual Cases

Case No.	A Agreement*	B Conformity†	C Resistance†	D Reaction†
1	2	4	6	0
2	2	9	8	1
3	1	0	8	9
4	1	11	1	3
5	3	5	2	4
6	5	2	6	2
7	7	4	2	2
8	8	5	2	0
9	3	7	1	2
10	0	6	7	2
11	2	9	4	1
12	0	7	3	6
13	0	5	5	2
14	1	10	8	6
15	3	5	1	3
16	2	5	1	4
17	3	3	5	2
18	4	2	6	8
19	5	13	0	0
20	6	7	0	0
21	3	8	2	1
22	2	5	3	3
23	6	8	0	0
24	1	3	2	6
Total	70	143	83	67

* These figures indicate the number of *items* out of the 12 where the person's private opinion agreed with his conception of the group norms.
† These figures represent the number of degrees of discrepancy on the five-point response.

formula, and the nonconformists were the two lowest. Applying the formula to the cases in Table 5, we find Cases 19 and 23 to be the conformists and Cases 3 and 18 to be the nonconformists.

Case Study Materials

The writer does not claim that the evidence presented by the case study materials is conclusive, nor does he claim that it was collected in such a manner that the collection of this portion of the data could be precisely repeated and verified. However, the writer feels that after having an intimate acquaintance with the personalities, through living in close contact with them for more than a year and systematically gathering case materials for over three months, some significant insights have been gained.

Case 3 (*nonconformist*). Mr W is a 25-year-old part-time student who is working on a full-time job. He is highly intelligent. He is not closely identified with the co-operative living group, but belongs to a small gang of high school buddies with whom he plays cards and drinks. He mentioned that he craved recognition, which he found hard to get in the co-op group, but liked living there because he 'hated to live alone, and besides I need someone around to kick me out of bed in the morning or to call the boss and tell him I'm sick and can't work.'

The writer has observed Mr W taking opposite sides on the same issue from time to time, and he admits 'getting a kick' out of showing his knowledge and shocking people with his views. He also feels there is no great penalty for having contrary views: 'No one gives a damn what you say or do as long as you get your work-job done. Everyone here is liberal, or at least thinks he is.'

In this case we find three important factors which seem to account for Mr W's nonconformity. First, he is more closely identified with his high school gang and does not depend heavily upon the co-op group for intimate response. Second, he admits craving recognition, 'but I don't get it here at the co-op; I'm just a plain old Joe here, and a prize dope.' Perhaps his apparent negativistic shifting of sides, to show off his knowledge and shock people, is an attempt to obtain this recognition. Third, he conceives the group sanctions to be mild and tolerant.

Case 18 (*nonconformist*). Miss X is a professional worker, 25 years of age, who has lived at the co-op house for about a year. She was born in Austria and spent a few years in England. According to her own testimony, most of her social contacts are in this group. 'I came hoping that the informal atmosphere would help me get rid of some of my inhibitions and peculiar reactions to the opposite sex. I don't belong to any cliques outside of the co-op. I have always lived in some peculiar circumstances where I have never really become sociable.'

She feels that the group is tolerant of deviations. She points out that although there is a wide range of opinions on vital matters, 'they all get along pretty well because both sides are tolerant and want to "live and let live ".'

Miss X is a socialist who in general seems to have a more moderate view of Russia than many. A statement which seems to represent her position is, 'Even the U.S.A. is not very democratic, and Russia is less so. I think the Labor Party in England will do a better job of balancing both economic and political power.'

Miss X, according to the observations of the writer, her friends, and her own testimony, has deep-seated negativistic reaction patterns: 'If they [men] think I am a "loose girl" I like to prove that I'm not; and if they think I am too prudish, I like to pretend that I really don't have any inhibitions but am just being coy. I'm not just trying to attract them, because as soon as they get interested then I change. Yet I don't want them to leave. I don't know why that is.'

We see that both Mr W and Miss X have personality traits which might increase the possibility of a negativistic reaction in the group. Both of them define the group as being tolerant. Both have superior intelligence and college degrees and no inferior feeling regarding personal appearance. Here the similarity ends. He is well integrated into an outside clique while she has her most intimate associations in the co-op group. However, her reaction to others is in many cases of a non-adjustive nature, and she is not well integrated into any social group. Perhaps her identification with the group is not great despite the fact that she does not have a greater degree of identification elsewhere.

Case 19 (*conformist*). Mr Y is 20 years old, and has not completed his high school education, which he is attempting to do on the G.I. Bill. He has been at the co-op house only two months. He is of Jewish background and is minority conscious. He is from a lower socio-economic class and has aspirations for upward mobility via education. He has a strong identification with the co-op group. He says, 'It is the first place that I have found since I came back from the army that made me feel at home. I don't have to worry about discrimination here and nobody is going to push me around. That's one reason why I want to get an education. . . . That's one reason I came to the co-op. There are lots of students here, and they are all smarter than I am. It is a good chance to learn a lot. . . . I don't know anything about Russia as it is today, even if my mother does tell me how things were when she was there forty years ago . . . and it sounds like a place where people get pushed around, but I don't know anything about it, so why should I show my ignorance?'

Mr Y's dependence on the group is obvious. He likes the group and feels it is a privilege to mingle with those who are 'smarter' than he is. He willingly and consciously conforms to a group who would 'never push me around'.

Case 23 (conformist). Miss Z is also a relatively new member in the house. She is 21 years old, attractive, Negro, and striving for upward social mobility by way of the teaching profession. She has finished college, dresses well, has 'good manners', and considers tact and diplomacy a very desirable trait in herself. She is gregarious and finds the co-op a 'haven of refuge' while waiting for a full-time teaching job. She expresses her attitude toward the group in the following manner:

'I was told before I came into the co-op that it didn't make any difference whether you were white, black, or something in between, and I've found that to be true. I have been so fed up on prejudice – even the Negroes are prejudiced against other Negroes and whites.'

In an informal interview after the experimental situation, she explained that she wasn't sure whether her statements in the group were the group's opinions or her own. 'I was left with no alternative but to assume or interpret what is meant by each statement without asking the interviewer, so I tried to interpret the meaning of each statement according to what I thought it meant to most of the other people in the house. . . . I know that there are some people in the house who are in political science and international relations who know a lot more about Russia than I do. I should know a lot more but I don't.'

In both cases (19 and 23) there is a strong identification with the group in the sense that it fulfills certain needs for the individual. Also, both people feel that their opinion on the matter is inferior to the others'. In Mr Y's case it seems that his conformity is more intentional, while in the case of Miss Z it takes the form of changed interpretation of the meaning of the questions in view of the probable meaning to others in the group. It is impossible to say why Mr Y conformed more than Miss Z, but one factor is that Miss Z did not conceive of the group norms as being so far from her anonymous opinion as did Mr Y. This fact places a limit upon the degree of conformity possible in her case.

In comparing the two most extreme conformists with the two most nonconformist members of this group, we find certain rather clear differences. First, the conformists had a number of factors which contributed to their need for security and acceptance into the group. Second, certain combinations of factors made them feel that their opinion was less important than their being accepted. And third, there was the implication that they could not deviate strongly from the group without jeopardizing their present or future status.

On the other hand, the nonconformists not only had certain personality factors which might predispose them toward a negative reaction to the group norms, but also it appears that they did not have so much to lose nor did they seem to feel that they would lose anything by nonconformity in this particular group. The writer, after living with the group for three years, feels that as people remain in the group longer, they become aware of a wider range of values and find that there is even more tolerance of ideas than they suspected. Among the older members there is not only tolerance of different ideas, whether conservative or radical, but a certain prestige value in being different if the difference is sincere.*

Summary and Conclusions

1. *Awareness of group pressure*

Both the symbolic responses of the members of the group and the more subtle nonsymbolic interaction in the group clearly indicate an acute awareness of the presence of the other members of the group when they are asked to express their opinion. Confused efforts to appear nonchalant, efforts to escape the situation, and attempts to prevent others from hearing one's response are all telltale signs of the awareness of pressure.

2. *Accuracy of estimate of group opinion*

Although there was a considerable range in the accuracy of individuals' estimates of the group opinion, certain general relationships were found. (*a*) As indicated in Table 1, nearly everyone in the group correctly estimated the *direction* of the group opinion in relation to his own private opinion. (*b*) But, as indicated in Table 2, there was a strong tendency to underestimate the degree of this discrepancy. In 20 out of 24 cases those who were above the median score for the group estimated the group opinion to be higher than it was or *vice versa*.

Here it is important to note that there was no significant or consistent difference in the accuracy of individual estimates of group opinion which could be related to the order in which the person was interviewed. This was true despite the fact that those who were

* The writer is acutely aware that no generalizations can be made from a rather impressionistic analysis of four extreme cases. It is also clear that the rough generalizations abstracted from these four cases are obscured or do not apply in other conforming or nonconforming cases.

interviewed last had heard many more responses from the members of the group upon which they could base an objective estimate. There are some possible explanations which would merit further investigation: (*a*) They may not have accepted the expressions of public opinion in the group as representing the real attitudes of the individual, or (*b*) the total effect may have been too confusing and therefore the respondent used some modification of his pre-conceived image of the group in estimating the group opinion. (*c*) Each respondent may have been interested only in the reactions of certain individuals in the group.

Although from one point of view it is important to understand the various factors influencing the accuracy of the estimate of the group opinion, the significant factor which influences the person's behavior in the group is his subjective feeling and imagery with regard to the group norms, regardless of how accurately this feeling and imagery may reflect the 'objective' situation.

3. *The effect of the definition of the situation*

We have already commented briefly upon the effect on the qualitative nonsymbolic interaction in the group, and will restrict the comments at this point to the effect upon the quantitative symbolic responses.

In general, the individuals tended to conform to their conception of the group norms when giving their public opinion. The typical pattern is for the individual to compromise between his private opinion and his conception of the group opinion when expressing his public opinion.

In addition to merely comparing the total scores, a more searching analysis of the data was made by making an item-by-item comparison of the three types of responses for each individual. This type of analysis indicated three types of adjustment to differences between the person's private opinion and his conception of the group norms. About 49% of these adjustments followed the conformity pattern, 28% followed the resistance pattern, and 22% followed the reaction pattern. Most of the individuals did not fall clearly into one of these adjustment patterns, but there was a wide variation in the proportion of each type of adjustment by each individual. However, there were three cases (see Cases 19, 20, and 23 in Table 5) who were pure conformists and one case (3) who showed no conformity in his adjustment pattern.

4. *Causes of the variation in adjustment patterns*

Since the reliability of the responses had not been established, only the two extreme conformists and the two extreme nonconformists were selected in an attempt to explain these apparently opposite types of adjustment. The following factors were felt by the writer to be significant in explaining the varying degrees of conformity and may serve as hypotheses for a more precise and controlled study: (*a*) the degree of the person's identification with the group, (*b*) his conception of the group's attitude toward nonconformity, (*c*) his conception of his own role in relation to the group, and (*d*) special personality traits such as negativism.

Part Three THEORY AND METHOD

The final part of the book is subdivided into two sections, the first on attitude theory and the second on the methodology of attitude measurement.

I Attitude Theory

During the twenties and thirties empirical research on attitudes was conducted more or less in a theoretical vacuum. In the great expansion of post-war work on the processes of attitude change, however, there developed a general interest in attitude structure and organization. This gave rise to various theoretical models. One major 'family' of theories which make use of a similar principle of 'consistency' in a cognitive framework is described and discussed here by Robert B. Zajonc. The theorists surveyed by Zajonc employ different terms, such as 'balance', 'dissonance', or 'congruity'; but these formulations are nonetheless a striking example of parallel theoretical development. A further theoretical contribution from Irving Sarnoff brings to the area of attitude organization the 'functional' point of view of modern psychoanalytic thought, emphasizing the role of attitudes in reducing tensions and resolving conflicts among motives.

23 R. B. Zajonc

Balance, Congruity and Dissonance

Reprinted from: R. B. Zajonc, *Public Opinion Quarterly*, Princeton, U.S.A., 1960, Vol. 24, 2, pp. 280–96.

Common to the concepts of balance, congruity, and dissonance is the notion that thoughts, beliefs, attitudes, and behavior tend to organize themselves in meaningful and sensible ways.[1] Members of the White Citizens' Council do not ordinarily contribute to NAACP. Adherents of the New Deal seldom support Republican candidates. Christian Scientists do not enroll in medical schools. And people who live in glass houses apparently do not throw stones. In this respect the concept of consistency underscores and presumes human *rationality*. It holds that behavior and attitudes are not only consistent to the objective observer, but that individuals try to appear consistent to themselves. It assumes that inconsistency is a noxious state setting up pressures to eliminate it or reduce it. But in the *ways* that consistency in human behavior and attitudes is achieved we see rather often a striking lack of rationality. A heavy smoker cannot readily accept evidence relating cancer to smoking;[2] a socialist, told that Hoover's endorsement of certain political slogans agreed perfectly with his own, calls him a 'typical hypocrite and a liar'.[3] Allport illustrates this irrationality in the following conversation:

Mr X: The trouble with Jews is that they only take care of their own group.

Mr Y: But the record of the Community Chest shows that they give more generously than non-Jews.

Mr X: That shows that they are always trying to buy favor and intrude in Christian affairs. They think of nothing but money; that is why there are so many Jewish bankers.

Mr Y: But a recent study shows that the per cent of Jews in banking is proportionally much smaller than the per cent of non-Jews.

Mr X: That's just it. They don't go in for respectable business. They would rather run night-clubs.[4]

Thus, while the concept of consistency acknowledges man's rationality, observation of the means of its achievement simultaneously unveils his irrationality. The psychoanalytic notion of

261

rationalization is a literal example of a concept which assumes both rationality and irrationality – it holds, namely, that man strives to understand and justify painful experiences and to make them sensible and rational, but he employs completely irrational methods to achieve this end.

The concepts of consistency are not novel. Nor are they indigenous to the study of attitudes, behavior, or personality. These concepts have appeared in various forms in almost all sciences. It has been argued by some that it is the existence of consistencies in the universe that made science possible, and by others that consistencies in the universe are a proof of divine power.[5] There is, of course, a question of whether consistencies are 'real' or mere products of ingenious abstraction and conceptualization. For it would be entirely possible to categorize natural phenomena in such a haphazard way that instead of order, unity, and consistency, one would see a picture of utter chaos. If we were to eliminate one of the spatial dimensions from the conception of the physical world, the consistencies we now know and the consistencies which allow us to make reliable predictions would be vastly depleted.

The concept of consistency in man is, then, a special case of the concept of universal consistency. The fascination with this concept led some psychologists to rather extreme positions. Franke, for instance, wrote, '. . . the unity of a person can be traced in each instant of his life. There is nothing in character that contradicts itself. If a person who is known to us seems to be incongruous with himself that is only an indication of the inadequacy and superficiality of our previous observations.'[6] This sort of hypothesis is, of course, incapable of either verification or disproof and therefore has no significant consequences.

Empirical investigations employing the concepts of consistency have been carried out for many years. Not until recently, however, has there been a programmatic and systematic effort to explore, with precision and detail, their particular consequences for behavior and attitudes. The greatest impetus to the study of attitudinal consistency was given recently by Festinger and his students. In addition to those already named, other related contributions in this area are those of Newcomb, who introduced the concept of 'strain toward symmetry',[7] and of Cartwright and Harary, who expressed the notions of balance and symmetry in a mathematical form.[8] These notions all assume inconsistency to be a painful or at least uncomfortable state, but they differ in the generality of application. The most restrictive and specific is the principle of congruity, since it restricts itself to the problems of the effects of information about objects and events on the attitudes toward the source of information. The most general is the notion of cognitive dissonance, since it considers consistency among any cognitions. In between are the notions of balance and symmetry, which consider attitudes toward people and objects in relation to one another, either within one person's cognitive structure, as in the case of Heider's theory of balance, or among a given group of individuals, as in the case of Newcomb's strain toward symmetry. It is the purpose of this paper to survey these concepts and to consider their implications for theory and research on attitudes.

The Concepts of Balance and Strain Toward Symmetry

The earliest formalization of consistency is attributed to Heider,[9] who was concerned with the way relations among persons involving some impersonal entity are cognitively experienced by the individual. The consistencies in which Heider was interested were those to be found in the ways people view their relations with other people and with the environment. The analysis was limited to two persons, labeled P and O, with P as the focus of the analysis and with O representing some other person, and to one impersonal entity, which could be a physical object, an idea, an event, or the like, labeled X. The object of Heider's inquiry was to discover how relations among P, O, and X are organized in P's cognitive structure, and whether there exist recurrent and systematic tendencies in the way these relations are experienced. Two types of relation, liking (L) and so-called U, or unit, relations (such as possession, cause, similarity, and the like) were distinguished. On the basis of incidental observations and intuitive judgment, probably, Heider proposed that the person's (P's) cognitive structure representing relations among P, O, and X are either what he termed 'balanced' or 'unbalanced'. In particular, he proposed, 'In the case of three entities, a balanced state exists if all three relations are positive in all respects or if two are negative and one positive.' Thus a balanced state is obtained when, for instance, P likes O, P likes X, and O likes X; or when P likes O, P dislikes X, and O dislikes X; or when P dislikes O, P likes X, and O dislikes X (see Figure 1). It should be noted that within Heider's conception a relation may be either positive or negative; degrees of liking cannot be represented. The fundamental assumption of balance theory is that an unbalanced state produces tension and generates forces to restore balance. This hypothesis was tested by Jordan.[10] He presented subjects with hypothetical situations involving two persons and an impersonal entity to rate for 'pleasantness'. Half the situations were by

263

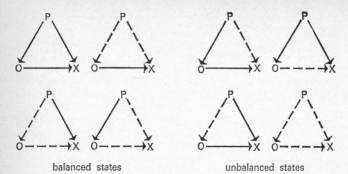

balanced states   unbalanced states

Figure 1 Examples of balanced and unbalanced states according to Heider's definition of balance. Solid lines represent positive, and broken lines negative, relations.

Heider's definition balanced and half unbalanced. Jordan's data showed somewhat higher unpleasantness ratings for the unbalanced than the balanced situations.

Cartwright and Harary[11] have cast Heider's formulation in graph-theoretical terms and derived some interesting consequences beyond those stated by Heider. Heider's concept allows either a balanced or an unbalanced state. Cartwright and Harary have constructed a more general definition of balance, with balance treated as a matter of degree, ranging from 0 to 1. Furthermore, their formulation of balance theory extended the notion to any number of entities, and an experiment by Morrissette[12] similar in design to that of Jordan obtained evidence for Cartwright and Harary's derivations.

A notion very similar to balance was advanced by Newcomb in 1953.[13] In addition to substituting A for P, and B for O, Newcomb took Heider's notion of balance out of one person's head and applied it to communication among people. Newcomb postulates a 'strain toward symmetry' which leads to a communality of attitudes of two people (A and B) oriented toward an object (X). The strain toward symmetry influences communication between A and B so as to bring their attitudes toward X into congruence. Newcomb cites a study in which a questionnaire was administered to college students in 1951 following the dismissal of General MacArthur by President Truman. Data were obtained on students' attitudes toward Truman's decision and their perception of the attitudes of their closest friends. Of the pro-Truman subjects 48 said that their closest friends favored Truman and none that their closest friends were opposed to his decision. Of the anti-Truman subjects only 2 said that their friends were generally pro-Truman, and 34 that they were anti-Truman. In a longitudinal study, considerably more convincing evidence was obtained in support of the strain-toward-symmetry hypothesis. In 1954 Newcomb set up a house at the University of Michigan which offered free rent for one semester for seventeen students who would serve as subjects. The residents of the house were observed, questioned, and rated for four to five hours a week during the entire semester. The study was then repeated with another set of seventeen students. The findings revealed a tendency for those who were attracted to one another to agree on many matters, including the way they perceived their own selves and their ideal selves, and their attractions for other group members. Moreover, in line with the prediction, these similarities, real as well as perceived, seemed to increase over time.[14]

Newcomb also cites the work of Festinger and his associates on social communication[15] in support of his hypothesis. Festinger's studies on communication have clearly shown that the tendency to influence other group members toward one's own opinion increases with the degree of attraction. More recently Burdick and Burnes reported two experiments in which measures of skin resistance (GSR) were obtained as an index of emotional reaction in the presence of balanced and unbalanced situations.[16] They observed significant differences in skin resistance depending on whether the subjects agreed or disagreed with a 'well-liked experimenter'. In the second experiment Burdick and Burnes found that subjects who liked the experimenter tended to change their opinions towards greater agreement with his, and those who disliked him, toward greater disagreement. There are, of course, many other studies to show that the attitude toward the communicator determines his persuasive effectiveness. Hovland and his co-workers have demonstrated these effects in several studies.[17] They have also shown, however, that these effects are fleeting; that is, the attitude change produced by the communication seems to dissipate over time. Their interpretation is that over time subjects tend to dissociate the source from the message and are therefore subsequently less influenced by the prestige of the communicator. This proposition was substantiated by Kelman and Hovland,[18] who produced attitude changes with a prestigeful communicator and retested subjects after a four-week interval with and without reminding the subjects about the communicator. The results showed that the permanence of the attitude change depended on the association with the source.

In general, the consequences of balance theories have up to now been rather limited. Except for Newcomb's longitudinal study, the experimental situations dealt mostly with subjects who responded to hypothetical situations, and direct evidence is scarce. The Burdick and Burnes experiment is the only one bearing more directly on the assumption that imbalance or asymmetry produces tension. Cartwright and Harary's mathematization of the concept of balance should, however, lead to important empirical and theoretical developments. One difficulty is that there really has not been a serious experimental attempt to *disprove* the theory. It is conceivable that some situations defined by the theory as unbalanced may in fact remain stable and produce no significant pressures toward balance. Festinger once inquired in a jocular mood if it followed from balance theory that since he likes chicken, and since chickens like chicken feed, he must also like chicken feed or else experience the tension of imbalance. While this counterexample is, of course, not to be taken seriously, it does point to some difficulties in the concepts of balance. It is not clear from Heider's theory of balance and Newcomb's theory of symmetry what predictions are to be made when attraction of both P and O toward X exists but when the origin and nature of these attractions are different. In other words, suppose both P and O like X but for different reasons and in entirely different ways, as was the case with Festinger and the chickens. Are the consequences of balance theory the same then as in the case where P and O like X for the same reasons and in the same way? It is also not clear, incidentally, what the consequences are when the relation between P and O is cooperative and when it is competitive. Two men vying for the hand of the same fair maiden might experience tension whether they are close friends or deadly enemies.

In a yet unpublished study conducted by Harburg and Price at the University of Michigan, students were asked to name two of their best friends. When those named were of opposite sexes, subjects reported they would feel uneasy if the two friends liked one another. In a subsequent experiment subjects were asked whether they desired their good friend to like, be neutral to, or dislike one of their strongly disliked acquaintances, and whether they desired the disliked acquaintance to like or dislike the friend. It will be recalled that in either case a balanced state obtains only if the two persons are negatively related to one another. However, Harburg and Price found that 39% desired their friend to be liked by the disliked acquaintance, and only 24% to be disliked. Moreover, faced with the alternative that the disliked acquaintance dislikes their friend, 55% as opposed to 25% expressed uneasiness. These results are quite inconsistent with balance theory. Although one may want one's friends to dislike one's enemies, one may not want the enemies to dislike one's friends. The reason for the latter may be simply a concern for the friends' welfare.

Osgood and Tannenbaum's Principle of Congruity

The principle of congruity, which is in fact a special case of balance, was advanced by Osgood and Tannenbaum in 1955.[19] It deals specifically with the problem of *direction* of attitude change. The authors assume that 'judgmental frames of reference tend toward maximal simplicity'. Thus, since extreme 'black-and-white', 'all-or-nothing', judgments are simpler than refined ones, valuations tend to move toward extremes or, in the words of the authors, there is 'a continuing pressure toward polarization'. Together with the notion of maximization of simplicity is the assumption of identity as being less complex than the discrimination of fine differences. Therefore, related 'concepts' will tend to be evaluated in a similar manner. Given these assumptions, the principle of congruity holds that when change in evaluation or attitude occurs it always occurs in the direction of increased congruity with the prevailing frame of reference. The paradigm of congruity is that of an individual who is confronted with an assertion regarding a particular matter about which he believes and feels in a certain way, made by a person toward whom he also has some attitude. Given that Eisenhower is evaluated positively and freedom of the press also positively, and given that Eisenhower (+) comes out in favor of freedom of the press (+), congruity is said to exist. But given that the *Daily Worker* is evaluated negatively, and given that the *Daily Worker* (—) comes out in favor of freedom of the press (+), incongruity is said to exist. Examples of congruity and incongruity are shown in Figure 2. The diagram shows the attitudes of a given individual toward the source and the object of the assertion. The assertions represented by heavy lines imply either positive or negative attitudes of the source toward the object. It is clear from a comparison of Figures 1 and 2 that in terms of their formal properties, the definitions of balance and congruity are identical. Thus, incongruity is said to exist when the attitudes toward the source and the object are similar and the assertion is negative, or when they are dissimilar and the assertion is positive. In comparison, unbalanced states are defined as having either one or all negative relations, which is of course equivalent to the above. To the extent that the person's attitudes are congruent with those

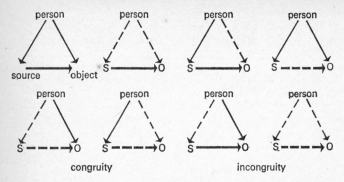

Figure 2 Examples of congruity and incongruity. Heavy lines represent assertions, light lines attitudes. Solid heavy lines represent assertions which imply a positive attitude on the part of the source, and broken heavy lines negative attitudes. Solid light lines represent positive, and broken light lines negative, attitudes.

implied in the assertion, a stable state exists. When the attitudes toward the person and the assertion are incongruent, there will be a tendency to change the attitudes toward the person and the object of the assertion in the direction of increased congruity. Tannenbaum obtained measures on 405 college students regarding their attitudes toward labor leaders, the *Chicago Tribune*, and Senator Robert Taft as sources, and toward legalized gambling, abstract art, and accelerated college programs as objects. Some time after the attitude scores were obtained, the subjects were presented with 'highly realistic' newspaper clippings involving assertions made by the various sources regarding the concepts. In general, when the original attitudes toward the source and the concept were both positive and the assertion presented in the newspaper clippings was also positive, no significant attitude changes were observed in the results. When the original attitudes toward the source and the concept were negative and the assertion was positive, again no changes were obtained. As predicted, however, when a positively valued source was seen as making a positive assertion about a negatively valued concept, the attitude toward the source became less favorable, and toward the concept more favorable. Conversely, when a negatively valued source was seen as making a positive assertion about a positively valued concept, attitudes toward the source became more favorable and toward the concept less favorable. The entire gamut of predicted changes was confirmed in Tannenbaum's data; it is summarized in the accompanying table, in which the direction of change is represented by either a plus or a minus sign, and the extent of change by either one or two such signs.

Change of Attitude toward the Source and the Object When Positive and Negative Assertions are Made by the Source

Original attitude toward the source	Positive assertion about an Object toward which the attitude is		Negative assertion about an object toward which the Attitude is	
	Positive	Negative	Positive	Negative
	Change of attitude toward the source			
Positive	+	——	——	+
Negative	++	—	—	++
	Change of attitude toward the object			
Positive	+	++	——	—
Negative	——	—	+	++

A further derivation of the congruity principle is that incongruity does not invariably produce attitude change, but that it may at times lead to incredulity on the part of the individual. When confronted by an assertion which stands in an incongruous relation to the person who made it, there will be a tendency not to believe that the person made the assertion, thus reducing incongruity.

There is a good deal of evidence supporting Osgood and Tannenbaum's principle of congruity. As early as 1921, H. T. Moore had subjects judge statements for their grammar, ethical infringements for their seriousness, and resolutions of the dominant seventh chord for their dissonance.[20] After two and one-half months the subjects returned and were presented with judgments of 'experts'. This experimental manipulation resulted in 62% reversals of judgments on grammar, 50% of ethical judgments, and 43% of musical judgments. And in 1935 in a study on a similar problem of prestige suggestion, Sherif let subjects rank sixteen authors for their literary merit.[21] Subsequently, the subjects were given sixteen passages presumably written by the various authors previously ranked. The subjects were asked to rank-order the passages for literary merit. Although in actuality *all* the passages were written by Robert Louis Stevenson, the subjects were able to rank the passages. Moreover, the correlations between the merit of the author and the merit of the passage ranged from between 0·33 to 0·53. These correlations are not very dramatic, yet they do represent some impact of attitude toward the source on attitude toward the passage.

With respect to incredulity, an interesting experiment was conducted recently by Jones and Kohler in which subjects learned statements which either supported their attitudes or were in disagreement with them.[22] Some of the statements were plausible and some implausible. The results were rather striking. Subjects whose attitudes favored segregation learned plausible pro-segregation statements and implausible anti-segregation statements much more rapidly than plausible anti-segregation and implausible pro-segregation statements. The reverse was of course true for subjects whose attitudes favored desegregation.

While the principle of congruity presents no new ideas, it has a great advantage over the earlier attempts in its precision. Osgood and Tannenbaum have formulated the principle of congruity in quantitative terms allowing for precise predictions regarding the extent and direction of attitude change – predictions which in their studies were fairly well confirmed. While balance theory allows merely a dichotomy of attitudes, either positive or negative, the principle of congruity allows refined measurements using Osgood's method of the semantic differential.[23] Moreover, while it is not clear from Heider's statement of balance in just what direction changes will occur when an unbalanced state exists, such predictions can be made on the basis of the congruity principle.

Festinger's Theory of Cognitive Dissonance

Perhaps the largest systematic body of data is that collected in the realm of Festinger's dissonance theory. The statement of the dissonance principle is simple. It holds that two elements of knowledge '. . . are in dissonant relation if, considering these two alone, the obverse of one element would follow from the other'.[24] It further holds that dissonance '. . . being psychologically uncomfortable, will motivate the person to try to reduce dissonance and achieve consonance' and '. . . in addition to trying to reduce it, the person will actively avoid situations and information which would likely increase the dissonance'.[25] A number of rather interesting and provocative consequences follow from Festinger's dissonance hypothesis.

First, it is predicted that all decisions or choices result in dissonance to the extent that the alternative not chosen contains positive features which make it attractive also, and the alternative chosen contains features which might have resulted in rejecting it. Hence after making a choice people seek evidence to confirm their decision and so reduce dissonance. In the Ehrlich experiment the finding was that new car owners noticed and read ads about the cars they had recently purchased more than ads about other cars.[26]

Post-decision dissonance was also shown to result in a change of attractiveness of the alternative involved in a decision. Brehm had female subjects rate eight appliances for desirability.[27] Subsequently, the subjects were given a choice between two of the eight products, given the chosen product, and after some interpolated activity (consisting of reading research reports about four of the appliances) were asked to rate the products again. Half the subjects were given a choice between products which they rated in a similar manner, and half between products on which the ratings differed. Thus in the first case higher dissonance was to be expected than in the second. The prediction from dissonance theory that there should be an increase in the attractiveness of the chosen alternative and decrease in the attractiveness of the rejected alternative was on the whole confirmed. Moreover, the further implication was also confirmed that the pressure to reduce dissonance (which was accomplished in the above experiment by changes in attractiveness of the alternatives) varies directly with the extent of dissonance.

Another body of data accounted for by the dissonance hypothesis deals with situations in which the person is forced (either by reward or punishment) to express an opinion publicly or make a public judgment or statement which is contrary to his own opinions and beliefs. In cases where the person actually makes such a judgment or expresses an opinion contrary to his own as a result of a promised reward or threat, dissonance exists between the knowledge of the overt behavior of the person and his privately held beliefs. Festinger also argues that in the case of noncompliance dissonance will exist between the knowledge of overt behavior and the anticipation of reward and punishment.

An example of how dissonance theory accounts for forced-compliance data is given by Brehm.[28] Brehm offered prizes to eighth-graders for eating disliked vegetables and obtained measures of how well the children liked the vegetables. Children who ate the vegetables increased their liking for them. Of course, one might argue that a simpler explanation of the results is that the attractiveness of the prize generalized to the vegetable, or that, even more simply, the vegetables increased in utility because a reward came with them. However, this argument would also lead one to predict that the increment in attraction under such conditions is a *direct* function of the magnitude of the reward. Dissonance theory makes the opposite prediction, and therefore a test of the validity of the two explanations is possible. Data collected by Festinger and Carlsmith[29] and by Aronson and Mills[30] support the dissonance point of view. In Festinger and Carlsmith's experiment subjects were offered either $20 or $1 for telling someone that an experience which had actually been quite boring had been rather enjoyable and interesting. When measures of the subjects' private opinions about their actual enjoyment of the task were taken, those who were to be paid only $1 for the false testimony showed considerably higher scores than those who were to be paid $20. Aronson and Mills, on the other hand, tested the effects of negative incentive. They invited college women to join a group requiring them to go through a process of initiation. For some women the initiation was quite severe, for others it was mild. The prediction from dissonance theory that those who had to undergo severe initiation would increase their attraction for the group more than those having no initiation or mild initiation was borne out.

A third set of consequences of the theory of dissonance deals with exposure to information. Since dissonance occurs between cognitive elements, and since information may lead to change in these elements, the principle of dissonance should have a close bearing on the individual's commerce with information. In particular, the assumption that dissonance is a psychologically uncomfortable state leads to the prediction that individuals will seek out information reducing dissonance and avoid information increasing it. The study on automobile-advertising readership described above is a demonstration of this hypothesis. [31] In another study Mills, Aronson, and Robinson gave college students a choice between an objective and an essay examination.[32] Following the decision, the subjects were given articles about examinations presumably written by experts, and they were asked if they would like to read them. In addition, in order to vary the intensity of dissonance, half the subjects were told that the examination counted 70% toward the final grade, and half that it counted only 5%. The data were obtained in the form of rankings of the articles for preference. While there was a clear preference for reading articles containing positive information about the alternative chosen, no significant selective effects were found when the articles presented arguments against the given type of examination. Also, the authors failed to demonstrate effects relating selectivity in exposure to information to the magnitude of dissonance, in that no significant differences were found between subjects for whom the examination was quite important (70% of the final grade) and those for whom it was relatively unimportant (5% of the final grade).

Festinger was able to account for many other results by means of the dissonance principle, and in general his theory is rather successful in organizing a diverse body of empirical knowledge by means of a limited number of fairly reasonable assumptions. Moreover, from these reasonable assumptions dissonance theory generated several nontrivial and nonobvious consequences. The negative relationship between the magnitude of incentive and attraction of the object of false testimony is not at all obvious. Also not obvious is the prediction of an increase in proselytizing for a mystical belief following an event that clearly contradicts it. Festinger, Riecken, and Schachter studied a group of 'Seekers' – people who presumably received a message from outer space informing them of an incipient major flood.[33] When the flood failed to materialize on the critical date, instead of quietly withdrawing from the public scene, as one would expect, the 'Seekers' summoned press representatives, gave extended interviews, and invited the public to visit them and be informed of the details of the whole affair. In a very recent study by Brehm, a 'nonobvious' derivation from dissonance theory was tested.[34] Brehm predicted that when forced to engage in an unpleasant activity, an individual's liking for this activity will increase more when he receives information essentially berating the activity than when he receives information promoting it. The results tended to support Brehm's prediction. Since negative information is said to increase dissonance, and since increased dissonance leads to an increased tendency to reduce it, and since the only means of dissonance reduction was increasing the attractiveness of the activity, such an increase would in fact be expected.

Conclusions

The theories and empirical work dealing with consistencies are mainly concerned with intra-individual phenomena, be it with relationships between one attitude and another, between attitudes and values, or information, or perception, or behavior, or the like. One exception is Newcomb's concept of 'strain toward symmetry'. Here the concern is primarily with the interplay of forces among individuals which results in uniformities or consistencies among them. There is no question that the concepts of consistency, and especially the theory of cognitive dissonance, account for many varied attitudinal phenomena. Of course, the various formulations of consistency do not pretend, nor are they able, to account completely for the phenomena they examine. Principles of consistency, like all other principles, are prefaced by the *ceteris paribus* preamble. Thus, when other factors are held constant, then the principles of consistency should be able to explain behavior and attitudes completely. But the question to be raised here is just what factors must be held constant and how important and significant, relative to consistency, are they.

Suppose a man feels hostile toward the British and also dislikes cricket. One might be tempted to conclude that if one of his attitudes were different he would experience the discomfort of incongruity. But there are probably many people whose attitudes toward the British and cricket are incongruent, although the exact proportions are not known and are hardly worth serious inquiry. But if such an inquiry were undertaken it would probably disclose that attitudes depend largely on the conditions under which they have been acquired. For one thing, it would show that the attitudes depend at least to some extent on the relationship of the attitude object to the individual's needs and fears, and that these may be stronger than forces toward balance. There are in this world things to be avoided and feared. A child bitten by a dog will not develop favorable attitudes toward dogs. And no matter how much he likes Popeye you can't make him like spinach, although according to balance theory he should.

The relationship between attitudes and values or needs has been explored, for instance, in *The Authoritarian Personality*, which appeared in 1950.[35] The authors of this work hypothesized a close relationship between attitudes and values on the one hand and personality on the other. They assumed that the ' . . . convictions of an individual often form a broad and coherent pattern, as if bound together by a mentality or spirit.' They further assumed that '. . . opinions, attitudes, and values depend on human needs and since personality is essentially an organization of needs, then personality may be regarded as a determinant of ideological preference.' Thus the *Authoritarian Personality* approach also stresses consistency, but while the concepts of congruity, balance, and dissonance are satisfied with assuming a general tendency toward consistency, the *Authoritarian Personality* theory goes further in that it holds that the dynamic of consistency is to be found in personality, and it is personality which gives consistency meaning and direction. Attitudes and values are thus seen to be consistent among themselves and with one another because they are both consistent with the basic personality needs, and they are consistent with needs because they are determined by them.

The very ambitious research deriving from the *Authoritarian Personality* formulation encountered many difficulties and, mainly because of serious methodological and theoretical shortcomings, has gradually lost its popularity. However, some aspects of this general approach have been salvaged by others. Rosenberg, for instance, has shown that attitudes are intimately related to the capacity of the attitude object to be instrumental to the attainment of the individual's values.[36] Carlson went a step further and has shown that, if the perceived instrumentality of the object with respect to a person's values and needs is changed, the attitude itself may be modified.[37] These studies, while not assuming a general consistency principle, illustrate a special instance of consistency, namely that between attitudes and utility, or instrumentality of attitude objects, with respect to the person's values and needs.

The concepts of consistency bear a striking historical similarity to the concept of vacuum. According to an excellent account by Conant,[38] for centuries the principle that nature abhors a vacuum served to account for various phenomena, such as the action of pumps, behavior of liquids in joined vessels, suction, and the like. The strength of everyday evidence was so overwhelming that the principle was seldom questioned. However, it was known that one cannot draw water to a height of more than 34 feet. The simplest solution of this problem was to reformulate the principle to read that 'nature abhors a vacuum below 34 feet'. This modified version of *horror vacui* again was satisfactory for the phenomena it dealt with, until it was discovered that 'nature abhors a vacuum below 34 feet only when we deal with water'. As Torricelli has shown, when it comes to mercury 'nature abhors a vacuum below 30 inches'. Displeased with the crudity of a principle which must accommodate numerous exceptions, Torricelli formulated the notion that it was the pressure of air acting upon the surface of the liquid which was responsible for the height to which one could draw liquid by the action of pumps. The 34-foot limit represented the weight of water which the air pressure on the surface of earth could maintain and the 30-inch limit represented the weight of mercury that air pressure could maintain. This was an entirely different and revolutionary concept, and its consequences had drastic impact on physics. Human nature, on the other hand, is said to abhor inconsistency. For the time being the principle is quite adequate, since it accounts systematically for many phenomena, some of which have never been explained and all of which have never been explained by one principle. But already today there are exceptions to consistency and balance. Some people who spend a good portion of their earnings on insurance also gamble. The first action presumably is intended to protect them from risks, the other to expose them to risks. Almost everybody enjoys a magician. And the magician only creates dissonance – you see before you an event which you know to be impossible on the basis of previous knowledge – the obverse of what you see follows from what you know. If the art of magic is essentially the art of producing dissonance, and if human nature abhors dissonance, why is the art of magic still flourishing? If decisions are necessarily followed by dissonance, and if nature abhors dissonance, why are decisions ever made? Although it is true that those decisions which would ordinarily lead to great dissonance take a very long time to make, they are made anyway. And it is also true that human nature does not abhor dissonance absolutely, as nature abhors a vacuum. Human nature merely avoids dissonance, and it would follow from dissonance theory that decisions whose instrumental consequences would not be worth the dissonance to follow would never be made. There are thus far no data to support this hypothesis, nor data to disprove it.

According to Conant, *horror vacui* served an important purpose besides explaining and organizing some aspects of physical knowledge. Without it the discomfort of 'exceptions to the rule' would never have been felt, and the important developments in theory might have been delayed considerably. If a formulation has then a virtue in being wrong, the theories of consistency do have this virtue. They do organize a large body of knowledge. Also, they point out exceptions, and thereby they demand a new formulation. It will not suffice simply to reformulate them so as to accommodate the exceptions. I doubt if Festinger would be satisfied with a modification of his dissonance principle which would read that dissonance, being psychologically uncomfortable, leads a person to actively avoid situations and information which would be likely to increase the dissonance, except when there is an opportunity to watch a magician. Also, simply to disprove the theories by counterexamples would not in itself constitute an important contribution. We would merely lose explanations of phenomena which had been explained. And it is doubtful that the theories of consistency could be rejected simply *because* of counterexamples. Only a theory which accounts for all the data that the consistency principles now account for, for all the exceptions to those principles and for all the phenomena which these principles should now but do not consider, is capable of replacing them. It is only a matter of time until such a development takes place.

References

1. The concepts of balance, congruity, and dissonance are due to Heider, Osgood and Tannenbaum, and Festinger, respectively. (F. Heider, 'Attitudes and Cognitive Organization', *Journal of Psychology*, Vol. 21, pp. 107–112, 1946. C. E. Osgood and P. H. Tannenbaum, 'The Principle of Congruity in the Prediction of Attitude Change', *Psychological Review*, Vol. 62, pp. 42–55, 1955. L. Festinger, *A Theory of Cognitive Dissonance*, Evanston, Ill., Row, Peterson, 1957.) For purposes of simplicity we will subsume these concepts under the label of consistency.
2. Festinger, op. cit., pp. 153-6.
3. H. B. Lewis, 'Studies in the Principles of Judgments and Attitudes: IV, The Operation of 'Prestige Suggestion', *Journal of Social Psychology*, Vol. 14, pp. 229–56, 1941.
4. G. W. Allport, *The Nature of Prejudice*, Cambridge, Mass., Addison-Wesley, 1954.
5. W. P. Montague, *Belief Unbound*, New Haven, Conn., Yale University Press, pp. 70–3, 1930.
6. R. Franke, 'Gang und Character', *Beihefte, Zeitschrift für angewandte Psychologie*, No. 58, p. 45, 1931.
7. T. M. Newcomb, 'An Approach to the Study of Communicative Acts', *Psychological Review*, Vol. 60, pp. 393–404, 1953.
8. D. Cartwright and F. Harary, 'Structural Balance: A Generalization of Heider's Theory', *Psychological Review*, Vol. 63, pp. 277–93, 1956.
9. Heider, op. cit.
10. N. Jordan, 'Behavioral Forces That Are a Function of Attitudes and of Cognitive Organization', *Human Relations*, Vol. 6, pp. 273–87, 1953.
11. Cartwright and Harary, op. cit.
12. J. Morrissette, 'An Experimental Study of the Theory of Structural Balance', *Human Relations*, Vol. 11, pp. 239–54, 1958.
13. Newcomb, op. cit.
14. T. M. Newcomb, 'The Prediction of Interpersonal Attraction', *American Psychologist*, Vol. 11, pp. 575–86, 1956.
15. L. Festinger, K. Back, S. Schachter, H. H. Kelley, and J. Thibaut, *Theory and Experiment in Social Communication*, Ann Arbor, Mich., University of Michigan, Institute for Social Research, 1950.
16. H. A. Burdick and A. J. Burnes, 'A Test of "Strain toward Symmetry" Theories', *Journal of Abnormal and Social Psychology*, Vol. 57, pp. 367–9, 1958.
17. C. I. Hovland, I. L. Janis, and H. H. Kelley, *Communication and Persuasion: Psychological Studies of Opinion Change*, New Haven, Conn., Yale University Press, 1953.
18. H. C. Kelman and C. I. Hovland, '"Reinstatement" of the Communicator in Delayed Measurement of Opinion Change', *Journal of Abnormal and Social Psychology*, Vol. 48, pp. 327–35, 1953.
19. Osgood and Tannenbaum, op. cit.
20. H. T. Moore, 'The Comparative Influence of Majority and Expert Opinion', *American Journal of Psychology*, Vol. 32, pp. 16–20, 1921.
21. M. Sherif, 'An Experimental Study of Stereotypes', *Journal of Abnormal and Social Psychology*, Vol. 29, pp. 371–5, 1935.

22. E. E. Jones and R. Kohler, 'The Effects of Plausibility on the Learning of Controversial Statements', *Journal of Abnormal and Social Psychology*, Vol. 57, pp. 315–20, 1958.

23. C. E. Osgood, 'The Nature and Measurement of Meaning', *Psychological Bulletin*, Vol. 49, pp. 197–237, 1952.

24. Festinger, op. cit., p. 13.

25. Ibid., p. 3.

26. D. Ehrlich, I. Guttman, P. Schönbach, and J. Mills, 'Post-decision Exposure to Relevant Information', *Journal of Abnormal and Social Psychology*, Vol. 54, pp. 98–102, 1957.

27. J. Brehm, 'Post-decision Changes in the Desirability of Alternatives', *Journal of Abnormal and Social Psychology*, Vol. 52, pp. 384–9, 1956.

28. J. Brehm, 'Increasing Cognitive Dissonance by a *Fait Accompli*', *Journal of Abnormal and Social Psychology*, Vol. 58, pp. 379–82, 1959.

29. L. Festinger and J. M. Carlsmith, 'Cognitive Consequences of Forced Compliance', *Journal of Abnormal and Social Psychology*, Vol. 58, pp. 203–10, 1959.

30. E. Aronson and J. Mills, 'The Effect of Severity of Initiation on Liking for a Group', *Journal of Abnormal and Social Psychology*, Vol. 59, pp. 177–81, 1959.

31. Ehrlich *et al.*, op. cit.

32. J. Mills, E. Aronson, and H. Robinson, 'Selectivity in Exposure to Information', *Journal of Abnormal and Social Psychology*, Vol. 59, pp. 250–3, 1959.

33. L. Festinger, J. Riecken, and S. Schachter, *When Prophecy Fails*, Minneapolis, University of Minnesota Press, 1956.

34. J. W. Brehm, 'Attitudinal Consequences of Commitment to Unpleasant Behavior', *Journal of Abnormal and Social Psychology*, Vol. 60, pp. 379–83, 1960.

35. T. W. Adorno, E. Frenkel-Brunswik, D. J. Levinson, and R. N. Sanford, *The Authoritarian Personality*, New York, Harper, 1950.

36. M. J. Rosenberg, 'Cognitive Structure and Attitudinal Affect', *Journal of Abnormal and Social Psychology*, Vol. 53, pp. 367–72, 1956.

37. E. R. Carlson, 'Attitude Change through Modification of Attitude Structure', *Journal of Abnormal and Social Psychology*, Vol. 52, pp. 256–61, 1956.

38. James B. Conant, *On Understanding Science*, New Haven, Conn., Yale University Press, 1947.

Social Attitudes and the Resolution of Motivational Conflict

Excerpt from: I. Sarnoff, *Personality Dynamics and Development*, Wiley, U.S.A., 1962.

The definition of attitude to be followed here is one about which a certain amount of agreement seems to exist among contemporary psychologists: *a disposition to react favorably or unfavorably to a class of objects*. This disposition may, of course, be inferred from a variety of observable responses made by the individual when he is confronted by a member of the class of objects toward which he has an attitude: facial expressions, postures, locomotions, sounds of voice and verbalizations. Moreover, an individual need not be aware of his attitude nor of the behaviors on the bases of which his attitude is inferred by others. However, insofar as psychologists have employed self-rating verbal scales as their operational measures of attitudes, they have been dealing with attitudes of which the individual – at least after filling out a questionnaire about his attitudes – is aware. In addition, verbalized attitudes of this sort tend to be couched in a set of cognitions about the attitudinal objects – articulate ideas and perceptions within which the favorable or unfavorable dispositions toward a given class of objects are imbedded.

Since attitudes are inferred from overt responses, and since overt responses are made in order to reduce the tension generated by motives, we may assume that attitudes are developed in the process of making tension-reducing responses to various classes of objects. In short, *an individual's attitude toward a class of objects is determined by the particular role those objects have come to play in facilitating responses that reduce the tension of particular motives and that resolve particular conflicts among motives*.

Attitudes and Consciously Acceptable Motives

Oriented in terms of his acceptable motives, the objects in the individual's environment fall into two classes:

1. Those to which he must have access and toward which he must make a specific overt response if the tension of a given motive is to be maximally reduced.

2. Those that facilitate or thwart the possibility of making the specific overt response necessary to reduce the tension of a motive. Frequently, these facilitating or thwarting objects either lead to or block the individual's access to those objects to which he must respond in a specific way if the tensions of his motives are to be maximally reduced.

Because attitudes are dispositions to respond favorably or unfavorably to objects, they should, *in the case of consciously acceptable motives*, be determined by the role that objects play in the maximal reduction of tension generated by the individual's motives. Thus, if an individual's motive is known to be acceptable to him, it should be possible to predict a variety of his attitudes toward objects in his environment. Let us suppose that Individual X has acquired an achievement motive. In order to reduce the tension generated by that motive, he is obliged to make quite specific responses under quite specific conditions. If Individual X fully accepts his achievement motive, we would expect him to have a favorable attitude toward: (*a*) those conditions of work that permit him to make the response upon which the criteria of achievement can be imposed; (*b*) those concrete objects, such as prizes, medals and certificates, that connote the fact of achievement; (*c*) those persons who provide the opportunity to make responses that reduce the tension of the achievement motive.

On the other hand, Individual X ought to have unfavorable attitudes toward: (*a*) those conditions of work that preclude or limit the possibility of making responses upon which the criteria of achievement can be imposed; (*b*) those concrete objects, such as low pay, that connote the failure to achieve; (*c*) those persons who create or threaten to create obstacles in the pursuit of achievement criteria.

In order to illustrate further the relationship between attitude and motive when the motive is consciously acceptable to the individual, let us consider two more of Individual X's motives: aggression and fear. The aggressive motive is often provoked by objects that thwart him in his attempts at motive satisfaction. Once it is induced, the aggressive motive can only be maximally reduced by making hostile or combative responses to those objects that provoked it. And since attitudes anticipate responses, it follows that the individual will develop an unfavorable attitude toward those objects to which he must respond with hostile acts in order to reduce maximally the tension of his aggressive motive.

Paradoxically enough, but in accordance with the formulation presented here, people will tend to develop favorable attitudes toward those objects that facilitate the maximal reduction of their aggressive motive. Thus, if someone in Individual X's office were to help him in bringing about the downfall or embarrassment of one of X's hated rivals, X would tend to have a favorable attitude toward his accomplice. It is conceivable that the reduction in prejudice which many white troops in integrated combat units appeared to experience in regard to their attitude toward Negroes (Stouffer *et al.*, 1949) may be attributable to the fact that they were in a position to observe directly Negroes in the process of reducing a strong motive that they shared with them: hatred of the enemy.

Quite frequently, the same objects that provoke aggression also provoke the fear motive. Thus, both fear and aggression are likely to be aroused when the individual is confronted by an object that directly threatens his survival. If the individual is able consciously to accept his fear, he attempts to make overt responses that will maximally reduce the tension of his fear. Accordingly, he will respond by attempting to separate himself from the feared object; and the unfavorableness of his attitude toward the threatening object ought to be influenced by his distance from it, that is, its capacity to harm him. The closer the object gets to him, the greater his fear of it, and, hence, the greater his unfavorable attitude toward it. As the threatening object loses its capacity to harm, the individual should grow less fearful of it and develop a more favorable attitude toward it. Similarly, the individual ought to develop favorable or unfavorable attitudes toward other objects that he perceives either to thwart or facilitate the making of those responses to the threatening object that will be maximally reductive of the fear induced by the object.

Even if all of the motives comprising a particular motivational conflict are consciously acceptable to him, the individual obviously cannot respond in any way that will provide simultaneous and maximal reduction of the tensions of all of his motives. On the contrary, in order to obtain a maximal reduction in tension for any one of his consciously acceptable motives, the individual must keep his responses to the other motives in abeyance. And the two kinds of responses that permit the postponement of maximal tension-reducing responses to consciously acceptable motives – inhibition and suppression – have already been discussed. It only remains to be pointed out, therefore, that attitudes may be formed in the process of facilitating the effect of these postponing responses as well as in the eventual process of reducing the tensions of the consciously acceptable motives *per se*. Considered from the standpoint of inhibition, for example, an individual's disposition to respond favorably or unfavorably to an object may be determined by the extent to which a given disposition is required if the individual is to avoid making an overt, tension-reducing response to the inhibited motive. Such phenomena as hypocrisy, duplicity and other types of interpersonal deception may involve just such a discrepancy between an individual's behavior (from which his ongoing attitude is inferred) and his conscious and inhibited motive.

Another, less anecdotal, example of attitudes that are formed in order to facilitate either inhibition or suppression may, perhaps, be found in Schanck's classical observation of discrepancies between publicly and privately expressed attitudes (Katz and Schanck, 1938). From the standpoint of the preceding discussion, an individual's publicly and privately expressed attitudes are equally 'real' or 'valid'. For they both facilitate the making of responses to motives. However, it is likely that the publicly expressed attitudes more often reflect the facilitation of inhibiting or suppressing responses to motives. Thus, if the verbalized attitude implies tension-reducing responses that the respondent believes might evoke unwanted disapproval, the respondent may wish to inhibit such responses when they are open to public scrutiny. One way of preventing the overt emergence of potentially punishable responses is to make them with less force; or, still better to make qualitatively different sorts of responses, ones that are not commonly associated with the inhibited motive. In private, however, when the individual feels free of potential punishment, he can permit the overt expression of those responses that are maximally reductive of the motive that he had inhibited or suppressed in public. Consequently, his attitude should change as he changes from a motive-inhibiting response to a motive-reducing response.

Attitudes and Consciously Unacceptable Motives

Because the individual cannot tolerate, by definition, the awareness of his consciously unacceptable motives, he is unable to use the devices of inhibition and suppression in connection with deferment of those motives. Instead, he develops the various mechanisms of ego defense whose operations are not discernible to the individual but whose effects, nevertheless, prevent him from becoming cognizant of the existence of motives that have traumatic implications for him.

Theoretically, different mechanisms of ego defense exert different effects on the unconscious motives whose banishment from consciousness those mechanisms insure; and, since these effects are wrought automatically, the individual remains unconscious of both the functioning of his ego defenses and the motives whose perception they obscure. It is evident, therefore, that the conceptual relationship between an attitude and a consciously unacceptable motive is considerably more complicated than that which exists between an attitude and a consciously acceptable motive. Certainly, knowledge of any given attitude *per se* would be an insufficient basis for imputing the specific consciously unacceptable motive to which it is functionally related; or, indeed, for inferring that the attitude in question is related to a consciously unacceptable motive rather than a consciously acceptable one. Thus, for example, Individual A, a Southern shopkeeper, may experience a motivational conflict between his conscious desire to promote his democratic ideals and his conscious desire to make money. Assuming that the motive to make money is more highly placed in his motivational hierarchy, Individual A may *consciously decide* to inhibit the public expression of his equalitarian feelings for Negroes. In fact, Individual A may *deliberately* behave in a manner that leads his prejudiced neighbours to infer that he shares their anti-Negro attitudes: he may, for instance, grin at anti-Negro jokes, nod his head at bigoted remarks made in his presence and offer his own negative pronouncements about Negroes. Approving of the anti-Negro sentiments that they see in this behavior, Individual A's neighbors patronize his store and help to reduce, thereby, the tensions of his motive to make money.

For Individual B, however, identical expressions of anti-Negro sentiments may be an indication of an ego-defensive response that functions to prevent his awareness of the existence of a consciously unacceptable motive. For example, he may be unable to accept consciously the fact that he possesses an aggressive motive. By means of the ego defense of projection Individual B may attribute that motive to Negroes and, hence, be spared the unpleasantness of seeing it in himself.

Since the individual's consciously unacceptable motives cannot be reliably predicted solely on the basis of his manifest attitudes, a precise determination of the functional relationship between an attitude and a consciously unacceptable motive involves:

1. A postulation of which *combination* of consciously unacceptable motive and ego defense might plausibly account for the *particular* overt response from which the attitude is inferred.
2. After conceptualizing this most plausible combination of ego

defense and consciously unacceptable motive, we must proceed to demonstrate *empirically* the relationship between that combination and the attitude it is presumed to support.

In general, such attempted empirical demonstrations have, in the past, employed correlational methods. Thus, as exemplified by the extremely influential research report, *The Authoritarian Personality* (Adorno *et al.*, 1950), responses to attitude scales are correlated with responses to personality scales, projective tests or interviews. The particular measures of personality are, of course, coded in terms of the motivational and ego-defensive categories required by the investigator's guiding hypotheses. The resulting correlations between the attitudinal and personality measures provide the evidence on the basis of which the hypotheses are evaluated.

The other method of testing hypotheses concerning the functional relationships between attitudes and consciously unacceptable motives is, of course, experimental. While the logical advantages of an experiment over a correlational approach are quite apparent, so are the difficulties of contriving adequate experimental manipulations for, and controls over, the complex variables involved. These difficulties may, perhaps, account for the fact that relatively few experiments have been conducted in this area. In any case, an experimental test of the functional relationship between an attitude and a consciously unacceptable motive would require, depending upon the particular prediction, either:

1. The manipulation of the ego defenses that presumably function to obliterate the perception of the consciously unacceptable motive whose functional relationship to the attitude had been postulated; or
2. The arousal of the motive against whose conscious perception the individual is supposed to be defending himself by use of a particular mechanism of ego defense.

If the theoretically suggested manipulation or arousal produces the predicted changes in those responses toward objects from which the attitude in question is inferred, the experiment is held to have supported the original hypothesis.

References
Adorno, T. W., Frenkel-Brunswik, E., Levinson, D. J., and Sanford, R. N., *The Authoritarian Personality*. New York: Harper, 1950.
Katz, D., and Schanck, R. L., *Social Psychology*. New York: Wiley, 1938.
Stouffer, S. A., Suchman, E. A., De Vinney, L. C., Star, Shirley A., and Williams, R. M., *The American Soldier*, Vol. I. Princeton: Princeton Univ. Press, 1949.

II Attitude Methodology

In the conduct of research at least three basic methodological decisions have to be made: the choice of research design, the method of data collection and quantification, and the logic of interpretation and inference. Each of these concerns is taken up by one of the selections which follow. Carl Hovland discusses the issues raised by discrepancies in findings between controlled experimental research carried out in the laboratory and sample surveys in which information is obtained from respondents by means of interviews or questionnaires. Hovland suggests reasons for the frequent divergence in findings and proposes an integration of the apparent conflicts. The major point is that the 'audience' exercises more initiative outside than inside the laboratory. Claire Selltiz and her colleagues provide a concise and clear exposition of various methods for the quantitative scaling of attitudes, dealing with the now classic approaches to scaling which are identified by the names of Thurstone, Likert, Bogardus and Guttman. Finally, an article by Cook and Selltiz presents a valuable survey of different types of measurement approaches, from the point of view of the kinds of evidence they provide as a basis for assessing attitudes and of the nature of the inferences involved.

25 C. I. Hovland

Reconciling Conflicting Results Derived from Experimental and Survey Studies of Attitude Change*

Reprinted from: *The American Psychologist*, Vol. 14, 1959, pp. 8–17.

Two quite different types of research design are characteristically used to study the modification of attitudes through communication. In the first type, the *experiment*, individuals are given a controlled exposure to a communication and the effects evaluated in terms of the amount of change in attitude or opinion produced. A base line is provided by means of a control group not exposed to the communication. The study of Gosnell (1927) on the influence of leaflets designed to get voters to the polls is a classic example of the controlled experiment.

In the alternative research design, the *sample survey*, information is secured through interviews or questionnaires both concerning the respondent's exposure to various communications and his attitudes and opinions on various issues. Generalizations are then derived from the correlations obtained between reports of exposure and measurements of attitude. In a variant of this method, measurements of attitude and of exposure to communication are obtained during repeated interviews with the same individual over a period of weeks or months. This is the 'panel method' extensively utilized in studying the impact of various mass media on political attitudes and on voting behavior (cf., e.g., Kendall and Lazarsfeld, 1950).

Generalizations derived from experimental and from correlational studies of communication effects are usually both reported in chapters on the effects of mass media and in other summaries of research on attitude, typically without much stress on the type of study from which the conclusion was derived. Close scrutiny of the results obtained from the two methods, however, suggests a marked difference in the picture of communication effects obtained from each. The object of my paper is to consider the conclusions derived from these two types of design, to suggest some of the factors responsible for the frequent divergence in results, and then

---

* This article, though primarily methodological, is clearly also relevant to problems of attitude change, and may be read in connexion with the earlier section on that topic. – Eds.

to formulate principles aimed at reconciling some of the apparent conflicts.

Divergence

The picture of mass communication effects which emerges from correlational studies is one in which few individuals are seen as being affected by communications. One of the most thorough correlational studies of the effects of mass media on attitudes is that of Lazarsfeld, Berelson, and Gaudet published in *The People's Choice* (1944). In this report there is an extensive chapter devoted to the effects of various media, particularly radio, newspapers, and magazines. The authors conclude that few changes in attitudes were produced. They estimate that the political positions of only about 5% of their respondents were changed by the election campaign, and they are inclined to attribute even this small amount of change more to personal influence than to the mass media. A similar evaluation of mass media is made in the recent chapter in the *Handbook of Social Psychology* by Lipset and his collaborators (1954).

Research using experimental procedures, on the other hand, indicates the possibility of considerable modifiability of attitudes through exposure to communication. In both Klapper's survey (1949) and in my chapter in the *Handbook of Social Psychology* (Hovland, 1954) a number of experimental studies are discussed in which the opinions of a third to a half or more of the audience are changed.

The discrepancy between the results derived from these two methodologies raises some fascinating problems for analysis. This divergence in outcome appears to me to be largely attributable to two kinds of factors: one, the difference in research design itself; and two, the historical and traditional differences in general approach to evaluation characteristic of researchers using the experimental as contrasted with the correlational or survey method. I would like to discuss, first, the influence these factors have on the estimation of overall effects of communications, and then turn to other divergences in outcome characteristically found by the use of the experimental and survey methodology.

Undoubtedly the most critical and interesting variation in the research *design* involved in the two procedures is that resulting from differences in definition of exposure. In an experiment the audience on whom the effects are being evaluated is one which is fully exposed to the communication. On the other hand, in naturalistic situations with which surveys are typically concerned, the outstanding phenomenon is the limitation of the audience to those who *expose themselves* to the communication. Some of the individuals in a captive audience experiment would, of course, expose themselves in the course of natural events to a communication of the type studied; but many others would not. The group which does expose itself is usually a highly biased one, since most individuals 'expose themselves most of the time to the kind of material with which they agree to begin with' (Lipset *et al.*, 1954, p. 1158). Thus one reason for the difference in results between experiments and correlational studies is that experiments describe the effects of exposure on the whole range of individuals studied, some of whom are initially in favor of the position being advocated and some who are opposed, whereas surveys primarily describe the effects produced on those already in favor of the point of view advocated in the communication. The amount of change is thus, of course, much smaller in surveys. Lipset and his collaborators make this same evaluation, stating that:

As long as we test a program in the laboratory we always find that it has great effect on the attitudes and interests of the experimental subjects. But when we put the program on as a regular broadcast, we then note that the people who are most influenced in the laboratory tests are those who, in a realistic situation, do not listen to the program. The controlled experiment always greatly overrates effects, as compared with those that really occur, because of the self-selection of audiences (Lipset *et al.*, 1954, p. 1158).

Differences in the second category are not inherent in the design of the two alternatives, but are characteristic of the way researchers using the two methods typically proceed.

The first difference within this class is in the size of the communication unit typically studied. In the majority of survey studies the unit evaluated is an entire program of communication. For example, in studies of political behavior an attempt is made to assess the effects of all newspaper reading and television viewing on attitudes toward the major parties. In the typical experiment, on the other hand, the interest is usually in some particular variation in the content of the communications, and experimental evaluations much more frequently involve single communications. On this point results are thus not directly comparable.

Another characteristic difference between the two methods is in the time interval used in evaluation. In the typical experiment the time at which the effect is observed is usually rather soon after exposure to the communication. In the survey study, on the other hand, the time perspective is such that much more remote effects are usually evaluated. When effects decline with the passage of time, the net outcome will, of course, be that of accentuating the effect obtained in experimental studies as compared with those obtained in survey researches. Again it must be stressed that the difference is not inherent in the designs as such. Several experiments, including our own on the effects of motion pictures (Hovland, Lumsdaine, and Sheffield, 1949) and later studies on the 'sleeper effect' (Hovland and Weiss, 1951; Kelman and Hovland, 1953), have studied retention over considerable periods of time.

Some of the difference in outcome may be attributable to the types of communicators characteristically used and to the motive-incentive conditions operative in the two situations. In experimental studies communications are frequently presented in a classroom situation. This may involve quite different types of factors from those operative in the more naturalistic communication situation with which the survey researchers are concerned. In the classroom there may be some implicit sponsorship of the communication by the teacher and the school administration. In the survey studies the communicators may often be remote individuals either unfamiliar to the recipients, or outgroupers clearly known to espouse a point of view opposed to that held by many members of the audience. Thus there may be real differences in communicator credibility in laboratory and survey researches. The net effect of the differences will typically be in the direction of increasing the likelihood of change in the experimental as compared with the survey study.

There is sometimes an additional situational difference. Communications of the type studied by survey researchers usually involve reaching the individual in his natural habitat, with consequent supplementary effects produced by discussion with friends and family. In the laboratory studies a classroom situation with low postcommunication interaction is more typically involved. Several studies, including one by Harold Kelley reported in our volume on *Communication and Persuasion* (Hovland, Janis, and Kelley, 1953), indicate that, when a communication is presented in a situation which makes group membership salient, the individual is typically more resistant to counternorm influence than when the communication is presented under conditions of low salience of group membership (cf. also, Katz and Lazarsfeld, 1955, pp. 48–133).

A difference which is almost wholly adventitious is in the types of populations utilized. In the survey design there is, typically, considerable emphasis on a random sample of the entire population. In the typical experiment, on the other hand, there is a consistent overrepresentation of high school students and college sophomores, primarily on the basis of their greater accessibility. But as Tolman has said: 'college sophomores may not be people'. Whether differences in the type of audience studied contribute to the differences in effect obtained with the two methods is not known.

Finally, there is an extremely important difference in the studies of the experimental and correlational variety with respect to the type of issue discussed in the communications. In the typical experiment we are interested in studying a set of factors or conditions which are expected on the basis of theory to influence the extent of effect of the communication. We usually deliberately try to find types of issues involving attitudes which are susceptible to modification through communication. Otherwise, we run the risk of no measurable effects, particularly with small-scale experiments. In the survey procedures, on the other hand, socially significant attitudes which are deeply rooted in prior experience and involve much personal commitment are typically involved. This is especially true in voting studies which have provided us with so many of our present results on social influence. I shall have considerably more to say about this problem a little later.

The differences so far discussed have primarily concerned the extent of overall effectiveness indicated by the two methods: why survey results typically show little modification of attitudes by communication while experiments indicate marked changes. Let me now turn to some of the other differences in generalizations derived from the two alternative designs. Let me take as the second main area of disparate results the research on the effect of varying distances between the position taken by the communicator and that held by the recipient of the communication. Here it is a matter of comparing changes for persons who at the outset closely agree with the communicator with those for others who are mildly or strongly in disagreement with him. In the naturalistic situation studied in surveys the typical procedure is to determine changes in opinion following reported exposure to communication for individuals differing from the communicator by varying amounts. This gives rise to two possible artifacts. When the communication is at one end of a continuum, there is little room for improvement for those who differ from the communication by small amounts, but a great deal of room for movement among those with large discrepancies. This gives rise to a spurious degree of positive relationship between the degree of discrepancy and the amount of change.

Regression effects will also operate in the direction of increasing the correlation. What is needed is a situation in which the distance factor can be manipulated independently of the subject's initial position. An attempt to set up these conditions experimentally was made in a study by Pritzker and the writer (1957). The method involved preparing individual communications presented in booklet form so that the position of the communicator could be set at any desired distance from the subject's initial position. Communicators highly acceptable to the subjects were used. A number of different topics were employed, including the likelihood of a cure for cancer within five years, the desirability of compulsory voting, and the adequacy of five hours of sleep per night.

The amount of change for each degree of advocated change is shown in Figure 1. It will be seen that there is a fairly clear progression, such that the greater the amount of change advocated the greater the average amount of opinion change produced. Similar results have been reported by Goldberg (1954) and by French (1956).

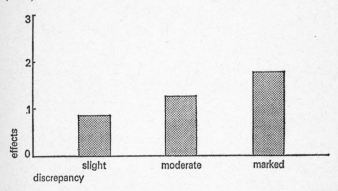

Figure 1 Mean opinion change score with three degrees of discrepancy (deviation between subject's position and position advocated in communication). [From Hovland & Pritzker, 1957]

But these results are not in line with our hunches as to what would happen in a naturalistic situation with important social issues. We felt that here other types of response than change in attitude would occur. So Muzafer Sherif, O. J. Harvey, and the writer (1957) set up a situation to simulate as closely as possible the conditions typically involved when individuals are exposed to major social issue communications at differing distances from their own position. The issue used was the desirability of prohibition. The study was done in two states (Oklahoma and Texas) where there is prohibition or local option, so that the wet-dry issue is hotly debated. We concentrated on three aspects of the problem: How favorably will the communicator be received when his position is at varying distances from that of the recipient? How will what the communicator says be perceived and interpreted by individuals at varying distances from his position? What will be the amount of opinion change produced when small and large deviations in position of communication and recipient are involved?

Three communications, one strongly wet, one strongly dry, and one moderately wet, were employed. The results bearing on the first problem, of *reception*, are presented in Figure 2. The positions

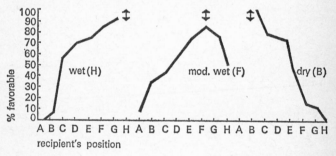

Figure 2 Percentage of favorable evaluations ('fair', 'unbiased', etc.) of wet (H), moderately wet (F), and dry (B) communications for subjects holding various positions on prohibition. Recipients position range from A (very dry) to H (very wet). Position of communications indicated by arrow. [From Hovland, Harvey & Sherif, 1957]

of the subjects are indicated on the abscissa in letters from A (extreme dry) to H (strongly wet). The positions of the communication are also indicated in the same letters, *B* indicating a strongly dry communication, *H* a strongly wet, and *F* a moderately wet. Along the ordinate there is plotted the percentage of subjects with each position on the issue who described the communication as 'fair' and 'unbiased'. It will be seen that the degree of distance between the recipient and the communicator greatly influences the evaluation of the fairness of the communication. When a communication is directed at the pro-dry position, nearly all of the dry

293

subjects consider it fair and impartial, but only a few per cent of the wet subjects consider the identical communication fair. The reverse is true at the other end of the scale. When an intermediate position is adopted, the percentages fall off sharply on each side. Thus under the present conditions with a relatively ambiguous communicator one of the ways of dealing with strongly discrepant positions is to *discredit* the communicator, considering him unfair and biased.

A second way in which an individual can deal with discrepancy is by distortion of what is said by the communicator. This is a phenomenon extensively studied by Cooper and Jahoda (1947). In the present study, subjects were asked to state what position they thought was taken by the communicator on the prohibition question. Their evaluation of his position could then be analyzed in relation to their own position. These results are shown in Figure 3

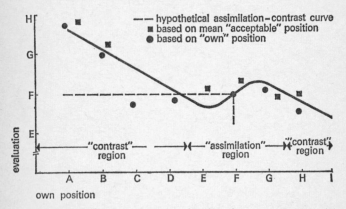

Figure 3 Average placement of position of moderately wet communication (F) by subjects holding various positions on the issue, plotted against hypothetical assimilation-contrast curve. [From Hovland, Harvey & Sherif, 1957]

for the moderately wet communication. It will be observed that there is a tendency for individuals whose position is close to that of the communicator to report on the communicator's position quite accurately, for individuals a little bit removed to report his position to be substantially more like their own (which we call an 'assimilation effect'), and for those with more discrepant positions to report the communicator's position as more extreme than it really was. This we refer to as a 'contrast effect'.

Now to our primary results on opinion change. It was found that individuals whose position was only slightly discrepant from the communicator's were influenced to a greater extent than those whose positions deviated to a larger extent. When a wet position was espoused, 28% of the middle-of-the-road subjects were changed in the direction of the communicator, as compared with only 4% of the drys. With the dry communication 14% of the middle-of-the-roaders were changed, while only 4% of the wets were changed. Thus, more of the subjects with small discrepancies were changed than were those with large discrepancies.

These results appear to indicate that, under conditions when there is some ambiguity about the credibility of the communicator and when the subject is deeply involved with the issue, the greater the attempt at change the higher the resistance. On the other hand, with highly respected communicators, as in the previous study with Pritzker using issues of lower involvement, the greater the discrepancy the greater the effect. A study related to ours has just been completed by Zimbardo (1959) which indicates that, when an influence attempt is made by a strongly positive communicator (i.e. a close personal friend), the greater the discrepancy the greater the opinion change, even when the experimenter made a point of stressing the great importance of the subject's opinion.

The implication of these results for our primary problem of conflicting results is clear. The types of issues with which most experiments deal are relatively uninvolving and are often of the variety where expert opinion is highly relevant, as for example, on topics of health, science, and the like. Here we should expect that opinion would be considerably affected by communications and furthermore that advocacy of positions quite discrepant from the individual's own position would have a marked effect. On the other hand, the types of issues most often utilized in survey studies are ones which are very basic and involve deep commitment. As a consequence small changes in opinion due to communication would be expected. Here communication may have little effect on those who disagree at the outset and function merely to strengthen the position already held, in line with survey findings.

A third area of research in which somewhat discrepant results are obtained by the experimental and survey methods is in the role of order of presentation. From naturalistic studies the generalization has been widely adopted that primacy is an extremely important factor in persuasion. Numerous writers have reported that what we experience first has a critical role in what we believe. This is particularly stressed in studies of propaganda effects in various countries when the nation getting across its message first is alleged to have a great advantage and in commercial advertising where 'getting a beat on the field' is stressed. The importance of primacy in political propaganda is indicated in the following quotation from Doob:

> The propagandist scores an initial advantage whenever his propaganda reaches people before that of his rivals. Readers or listeners are then biased to comprehend, forever after, the event as it has been initially portrayed to them. If they are told in a headline or a flash that the battle has been won, the criminal has been caught, or the bill is certain to pass the legislature, they will usually expect subsequent information to substantiate this first impression. When later facts prove otherwise, they may be loath to abandon what they believe to be true until perhaps the evidence becomes overwhelming (Doob, 1948, pp. 421–2).

A recent study by Katz and Lazarsfeld (1955) utilizing the survey method compares the extent to which respondents attribute major impact on their decisions about fashions and movie attendance to the presentations to which they were first exposed. Strong primacy effects are shown in their analyses of the data.

We have ourselves recently completed a series of experiments oriented toward this problem. These are reported in our new monograph on *Order of Presentation in Persuasion* (Hovland, Mandell, Campbell, Brock, Luchins, Cohen, McGuire, Janis, Feierabend, and Anderson, 1957). We find that primacy is often *not* a very significant factor when the relative effectiveness of the first side of an issue is compared experimentally with that of the second. The research suggests that differences in design may account for much of the discrepancy. A key variable is whether there is exposure to both sides or whether only one side is actually received. In naturalistic studies the advantage of the first side is often not only that it is first but that it is often then the only side of the issue to which the individual is exposed. Having once been influenced, many individuals make up their mind and are no longer interested in other communications on the issue. In most experiments on order of presentation, on the other hand, the audience is systematically exposed to both sides. Thus under survey conditions, self-exposure tends to increase the impact of primacy.

Two other factors to which I have already alluded appear significant in determining the amount of primacy effect. One is the nature of the communicator, the other the setting in which the communication is received. In our volume Luchins presents results indicating that, when the same communicator presents contradictory material, the point of view read first has more influence. On the other hand, Mandell and I show that, when two different communicators present opposing views successively, little primacy effect is obtained. The communications setting factor operates similarly. When the issue and the conditions of presentation make clear that the points of view are controversial, little primacy is obtained.

Thus in many of the situations with which there had been great concern as to undesirable effects of primacy, such as in legal trials, election campaigns, and political debate, the role of primacy appears to have been exaggerated, since the conditions there are those least conducive to primacy effects: the issue is clearly defined as controversial, the partisanship of the communicator is usually established, and different communicators present the opposing sides.

Time does not permit me to discuss other divergences in results obtained in survey and experimental studies, such as those concerned with the effects of repetition of presentation, the relationship between level of intelligence and susceptibility to attitude change, or the relative impact of mass media and personal influence. Again, however, I am sure that detailed analysis will reveal differential factors at work which can account for the apparent disparity in the generalizations derived.

Integration

On the basis of the foregoing survey of results I reach the conclusion that no contradiction has been established between the data provided by experimental and correlational studies. Instead it appears that the seeming divergence can be satisfactorily accounted for on the basis of a different definition of the communication situation (including the phenomenon of self-selection) and differences in the type of communicator, audience, and kind of issue utilized.

But there remains the task of better integrating the findings associated with the two methodologies. This is a problem closely akin to that considered by the members of the recent Social Science Research Council summer seminar on *Narrowing the Gap Between Field Studies and Laboratory Studies in Social Psychology* (Riecken, 1954). Many of their recommendations are pertinent to our present problem.

What seems to me quite apparent is that a genuine understanding of the effects of communications on attitudes requires both the survey and the experimental methodologies. At the same time there appear to be certain inherent limitations of each method which must be understood by the researcher if he is not to be blinded by his preoccupation with one or the other type of design. Integration of the two methodologies will require on the part of the experimentalist an awareness of the narrowness of the laboratory in interpreting the larger and more comprehensive effects of communication. It will require on the part of the survey researcher a greater awareness of the limitations of the correlational method as a basis for establishing causal relationships.

The framework within which survey research operates is most adequately and explicitly dealt with by Berelson, Lazarsfeld, and McPhee in their book on *Voting* (1954). The model which they use, taken over by them from the economist Tinbergen, is reproduced in the top half of Figure 4. For comparison, the model used by

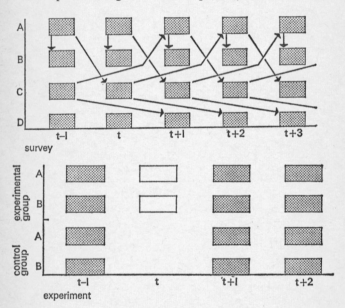

Figure 4 Top Half: 'Process analysis' schema used in panel research. (Successive time intervals are indicated along abscissa. Letters indicate the variables under observation. Arrows represent relations between the variables.) [From Berelson, Lazarsfeld, & McPhee, 1954.] Bottom Half: Design of experimental research. (Letters on vertical axis again indicate variables being measured. Unshaded box indicates experimentally manipulated treatment and blank absence of such treatment. Time periods indicated as in top half of chart.)

experimentalists is presented in the lower half of the figure. It will be seen that the model used by the survey researcher, particularly when he employs the 'panel' method, stresses the large number of simultaneous and interacting influences affecting attitudes and opinions. Even more significant is its provision for a variety of 'feedback' phenomena in which consequences wrought by previous influences affect processes normally considered as occurring earlier in the sequence. The various types of interaction are indicated by the placement of arrows showing direction of effect. In contrast the experimentalist frequently tends to view the communication process as one in which some single manipulative variable is the primary determinant of the subsequent attitude change. He is, of course, aware in a general way of the importance of context, and he frequently studies interaction effects as well as main effects; but he still is less attentive than he might be to the complexity of the influence situation and the numerous possibilities for feedback loops. Undoubtedly the real life communication situation is better described in terms of the survey type of model. We are all familiar, for example, with the interactions in which attitudes predispose one to acquire certain types of information, that this often leads to changes in attitude which may result in further acquisition of knowledge, which in turn produces more attitude change, and so on. Certainly the narrow question sometimes posed by experiments as to the effect of knowledge on attitudes greatly underestimates these interactive effects.

But while the conceptualization of the survey researcher is often very valuable, his correlational research design leaves much to be desired. Advocates of correlational analysis often cite the example of a science built on observation exclusively without experiment: astronomy. But here a very limited number of space-time concepts are involved and the number of competing theoretical formulations is relatively small so that it is possible to limit alternative theories rather drastically through correlational evidence. But in the area of communication effects and social psychology generally the variables are so numerous and so intertwined that the correlational methodology is primarily useful to suggest hypotheses and not to establish causal relationships (Hovland *et al.*, 1949, pp. 329–40; Maccoby, 1956). Even with the much simpler relationships involved in biological systems there are grave difficulties of which we are all aware these days when we realize how difficult it is to establish through correlation whether eating of fats is or is not a cause of heart disease or whether or not smoking is a cause of lung cancer. In communications research the complexity of the problem makes it inherently difficult to derive causal relationships from correlational analysis where experimental control of exposure is not possible. And I do not agree with my friends the Lazarsfelds (Kendall and Lazarsfeld, 1950) concerning the effectiveness of the panel method in circumventing this problem since parallel difficulties are raised when the relationships occur over a time span.

These difficulties constitute a challenge to the experimentalist in this area of research to utilize the broad framework for studying communication effects suggested by the survey researcher, but to employ well controlled experimental design to work on those aspects of the field which are amenable to experimental manipulation and control. It is, of course, apparent that there are important communication problems which cannot be attacked directly by experimental methods. It is not, for example, feasible to modify voting behavior by manipulation of the issues discussed by the opposed parties during a particular campaign. It is not feasible to assess the effects of communications over a very long span of time. For example, one cannot visualize experimental procedures for answering the question of what has been the impact of the reading of *Das Kapital* or *Uncle Tom's Cabin*. These are questions which can be illuminated by historical and sociological study but cannot be evaluated in any rigorous experimental fashion.

But the scope of problems which do lend themselves to experimental attack is very broad. Even complex interactions can be fruitfully attacked by experiment. The possibilities are clearly shown in studies like that of Sherif and Sherif (1953) on factors influencing cooperative and competitive behavior in a camp for adolescent boys. They were able to bring under manipulative control many of the types of interpersonal relationships ordinarily considered impossible to modify experimentally, and to develop motivations of an intensity characteristic of real-life situations. It should be possible to do similar studies in the communication area with a number of the variables heretofore only investigated in uncontrolled naturalistic settings by survey procedures.

In any case it appears eminently practical to minimize many of the differences which were discussed above as being not inherent in design but more or less adventitiously linked with one or the other method. Thus there is no reason why more complex and deeply-involving social issues cannot be employed in experiments rather than the more superficial ones more commonly used. The resistance to change of socially important issues may be a handicap in studying certain types of attitude change; but, on the other hand, it is important to understand the lack of modifiability of opinion with highly-involving issues. Greater representation of the diverse types of communicators found in naturalistic situations can also be achieved. In addition, it should be possible to do experiments with a wider range of populations to reduce the possibility that many of our present generalizations from experiments are unduly affected by their heavy weighting of college student characteristics, including high literacy, alertness, and rationality.

A more difficult task is that of experimentally evaluating communications under conditions of self-selection of exposure. But this is not at all impossible in theory. It should be possible to assess what demographic and personality factors predispose one to expose oneself to particular communications and then to utilize experimental and control groups having these characteristics. Under some circumstances the evaluation could be made on only those who select themselves, with both experimental and control groups coming from the self-selected audience.

Undoubtedly many of the types of experiments which could be set up involving or simulating naturalistic conditions will be too ambitious and costly to be feasible even if possible in principle. This suggests the continued use of small-scale experiments which seek to isolate some of the key variables operative in complex situations. From synthesis of component factors, prediction of complex outcomes may be practicable. It is to this analytic procedure for narrowing the gap between laboratory and field research that we have devoted major attention in our research program. I will merely indicate briefly here some of the ties between our past work and the present problem.

We have attempted to assess the influence of the communicator by varying his expertness and attractiveness, as in the studies by Kelman, Weiss, and the writer (Hovland and Weiss, 1951; Kelman and Hovland, 1953). Further data on this topic were presented earlier in this paper.

We have also been concerned with evaluating social interaction effects. Some of the experiments on group affiliation as a factor affecting resistance to counternorm communication and the role of salience of group membership by Hal Kelley and others are reported in *Communication and Persuasion* (Hovland *et al.*, 1953).

Starting with the studies carried out during the war on orientation films by Art Lumsdaine, Fred Sheffield, and the writer (1949), we have had a strong interest in the duration of communication effects. Investigation of effects at various time intervals has helped to bridge the gap between assessment of immediate changes with those of longer duration like those involved in survey studies. More recent extensions of this work have indicated the close relationship between the credibility of the communicator and the extent of post-communication increments, or 'sleeper effects' (Hovland and Weiss, 1951; Kelman and Hovland, 1953).

The nature of individual differences in susceptibility to persuasion via communication has been the subject of a number of our recent studies. The generality of persuasibility has been investigated by Janis and collaborators and the development of persuasibility in children has been studied by Abelson and Lesser. A volume concerned with these audience factors to which Janis, Abelson, Lesser, Field, Rife, King, Cohen, Linton, Graham, and the writer have contributed will appear under the title *Personality and Persuasibility* (1959).

Lastly, there remains the question on how the nature of the issues used in the communication affects the extent of change in attitude. We have only made a small beginning on these problems. In the research reported in *Experiments on Mass Communication*, we showed that the magnitude of effects was directly related to the type of attitude involved: film communications had a significant effect on opinions related to straightforward interpretations of policies and events, but had little or no effect on more deeply entrenched attitudes and motivations. Further work on the nature of issues is represented in the study by Sherif, Harvey, and the writer (1957) which was discussed above. There we found a marked contrast between susceptibility to influence and the amount of ego-involvement in the issue. But the whole concept of ego-involvement is a fuzzy one, and here is an excellent area for further work seeking to determine the theoretical factors involved in different types of issues.

With this brief survey of possible ways to bridge the gap between experiment and survey I must close. I should like to stress in summary the mutual importance of the two approaches to the problem of communication effectiveness. Neither is a royal road to wisdom, but each represents an important emphasis. The challenge of future work is one of fruitfully combining their virtues so that we may develop a social psychology of communication with the conceptual breadth provided by correlational study of process and with the rigorous but more delimited methodology of the experiment.

References
Berelson, B. R., Lazarsfeld, P. F., and McPhee, W. N., *Voting: A study of opinion formation in a presidential campaign.* Chicago: Univer. Chicago Press, 1954.

Cooper, Eunice, and Jahoda, Marie, The evasion of propaganda: How prejudiced people respond to anti-prejudice propaganda. *J. Psychol.*, **23**, 15–25, 1947.

Doob, L. W., *Public opinion and propaganda*. New York: Holt, 1948.

French, J. R. P., Jr., A formal theory of social power. *Psychol. Rev.*, **63**, 181–94, 1956.

Goldberg, S. C., Three situational determinants of conformity to social norms. *J. abnorm. soc. Psychol.*, **49**, 325–9, 1954.

Gosnell, H. F., *Getting out the vote: An experiment in the stimulation of voting*. Chicago: Univer. Chicago Press, 1927.

Hovland, C. I., Effects of the mass media of communication. In G. Lindzey (ed.), *Handbook of social psychology*. Vol. II. *Special fields and applications*. Cambridge, Mass.: Addison-Wesley, pp. 1062–1103, 1954.

Hovland, C. I., Harvey, O. J., and Sherif, M., Assimilation and contrast effects in reactions to communication and attitude change. *J. abnorm. soc. Psychol.*, **55**, 244–52, 1957.

Hovland, C. I., Janis, I. L., and Kelley, H. H., *Communication and persuasion*. New Haven: Yale Univer. Press, 1953.

Hovland, C. I., Lumsdaine, A. A., and Sheffield, F. D., *Experiments on mass communication*. Princeton: Princeton Univer. Press, 1949.

Hovland, C. I., Mandell, W., Campbell, Enid H., Brock, T., Luchins, A. S., Cohen, A. R., McGuire, W. J., Janis, I. L., Feierabend, Rosalind L., and Anderson, N. H., *The order of presentation in persuasion*. New Haven: Yale Univer. Press, 1957.

Hovland, C. I., and Pritzker, H. A., Extent of opinion change as a function of amount of change advocated. *J. abnorm. soc. Psychol.*, **54**, 257–61, 1957.

Hovland, C. I., and Weiss, W., The influence of source credibility on communication effectiveness. *Publ. Opin. Quart.*, **15**, 635–50, 1951.

Janis, I. L., Hovland, C. I., Field, P. B., Linton, Harriett, Graham, Elaine, Cohen, A. R., Rife, D., Abelson, R. P., Lesser, G. S., and King, B. T., *Personality and persuasibility*. New Haven: Yale Univer. Press, 1959.

Katz, E., and Lazarsfeld, P. F., *Personal influence*. Glencoe, Ill.: Free Press, 1955.

Kelman, H. C., and Hovland, C. I., 'Reinstatement' of the communicator in delayed measurement of opinion change. *J. abnorm. soc. Psychol.*, **48**, 327–35, 1953.

Kendall, Patricia L., Lazarsfeld, P. F., Problems of survey analysis. In R. K. Merton and P. F. Lazarsfeld (Eds.), *Continuities in social research: Studies in the scope and method of 'The American Soldier'*, Glencoe, Ill.: Free Press, pp. 133–96, 1950.

Klapper, J. T., *The effects of mass media*. New York: Columbia Univer. Bureau of Applied Social Research, 1949. (Mimeo).

Lazarsfeld, P. F., Berelson, B., and Gaudet, Hazel, *The people's choice*. New York: Duell, Sloan and Pearce, 1944.

Lipset, S. M., Lazarsfeld, P. F., Barton, A. H., and Linz, J., The psychology of voting: An analysis of political behavior. In G. Lindzey (Ed.), *Handbook of social psychology*. Vol. II. *Special fields and applications*. Cambridge, Mass.: Addison-Wesley, pp. 1124–75, 1954.

Maccoby, Eleanor E., Pitfalls in the analysis of panel data: A research note on some technical aspects of voting. *Amer. J. Sociol.*, **59**, 359–62, 1956.

Riecken, H. W. (Chairman), Narrowing the gap between field studies and laboratory experiments in social psychology: A statement by the summer seminar. *Items Soc. Sci. Res. Council*, **8**, 37–42, 1954.

Sherif, M., and Sherif, Carolyn W., *Groups in harmony and tension: An integration of studies on intergroup relations*. New York: Harper, 1953.

Zimbardo, P. G., Involvement and communication discrepancy as determinants of opinion change. Unpublished doctoral dissertation, Yale University, 1959.

Attitude Scaling

Excerpt from: C. Selltiz *et al.*, *Research Methods in Social Relations*,
Holt Rinehart, U.S.A., 1959.

Attitude scales differ in method of construction, method of response, and basis for interpreting scores. Different types of attitude scale will be discussed in this section.

The separate items or questions in an attitude scale are usually not of interest in themselves; the interest is, rather, in the total score or in subscores that result for each individual from the combination of his responses to various items. In effect, any set of items works as well as any other set provided they give the same final scores on the particular attitude being measured.

In selecting items for inclusion in a scale, two criteria are commonly used. First, the items must elicit responses that are psychologically related to the attitude being measured. For example, in a scale measuring anti-semitism, the following item has a *manifest* relation to the attitude being measured: 'Anyone who employs many people should be careful not to hire a large percentage of Jews' (Adorno *et al.*, 1950). However, the relationship does not necessarily have to be so evident. In fact, there is a considerable advantage in using items that, on the surface, have no bearing on the attitude being measured. This may prevent the respondent from concealing or distorting his attitude. Thus, in their study of anti-democratic ideology, Adorno *et al.*, used many items that have no apparent relationship to this attitude – e.g. 'When a person has a problem or worry, it is best for him not to think about it, but to keep busy with more cheerful things'. This item is one of several that indicate an individual's readiness or lack of readiness to adopt a psychologically insightful view of other people and of himself. The theory is that people who are lacking in psychological insight and understanding have a personality structure (e.g. greater repressed hostility, weaker ego, etc.) that predisposes them to an anti-democratic ideology.*

* Such indirect items cannot, of course, be used as measures of the attitude being studied simply on the basis of theoretical assumptions about their relation to the attitude. Before they are accepted as adequate measures, their relation to the attitude must be demonstrated. (This statement is equally true for items that seem to have a *manifest* relation to the attitude

The second criterion requires that the scale differentiate among people who are at different points along the dimension being measured. To discriminate not merely between opposite extremes in attitude but also among individuals who differ slightly, items that discriminate at different points on the scale are usually included. Thus, a test of opinions about child-rearing practices, along the dimension 'permissiveness-strictness', would contain not only items representing a very strict approach and others representing a very permissive approach, but intermediate items representing moderate strictness, moderate permissiveness, etc. Some types of scale, however, provide for the identification of moderate positions by permitting the expression of various degrees of agreement or disagreement with extreme items rather than by the inclusion of intermediate items.

The way in which a scale discriminates among individuals depends on the construction of the scale and the method of scoring. In some scales the items form a gradation of such a nature that the individual agrees with only one or two, which correspond to his position on the dimension being measured, and disagrees with statements on either side of those he has selected. Such scales, in which a person's response localizes his position, are sometimes called *differential* scales. In other scales, the individual indicates his agreement or disagreement with each item, and his total score is computed by adding the subscores assigned to his responses to all the separate items; such scales are sometimes called *summated* scales. Still others are set up in such a way that the items form a *cumulative* series; theoretically, an individual whose attitude is at a certain point on the dimension being measured will answer favorably all the items on one side of that point and answer unfavorably all those on the other side. Each of these types of scale is discussed in more detail in the following paragraphs.

Differential Scales

Differential scales for the measurement of attitudes are closely associated with the name of L. L. Thurstone. The methods he devised represent attempts to approximate interval scales. An interval scale is one on which the distances between points on the

---

being studied.) Thus, in the study of anti-democratic ideology, the hypothesis that items such as the one quoted were related to anti-democratic ideology was tested – and borne out – by analysis of the difference between responses to such items made by people known on other grounds to have a democratic ideology and those made by people known to have an anti-democratic ideology.

measuring instrument are known, and on which equal numerical distances represent equal distances along the continuum being measured. Such a scale enables one to compare differences or changes in attitude, since the difference between a score of 3 and a score of 7 is equivalent to the difference between a score of 6 and a score of 10 and to the difference between any other two scores that are four points apart.

A differential scale consists of a number of items whose position on the scale has been determined by some kind of ranking or rating operation performed by judges. Various methods of securing judgments of scale position have been used: the method of *paired comparisons* (see Thurstone, 1927, 1928); the method of *equal-appearing intervals* (see Thurstone, 1929, 1931, and Thurstone and Chave, 1929); and the method of *successive intervals* (see Saffir, 1937). It is beyond the scope of this volume to give the details of these procedures; we shall only present in broad outline the method of *equal-appearing intervals*, which is the most commonly used.

In selecting the items for the scale and assigning values to them, the following procedure is used: (1) The investigator gathers several hundred statements conceived to be related to the attitude being investigated. (2) A large number of judges – usually from 50 to 300 – working independently, classify these statements into eleven groups. In the first pile the judge places the statements he considers most favorable to the object; in the second, those he considers next most favorable; and in the eleventh pile, the statements he considers most unfavorable. The sixth, or 'neutral', position is defined as the point at which there is neither 'favorableness' nor 'unfavorableness'.* (3) The scale value of a statement is computed as the median position (or pile) to which it is assigned by the group of judges. Statements that have too broad a scatter are discarded as ambiguous or irrelevant. (4) A final selection is made, taking items that are spread out evenly along the scale from one extreme position to the other. It is often possible to construct duplicate forms of the scale from items not used on the original form.

* Throughout this section, for the sake of simplicity, the discussion is worded in terms of scales measuring favorableness-unfavorableness toward some object. A scale may, of course, be concerned with some other dimension; for example, liberalism-conservatism of social, political, or economic views; permissiveness-strictness of views on child-rearing, etc. In developing Thurstone scales, the instructions to the judges specify the dimension along which the items are to be placed. Thus, in developing a scale to measure liberalism-conservatism, the judges would be instructed to place in the first pile the items they consider most liberal, in the eleventh those they consider most conservative. The same principles and procedures apply whether the dimension to be measured is favorableness-unfavorableness or some other.

The resulting Thurstone-type scale is a series of statements, usually about twenty; the position of each statement on a scale of favorable-unfavorable attitude toward the object has been determined by the judges' classification. The subjects, in filling out the questionnaire, are asked either to check each statement with which they agree or to check the two or three items that are closest to their position.

The following illustration of items from a Thurstone-type scale is taken from MacCrone's study of attitudes toward natives in South Africa (1937):

Scale value	Item no.	
10·3	1	I consider that the native is only fit to do the 'dirty' work of the white community.
10·2	2	The idea of contact with the black or dark skin of the native excites horror and disgust in me.
8·6	15	I do not think that the native can be relied upon in a position of trust or of responsibility.
8·4	17	To my mind the native is so childish and irresponsible that he cannot be expected to know what is in his best interest.
3·8	22	I consider that the white community in this country owe a real debt of gratitude to the missionaries for the way in which they have tried to uplift the native.
3·1	3	It seems to me that the white man by placing restrictions such as the 'Colour Bar' upon the native is really trying to exploit him economically.
0·8	11	I would rather see the white people lose their position in this country than keep it at the expense of injustice to the native.

The scale values, of course, are not shown on the questionnaire, and the items are usually arranged in random order rather than in order of their scale value. The mean (or median)* of the scale values of the items the individual checks is interpreted as indicating his

---

* Thurstone, on the assumption that scales constructed by this method were true interval scales, advocated the use of statistics appropriate to interval scales – the mean and the standard deviation. Other investigators, operating on the more cautious assumption that the intervals are not truly equal, have favored the use of the median as appropriate to ordinal scales. For a discussion of whether the assumption that these are true interval scales is justified, see pages 311–12.

position on a scale of favorable-unfavorable attitude toward the object.

Theoretically, if a Thurstone-type scale is completely reliable and if the scale is measuring a single attitude rather than a complex of attitudes, an individual should check only items that are immediately contiguous in scale value – e.g. items 15 and 17 above. If the responses of an individual scatter widely over noncontiguous items, his attitude score is not likely to have the same meaning as a score with little scatter. The scattered responses may indicate that the subject has *no* attitude or that his attitude is not organized in the manner assumed by the scale. There is no *a priori* reason to expect that all people have attitudes toward the same things or that attitudinal dimensions are the same for all.

The Thurstone method of equal-appearing intervals has been widely used. Scales have been constructed to measure attitudes toward war, toward the church, toward capital punishment, toward the Chinese, toward Negroes, toward whites, etc. In addition, an attempt has been made by Remmers and his colleagues (1934) to develop generalized Thurstone scales that might be used to measure attitudes toward any group, social institution, etc. For example, the Kelley-Remmers 'Scale for Measuring Attitudes Toward Any Institution' consists of forty-five statements, ranging from 'The world could not exist without this institution', through such items as 'Encourages moral improvement' and 'Is too radical in its views and actions', to 'Is the most hateful of institutions'. In applying this generalized scale to the measurement of attitudes toward a given institution (war, the family, the church, advertising, or whatever), the subject is instructed to check each of the statements with which he agrees in reference to the given institution, or the statements may be reworded to include mention of the specific institution being considered (e.g. 'War is the most hateful of institutions').

The Wright-Nelson study of editorial positions of newspapers concerning Japan and China (1939) illustrates an application of Thurstone-type scaling to the analysis of available data. In this study, the sorting of statements by the judges served simultaneously to establish the position of each item on a scale of favorableness-hostility and to determine the scores of the various newspapers. In effect, each newspaper was treated as having 'checked' all the statements selected from its editorials; its score was obtained by averaging the score values of the specific statements.

Several objections have been raised against the Thurstone-type scale. First, many have objected to the amount of work involved in constructing it. Undoubtedly, the procedure is cumbersome. However, Edwards (1957) has expressed the opinion that, in view of recent developments in time-saving techniques, the amount of time and labor involved in constructing a scale by the method of equal-appearing intervals is not substantially different from that involved in constructing a summated scale. In any case, it is doubtful that simple methods for the rigorous construction of scales will ever be developed. The precise measurement of attitudes is perhaps inevitably a complex affair.

A second criticism has been that, since an individual's score is the mean or median of the scale values of the several items he checks, essentially different attitudinal patterns may be expressed in the same score. For example, on the scale of attitudes toward natives of South Africa given earlier, an individual who checks the two moderately 'anti' items 15 and 17 receives a score of 8·5 (the median of their scale values). Another individual, who checks items 1, 15, 17 and 22 (perhaps because 22 has a meaning for him which is different from that which it had for the judges), also receives a score of 8·5 (the median of the scale values of these items). The two individuals are rated as having the same degree of prejudice, even though the latter checked the most unfavorable item in the scale and the former did not. Dudycha (1943), after six years' use of the Peterson test of attitude toward war (a test constructed by the method of equal-appearing intervals) with college students, reported that the average student, instead of checking only two or three contiguous items, covered more than a third of the scale; some students endorsed statements ranging from those placed at the 'strongly favorable' end of the scale to statements at the 'strongly opposed' end. (One must, of course, consider the possibility that such students had no clear attitude toward war and that it was therefore inappropriate to try to measure their attitude by *any* technique.) Dudycha questioned the meaning to be given to a median derived from such a range of responses. However, the criticism that identical scores do not necessarily indicate identical patterns of response is not unique to the Thurstone-type scale; it applies at least as strongly, as we shall see, to summated scales.*

A still more serious question has to do with the extent to which the scale values assigned to the items are influenced by the attitudes

* The fact that different patterns may lead to identical scores is not necessarily as serious a limitation as it might seem. This point is discussed on pages 316–17.

of the judges themselves. Do the attitudes and backgrounds of the judges affect the position of the various items on the scale? This obviously is a matter that is open to experimental inquiry. A number of early studies supported the view that the scale values assigned did *not* depend on the attitude of the judges. Hinckley (1932) found a correlation of 0·98 between the scale positions assigned to 114 items measuring prejudice toward Negroes by a group of Southern white students in the United States who were prejudiced against Negroes and those assigned by a group of unprejudiced Northern students. Similarly, MacCrone (1937), in the study of race attitudes in South Africa referred to earlier, found that the scale positions assigned various items by South Africans of European background and by educated Bantus, natives of South Africa, were similar except for a few items. Studies of the construction of scales measuring attitudes toward a particular candidate for political office (Beyle, 1932), toward war (Ferguson, 1935), toward 'patriotism' (Pinter and Forlano, 1937), and toward Jews (Eysenck and Crown, 1949) all found correlations of 0·98 or higher between the scale positions assigned to the items by groups of judges with opposed attitudes toward the object of the scale.

More recent research, however, has sharply challenged the conclusions of these studies. Hovland and Sherif (1952), using the items employed in the Hinckley study mentioned above, found marked differences between the scale values assigned to items by anti-Negro white judges on the one hand, and those assigned by pro-Negro white judges and Negro judges, on the other. Items rated as 'neutral' or moderately favorable by Hinckley's subjects were likely to be seen as unfavorable by the pro-Negro white judges and the Negro judges. This discrepancy between the earlier and the later findings can be accounted for by the different procedures used. Hinckley followed a rule suggested by Thurstone, that any judge who placed more than one fourth of the statements in a single category should be eliminated as 'careless'. Hovland and Sherif, however, found that judges with extreme attitudes tended to place many statements in the same category; checks within their procedure convinced these investigators that this was not a matter of carelessness. Application of the rule followed by Hinckley would have eliminated over three fourths of their Negro judges and two thirds of their pro-Negro white judges; when they did eliminate these judges, they found that the scale values assigned by the remaining white judges were very close to those assigned by Hinckley's judges. These findings strongly suggest that Hinckley's procedure had the effect of ruling out judges with extreme attitudes.

A subsequent study by Kelley *et al.* (1955), using twenty of the Hinckley items, found marked differences between the scale values assigned to items by white and by Negro judges, with the statements fairly evenly distributed from 'favorable' to 'unfavorable' by the white judges, but bunched at the two ends of the continuum by the Negro judges.* Granneberg (1955), in constructing a scale of attitudes toward religion, found not only that a religious group and a nonreligious group differed significantly in the scale values they assigned to items, but that judges of superior and of low intelligence differed, and that there was an interaction between attitude and intelligence which affected the scale position to which items were assigned.

Such findings, of course, cast serious doubt on the meaning of the scale positions and the distances between them. It should be noted, however, that even those studies that found marked differences between groups of judges in the absolute scale values they assigned to items found high agreement in the *rank order* in which judges with differing attitudes arranged the items along the favorable-unfavorable continuum. Thus, although the assumption that Thurstone-type scales are true interval scales seems dubious, it is still possible for them to constitute reasonably satisfactory ordinal scales; that is, they provide a basis for saying that one individual is more favorable or less favorable than another. If in practice individuals agreed with only a few contiguous items, so that a given score had a clear meaning, the Thurstone methods would provide highly satisfactory ordinal scales. But, as noted above, individuals may agree with items quite widely spaced on the scale, and in such cases the median of the items checked may not provide a meaningful basis for ranking the individual in relation to others.

Summated Scales

A summated scale, like a differential scale, consists of a series of items to which the subject is asked to react. However, no attempt is made to find items that will be distributed evenly over a scale of favorableness-unfavorableness (or whatever dimension is to be measured). Rather, only items that seem to be either definitely favorable or definitely unfavorable to the object are used, not neutral or 'slightly' favorable or unfavorable items. Rather than

---

* These investigators found that other methods of constructing Thurstone-type scales were less subject than the equal-interval technique to the effect of extreme attitudes on the part of the judges. The method of successive intervals showed less difference between white and Negro judges, and the method of paired comparisons eliminated the differences almost entirely.

checking only those statements with which he agrees, the respondent indicates his agreement or disagreement with each item. Each response is given a numerical score indicating its favorableness or unfavorableness; often, favorable responses are scored plus, unfavorable responses, minus. The algebraic summation of the scores of the individual's responses to all the separate items gives his total score, which is interpreted as representing his position on a scale of favorable-unfavorable attitude toward the object. The rationale for using such total scores as a basis for placing individuals on a scale seems to be as follows: The probability of agreeing with any one of a series of favorable items about an object, or of disagreeing with any unfavorable item, varies directly with the degree of favorableness of an individual's attitude. Thus, one could expect an individual with a favorable attitude to respond favorably to many items (that is, to agree with many items favorable to the object and to disagree with many unfavorable ones); an ambivalent individual to respond unfavorably to some and favorably to others; an individual with an unfavorable attitude to respond unfavorably to many items.

The type of summated scale most frequently used in the study of social attitudes follows the pattern devised by Likert (1932) and is referred to as a *Likert-type scale*. In such a scale, the subjects are asked to respond to each item in terms of several degrees of agreement or disagreement; for example, (1) strongly approve, (2) approve, (3) undecided, (4) disapprove, (5) strongly disapprove.* Reproduced below are several items, with directions, from a Likert-type scale, the so-called 'Internationalism Scale' used by Murphy and Likert (1938).

Directions: The following list of sentences is in the form of what should or should not be done. If you strongly approve of the statement as it stands, underscore the words 'strongly approve', and so on, with regard to the other attitudes (approve, undecided, disapprove, strongly disapprove).

18. In the interest of permanent peace, we should be willing to arbitrate absolutely all differences with other nations which we cannot readily settle by diplomacy.

Strongly approve (5)	Approve (4)	Undecided (3)	Disapprove (2)	Strongly disapprove (1)

* Although Likert used five categories of agreement-disagreement, some investigators have used a smaller and some a larger number of categories. Many summated scales call simply for an expression of agreement or disagreement, without indication of degree.

19. A person who loves his fellow men should refuse to engage in any war, no matter how serious the consequences to his country.

Strongly approve (5)	Approve (4)	Undecided (3)	Disapprove (2)	Strongly disapprove (1)

22. We must strive for loyalty to our country before we can afford to consider world brotherhood.

Strongly approve (1)	Approve (2)	Undecided (3)	Disapprove (4)	Strongly disapprove (5)

The numbers under the scale positions do not appear on the questionnaire given to the respondents. They are shown here to indicate the scoring system.

The procedure for constructing a Likert-type scale is as follows: (1) The investigator assembles a large number of items considered relevant to the attitude being investigated and either clearly favorable or clearly unfavorable. (2) These items are administered to a group of subjects representative of those with whom the questionnaire is to be used. The subjects indicate their response to each item by checking one of the categories of agreement-disagreement. (3) The responses to the various items are scored in such a way that a response indicative of the most favorable attitude is given the highest score. It makes no difference whether 5 is high and 1 is low or vice-versa. The important thing is that the responses be scored consistently in terms of the attitudinal direction they indicate. Whether 'approve' or 'disapprove' is the favorable response to an item depends, of course, upon the content and wording of the item. (4) Each individual's total score is computed by adding his item scores. (5) The responses are analyzed to determine which of the items discriminate most clearly between the high scorers and the low scorers on the total scale. For example, the responses of those subjects whose total scores are in the upper quarter and the responses of those in the lower quarter may be analyzed in order to determine for each item the extent to which the responses of these criterion groups differ. Items that do not show a substantial correlation with the total score, or that do not elicit different responses from those who score high and those who score low on the total test, are eliminated to ensure that the questionnaire is 'internally consistent' – that is, that every item is related to the same general attitude.

The Likert-type scale, like the Thurstone scale, has been used widely in studies of morale, of attitudes toward Negroes, of attitudes toward internationalism, etc. It has several advantages over the Thurstone scale. First, it permits the use of items that are not manifestly related to the attitude being studied. In the Thurstone method, the necessity of agreement among judges tends to limit items to content that is obviously related to the attitude in question; in the Likert method, any item that is found empirically to be consistent with the total score can be included. Second, a Likert-type scale is generally considered simpler to construct. Third, it is likely to be more reliable than a Thurstone scale of the same number of items. Within limits, the reliability of a scale increases as the number of possible alternative responses is increased; the Likert-type scale item permits the expression of several (usually five) degrees of agreement-disagreement, whereas the Thurstone scale item allows a choice between two alternative responses only. Fourth, the range of responses permitted to an item given in a Likert-type scale provides, in effect, more precise information about the individual's opinion on the issue referred to by the given item.*

The Likert-type scale does not claim to be more than an ordinal scale; that is, it makes possible the ranking of individuals in terms of the favorableness of their attitude toward a given object, but it does not provide a basis for saying *how much* more favorable one is than another, nor for measuring the *amount* of change after some experience. From the point of view of the level of measurement we would like our instruments to provide, this is, of course, a disadvantage. Whether it constitutes a disadvantage of the Likert scale in comparison with the Thurstone scale depends on one's judgment of whether Thurstone scales really meet the criteria for interval scales.

Another disadvantage of the Likert-type scale is that often the total score of an individual has little clear meaning, since many patterns of response to the various items may produce the same score. We have already noted that Thurstone-type scales are also subject to this criticism, but it applies even more strongly to the Likert scales since they provide a greater number of response possibilities. Using the three items in our illustration of the Likert-type scale, for example, an individual may obtain a total score of 6 by indicating: (*a*) disapproval of 18 and 19, approval of 22; (*b*) approval of 18, strong disapproval of 19, and strong approval of 22; (*c*) indecision on 18, disapproval of 19, and strong approval of

* For a detailed comparison of the Thurstone and Likert methods, see Edwards and Kenney (1946) and Edwards (1957).

22; (*d*) other combinations of responses. It seems reasonable to suppose that, although the total scores are the same, their meanings may be markedly different. Thus one may raise a serious question whether the Likert-type scale actually conforms to the requirements of an ordinal, much less an interval, scale. Despite the lack of theoretical rationale for scalability, however, pragmatically the scores on the Likert-type questionnaire often provide the basis for a rough ordering of people on the characteristic being measured.

The fact that different patterns of response may lead to identical scores on either a Thurstone or a Likert scale is not necessarily as serious a drawback as it may at first appear. Some of the differences in response patterns leading to a given score may be attributable to random variations in response. Others may arise because specific items involve not only the attitude being measured but also extraneous issues that may affect the response. Thus some of the differences in response patterns leading to the same score may be thought of as errors from the point of view of the attitude being measured, rather than as true differences in attitude that are being obscured by identical scores. The fact that the scale contains a number of items means that these variations on individual items unrelated to the attitude being measured may cancel each other out.

Moreover, different ways of getting to the same place may be equivalent from the point of view of the measurement goal that is being served. For example, if one weights addition and subtraction equally in a concept of arithmetic ability, it makes sense to score two individuals as equivalent in arithmetic ability, even though one is relatively strong in addition and the other relatively strong in subtraction. Similarly, it may make sense to say that the net degree of animosity toward a given attitudinal object is the same in two individuals even though the animosity expresses itself differently.

The problem is to determine when the fact that the same score can be arrived at in different ways has consequences for the meaningfulness of the score, and when it does not. In part, this problem is one of conceptual clarity; in part, it involves questions of fact. If the investigator is not clear about what he is trying to measure, and why, this will be only one of many problems with which he will be unable to cope. But even if his concepts are clear, he will still want to know (although, unfortunately, he may not be in a position to find out) the answers to such questions as: Do the response patterns of individuals remain stable over time? If alternate forms of the test are available, do individuals receive the same scores on different forms? Do different individuals achieving the same score in different ways react in the same way to particular stimuli, problems, incentives, etc.?

Ultimately what is involved is a question of the validity of the scale. Questions of validity always involve questions of fact, which cannot be settled by armchair argument. The problem of whether different combinations of responses can meaningfully be assigned the same score is one for empirical investigation.

Cumulative Scales

Cumulative scales, like differential and summated scales, are made up of a series of items with which the respondent indicates agreement or disagreement. In a cumulative scale, the items are related to one another in such a way that, ideally, an individual who replies favorably to item 2 also replies favorably to item 1; one who replies favorably to item 3 also replies favorably to items 1 and 2; etc. Thus, all individuals who answer a given item favorably should have higher scores on the total scale than the individuals who answer that item unfavorably. The individual's score is computed by counting the number of items he answers favorably. This score places him on the scale of favorable-unfavorable attitude provided by the relationship of the items to one another.

Sometimes the items as they appear in the scale are arranged in order of favorableness; sometimes they are randomly arranged. Ordinarily, no attempt is made to determine whether the intervals between items are equal, thus, in practice, cumulative scales are ordinal scales.

One of the earliest scales used in the measurement of attitudes, the Bogardus social-distance scale (see Bogardus, 1925, 1928, 1933), was intended to be of the cumulative type. The social-distance scale, which has become a classic technique in the measuring of attitudes toward ethnic groups, lists a number of relationships to which members of the group might be admitted. The respondent is asked to indicate, for specified nationality or racial groups, the relationships to which he would be willing to admit members of each group. His attitude is measured by the closeness of relationship that he is willing to accept. The Bogardus-type scale is illustrated below:

Directions: For each race or nationality listed below, circle each of the classifications to which you would be willing to admit the average member of that race or nationality (not the best members

317

you have known, nor the worst). Answer in terms of your first feeling reactions.

	To close kinship by marriage	To my club as personal chums	To my street as neighbors	To employment in my occupation	To citizenship in my country	As visitors only to my country	Would exclude from my country
English	1	2	3	4	5	6	7
Negro	1	2	3	4	5	6	7
French	1	2	3	4	5	6	7
Chinese	1	2	3	4	5	6	7
Russian	1	2	3	4	5	6	7
etc.							

The items used in the Bogardus scale (that is, the column headings in the illustration above) were selected on logical grounds. It seems reasonable to expect that an individual who circles 4 in relation to Chinese, indicating that he would be willing to accept them to employment in his occupation, would ordinarily also circle 5 and not circle 6 or 7. (Here, as in other scales, the content of the item must be taken into account in deciding whether a 'Yes' response is to be scored as favorable or unfavorable. Since 6 and 7 are essentially statements of exclusion, *absence* of a circle constitutes the favorable response to these two items. Thus, neither 6 nor 7 should be circled for a given group if any of the other numerals is circled.) If the individual did not circle 3 (willing to admit to my street as neighbors), one would expect, on logical grounds, that he would also not circle 2 or 1.

On the whole, the assumption that these items form a cumulative scale has been borne out. Nevertheless, in practice some reversals do occur. Some individuals, for example, who would object to living in a building with Puerto Ricans would not object to having Puerto Ricans in an informal social club (see Deutsch and Collins, 1951). Although individuals not infrequently show such reversals in replies on the social-distance scale, it is relatively uncommon to find an entire group reversing items. Thus the social-distance scale has been used rather effectively in comparing the attitudes of different groups of people toward various nationalities. It may be noted that reversals can almost always be interpreted by postulating the intrusion of some factor other than the individual's own attitude toward the group in question – e.g. the respondent's image of how other people would interpret his living in a certain neighborhood, or his expectation concerning the impact on real estate values of admitting minority group members to residence on his street, etc.

With the appearance of the Thurstone and Likert scaling methods in the late nineteen-twenties and early thirties, attention shifted away from cumulative scales. However, the forties saw a revival of interest and a rapid development of techniques for determining whether the items of a scale do in fact have a cumulative relationship, regardless of whether they appear cumulative in commonsense terms. This renewed interest was linked to an emphasis on the development of *unidimensional* scales – that is, scales consisting of items that do not raise issues, or involve factors, extraneous to the characteristic being measured.

A number of investigators had pointed out that the Thurstone and Likert scales, although ostensibly measuring 'an attitude', contained statements about various aspects of the object under consideration. Thus, Carter (1945) pointed out that Form A of the Peterson scale of attitude toward war (a Thurstone-type scale) had as its most favorable statement, 'War is glorious'; as its most unfavorable statement, 'There is no conceivable justification for war'; and as its mid-point, 'I never think about war and it doesn't interest me'. He commented that it is difficult to think of these statements as falling along a straight line. He suggested that such statements as, 'The benefits of war rarely pay for its losses even for the victor' and 'Defensive war is justified but other wars are not', belong on two different scales, one having to do with the economic results of war, the other with the ethics of war activity. It was argued that combining items referring to different aspects of the object made it impossible to specify exactly what the scale was measuring, and also accounted for the scattering of responses, which made it difficult to assign any clear meaning to the score based on the median of the items checked.

There have been several approaches to this problem. We shall discuss here only the technique developed by Guttman, commonly called *scale analysis* or the *scalogram method*.* One of the main purposes of this technique is to ascertain whether the attitude or characteristic being studied (technically termed the 'universe of content' or the 'universe of attributes') actually involves only a

* For a more comprehensive discussion of the Guttman technique, see Stouffer *et al.* (1950). For critiques of it, and alternative approaches to the same problem, see Festinger (1947) and Loevinger (1948).

single dimension. In the Guttman procedure, a 'universe of content' is considered to be unidimensional only if it yields a perfect, or nearly perfect, cumulative scale – that is, if it is possible to arrange all the responses of any number of respondents into a pattern of the following sort:

Score	Says 'Yes' to item			Says 'No' to item		
	3	2	1	3	2	1
3	x	x	x			
2		x	x	x		
1			x	x	x	
0				x	x	x

The important thing about this pattern is that, if it holds, a given score on a particular series of items always has the same meaning; knowing an individual's score makes it possible to tell, without consulting his questionnaire, exactly which items he endorsed. Consider, for example, the following items, with which respondents are asked either to agree or to disagree:

1. A young child is likely to face serious emotional problems if his parents get divorced.
2. Even if a husband or wife or both are unhappy in their marriage, they should remain together as long as they have any young children.
3. Divorce laws in this state should be changed to make it more difficult to get a divorce.

If these items were found to form a perfect cumulative scale, we would know, for example, that *all* individuals with a score of 2 on the scale believe that divorce of the parents presents serious emotional problems for a young child and that a couple with young children should remain together even if they are unhappy, but do *not* believe that the divorce laws should be made more stringent.

In practice, perfect cumulative, or unidimensional, scales are rarely or never found in social research, but approximations to them can often be developed. Scalogram analysis uses several criteria for deciding whether or not a particular series of items may be usefully regarded as approximating a perfect unidimensional scale. The most important of these is the *reproducibility* of the responses – the proportion of responses of a large number of subjects which actually fall into the pattern presented above.* This pattern contains all the responses to particular items that would be predicted from a knowledge of the individual's total score on the series of items (his 'scale type'). Thus the proportion of actual responses which fall into the pattern provides a measure of the extent to which particular responses are 'reproducible' from the total score. Guttman and his co-workers have set 0·90 as the minimal reproducibility necessary for a series of items to be regarded as approximating a perfect scale. Examples of such scales are presented in Stouffer *et al.* (1950).

The Guttman technique is a method of determining whether a set of items forms a unidimensional scale; as a number of writers have pointed out, it offers little guidance for selecting items that are likely to form such a scale. Edwards and Kilpatrick (1948)† have suggested a method of selecting a set of statements likely to form a unidimensional scale. Called the *scale-discrimination technique*, it combines aspects of the Thurstone and Likert approaches to scale construction, in the following steps: (1) A large assortment of items dealing with the issue of study is collected. Items that are ambiguous, irrelevant, neutral, or too extreme are eliminated by inspection. (2) As in the Thurstone method of equal-appearing intervals, a large number of judges place the remaining items in eleven piles, according to their judged favorableness or unfavorableness toward the issue. The extent to which the judges agree on the placement of each item is determined, and the half of the items on which there is greatest variability or scatter of judgments is eliminated. Each of the remaining items is assigned a scale value corresponding to the median position in which it has been placed by the judges. (3) These items are then transformed into a Likert-type scale by providing for the expression of five or six degrees of agreement-disagreement in response to each item. This scale is administered to a large group of subjects, and their responses are analyzed to determine which of the items discriminate most clearly between the high scorers and the low scorers on the total scale. The resulting 'discriminatory coefficients' of the various items are then plotted against their scale values. From the total list of items, twice the number wanted in the final scale are selected. The items selected are those which have the highest discriminatory coefficients in their scale interval; for example, of all the items with scale values between 8·0 and 8·9, those with the highest discriminatory

---

* For a detailed discussion of this and other methods of determining whether a scale is unidimensional, see White and Saltz (1957).
† This article appears also, with minor changes, in Edwards (1957).

coefficients are selected. An equal number of items is selected for each interval. (4) The items in the resulting list are arranged in order of their scale value. The list is then divided into two equated forms of the questionnaire by assigning all the odd-numbered items to one form and all the even-numbered items to the other.

The Guttman and related techniques represent major contributions to the methodology of questionnaire construction and analysis. However, two qualifications related to the use of unidimensional scales should be kept in mind: (1) Such a scale may not be the most effective basis either for measuring attitudes toward complex objects or for making predictions about behavior in relation to such objects; (2) a given scale may be unidimensional for one group of individuals but not for another.

Let us consider the first reservation. Suppose we have devised a unidimensional scale to measure attitude toward the economic results of war, another to measure attitude concerning the ethics of war activity, still others to measure whatever other aspects of attitude toward war can be identified and measured by unidimensional scales. No single one of these scales may give an accurate reflection of an individual's attitude toward the complex concept 'war', or provide a basis for predicting how he would vote on the question of his country's participation in a specific war; a complex measure may be needed as a basis for predicting complex behavior.

As for the second reservation, it is sometimes assumed that unidimensionality is a property of a measuring instrument, rather than of the patterning of an attitude among a given group of individuals. For one group, a number of items may be arranged unidimensionally in a given order; for another group, the same items may fall into a different order; for still another group, they may not form a unidimensional pattern at all. The way in which the experiences of different groups can lead to different patternings of items is illustrated in a study by Harding and Hogrefe (1952). These investigators interviewed three groups of white department-store employees. The members of Group I worked in departments in which there was at least one Negro in a job equal in status to their own, or of higher status than their own; those in Group II worked in departments in which all the Negroes were in jobs of lower status than their own; those in Group III were in departments where there were no Negroes. The interviews included six 'social-distance' questions, having to do with: sitting next to Negroes in buses or trains, sitting at the same table with a Negro in a lunchroom, taking a job in which there were both Negroes and white people doing the same kind of work as you, working under a Negro supervisor, living in a building in which there were both white and Negro families, and having a Negro for a personal friend. The investigators found that these six questions formed satisfactory Guttman-type scales for each of the three groups, but that the question about taking a job in which there were both Negroes and white people doing the same kind of work as the respondent fell in a different position for each of the three groups. For Group I – the people who were actually in this situation – this question tied with the one about buses and trains for the 'most acceptable' position. For Group II – those working in departments with Negroes, but in positions of unequal status – sitting next to Negroes in trains and buses was more acceptable than working with them on an equal status. For those in all-white departments, both sitting next to Negroes in buses and trains and sitting at the same table with a Negro in a lunchroom were more acceptable than working with them on an equal status.

In other words, as Coombs (1948) has pointed out:

. . . in a highly organized social order with standardized education, there will tend to be certain traits generated which will be common to the population subjected to the same pattern of forces. There is, however, at the same time, opposition, contradiction, and interaction of these forces on organisms that are not equally endowed in the first place – with the result that the structuring of a psychological trait is less complete in some individuals than in others. . . . A psychological trait, in other words, may or may not be a functional unity and it may or may not be general, i.e. common to a large number of individuals.

References

Adorno, T. W., Frenkel-Brunswik, E., Levinson, D. J., and Sanford, R. N., *The authoritarian personality*. Harper, 1950.

Beyle, H. C., A scale for the measurement of attitude toward candidates for elective government office. *American Political Science Review*, **26**, 527–44, 1932.

Bogardus, E. S., Measuring social distances. *J. Applied Sociology*, **9**, 299–308, 1925.

Bogardus, E. S., *Immigration and race attitudes*. Heath, 1928.

Bogardus, E. S., A social distance scale. *Sociology and Social Research*, **17**, 265–71, 1933.

Carter, H., Recent American studies in attitudes toward war: a summary and evaluation. *American Sociological Review*, **10**, 343–52, 1945.

Coombs, C. H., Some hypothesis for the analysis of qualitative variables. *Psychological Review*, **55**, 167–74, 1948.

Deutsch, M., and Collins, M. E., *Interracial housing: a psychological evaluation of a social experiment*. Univ. of Minnesota, 1951.

Dudycha, G. J., A critical examination of the measurement of attitude toward war. *J. Social Psychology*, **39**, 846–60, 1943.

Edwards, A. L., *Techniques of attitude scale construction*. Appleton-Century-Crofts, 1957.

Edwards, A. L., and Kennedy, K. C., A comparison of the Thurstone and Likert techniques of attitude scale construction. *J. Applied Psychology*, **30**, 72–83, 1946.

Edwards, A. L., and Kilpatrick, F. P., A technique for construction of attitude scales. *J. Applied Psychology*, **32**, 374–84, 1948.

Eysenck, H. J., and Crown, S., An experimental study in opinion-attitude methodology. *International J. Opinion and Attitude Research*, **3**, 47–86, 1949.

Ferguson, L. W., The influence of individual attitudes on construction of an attitude scale. *J. Social Psychology*, **6**, 115–17, 1935.

Festinger, L., The treatment of qualitative data by scale analysis. *Psychological Bulletin*, **44**, 149–61, 1947.

Granneberg, R. T., The influence of individual attitude and attitude-intelligence interaction upon scale values of attitude items. *American Psychologist*, **10**, 330–1, Abstract, 1955.

Harding, J., and Hogrefe, R. Attitudes of white department store employees toward Negro co-workers. *J. Social Issues*, **8**, 1, 18–28, 1952.

Hinckley, E. D., The influence of individual opinion on construction of an attitude scale. *J. Social Psychology*, **3**, 283–96, 1932.

Hovland, C. I., and Sherif, M., Judgmental phenomena and scales of attitude measurement: item displacement in Thurstone scales. *J. Abnormal and Social Psychology*, **47**, 822–32, 1952.

Kelley, H. H., Hovland, C. I., Schwartz, M., and Zbelson, R. P., The influence of judges' attitudes in three methods of attitude scaling. *J. Social Psychology*, **42**, 147–58, 1955.

Likert, R., A technique for the measurement of attitudes. *Archives Psychology*, No. 140, 1932.

Loevinger, J., The technique of homogeneous tests compared with some aspects of 'scale analysis' and factor analysis. *Psychological Bulletin*, **45**, 507–29, 1948.

MacCrone, I. D., *Race attitudes in South Africa*. Oxford, 1937.

Murphy, G., and Likert, R., *Public opinion and the individual*. Harper, 1938.

Pinter, R., and Forlano, G., The influence of attitude upon scaling of attitude items. *J. Social Psychology*, **8**, 39–45, 1937.

Remmers, H. H., (ed.), Studies in attitudes. Purdue University studies in higher education, 26. *Bulletin of Purdue University*, **35**, No. 4, 1934.

Saffir, M. A., A comparative study of scales constructed by three psychophysical methods. *Psychometrika*, **2**, 179–98, 1937.

Stouffer, S. A., *et al.*, *Measurement and prediction. Studies in Social Psychology in World War II, Vol. IV*. Princeton University, 1950.

Thorstone, L. L., The method of paired comparisons for social values. *J. Abnormal and Social Psychology*, **21**, 384–400, 1927.

Thurstone, L. L., An experimental study of nationality preferences. *J. Genetic Psychology*, **1**, 405–25, 1928.

Thurstone, L. L., Theory of attitude measurement. *Psychological Bulletin*, **36**, 222–41, 1929.

Thurstone, L. L., The measurement of social attitudes. *J. Abnormal and Social Psychology*, **26**, 249–69, 1931.

Thurstone, L. L., and Chave, E. J., *The measurement of attitude*. University of Chicago, 1929.

White, B. W., and Saltz, E., Measurement of reproducibility. *Psychological Bulletin*, **54**, 81–99, 1957.

Wright, Q., and Nelson, C. J., American attitudes toward Japan and China, 1937–38. *Public Opinion Quarterly*, **3**, 46–62, 1939.

27   S. W. Cook and C. Selltiz

A Multiple Indicator Approach to Attitude Measurement

Reprinted from: S. W. Cook and C. Selltiz, *Psychological Bulletin*, American Psychological Assoc., U.S.A., 1964, Vol. 62, Chapter 1, pp. 36-55.

At least since LaPiere's report (1934) of the discrepancy between the actual reception accorded him and a Chinese couple and the answers to a questionnaire about accepting Chinese as guests, investigators have been concerned with the fact that different procedures designed to assess the same attitudes have often led to quite different placements of the same individuals, and that observed behavior toward a social object (person, group, etc.) is frequently not what would have been predicted from a given instrument intended to measure attitude toward that object.* There have been several types of reaction to such observed discrepancies. One has been to assume that there is a 'true' attitude toward the object, which one or both measures have failed to gauge correctly. A second has been to assume that there are different 'classes' of attitudes toward a given object – for example, 'verbal attitudes' and 'action attitudes' – which should not necessarily be expected to correspond. Another has been to equate attitude with behavior, using 'attitude' simply as a descriptive term summarizing observed consistencies in behavior. Still another reaction has been to think of attitude as an underlying disposition which enters, along with other influences, into the determination of a variety of behaviors toward an object or class of objects, including statements of beliefs and feelings about the object and approach-avoidance actions with respect to it.

We prefer the latter position; first, because for us, as for others (e.g. Allport, 1954) the observation of regularities in social behavior seems to point to the operation of relatively stable underlying dispositions toward classes of objects. Further, we believe that apparent inconsistencies in social behavior may often best be understood in terms of the operation of such stable underlying

* The initial discussion here, and to some extent the whole article in its concern with the nature of the inferences involved in assessing attitudes, is useful in relation to the problem of discrepancies between attitudes and behavior, as taken up in the earlier section, 'Focus on Behavior'. – Eds.

dispositions in shifting relation to other influences on behavior. Finally, if validly distinguished, a dispositional concept has, by its very nature, a wider range of situational relevance – including projectability into relatively novel situations – than a simple descriptive concept equating attitude with behavior in specified situations.

We assume that two classes of variables, in addition to an individual's attitudinal disposition toward a given object or class of objects, influence his behavior in situations involving the object or symbols of the object (including the behavior constituting his responses to instruments designed to measure attitude toward the object): (a) *other characteristics of the individual*, including his dispositions toward other objects represented in the situation, values he holds that are engaged by the situation, his motivational state, his expressive style, and so on; (b) *other characteristics of the situation*, including its prescriptions as to appropriate behavior, the expectations of others in the situation with respect to the individual's behavior, the possible or probable consequences of various acts on his part, and so on.

In this view, an attitude cannot be measured directly, but must always be inferred from behavior – whether the behavior be language in which the individual reports his feelings about the attitude-object, performance of a task involving material related to the object (e.g. recall of statements which take a position with respect to the object), or actions toward a representative of the object-class (e.g. avoidance of such an individual). Lazarsfeld (1959) takes a similar position in his discussion of latent structure analysis. He points out that there is a probability relation between an indicator and the underlying trait of which it is taken as an indication; that is, a given trait does not invariably produce a given behavior. He stresses that, in consequence, some inconsistency will always be found between different measures of a hypothesized trait, and that the task of the investigator is to combine them into an 'index' or 'measurement' which represents the best inference that can be made from the manifold of empirical operations to the underlying characteristic they are assumed to reflect.

This orientation leads to emphasis on the need for a number of different measurement approaches to provide a basis for estimating the common underlying disposition, and to the expectation that data from these approaches will not be perfectly correlated. However, it seems to us that it should be possible to increase the correspondence among the indicators by careful analysis of other factors that are likely to affect response to a given measuring instrument and by efforts to reduce or control the influence of those factors. Ideally, the goal would be to develop one or more measures from which the effects of all probable response determinants other than attitude toward the relevant object would be removed. This goal, however, seems unlikely of achievement; therefore it seems to us important to work with a number of different measures, in each of which an effort is made to eliminate or control in some systematic way some identifiable influence on response other than the attitude in question. Since different influences will be controlled in different measures – and thus, conversely, different influences in addition to attitude will affect responses on the different measures – there will remain a lack of full correspondence among scores on the different measures.

Social scientists have long recognized that factors other than an individual's attitude toward an object may influence both his response to instruments designed to measure the attitude and his behavior toward the object in everyday life. Much recent work in the field of both personality and attitude measurement has been concerned with identifying the effects of such 'extraneous' variables as the tendency to agree (or to disagree) with statements regardless of their content (e.g. Bass, 1955; Cronbach, 1946, 1950) or the wish to give a socially acceptable picture of oneself (e.g. Edwards, 1953, 1957; Taylor, 1961). Another interest has been in the development of indirect methods of attitude assessment (for a review of such methods, see Campbell, 1950). But attempts to develop indirect measures have, for the most part, been sporadic, and there has been little effort to examine systematically the relation of different indirect measures to each other or their relative susceptibility to such influences as agreeing response set or social norms.

Despite the general awareness of measurement problems, examination of reports of experimental research on attitudes shows the following picture: First, even investigators who hold very sophisticated theoretical positions about the nature and functions of attitudes and the conditions for attitude change commonly use only a single attitude measure – typically quite crude – in testing hypotheses derived from those theoretical positions. Second, most investigators are aware of the possibility that responses to these instruments may be influenced by factors other than the attitudes they are intended to measure. Third, efforts are made to guard against the intrusion of such factors or to rule out interpretations based on the possibility that they have been operative. These safeguards usually take one or more of the following forms:

sampling (e.g. selection of groups of subjects believed to differ in susceptibility to the extraneous influences most likely to be operative in the measurement situation), experimental design (e.g. the introduction of control groups), internal analysis of the data (e.g. considering how the responses of subgroups of subjects might be expected to differ if one determinant rather than another were operative).

We do not mean to minimize the importance of such procedures. In any given study they may quite convincingly rule out the possibility that responses have been influenced by factors other than subjects' attitudes toward the object in question. Nevertheless, it seems to us that effort directed toward improving measuring instruments might be at least equally useful.

An Examination of Different Types of Measuring Instruments in Terms of the Kinds of Evidence They Provide as a Basis for Inferences about Attitude.

In most current research on attitudes, efforts directed specifically toward improving measuring techniques are limited to such matters as assuring anonymity, attempting to separate the measurement from the experimental sessions, varying the order of presentation of items or the context in which they are embedded. If we are to go beyond such limited steps, a more systematic analysis of the characteristics of measuring instruments is needed than is yet available. This paper is a first step toward such an analysis. Our purpose is not to present a detailed review of the different kinds of instruments that have been used to measure attitudes; this has been well done by others (Campbell, 1950; Deri, Dinnerstein, Harding, and Pepitone, 1948; Weschler and Bernberg, 1950). Rather, we propose to examine broad classes of measurement techniques from the point of view of the kinds of evidence they provide and thus the nature of the inferences involved in estimating attitude. By 'the nature of the inferences involved' we mean the grounds for believing that attitude toward the presumed object is a determinant of responses to the measuring instrument, and the bases for inferring the nature of the attitude from the characteristics of the responses (i.e. for considering a given response as indicative of a positive or a negative disposition toward the object).

We have found it useful to think in terms of five major groupings: (a) measures in which the material from which inferences are drawn consists of self-reports of beliefs, feelings, behavior, etc., toward an object or class of objects; (b) measures in which inferences are drawn from observed overt behavior toward the object;

(c) measures in which inferences are drawn from the individual's reactions to or interpretations of partially structured material relevant to the object; (d) measures in which inferences are drawn from performance on objective tasks where functioning may be influenced by disposition toward the object; and (e) measures in which inferences are drawn from physiological reactions to the object. Not all of the measures discussed have been used as attitude tests in the formal sense, but for each of them there is reason to believe that attitude may be an important determinant of response and thus that the technique could serve as a basis for inferences about attitude.

In assessing the adequacy of an instrument as an indicator of attitude, consideration of its susceptibility to other influences is as important as consideration of the grounds for believing that underlying disposition toward the object is a determinant of response. In examining measuring instruments from the point of view of the possible influence of factors other than attitude, we shall consider two major aspects: (a) the probability that overt responses may deviate from 'private' responses – that is, the ease with which an individual can alter his responses to present a certain picture of himself; (b) the probability that private responses may be influenced by determinants other than attitude, in the absence of any attempt to distort responses.

Possibilities of influence of private response by factors other than attitude are, of course, almost limitless; we shall discuss only those that seem most probable with respect to each type of instrument. Susceptibility of overt response to distortion – that is, the possibility of discrepancy between private and overt response – would seem to be a function of three characteristics of the instrument: the extent to which its purpose is apparent, the extent to which the implications of specific responses are clear, and the extent to which responses are subject to conscious control.

In discussing the susceptibility of measures to distortion of responses and techniques developed to lessen the probability of distortion, we assume that with respect to many attitudes the settings in which tests are usually administered tend to exert pressures in a constant direction. It seems reasonable to suppose that most respondents, presented with tests in an academic setting or under the auspices of some other 'respectable' organization, will assume that the responses which will place them in the most favorable light are those which represent them as well adjusted, unprejudiced, rational, open-minded, and democratic. Moreover, since these are ideal norms at least in much of the American middle class,

329

the pressures specific to the test situation are likely to coincide with inner pressures toward maintaining an image acceptable to the self as well as to others. By 'controversial social attitudes' we mean attitudes with respect to which such norms are operative. Some of our discussion, and especially some of our examples, concern techniques for making it easier for the individual to reveal himself as not well adjusted, not unprejudiced, etc., or for making it harder for him to portray himself, falsely, as well adjusted, unprejudiced, etc. While some assumption as to the probable direction of pressures operating in the situation is necessary for the concrete details of certain techniques, the principles involved do not hinge on the specific direction of pressures; given testing situations in which there is reason to believe that the pressures are predominantly in a different direction, the techniques can be modified accordingly. And many of the techniques require no assumption about the probable direction of pressures, being designed to reduce the effects of extraneous influences in any direction.

Measures in which inferences are drawn from self-reports of beliefs, feelings, behaviors, etc.

By far the most frequently used method of securing material from which to make inferences about an attitude is to ask an individual to reveal – either in his own words or through acceptance or rejection of standardized items – his beliefs about the attitudinal object, how he feels toward it, how he behaves or would behave toward it, how he believes it should be treated.

The basis for inference is clear: it is axiomatic in all definitions that an individual's attitude toward an object is indicated by his beliefs, feelings, and action orientation toward it. The nature of the inference is also clear: it is assumed that the relationship between attitude and expression is a direct one and that the attitude corresponds to the manifest, common-sense implications of the stated belief or feeling. For example, a stated belief that the object has characteristics usually considered desirable is taken as reflecting a favorable disposition toward it, and a stated belief that it has characteristics usually considered undesirable is taken as reflecting an unfavorable disposition. Similarly, a report that the person avoids contact with the object is taken as indicating an unfavorable disposition toward it, while a report that he does or would willingly enter into contact with it is taken as indicating a favorable disposition.

In some definitions, attitude is considered identical with, or simply a summary of, beliefs, feelings, behavior, etc., toward the object; thus no problem of inference arises. However, in such definitions some criteria must be adopted for choosing which behavior constitutes the population of 'attitudinal responses' to be sampled. The choice of such criteria would, we believe, depend upon an analysis essentially similar to our consideration of 'extraneous influences' in the remainder of this paper.

Self-report measures have a number of characteristics that make them susceptible to distortion of overt responses. The purpose of the instrument is obvious to the respondent; the implications of his answers are apparent to him; he can consciously control his responses. Thus a person who wishes to give a certain picture of himself – whether in order to impress the tester favorably, to preserve his own self-image, or for some other reason – can rather easily do so. This difficulty has long been recognized, and in recent years it has been extensively investigated under the rubric of 'social desirability'. A number of techniques have been devised to make the purpose of the instrument or the implications of the responses less apparent; to make it easier to give answers that may be considered undesirable; and to make it harder to give, falsely, answers that may be considered desirable. Some of these techniques are focused primarily on reducing the likelihood that responses will be distorted in an attempt to meet the investigator's expectations or to please him; others are addressed to reducing the influence on responses of a desire to maintain a certain self-image as well as that of a desire to please or impress the investigator.

One of the simplest approaches to making the purpose of the instrument less apparent is the inclusion of items not relevant to the attitudinal object in which the investigator is interested. A variation of this approach is to include in each of the items a number of aspects in addition to that in which the investigator is interested; for example, if the investigator is interested in attitudes toward one or more racial groups, each item may refer to a hypothetical person characterized not only in terms of race but of age, sex, religion, occupation, etc. Approaches of either sort serve only to make the purpose of the test less obvious. They do not completely conceal or disguise it, nor can they do so within the format of self-report measures, which by definition call for the individual's own account of his reactions to the attitudinal object.

Among the simplest, and most frequently used, approaches to making it easier to give answers that may be considered undesirable are assurances of anonymity, statements to the effect that 'there are no right or wrong answers' or that 'people differ in their views on these things', emphasis on the importance of honest answers in order to contribute to scientific knowledge or some other presumably desirable outcome, efforts to build up rapport between questioner and respondent and to create the impression that the questioner will not disapprove of whatever views may be expressed.

Other approaches are built into the instrument itself: including items to which an unfavorable reply is likely to be considered acceptable (e.g. 'Would you be willing to have a ditch digger as U.S. Congressman from your district?' – Westie, 1952, 1953), in order to break down a possible set to give uniformly favorable replies; including in the statement of a view that may be considered undesirable a qualification or a justification of it (e.g. 'It is best that Jews should have their own fraternities and sororities, since they have their own particular interests and activities which they can best engage in together, just as Christians get along best in all-Christian fraternities' – Adorno, Frenkel-Brunswik, Levinson, and Sanford, 1950); wording questions in such a way that they assume the respondent holds certain views or has engaged in certain kinds of behavior (e.g. 'When did you first . . .?' – Kinsey, Pomeroy, and Martin, 1948).

Other approaches are designed to make it difficult to give, falsely, what may be considered a desirable answer. In the measurement of personality, a major effort in this direction has been the use of forced-choice tests, where the respondent is asked to indicate which of two statements, matched in terms of social desirability but differing in their implications with respect to traits or needs, is closer to his own views or more descriptive of his own behavior. This approach has not been extensively used in the measurement of attitudes.

In addition to their susceptibility to conscious distortion in order to give the picture the individual wishes to present of himself, responses to self-report measures may be influenced by another set of characteristics presumably unrelated to attitude toward the object in question – characteristics frequently labeled 'response set' or 'expressive style'. It has long been noted that some individuals have a consistent tendency to agree (or to disagree) with items presented to them, regardless of their content; or to select, with more than chance frequency, the alternative which appears in a given position; or to give extreme (or moderate) answers.

A number of techniques have been devised to reduce the effects of such tendencies on scores that are to be taken as indicative of attitudes. Perhaps the simplest and the most common approach to the problem of influence by a tendency to agree (or to disagree) is to vary the wording of items in such a way that for approximately half of them agreement represents a favorable response to the attitudinal object, and for half an unfavorable response. Other approaches to this problem involve setting up the instrument in such a way that responses do not take the form of expressing agreement or disagreement with one statement at a time. The instrument may consist of pairs of statements representing roughly opposed points of view on a given issue, both statements being worded positively or both worded negatively; the subject is asked to indicate which is nearer his own position, or to indicate his position on a scale running between the two statements. The following pair of items from an unpublished scale of attitudes toward freedom of speech, developed by students of Donald T. Campbell at Northwestern University, illustrate this approach:

A. Fascists and Communists are entitled to preach their beliefs in this country.
B. Only those who are in agreement with this country's philosophy of government are entitled to preach their beliefs.

In other instruments, the problem, at least in its obvious form, is avoided by using items that call for free response – open-ended questions, sentence stubs to be completed with the individual's own responses, etc.

An approach to correcting for the effects of a tendency to give extreme answers, or moderate answers, consists in providing matched pairs of items, one referring to the attitudinal object, the other referring to some control object, and scoring in terms of the discrepancy between the two responses. For example, if respondents were asked only, 'Would you be willing to have a Negro bookkeeper live in the same apartment building you live in?' and are provided with a 5-point response scale, it is impossible to determine whether respondents who answer 'very willing' differ from those who answer simply 'willing' in attitude, in response style, or in both. Providing a parallel item with respect to a white bookkeeper and scoring on the basis of discrepancy between an individual's responses to the Negro and the white removes the effects of response style from the score (Westie, 1953).

Susceptibility of self-report measures to the two kinds of influences discussed so far – desire to present a certain picture of oneself, and response sets unrelated to the content of items – clearly leads to the possibility of distortion of responses in the obvious sense of lack of correspondence between the overt responses and the individual's private beliefs, feelings, policy views,

333

etc. Still other factors, however, may influence his private beliefs and feelings as well as his overt responses. While private beliefs, feelings, and action orientations with respect to an object are by definition at least partially determined by the individual's attitude toward the object, they may be influenced by other factors as well — for example, by the availability of information, or by other values the individual holds. Thus, a person who has an essentially devaluing attitude toward Negroes may nevertheless have learned and state as his belief that there is no difference in the chemical composition of the blood of Negroes and whites; on the other hand, a person whose disposition toward Negroes is not devaluing may know and state as his belief that the average scholastic achievement of Negroes in the United States is lower than that of whites. A person with a devaluing attitude toward Negroes may nevertheless believe that they should not be deprived of the right to vote, because he sees this right as an essential ingredient of democracy; a person whose attitude toward Negroes is not devaluing may be opposed to laws forbidding discrimination in the sale and rental of housing because he places great store on the right of an owner to do with his property as he sees fit.

To the extent that such other influences affect different items differently, or affect only certain items, this problem has been attacked by examining responses for consistency, eliminating items which show low agreement with total scores, or eliminating those to which responses do not fall on a unidimensional scale.

A given technique may help to reduce or correct for extraneous influence from more than one source. For example, scoring in terms of discrepancy between responses to items concerning the attitudinal object and comparable items about a control object may provide a correction for the effects of other values or meanings engaged by the items as well as for response sets. Asking the respondents to choose which of two statements is closer to his views may help to eliminate the influence both of response set and of concern with the acceptability of responses, if the alternatives provided are equivalent in both respects.

Not only may a given technique serve more than one function; a given instrument may embody a number of techniques designed to reduce the influence of extraneous factors. For example, in Westie's (1953) Summated Differences Test, the subject is presented with hypothetical persons of specified race (Negro or white) and occupation (eight occupations, ranging from ditch digger to banker, plus 'the average man'), and asked to indicate, on 5-point scales, his willingness to accept each of these 18 hypothetical persons in each of 24 relationships – a total of 432 items. Some of the items are such that a negative answer is likely to be considered acceptable by most people (e.g. unwillingness to vote for a machine operator, whether white or Negro, as President of the United States is not likely to be seen as an expression of 'prejudice'), thus presumably breaking down a possible tendency to give uniformly favorable answers whether through an acquiescent response set or through a desire to give a picture of oneself as unprejudiced. The large number of items, and the format of the questionnaire, make it extremely unlikely that the subject can remember or check his response to a given item with respect to one racial group when he is answering the comparable item concerning the other group. Scoring on the basis of discrepancy between parallel items referring to whites and Negroes takes account both of possible response sets and of the influence of the specified occupation and the specified situation. Thus, this instrument adds to the basic social distance questionnaire a number of techniques designed to make the focus of the investigator's interest less apparent, to make it easier to give answers that might be considered undesirable, to correct for possible response sets, and to some extent to take account of other values or meanings that may affect responses.

Measures in which inferences are drawn from observation of overt behavior

Many investigators have pointed out the desirability of using measures in which overt behavior toward members of a class of objects would serve as a basis for inferences about attitude toward the object-class. As with self-report measures, the basis for inference is clear; all definitions of attitude specify that behavior can be taken as an indicator of attitude. And, as in the case of self-report measures, the usual assumption is that there is a simple correspondence between the nature of the behavior and the nature of the underlying attitude; for example, that friendly behavior toward a member of a given class of objects indicates a favorable attitude toward the object-class.

There has been much less extensive development of measures of this sort than of self-report measures. Situations capable of eliciting behavior toward an attitudinal object are more difficult to devise and to standardize, and more time-consuming and costly to administer, than self-report measures. Although some measures of this type have been devised, they have not been widely enough used to provide much evidence as to their specific strengths and weaknesses nor to stimulate efforts to correct for shortcomings.

However, analysis of their characteristics can provide estimates as to their probable susceptibility to influences other than attitude and possibilities of reducing such susceptibility.

Attempts to develop behavioral measures have followed three general lines. One consists in presenting subjects with standardized situations that they are led to believe are unstaged, in which they believe that their behavior will have consequences, and in which the attitudinal object is represented in some way other than by the actual presence of a member of the object-class. For example, subjects may be asked to sign a petition on behalf of an instructor, about to be discharged for membership in the Communist party, to contribute money for the improvement of conditions for migratory workers, to indicate whether they would be willing to have a Negro roommate. DeFleur and Westie (1958) have attempted to develop a measure of this sort which is appropriate for use in many different testing situations. In their procedure, as part of a larger program of research, white subjects viewed a number of colored photographic slides showing a young Negro man and a young white woman, or a young white man and a young Negro woman, in a social setting; subjects described the pictures and answered specific questions about them. At the close of an interview following this session the measurement procedure being discussed here was introduced. DeFleur and Westie describe the procedure as follows: The subject was told that another set of such slides was needed for further research, was asked if he (or she) would be willing to be photographed with a Negro of the opposite sex, and then was given 'a standard photograph release agreement', containing a variety of uses to which such a photograph would be put, ranging from laboratory experiments where it would be seen only by professional sociologists, to a nationwide publicity campaign advocating racial integration. The subject was asked to sign his name to each use of the photograph which he would permit. These investigators report that subjects 'uniformly perceived the behavioral situation posed for them as a highly realistic request'.

Such devices differ from self-report measures with similar content in that, in the behavioral measures, the subject either actually carries out the behavior (signs a petition, makes a contribution, etc.) or is led to believe that his agreement to do so will lead to real-life consequences (being asked to pose for a photograph to be put to specified uses, being assigned a Negro roommate, etc.).

Another approach is to present the subject with an admittedly staged situation and ask him to play a role – perhaps to behave as he would in such a situation in real life, perhaps to take the part of someone else or to act in some specified way. Stanton and Litwak (1955) presented actual and potential foster parents with situations of interpersonal stress in which they were instructed to behave in a given way (defined as not manifesting specified undesirable or neurotic kinds of behavior); for example, in one scene the subject was instructed that he was to play the role of a married man, having dinner with his parents; the investigator, playing the role of the man's father, treated his son like a child, criticized his wife, and put him in the wrong. These investigators found that ratings based on a half-hour's role playing were better predictors of subjects' behavior as foster parents (as rated by case workers who had sustained contact with them) than were ratings based on 12 hours of intensive interviewing by a trained social worker. Stanton, Back, and Litwak (1956) reported that a role-playing approach was successful in discovering the limits of positive and negative feelings about public housing projects on the part of slum dwellers in Puerto Rico. These investigators have stressed the importance of designing the scene specifically to elicit responses relevant to the particular behavior or attitude in which the investigator is interested.

A third behavioral approach, used in the study of attitudes toward social groups, has been to ask for sociometric choices among individuals some of whom are members of the object group, preferably under circumstances that lead the participants to believe that such choices will have consequences in the form of subsequent assignment in some situation. Early applications of this technique to the study of intergroup attitudes were made in studies by Moreno (see 1943) and by Criswell (1937, 1939), in which patterns of choices by school children were analyzed in terms of the development of cleavage along racial lines. Subsequently, sociometric techniques have been used in research evaluating the effects of certain experiences on attitudes (e.g. Mann, 1959a; Mussen, 1950a, 1950b) and of the relations among different aspects of attitudes (e.g. Mann, 1959b).

There are differences among these three kinds of behavioral measures – situations appearing to the subject to be unstaged, role playing, and sociometric choice – in characteristics that affect the probability that overt responses will correspond to responses that would be shown if the individual were not concerned with presenting (to others or to himself) a certain picture of himself. Let us consider first the extent to which their purpose is apparent to the respondent. To the extent that the purportedly unstaged situations are accepted as genuine, the respondent will not see them as designed to get information about his attitudes; thus one possible source of pressure to give responses that are likely to be considered desirable is eliminated. Nevertheless, the implications of his behavior as revealing certain characteristics may be apparent to him; even if he accepts a question about his willingness to pose with a Negro or to have a Negro roommate as genuine, he may be aware that a positive answer will have the effect of presenting him as unprejudiced, a negative answer as prejudiced. Thus, even in the absence of awareness that he is being tested, an individual may be motivated to give a response that differs from his spontaneous private one, in order to present himself to the questioner as unprejudiced or to maintain his own image of himself as one who behaves in an unprejudiced way. The sociometric choice method would appear to be similar in these respects, though it may perhaps be assumed that, in the absence of special influences calling attention to racial or ethnic group membership, the implications of the choices are less likely to be apparent. In the case of role playing, the extent to which the purpose of the situation and the implications of responses are clear presumably depends on the convincingness with which the situation can be presented as a measure of some other characteristic, such as acting ability.

All of these behavioral approaches have characteristics that may operate to make it easier to respond in ways that may be considered undesirable. In many situations it is possible to justify a negative response on neutral or acceptable grounds: one does not believe in signing petitions, or he does not like to have his picture taken, or he prefers Persons A and B to X and Y because they share his interest in music. Or, in the role-playing situation, his behavior is shaped not by his own reactions toward the attitudinal object but by interest in the dramatic requirements of the situation. (To the extent that these alternative explanations are real possibilities, however, they introduce other problems about interpretation of the behavior as an indicator of the attitude in which the investigator is interested.)

Some characteristics of the behavioral approaches may reduce the probability that the individual will modify his behavior in order to present an acceptable picture of himself. When responses are expected to have real-life consequences, the anticipation of such consequences may counterbalance the wish to make a good impression. In a social distance questionnaire, if one wishes to present himself (to the tester, or to himself, or both) as unprejudiced, there is little effective pressure against saying that one would be willing to work with a Negro, or to have a Negro roommate;

but if the question is posed in a context where a positive reply is seen as leading to assignment of a Negro as a co-worker or a roommate, one must weigh his willingness to accept that consequence against his wish to appear unprejudiced. In role playing, the pressure for quick response to unanticipated stimulus situations probably operates to lessen conscious control of behavior in order to produce a desired impression. Faced with the necessity of doing or saying something to keep the situation going, the individual may not have time to consider the impression he is making; to the extent that this is so, this approach may be thought of as reducing the individual's conscious selection of his response.

Thus behavioral measures seem to be less susceptible than simple self-report measures to distortion of response in the interest of presenting a certain picture of the self. But they are at least as susceptible as self-report measures to the effects of other extraneous influences. It has sometimes been suggested that the model of behavioral measures would be apparently unstaged situations in which a member of the object-class is present. But it is clear that behavior in everyday life situations (which this model seeks to approximate) is not determined exclusively by attitude toward the presumed attitudinal object. In the case of behavior toward minority groups, for example, social custom is a major determinant; in communities with segregated transportation systems, almost all white people – regardless of their attitudes toward Negroes or toward segregation – sit in the white section, whereas in communities with unsegregated transportation systems, very few white people – regardless of their attitudes – refuse to sit next to Negroes. Other values may override attitudes toward the presumed object; an individual who feels physical revulsion at the experience of eating with Negroes may nevertheless do so because he has come to believe that the ideals of democracy, or religious principles of brotherhood, or the position of the United States in the eyes of the world, require that all men be treated as equals. Finally, other characteristics of the object individuals may predominate over their ethnic identification in determining response to them. Thus, LaPiere (1934) concluded that the factors which most influenced the behavior of hotel and restaurant personnel to the Chinese couple with whom he was traveling 'had nothing to do with race'; rather, it was the quality and condition of their clothing, the appearance of their baggage, their cleanliness and neatness, and above all, their self-confident and pleasant manner, that determined reactions. Observations such as this suggest that, to the extent that one is interested in tapping generalized dispositions toward a given group rather than in predicting behavior in specific situations, behavioral measures that call for response to a symbolic representation of the group may be less subject to influence by extraneous factors than measures that call for response to members of the group who are physically present.

Campbell (1961) has suggested an approach to the use of behavior measures which is based on the premise that different situations have different thresholds, for the manifestation of hostile, avoidant, or discriminatory behavior. He suggests that, in order to secure evidence about an individual's attitude, it is necessary to place him in a number of situations with differing thresholds – ranging, for example, from eating with a Negro at a business men's luncheon club (assumed to be a situation with a low threshold for nondiscriminatory behavior – in other words, one in which it is easy to behave in an unprejudiced way) to renting one's house to a Negro (assumed to have a high threshold for nondiscriminatory behavior). The lowest-threshold situation in which an individual exhibits discriminatory behavior would indicate his position on a scale of attitude with respect to the group in question. Such a procedure would be effective in taking account of pressures that are constant for all, or most, individuals; it would not, it seems to us, rule out the effects of differences in the strength for different individuals of such influences as concern with social approval, other values seen as relevant to the situation, etc.

Measures in which inferences are drawn from the individual's reaction to or interpretation of partially structured stimuli

The characteristic common to techniques in this category is that, while there may be no attempt to disguise the reference to the attitudinal object, the subject is not asked to state his own reactions directly; he is ostensibly describing a scene, a character, or the behavior of a third person. He may be presented with a photograph of a member of the object-class (usually a person of a given social group) and asked to describe his characteristics; or he may be presented with a scene in which members of the object-class are present and asked to describe it, to tell a story about it, to predict the behavior of one of the characters, etc. The stimulus material may be verbal rather than pictorial; for example, the subject may be asked to complete sentence stubs referring to a hypothetical third person.

The bases for inferences about attitudes are those common to all projective tests: assumptions that perception of stimuli that are not clearly structured is influenced by the perceiver's own needs and dispositions; that, asked to provide an explanation or interpretation for which the stimulus presented gives no clear clue, the subject must draw on his own experience or his own dispositions or his own definitions of what would be probable or appropriate; that, asked to attribute behavior to others, especially under speed conditions, the most readily accessible source of hypotheses is the individual's own response disposition. As in self-report and behavioral tests, the usual assumption is that the expressed response corresponds directly to the individual's attitude; for example, that attribution of desirable characteristics to a member of a given group represents a favorable attitude toward that group, that interpretation of a scene as one in which there is hostility toward a member of a given group represents a hostile attitude toward the group, that attribution of a positive (or a negative) response to a hypothetical third person with respect to a given object reflects a positive (or a negative) disposition toward the object in question.

A major reason for the development of such techniques is the assumption that, by disguising the purpose of the instrument and the implications of responses, they lessen the probability of distortion of responses in the interest of presenting a certain picture of the self. They are presented to the respondent not as measures of attitudes but as tests of imagination, verbal fluency, ability to judge character, social sensitivity, or some such characteristic. To the extent that the respondent accepts these explanations, he presumably is unaware not only of the purpose of the test but of the implications of his responses as revealing his own attitudes. Even if the subject does realize that he is expressing his own attitude, it is assumed that it may be easier to express views that may be considered undesirable if one does not explicitly acknowledge them as his own. In some instances the questions asked are nonevaluative, so that the implications of one or another response are quite unlikely to be apparent to the respondent; for example, 'What is the [nonexistent] colored man in the corner doing?' [Horowitz and Horowitz, 1938.]'

Questions have been raised, however, about the validity of the assumption that responses, even though spontaneous and undistorted, reflect the individual's own attitude toward the object. While it seems clearly established that an individual's response may reflect his own disposition, it is not certain that it necessarily does so. Given a scene in which the roles of Negro and white are ambiguous, an individual who describes the Negro as being in a menial position may be reflecting his own devaluing disposition toward Negroes; on the other hand, he may simply be reporting the arrangement most commonly observed in our culture. Similarly, the responses he attributes to a hypothetical third person may be based either on his own response disposition or on his estimate of how most people would react in such a situation.

Attempts to secure evidence as to whether responses to instruments of this type do in fact reflect the individual's own attitudes have followed two lines: examination of the correspondence between estimates of attitude based on these measures and estimates based on other measures (usually of the self-report type); and examination of data secured from instruments of this sort in the light of predictions about patterns of results.

Several studies have found significant correspondence between results of measures of this type and scores on self-report measures. Proshansky (1943) found high correlations between scores based on a standard self-report scale for measuring attitude toward organized labor and scores based on descriptions of briefly-exposed ambiguous pictures of relevant social situations. Riddleberger and Motz (1957) found that subjects who scored high and those who scored low on a self-report measure of attitude toward Negroes differed in their explanations of how the people in a picture interracial group had met. Sommer (1954), using a modified form of Brown's (1947) adaptation of the Rosenzweig Picture-Frustration Test, was able to identify with considerable success not only individuals who scored high and those who scored low on a self-report scale of attitude toward Negroes but a subgroup who had been instructed to respond to the Picture-Frustration Test as if they were unprejudiced, even though their self-report scores were unfavorable.

However, in view of the assumption that an important characteristic of tests of this type is their relative lack of susceptibility, as compared with self-report measures, to efforts to present a certain picture of the self, correspondence with scores based on self-report measures is a dubious criterion. Getzels (1951), recognizing this fact, approached the problem by predicting conditions under which speeded completions of third-person sentence stubs would differ from completions, by the same respondents, of the same sentence stubs presented in the first person. He made two predictions: (a) that first- and third-person responses would differ on items subject to strong social norms not fully internalized by all members of the group and would not differ on items not subject to such norms; and (b) that in the case of the former items, more socially acceptable answers would be given on the first-person form than on the third-person form. Both predictions were strongly supported. Getzels recognized the possibility that responses to the third-person form might be based on estimates of how most people would respond rather than on the subjects' own response dispositions. Accordingly, he asked the subjects to estimate how most people would respond to the items about Negroes, and found no difference between the average estimates made by those whose third-person responses had been favorable and those whose third-person responses had been unfavorable.

A number of techniques involving perception – in a more literal sense – of ambiguous or unstructured material may be considered in this category. For example, a number of psychologists have been investigating the possible relation of attitudes to perception of stimuli presented under stereoscopic conditions of binocular rivalry. Bagby (1957), presenting pairs of cards differing in cultural content (e.g. a bullfighter and a baseball player) to subjects from Mexico and the United States, found that Mexicans tended to see the card with Mexican content, North Americans those with content familiar in the United States. Pettigrew, Allport, and Barnett, (1958), presenting to residents of South Africa pairs of pictures of individuals from different racial groups, found that Afrikaners deviated most consistently from other groups in their responses, overusing the 'European' and 'African' categories, underusing 'Colored' or 'Indian'.

A study by Bray (1950) made use of unstructured visual material in a different way. Taking off from Sherif's (1935) finding that estimates of movement in the autokinetic phenomenon are markedly influenced by the estimates given by others, Bray investigated the effects of estimates by confederates who were identified as members of minority groups. He had the hypothesis that the extent and direction of such effects would be influenced by the subject's attitude toward the minority group. Here the unstructured perceptual material did not refer to the attitudinal object, but simply provided an opportunity for expressing indirectly a response to the attitudinal object – the physically present, minority-group member.

Again, there are problems about the nature of the inferences that can be drawn. Bray, for example, did not find the direct relationship he had predicted between attitude toward the minority group (as measured by self-report scales) and responses to the minority-group members' estimates. In the case of binocular rivalry, in what way, if at all, does attitude influence perception? Does one see the picture with the most familiar content? Does one see the member of the racial group toward which he is most favorable, or the one toward which he is most hostile, or of which he is most afraid?

Questions such as these point both to the need for further research on the usefulness of these techniques as measures of attitude and to potentially fruitful lines of investigation of the relation between attitudes and response to various kinds of materials under various conditions.

Measures in which inferences are drawn from performance of 'objective' tasks

Approaches in this category present the respondent with specific tasks to be performed; they are presented as tests of information or ability, or simply as jobs that need to be done. The assumption common to all of them is that performance may be influenced by attitude, and that a systematic bias in performance reflects the influence of attitude.

For example, the subject may be asked to memorize material, some of which is favorable to the attitudinal object, some unfavorable, perhaps some neutral or irrelevant. The assumption is that material congenial with the subject's own position will be learned more quickly and remembered longer. Some empirical support is available for this assumption; for example, in a study by Levine and Murphy (1943), using material about the Soviet Union, and one by Jones and Kohler (1958) using statements about segregation. Or the subject is given a test of 'information', in which at least some of the items referring to the attitudinal object either have no correct answers or are so unfamiliar that it can be assumed that few if any respondents will know the correct answers; alternative responses believed (by the investigator) to indicate relatively favorable or relatively unfavorable dispositions toward the object are provided. The assumption here is that, when forced to make a guess on ostensibly factual questions where he has no objective basis for an answer, the subject is likely to choose the alternative most consistent with his own attitudinal disposition. This assumption, too, is supported by some empirical evidence; for example, studies by Hammond (1948) and Weschler (1950) of attitudes toward labor and toward Russia, and by Rankin and Campbell (1955) of attitude toward Negroes. Or the task may be a test of 'reasoning', in which syllogisms or other logical forms are presented, and the subject is asked to indicate which of a number of conclusions can appropriately be drawn. Items referring to the attitudinal object are paralleled by similar items with neutral or abstract content; scoring is on the basis of the number and direction of errors on the attitudinally relevant items as compared with the control items. The assumption is that reasoning may be swayed by attitudinal disposition, and thus that errors on the attitudinally relevant items reflect the individual's own position, if the parallel neutral items have been answered correctly. Watson (1925), Morgan (1945), and Thistlethwaite (1950), among others, have developed instruments of this type. Thistlethwaite found a significant difference between Northern and Southern college students in frequency of errors on items dealing with Negroes (as compared with errors on the neutral items), and no corresponding difference on items dealing with Jews, women, or patriotism.

Other measures place the emphasis on the material being judged or on the outcome to be achieved rather than on the ability involved in achieving it. For example, the subject is asked to sort items about the attitudinal object in terms of their position on a scale of favorableness-unfavorableness, ostensibly in order to help in the construction of a Thurstone-type scale. The assumption here is that the rater's own attitude toward the object – especially if it is extreme – influences his judgments of the favorableness of statements about the object. Despite the earlier belief that ratings of items for Thurstone scales are not affected by the raters' own attitudes, a number of recent studies (e.g. Hovland and Sherif, 1952) have found such effects.

It seems reasonable to suppose that most subjects accept these tasks at face value; presumably only someone with rather sophisticated knowledge of research techniques in the social sciences would be aware of their attitudinal implications. Thus it seems reasonable to suppose that they may be relatively impervious to distortion in the interest of presenting a desired picture of the self.

Again, however, there are questions about the nature of the inferences to be drawn. If a subject shows marked and consistent bias, it seems reasonable to infer that he has an attitude toward the object strong enough to affect his performance. If he does not show consistent bias, however, are we to infer that his attitude is not strong, or not consistent? In other words, how sensitive are such measures? Is it possible that individuals with equivalent attitudes differ in the extent to which their performance on such tasks is influenced by those attitudes?

Another problem has to do with the direction in which attitude influences the response, and, conversely, with the nature of the inference to be drawn from a given response. Responses may reflect either wishes or fears; a member of the Communist party may overestimate the number of Communists in the United States, but so may a member of the John Birch Society. A person who under-estimates the number of Negro doctors in the United States may do so on the basis of his feeling that Negroes do not have the ability to become doctors, or he may do so on the basis of his belief that opportunities for Negroes to obtain medical training are limited.

Judgments of the favorableness or unfavorableness of state-ments are subject to a similar problem of interpretation. Hovland and Sherif (1952), working with items about Negroes, found that ratings by Negro subjects and by white subjects who actively supported desegregation differed from ratings by 'average' and by anti-Negro white subjects. However, other investigators (e.g. Manis, 1960; Weiss, 1959), working with statements about different attitudinal objects, found that subjects with extreme attitudes – whether favorable or unfavorable – showed similar patterns of ratings, which differed from those made by subjects with moderate attitudes.

As with the preceding category, these problems of interpretation point to the need for caution in inferring the attitude of a given individual from a single test of this sort, but they seem to point also to the probable usefulness of further empirical investigation of the relation of scores based on such measures to those based on tests providing other grounds for inference.

Another group of measures presented as objective tasks or tests of ability focus on the extent to which the attitudinal object figures prominently in the subject's organization of his environment, that is, its salience for him. The kinds of data appropriate for inference about the salience of an attitudinal object differ in some respects from the kinds appropriate for inference about the nature or direction of the attitude. Measures of salience have been developed primarily with respect to attitudes toward social groups. They are of two types: techniques for assessing the tendency to classify individuals in terms of group membership, and techniques for assessing the tendency to subordinate individual differences to group identification.

One technique for assessing the tendency to classify individuals in terms of group membership, originated by Horowitz and Horowitz (1938), may be presented as a test of concept formation. It consists in presenting to a subject sets of photographs of indi-viduals differing in race, sex, age, and socioeconomic status and asking him to select those which 'belong together'. For example, one set may contain photographs of three white boys, one white girl, and one Negro boy. If the subject replies that the white girl does not belong, this is taken to mean that for him sex is a more important basis for classification than race; if he replies that the Negro boy does not belong, the inference is that race is a more important category for him than sex.

Another technique for assessing the tendency to classify individuals in terms of group membership, presented as a test of memory, involves the clustering, in recall, of verbal symbols for which alternative classificatory principles are available. This technique rests on the finding from studies of verbal behavior that when words drawn from various categories are presented in random order, subjects tend to recall them in clusters, with several words representing a given category being recalled together even though they were not next to each other in the list presented. In studying the salience of race as a basis for classification, a subject would be presented, in random order, with names of people from several different occupational categories – for example, baseball players, musicians, political figures, actors, one name in each category being that of a Negro. The extent to which names of Negroes are grouped together in recall would provide the basis for inference as to the salience of race as a basis for classifying individuals.

A measure of the tendency to subordinate individual differences to group identification, originated by Horowitz and Horowitz (1938), consists in showing the subject a number of photographs of individuals of different ethnic groups and then asking him to identify, from a larger number of photographs, those he has already seen. The task is presented as one involving perception and/or memory. Scoring is in terms of the proportion of correct responses to individuals of a given social group as compared with the proportion of correct responses with respect to individuals of other groups. The inference here is that accuracy in identifying whether or not pictures of specific individuals of a given social group have previously been seen is decreased by the tendency to subordinate individual differences to group identification.

Seeleman (1940–41), using pictures of whites and Negroes, found a high correlation between scores on this measure and scores on a self-report questionnaire designed to measure attitude toward Negroes, with the less-favorable subjects less accurate in identifying whether the Negro pictures had previously been exposed. The question whether there is, in general, a correlation between salience of an attitudinal object and favorableness of disposition toward it is an interesting problem for empirical investigation.

347

Measures in which inferences are drawn from physiological reactions to the attitudinal object or representations of it

At the opposite extreme from measures relying on a subject's verbal report of his beliefs, feelings, etc., are those relying on physiological responses not subject to conscious control. These may be measures of a subject's reaction – for example, galvanic skin response (GSR), vascular constriction – to the presence of a member of the object group or to pictorial representations of situations involving members of the object group. For example, Rankin and Campbell (1955) compared GSRs obtained when the experimenter was a Negro with those obtained when the experimenter was white; Westie and DeFleur (1959) recorded GSR, vascular constriction of finger, amplitude and duration of heartbeat, and duration of heart cycle, while the subjects were viewing pictures of white and Negroes in social situations. Hess and Polt (1960) have photographed pupillary constriction in response to unpleasant stimuli and pupillary dilation in response to pleasant stimuli.

Or the measures may involve responses, such as salivation, blinking, vascular constriction, that have been conditioned to a verbal stimulus, and, by a process of semantic generalization appear in response to words or concepts that are similar in meaning to the original stimulus. For example, Volkova (1953) has reported a series of experiments in Russia in which subjects were conditioned to salivate in response to the word GOOD; subsequently, such statements as 'The Young Pioneer helps his comrade' brought maximum salivation, while such statements as 'The Fascists destroyed many cities' brought minimum salivation.

In the case of unconditioned physiological responses to the presence or the representation of the attitudinal object, the basis for inference comes directly from the concept of attitude. Just as all definitions of attitude include beliefs, feelings, and overt behavior as indicators of attitude, so do all definitions, explicitly or implicitly, include physiological responses. It is assumed that the magnitude of the physiological reaction is directly and positively related to the extent of arousal or the intensity of feeling; thus, the greater the physiological response, the stronger and/or more extreme the attitude is presumed to be. Here again, however, there are problems in inferring the nature of the attitude being reflected. Most measures of physiological reaction give direct indications only of the extent of arousal; they do not reveal whether the corresponding emotion is pleasurable or unpleasurable. In general, in attempts to assess attitudes toward social groups via measurement of physiological responses, it has been assumed that the range of affect is not from strongly favorable to strongly unfavorable but rather from accepting, or neutral, to strongly unfavorable; thus the inference has been drawn that the greater the physiological response, the more unfavorable the attitude. If Hess' technique of photographing pupillary constriction-dilation can be adapted to the study of attitudes, it would provide a much firmer basis for inferences about the direction of attitude, since the reaction being measured shows a differential response to pleasant and unpleasant stimuli.

In the case of the conditioned physiological responses, the basis for inference eis somwhat different, stemming from learning theory. A response that has been conditioned to a given stimulus tends to generalize to stimuli that are similar. Thus, if a response that has been conditioned to the concept 'good' appears when the attitudinal object is presented, the inference is that the subject considers the object good – that is, that his attitude toward it is favorable; if the response does not appear when the attitudinal object is presented, the inference is that the subject does not consider it good – that is, that his attitude toward it is not favorable.

The purpose of the physiological measures may or may not be apparent to the subject. In the Westie and DeFleur (1959) study, for example, subjects presumably realized that the physiological measures were being used as indicators of their reactions to the interracial pictures. In the Rankin and Campbell (1955) experiment, on the other hand, subjects were led to believe that they were taking part in a word-association study and that it was their GSRs to the stimulus words (rather than to the Negro and white experimenters) that were being investigated. Whether or not the purpose is clear to the subject, the fact that the responses measured are not subject to conscious control would seem to eliminate the possibility of modification of responses in order to present a certain picture of the self.

However, physiological responses may be quite sensitive to influences other than those in which the investigator is interested – both to other aspects of the stimulus material and to other environmental influences. It is difficult to control the experimental situation so completely that other factors are ruled out as possible determinants of the response.

Again, questions such as these point to the need for extreme caution in drawing inferences about the attitude of a given individual from a measure of this type. But, again, they point to encouraging possibilities for empirical research and to the opportunity to greatly increase our understanding of attitudes and their relation to various kinds of response, by the use of instruments yielding different types of evidence.

References

Adorno, T. W., Frenkel-Brunswik, Else, Levinson, D. J., and Sanford, R. N., *The authoritarian personality*. New York: Harper, 1950.

Allport, G. W., The historical background of modern social psychology. In G. Lindzey (Ed.), *Handbook of social psychology*. Vol. 1. *Theory and method*. Cambridge, Mass.: Addison-Wesley, pp. 3–56, 1954.

Bagby, J. W., A cross-cultural study of perceptual predominance in binocular rivalry. *J. abnorm. soc. Psychol.*, **54**, 331–4, 1957.

Bass, B. M., Authoritarianism or acquiescence? *J. abnorm. soc. Psychol.*, **51**, 616–23, 1955.

Bray, D., The prediction of behavior from two attitude scales. *J. abnorm. soc. Psychol.*, **45**, 64–84, 1950.

Brown, J. F., A modification of the Rosenzweig Picture-Frustration Test to study hostile interracial attitudes. *J. Psychol.*, **24**, 247–72, 1947.

Campbell, D. T., The indirect assessment of social attitudes. *Psychol. Bull.*, **47**, 15–38, 1950.

Campbell, D. T., Social attitudes and other acquired behavioral dispositions. In S. Koch (Ed.), *Psychology: A study of a science*. Vol. 6. *Investigations of man as socius: Their place in psychology and the social sciences*. New York: McGraw-Hill, 1961.

Criswell, Joan H., Racial cleavages in Negro-white groups. *Sociometry*, **1**, 87–9, 1937.

Criswell, Joan H., Social structure revealed in a sociometric retest. *Sociometry*, **2**, 69–75, 1939.

Cronbach, L. J., Response sets and test validity. *Educ. psychol. Measmt.*, **6**, 475–94, 1946.

Cronbach, L. J., Further evidence on response sets and test design. *Educ. psychol. Measmt.*, **10**, 3–31, 1950.

DeFleur, M. L., and Westie, F. R., Verbal attitudes and overt acts: An experiment on the salience of attitudes. *Amer. sociol. Rev.*, **23**, 667–73, 1958.

Deri, Susan, Dinnerstein, Dorothy, Harding, J., and Pepitone, A. D., Techniques for the diagnosis and measurement of intergroup attitudes and behavior. *Psychol. Bull.*, **45**, 248–71, 1948.

Edwards, A. L., The relationship between the judged desirability of a trait and the probability that the trait will be endorsed. *J. appl. Psychol.*, **37**, 90–3, 1953.

Edwards, A. L., *The social desirability variable in personality assessment and research*. New York: Dryden Press, 1957.

Getzels, J. W., The assessment of personality and prejudice by the method of paired direct and projective questions. Unpublished doctoral dissertation, Harvard University, 1951.

Hammond, K. R., Measuring attitudes by error-choice: An indirect method. *J. abnorm. soc. Psychol.*, **43**, 38–48, 1948.

Hess, E. H., and Polt, J. M., Pupil size as related to interest value of visual stimuli. *Science*, **132**, 349–50, 1960.

Horowitz, E. L., and Horowitz, Ruth E., Development of social attitudes in children. *Sociometry*, **1**, 301–38, 1938.

Hovland, C. I., and Sherif, M., Judgmental phenomena and scales of attitude measurement: Item displacement in Thurstone scales. *J. abnorm. soc. Psychol.*, **47**, 822–32, 1952.

Jones, E. E., and Kohler, Rika. The effects of plausibility on the learning of controversial statements. *J. abnorm. soc. Psychol.*, **57**, 315–20, 1958.

Kinsey, A. C., Pomeroy, W. B., and Martin, C. E., *Sexual behavior in the human male*. Philadelphia, Pa.: Saunders, 1948.

LaPiere, R. T., Attitudes vs. actions. *Soc. Forces*, **14**, 230–7, 1934.

Lazarsfeld, P. F., Latent structure analysis. In S. Koch (Ed.), *Psychology: A study of a science*. Vol. 3. *Formulations of the person and the social context*. New York: McGraw-Hill, 1959.

Levine, J. M., and Murphy, G., The learning and forgetting of controversial material. *J. abnorm. soc. Psychol.*, **38**, 507–17, 1943.

Manis, M., The interpretation of opinion statements as a function of recipient attitude. *J. abnorm. soc. Psychol.*, **60**, 340–4, 1960.

Mann, J. H., The effect of inter-racial contact on sociometric choices and perceptions. *J. soc. Psychol.*, **50**, 143–52, (a) 1959.

Mann, J. H., The relationship between cognitive, affective and behavioral aspects of racial prejudice. *J. soc. Psychol.*, **49**, 223–8, (b) 1959.

Moreno, J. L., *Who shall survive?* (Orig. publ. 1934) (Rev. ed.) Beacon, N. Y.: Beacon House, 1943.

Morgan, J. J. B., Attitudes of students toward the Japanese. *J. soc. Psychol.*, **21**, 219–27, 1945.

Mussen, P. H., The reliability and validity of the Horowitz Faces Test. *J. abnorm. soc. Psychol.*, **45**, 504–6, (a) 1950.

Mussen, P. H., Some personality and social factors related to changes in children's attitudes toward Negroes. *J. abnorm. soc. Psychol.*, **45**, 423–41, (b) 1950.

Pettigrew, T. F., Allport, G. W., and Barnett, E. O., Binocular resolution and perception of race in South Africa. *Brit. J. Psychol.*, **49**, 265–78, 1958.

Proshansky, H. M., A projective method for the study of attitudes. *J. abnorm. soc. Psychol.*, **38**, 393–5, 1943.

Rankin, R. E., and Campbell, D. T., Galvanic skin response to Negro and white experimenters. *J. abnorm. soc. Psychol.*, **51**, 30–3, 1955.

Riddleberger, Alice B., and Motz, Annabelle B., Prejudice and perception. *Amer. J. Sociol.*, **62**, 498–503, 1957.

Seeleman, Virginia, The influence of attitude upon the remembering of pictorial material. *Arch. Psychol., N.Y.*, **36** (No. 258), 1940–41.

Sherif, M., A study of some social factors in perception. *Arch. Psychol., N. Y.*, No. 187, 1935.

Sommer, R., On the Brown adaptation of the Rosenzweig P-F for assessing social attitudes. *J. abnorm. soc. Psychol.*, **49**, 125–8, 1954.

Stanton, H., Back, K. W., and Litwak, E., Role-playing in survey research *Amer. J. Sociol.*, **62**, 172–6, 1956.

Stanton, H. R., and Litwak, E., Toward the development of a short form test of inter-personal competence. *Amer. sociol. Rev.*, **20**, 668–74, 1955.

Taylor, J. B., What do attitude scales measure: The problem of social desirability. *J. abnorm. soc. Psychol.*, **62**, 386–90, 1961.

Thistlethwaite, D., Attitude and structure as factors in the distortion of reasoning. *J. abnorm. soc. Psychol.*, **45**, 442–58, 1950.

Volkova, B. D., Some characteristics of conditioned reflex formation to verbal stimuli in children. *Sechenov physiol. J. USSR*, **39**, 540–8, 1953.

Watson, G. B., The measurement of fairmindedness. *Teachers Coll. Columbia U. Contr. Educ.*, No. 176, 1925.

Weiss, W., The effects on opinions of a change in scale judgments. *J. abnorm. soc. Psychol.*, **58**, 329–34, 1959.

Weschler, I. R., An investigation of attitudes toward labor and management by means of the error-choice method. *J. soc. Psychol.*, **32**, 51–67, 1950.

Weschler, I. R., and Bernberg, R. E., Indirect methods of attitude measurement. *Int. J. Opin. attit. Res.*, **4**, 209–28, 1950.

Westie, F. R., Negro-white status differentials and social distance. *Amer. sociol. Rev.*, **17**, 550–8, 1952.

Westie, F. R., A technique for the measurement of race attitudes. *Amer. sociol. Rev.*, **18**, 73–8, 1953.

Westie, F. R., and DeFleur, M. L., Autonomic responses and their relationship to race attitudes. *J. abnorm. soc. Psychol.*, **58**, 340–7, 1959.

Further Reading

General

These books are recommended to the student as of general usefulness in the area of attitudes.

Sherif, M., Sherif, C., and Nebergall, N.C., *Attitude and Attitude Change*. Saunders. 1965 – *a review of the area which includes well thought-out criticisms of some current approaches and presents new methods of measuring commitment to an attitude.*

Newcomb, T. M., Turner, R. H., and Converse, P. E., *Social Psychology: the study of human interaction*. New York and London: Holt. 1965, Tavistock Publications: Routledge & Kegan Paul. 1952 – *a comprehensive textbook of social psychology which treats attitude as the core concept and has a useful appendix on attitude measurement.*

Secord, P. F., and Backman, C. W., *Social Psychology*. New York and London: McGraw-Hill. 1964 – *Part Two of this textbook is a valuable account of research and theory in attitude and attitude change.*

Smith, M. B., Bruner, J. S., and White, R. W., *Opinions and Personality*. New York: Wiley. 1956 – *a study in depth of the complex interweaving of attitudes and personality in a small number of subjects.*

Allport, G. W., *The Nature of Prejudice*. Addison-Wesley. 1954 – *a very comprehensive survey covering many approaches to the understanding of prejudice.*

Adorno, T. W. *et al.*, *The Authoritarian Personality*. New York: Harper. 1950 – *report of the now-classic studies of authoritarianism.*

The Concept of Attitude

Defleur, M. L., and Westie, F. R., Attitude as a scientific concept. *Social Forces*, 42, 1963, 17–31 – *an analysis of the logical implications of different conceptions of 'attitude'.*

Katz, D., and Stotland, E., A preliminary statement to a theory of attitude structure and change. In S. Koch (ed.), *Psychology: A study of a science*. Vol. 3. New York: McGraw-Hill. 1959 – *an analysis of the motivational basis of attitudes in a functionalist framework.*

353

Campbell, D. T., Acquired behavioural dispositions. In S. Koch (ed.), *Psychology: A study of a science.* Vol. 3. New York: McGraw-Hill. 1959 – *an insightful examination of the attitude construct and its theoretical alternatives, with general implications for concept formation and theory construction.*

Focus on Origins

Clark, K. B., and Clark, Mamie P., Racial Identification and Preference in Negro children. In Maccoby, Eleanor E., Newcomb, T. M., and Hartley, E. L. (eds.), *Readings in Social Psychology.* New York: Holt. 1961 – *an analysis of the genesis and development of racial identification in the self-concept of Negro children.*

Eysenck, H. J., The inheritance of extraversion-introversion., *Acta Psychol.,* 12, 1965, 95–110 – *a view of hereditary factors as the basis of social attitudes.*

Staats, A. W., and Staats, C. K., Attitudes established by classical conditioning. *J. Abnorm. Soc. Psych.,* 57, 1958, 37–40 – *an experimental demonstration of a behaviourist conception of attitude acquisition.*

Katz, E., The two-step flow of communication: an up-to-date report on a hypothesis. *Public Opinion Quarterly,* 21, 1957, 61–78 – *deals with the formation and modification of attitudes by mass communications through the mediation of 'opinion leaders'.*

Focus on Change

Hovland, C. I., Janis, I. L., and Kelley, H. H., *Communication and Persuasion.* London: Oxford U. P. 1953 – *an important report of the Yale programme of experimental research in attitude and opinion change.*

Hovland, C. I., and Janis, I. L., *Personality and persuasibility.* New Haven and London: Yale U.P. 1959 – *further research from the same programme, this time on 'general persuasibility' as a dispositional factor.*

Rosenberg, M. J. *et al., Attitude Organization and Change.* New Haven, Conn.: Yale U.P. 1960 – *a later volume from the Yale research team, notable for its sophisticated theoretical crystallizations.*

Brehm, J. W. and Cohen, A. R., *Explorations in cognitive dissonance.* New York and London: Wiley. 1962 – *much of the work reported is directly relevant to attitude change.*

Schein, E. H., The Chinese indoctrination program for prisoners of war: a study of attempted 'brainwashing'. In Maccoby, Eleanor E., Newcomb, T. M., and Hartley, E. L. (eds.), *Readings in Social Psychology*. New York: Holt. 1961 – *the best known of the studies of 'brainwashing'*.

Rosenberg, M. J., Cognitive reorganization in response to the hypnotic reversal of attitudinal affect. *J. Personality*, 28, 1960, 39–63 – *a study of the effects of changing (by hypnosis) one element of an attitudinal structure on other elements of the structure*.

Klapper, J. T., *The Effects of Mass Communication*. New York: Free Press. 1961 – *the best review to date of the way in which the mass media may shape or influence attitudes and opinions*.

Focus on Behaviour

The following three studies are frequently cited when the correspondence between verbal attitudes and overt behaviour is discussed. It is probably fair to say, as an indication of the sparseness of research in this area, that very few other investigations of this kind are available.

Lapiere, R. T., Attitudes vs. Actions. *Social Forces*, 13, 1934, 230–7.

Schank, R. L., A study of a community and its groups and institutions conceived of as behaviours of individuals. *Psychological Monographs*, 43, 1932, No. 2.

Kutner, B., Wilkins, Carol, and Yarrow, Penny, Verbal attitudes and overt behaviour involving racial prejudice. *J. Abnorm. Soc. Psych.*, 47, 1952, 649–52.

Festinger, L., *A theory of cognitive dissonance.*, New York: Harper. 1957 – *a theory which attempts to treat attitudes and behaviour separately and directs attention to the function of discrepancies between them.* (*v. also* Brehm and Cohen, *op. cit. above*)

Campbell, D. T., Op. cit. above – *a discussion which in part treats systematically the relationship between attitudes and behaviour.*

Defleur, M. L., and Westie, F. R., Op. cit. above – *an analysis of different conceptions of attitude, suggesting that the expectation of correspondence between attitudes and action may be due to faulty conceptualization.*

355

Wilner, D. M., Walkley, Rosabelle, P., and Cook, S. W., *Human relations in interracial housing projects.* Minneapolis: U. Minnesota Press. 1955 – *a study of the way in which the physical ecology affects social contact, communication and attitudes.*

Festinger, L., Schachter, S., and Back, K., *Social pressures in informal groups.* New York: Harper. 1950 – *another demonstration of the effects of physical arrangements on eventual attitudes.*

Attitude Theory

Brown, R., Models of attitude change. In T. M. Newcomb (ed.), *New Directions in Psychology.* New York: Holt. 1963 (v. also Brown, R., *Social Psychology.* Free Press. 1965) – *an alternative review, in a delightful style, of the 'cognitive consistency' theories of attitude organization and change.*

Katz, D., and Stotland, E., Op. cit. above – *a comprehensive statement of the functional approach.*

Abelson, R. P., and Rosenberg, M. J., Symbolic psychologic: a model of attitudinal cognition. *Behav. Sci.*, 3, 1958, 1–13 – *a formal statement of a theory of attitude structure.*

Peak, Helen., Attitude and Motivation. In M. R. Jones (ed.), *Nebraska Symposium on Motivation*, 1955. Lincoln, Neb.: Univ. of Nebraska Press. 1955 – *a theoretical overview of attitude structure, motive structure, and their interrelationship.*

Attitude Methodology

Stouffer, S. A., *et al.*, *Measurement and Prediction.* Princeton: Princeton U. Press. 1950 – *in particular, the articles by Suchman, Lazarsfeld, Guttman and Stouffer.*

Green, B. F., Attitude measurement. In Lindzey, G. (ed.), *Handbook of Social Psychology.* Cambridge, Mass.: Addison-Wesley. 1954 – *a compact and thorough, if at times over-concise, summary.*

Osgood, C. E., Suci, G. J., and Tannenbaum, P. H., *The measurement of meaning.* Urbana, Ill.: U. of Illinois Press. 1957 – *an exposition of the semantic differential, which can be used as an attitude scale.*

Kelly, G. A., *The psychology of personal constructs.* New York: Norton. 1955 – *an exposition of the repertory grid technique, which may also be used in attitude measurement.*

Sherif, M., Sherif, C., and Nebergall, N. C., Op. cit. above – *presents methods for determining degree of commitment to an attitude.*

Edwards, A. L., *The social desirability variable in personality assessment and research.* New York: Holt. 1957 – *a discussion of a major methodological pitfall in questionnaire research.*

Bauer, R. A., The obstinate audience. *Amer. Psychologist*, 19, 1964, 319–28 – *a critical examination of social and psychological models behind the design of research in communication ond attitude change.*

Eysenck, H. J. *The psychology of politics.* London: Routledge & Kegan Paul. 1954 – *presents a study of attitudes which is a good example of the statistical method of factor analysis used with questionnaire data.*

Acknowledgements

Acknowledgements are due to the following for permission to publish extracts in this volume: Academic Press Inc., L. Berkowitz (ed.), *Advances in Experimental Social Psychology*, W. J. McGuire, 'Inducing resistance to persuasion'; Addison-Wesley Publishing Co., G. Lindzey (ed.), *Handbook of Social Psychology*, G. W. Allport, 'Attitudes in the history of social psychology', Vol. 1, 1954; American Psychological Association, *Journal of Abnormal and Social Psychology*, I. L. Janis, B. T. King, 'The Influence of role-playing on opinion change', Vol. 49, 1954, A. E. Siegel, S. Siegel, 'Reference groups, membership groups and attitude change', Vol. 55, 1957; *Psychological Bulletin*, S. W. Cook, Claire Selltiz, 'A multiple indicator approach to attitude measurement', Vol. 62, No. 1, 1964; American Sociological Association, *American Sociological Review*, R. L. Gorden, 'Attitude and the definition of the situation', Vol. 17, 1952, M. L. Defleur, F. R. Westie, 'Verbal attitudes and overt acts', Vol. 23, 1958; British Psychological Society, *British Journal of Social and Clinical Psychology*, R. Lynn and I. E. Gordon, 'Maternal attitudes to child socialisation', Vol. 1, 1962; Free Press of Glencoe, Illinois and Tavistock Publications, J. Gould, W. L. Kolb (eds.), *A Dictionary of the Social Sciences*, T. M. Newcomb, 'On the definition of attitude', 1964; M. Argyle, Religious Behavior, © Michael Argyle, 1958, First published in U.S.A. 1959 by The Free Press Corporation; Holt, Rinehart and Winston, Inc., C. Selltiz, M. Jahoda, M. Deutsch, S. W. Cook, *Research Methods in Social Relations*, 'Attitude scaling', 1959; John Wiley & Sons Inc., Irving Sarnoff, *Personality Dynamics and Development*, 'Social attitudes and the resolution of motivational conflict', 1962; Journal Press, *Journal of Genetic Psychology*, L. Bloom, 'Piaget's theory of the development of moral judgement', Vol. 95, 1959; Logos Press Inc., J. L. McCary (ed.), *Psychology of Personality*, N. Sanford, 'The genesis of authoritarianism', 1959; McGraw-Hill Book Company, S. Koch (ed.), *Psychology: A Study of a Science*, D. T. Campbell, 'Acquired Behavioural Dispositions', Vol. 6, 1963; Nuffield Foundation, H. T. Himmelweit, A. N. Oppenheim, P. Vince, *Television and the Child*, 'The influence of television on ideas about foreigners'; Prentice-Hall Inc., S. E. Asch, *Social Psychology*, 'Attitudes as cognitive structures', 1952; Princeton University Press, C. I. Hovland, I. L. Janis, H. H. Kelley, *Communication and Persuasion*, 'A summary of experimental studies of opinion change', published by O.U.P. on behalf of Princeton University Press in 1953; *Public Opinion Quarterly*, H. C. Kelman, 'Three processes of social influence', Vol. 25, 1961, R. B. Zajonc, 'Balance, congruity and dissonance', Vol. 24, No. 2, 1960; Routledge & Kegan Paul Ltd, British Journal of Sociology, C. C. Moskos, W. Bell, 'Attitudes towards democracy among leaders in four emergent nations', Vol. 14, No. 4, 1964, M. Argyle *Religious Behaviour*, 1958; Schenkman Publishing Co., J. B. Cooper, J. L. McGaugh, *Integrating Principles of Social Psychology*, 'Attitude and related concepts'; Scientific American, B. Bettelheim, M. Janowitz, 'Prejudice', October 1950, Copyright © 1965 by Scientific American, Inc. All Rights Reserved; Society for Psychological Study of Social Issues, *Journal of Social Issues*, R. J. Lifton, 'Thought reform of Chinese intellectuals', Vol. 13, 1957, M. B. Freedman, 'Changes in attitudes and values over six decades', Vol. 17, No. 1, 1961; Verlag für

ACKNOWLEDGEMENTS

Demoskopie Allensbach, M. Jahoda, P. F. Lazarsfeld, H. Zeisel, *Die Arbeitslosen von Marienthal*, 'Attitudes under conditions of unemployment', 2nd edition 1960.

Author Index

Author Index

367

Subject Index

Subject Index

Penguin Modern Psychology Readings

More titles in this series are:

MOTIVATION Ed. Dalbir Bindra and Jane Stewart
UPS1
A collection of papers which deal most directly with the three
central problems of motivation: *drive* (what instigates an organism
to action?); *goal direction* (what directs behaviour toward certain
ends?); *reinforcement* (what precisely makes certain events rewarding
and others punishing?).

EXPERIMENTS IN VISUAL PERCEPTION
Ed. M. D. Vernon.
UPS2
The volume reviews four central topics—
the perception of form, space and distance, 'constancy'
phenomena: and then explains the variations in perception which
occur within the individual and between individuals. Four excerpts
from Piaget on perception in infancy complete the volume.

PERSONALITY ASSESSMENT Ed. Boris Semeonoff
UPS4
Readings on variations in normal personality, which include Galton
and the early writings on typology, the applications of
psychometric methods and of controlled observations in selection
procedures.

Titles to be published in 1967 are:

ABNORMAL PSYCHOLOGY Ed. M. Hamilton

ANIMAL PROBLEM SOLVING Ed. A. J. Riopelle

INTELLIGENCE AND ABILITY Ed. Stephen Wiseman

PERSONALITY Ed. R. S. Lazarus and E. Opton Jr.

Studies in Social Pathology

General Editor G. M. Carstairs

Psychology in Pelicans

FREUD AND THE POST-FREUDIANS

J. A. C. Brown

Freud and the Post-Freudians explains the main concepts of Freudian psychology and goes on to review the theories of Adler, Jung, Rank, and Stekel. Later developments in the orthodox Freudian school are also discussed, as are those of the American Neo-Freudians and the Post-Freudians in England.

This is the first book published in Britain to bring together all these psychological and sociological schools and criticize them, both from the Freudian standpoint and that of the scientific psychologists.

New Horizons In Psychology

Edited by Brian M. Foss

Psychology as a science of observation and experiment is 100 years old. In the last decade it has expanded greatly, exploring new fields of human behaviour and using new techniques.

New Horizons in Psychology is both a progress report and a guide to exciting developments in coming years. All of them will affect scientific thinking in many fields and some of them will influence the way we live.

Visual illusions, information theory, creativity – genetics, motivation, drugs – operant conditioning, programmed learning, behaviour therapy – personal construct psychology, small groups, cross cultural studies – psychology is seething with new ideas and methods today. These and many others are explained here by a distinguished team of experimental psychologists. A linking commentary by the editor, Professor Foss, paints the conceptual background to each topic.

The Psychology of Perception
M. D. Vernon

When we look at the world with our eyes, do we see it *as it really is*? In this authoritative study the Professor of Psychology at the University of Reading shows how, behind the retina of the eye, many more fallible mental processes cause errors and inconsistencies to creep into our perceptions. We are seldom aware of these.

Here then is a non-technical outline of the psychological processes which have been shown to be involved in our visual perceptions of things around us. These perceptions of shape, colour, movement, and space develop gradually from infancy upwards. Special processes also emerge to enable us to deal with symbolic material such as printed words and diagrams, for the purpose, in particular, of reading.

Finally this book, which is based on over thirty years of psychological research at Cambridge and elsewhere, shows how the perceptions of different people are not always alike: they vary with attention, interest, and individual personality factors.

Other books on psychology published in Pelicans which are of particular interest to students of psychology are:

A271 CHILD CARE AND THE GROWTH OF LOVE (2nd edition 1965)
John Bowlby and Margaret Fry

A346 HUMAN GROUPS
W. J. H. Sprott

A405 MEMORY (2nd edition 1964)
Ian M. L. Hunter

A262 PSYCHIATRY TODAY (2nd edition 1963)
David Stafford-Clark

A743 SLEEP
Ian Oswald

A296 THE SOCIAL PSYCHOLOGY OF INDUSTRY
J. A. C. Brown

A281 USES AND ABUSES OF PSYCHOLOGY
H. J. Eysenck